Peshmerga Loyalty Oath

I swear by God my loyalty will be only for my country,

and I will protect my people until my last breath.

Peshmerga forces fleeing Shingal ahead of Yezidis, August 3, 2014

D1250384

The Last Yezidi Genocide

Amy L. Beam, PhD, author
amybeam@yahoo.com

non-fiction
keywords: *genocide, war crimes, crimes against humanity, Shingal, Iraq, Middle East, Kurdistan, Peshmerga, Yezidis, sexual violence, rape as a weapon of war, human rights, human trafficking, immigration, asylum, refugees, displaced persons, Islamic State, Daesh, ISIS, ISIL, terrorism, extremism, Islam*

ISBN 978-0-9790835-1-8
Adinolfi Books

Preface

On August 3, 2014, and again on August 15, the Islamic State terrorist organization, known in Iraq as Daesh, attacked Yezidis in Shingal, northern Iraq. Daesh killed or abducted at least 6417 Yezidis. The women and girls were held as prisoners and raped. Their men were killed. The entire population of 360,000 was displaced from Shingal in twelve hours. Daesh publicly stated its goal was to destroy the Yezidis, a non-Muslim ethno-religious people. Those who were captured were given the choice to convert to Islam or be killed.

Kurdish Peshmerga defense forces withdrew from Shingal in the early morning hours of August 3, 2014, leaving Yezidis defenseless against the attack. Daesh gangs were their own Sunni Arab neighbors, as well as some Kurdish neighbors, joined by foreign fighters from 80 countries.

Article 6 of the Rome Statute defines "genocide" as *the intent to destroy, in whole or in part, a national, ethnical, racial or religious group.* The United Nations and other countries took two years to recognize the Yezidi genocide. The U.N. did not pass a resolution calling for an investigation and prosecution of Daesh crimes until 2017, three years after the attack.

While the U.N. was thinking it over, I was investigating the crimes of genocide against the Yezidis. For more than five years I obtained Iraqi passports for hundreds of witnesses and survivors of kidnapping, rape, and torture.

Many of them wanted to share their story with me, because they want the world to know the truth. This book is the result of my investigation. It contains testimony of courageous Yezidis who have allowed me to use their real names. I wrote their stories in first person based on my interviews with them. They reviewed their statements for accuracy. For two years, I continued to have several hundred readers review this book and make corrections and additions so that the historical record is accurate. There are 300,000 more stories like these.

It is time for action, prosecutions, and compensation. The Yezidi voices cry out for help to a world that has fallen deaf. To save the Yezidi nation, they need asylum and international protection of Shingal with massive reconstruction funds.

The UN Investigative Team to Promote Accountability for Crimes Committed by Daesh (UNITAD) received funding in January 2019 and exhumed its first mass grave site in Kocho, Shingal, on March 16, 2019. UNITAD created a database to use in prosecutions against Daesh criminals. Nearly 3000 Ezidis are missing.

Amy L. Beam, Ph.D.
Shingal, Iraq
January 3, 2021
amybeam@yahoo.com

Contents

Understanding Names and Spellings

Under Saddam Hussein, all school was taught in Arabic. Now in Kurdistan, school is taught in Kurdish. The official language used in Kurdistan government is Sorani, the dialect of Kurdish spoken predominantly in Sulaymaniyah and Erbil (or Arbil or Irbil). Kurmanji is spoken in Duhok and Turkey. Yezidis speak both Arabic and Ezidian, another dialect of Kurdish. The Ezidian dialect is spoken the same by Yezidis world-wide and is closest to the Kurdish spoken in Turkey. Turkey was the previous homeland of Yezidis before being driven out by numerous previous genocides.

Both Arabic and Kurdish are written in an Arabic script alphabet. Translation to English spelling is done phonetically. Therefore, a word or name may literally be spelled a dozen different ways in English. These spellings may also differ depending on the Kurdish dialect.

For example, a person's name may be spelled Bissee or Pissee. depending on the dialect. The village of Kocho may be spelled Kojo. Some pronounce it with "ch" sound, others with "j" sound.

Some sounds in the Kurdish language are not used in the English language, such as "Kh" also spelled with an "x". This sound is made deep in the throat, like a person hacking up phlegm. For example, Siba Shex Khudir and Siba Sheikh Khudir is the same place. Additionally, the Kurdish language has fewer vowels, or more consonant clusters, as in the word "hashd" which rhymes with smashed. Double vowels are both pronounced, so the name Saad is pronounced "Sa-ahd". Each of the letters "a" gets pronounced. The name Said is two syllables, pronounced as "Sa-eed" with the "i" having a long "e" sound.

In addition, the villages and cities of Shingal have both an Arabic name and a Kurdish name. Throughout this book, Kurdish place names are usually used. There is a city named Shingal and a region named Shingal. Like New York city, New York. So in this book **"Sinjar" is used to refer to Sinjar the city, while Shingal is used to refer to the entire region.** The main Yezidi villages which were attacked are:

Arabic	Kurdish
Erbil, Irbil, Arbil	Hawler (capitol of Kurdistan, not attacked)
Sinjar	Shingal, Shengal
Adnania	Gir Zerik, Gir Zarik, Gerzerik, Gurzurik
Tal Ezeer, Qatania, Qataniya	Gir Azeer
Jazeera	Siba Sheikh Khudir, Siba Shex Khuder
Mujahma al Whaleed, Tal Banat	
Mujahma al Baath, Tal Qassab	
	Qapousi, Qapusi, Kapoosi
	Kocho, Kojo
	Hatamia, Hatamiya
Andulous	Gohbal
Hatten	Duguri, Dugery
Nahiat Shimal	Snoni, Sunoni, Sinoni
Yermuke	Borek, Borik, Bork
Tamime	Khanasor, Khanasur
	Hamadan
	Hardan
	Gurmiz, Gurmis
	Zorava, Zorova

Vian Dakhil Pleas to Parliament

I was in Sirnak, southeast Turkey, watching TV on August 5, 2014. Who was this woman standing in the back, shouting out to a room full of men in suits and starched white shirts? I could not understand her words, but in any language I could understand something was terribly wrong.

The Speaker interrupted, tried to shut her down, "Madam MP, please abide by the statement that was agreed upon ..."

Her voice cut him off and rose an octave to a shrill, strident demand. The men in the room stood up and began muttering objections. In the Middle East it is an unforgivable transgression for a woman to raise her voice to a man. It is cause for permanent banishment. Here she was shouting and stabbing the air with her finger. The men were not going to tolerate this unbecoming breach of protocol. But she would not be silenced.

She did what women all over the world have learned to do since time immemorial when they are not being taken seriously: she became hysterical. Tears wet her flushed red cheeks. She clutched her handkerchief as her words gained momentum like a bullet train.

The men were chastised into silence. No one moved, no one dared to whisper, until after two minutes and fifteen seconds, grief overcame her, and with a sob in mid-sentence, she fainted into the arms of the women surrounding her. In any language, I understood she was raising an alarm for help. But what was the crisis? *What? What? What?*

This was Vian Dakhil's plea to the Iraqi Parliament:

There are Yezidis who now are living in Sinjar Mountain. Mr. Speaker, we are being slaughtered under the banner of 'there is no god but Allah'. Mr. Speaker, until now 500 Yezidi men have been slaughtered.

Speaker: "Madam MP, please abide by the statement that was agreed upon."

Mr. Speaker, our women are being taken as slaves and sold in the slave market.

(shouting at her from the floor)

Please, brothers. There is now a campaign of genocide being waged on the Yezidi constituent.

(interruption again by the Speaker)

Yes, Mr. Speaker, I am abiding [by the statement]. Please, Mr. Speaker, my people are being slaughtered just as all Iraqis were slaughtered. The Shias, the Sunnis, the Christians, the Turkmen, and the Shabak were slaughtered. And today, the Yezidis are being slaughtered. Brothers, away from all political disputes, we want humanitarian solidarity. I speak here in the name of humanity. Save us! Save us! For 48 hours, 30,000 families have been besieged in Sinjar Mountain without water and food. They are dying. Seventy babies have died so far from thirst and suffocation. Fifty old people have died from the deteriorating conditions. Our women are taken as slaves and sold in the slave market.

Mr. Speaker, we demand that the Iraqi Parliament intervene immediately to stop this massacre. There have been 72 genocide campaigns on the Yezidis, and now it is being repeated in the 21st century. We are being slaughtered. We are being exterminated. An entire religion is being exterminated from the face of the earth. Brothers, I appeal to you in the name of humanity to save us! Mr. Speaker, I want . . . [breaks into a sob and faints]

Within hours Vian Dakhil's impassioned plea to rescue the Yezidis on Shingal Mountain went viral and was translated into many languages. Vian Dakhil, at age 43, was a Yezidi member of the Iraqi parliament. She was honored as the person who alerted the world to the Yezidi genocide. On August 8, President Obama ordered the United States to drop water on Shingal Mountain. Unfortunately, many of the plastic bottles broke open upon impact. The rescue mission was a nightmare that has not yet ended for Yezidis.

That day was the first time I heard the word "Yezidi". Like the rest of the world, I wondered, "What's a Yezidi?"

They Died for Shame

There is a deeply ingrained culture of shame in the Kurdish, Muslim and Yezidi cultures. In America, when one murmurs "What a shame," it means "what a pity." It expresses regret and sadness. It is offered as a condolence, meaning, "I am sorry for your bad fortune." But for Yezidis, *shame* means *disgrace;* a disgrace so big that it is unforgettable and often unforgivable. In many situations, Daesh effectively relied on this culture of shame to control and capture the Yezidis.

The greatest shame is for a single woman to have sexual relations before marriage. Such a transgression will bring dishonor to her entire extended family, possibly banishment to another town. A family's honor is wrapped up in their daughters' virginity. If the town's people knew that a girl was not a virgin, not only would no one marry her, but no one would marry her sisters or brothers, either. The entire family bore the burden of shame. The family may be shunned; their business boycotted.

Not only are premarital relations forbidden, but a myriad of lesser infringements. It is a shame for a woman to expose her ankles, bosom, or upper arms even in 115F degrees; a shame to post her photo on her internet FaceBook page; a shame to walk down the street eating an ice cream cone; a shame to wear blue; a shame for a woman to go out without a male relative accompanying her; a shame for a woman to raise her voice against a man; a shame for a husband and wife to hold hands in public; a shame for a woman to sit next to an unknown man in a shared taxi or waiting room of a government office.

In western cultures, the fear of legal prosecution curbs people's inappropriate impulses and makes them toe the line of acceptable societal behavior. But in the Yezidi culture, where they have endured persecution and genocide for centuries, they do not look to the Iraqi legal system for justice.

In Yezidi culture, it is the fear of bringing shame to one's family honor that keeps people in line. *What the neighbors think* is paramount. For example, there is virtually no stealing, because that is a shame. Possibly Yezidis have one of the lowest crime rates of theft in the world.

It is a shame for a younger person to question the authority of one's elders. Within the Yezidi family unit, the eldest man is considered the wise man and protector. He is the final word and rules over his wife, daughters, sons, daughters-in-law, and grandchildren.

His decisions and advice, based on his experience, must be obeyed. Family or community councils among the males may be held, but the final decision always lies with the tribal or town manager called the muhktar. Within a Yezidi village, there is no elected mayor. The eldest man is the village muhktar. This responsibility of leadership is often passed down from father to eldest son.

The village muhktar is given great love and respect. This form of leadership might be thought of as benevolent dictatorship. It is demonstrated through fierce loyalty and unquestioning obedience. To challenge a final decision is considered shameful. This moral imperative to trust and obey the leader is how Yezidis from the Azawi tribe in Tal Banat ended up massacred in Zuleyli valley on August 4, 2014.

Tal Banat lies south of Mount Shingal. In the morning of August 3, its residents fled to the mountain where they stopped to rest in the shade of Zuleyli valley.

Sunni Arabs from neighboring Kheillo and Ain Ghazal villages came and told them to fly white flags. They told the Yezidis "You are our friends and neighbors. No one will hurt you. We will return and take you back to your village of Tal Banat."

Not only did their ancestral culture of obedience and shame compel the Tal Banat residents to follow their muhktar's instructions and wait for Daesh to return, but, this was coupled with an utter disbelief that their own Arab neighbors, with whom they had been friends for years, with whom they had shared circumcision ceremonies of their sons, making them "blood" brothers, would turn into betrayers and slaughter them. One might as well ask them to believe that the sun would rise in the west. The treachery awaiting them was inconceivable.

When they ran from their village, they thought they might be gone for only a few hours; possibly a few days . . . certainly not for the rest of their lives. Many did not grab so much as a bottle of water as they ran out the door. So they waited with cautious optimism in the oppressive heat for their Arab neighbors to return with an answer to their fate.

Paymon, a twenty-five-year-old Yezidi mother from Tal Banat, Shingal, had the courage, fueled by fear, to defy her uncle's instructions to stay in Zuleyli valley. She fled to the mountain with her family and 200 others who followed her.

Two hours later Daesh returned to Zuleyli. They separated the men from the women and children. Daesh told the men if they would convert to Islam, they would not kill them. The men did not agree to convert. Then Daesh shot between 70 and 140 men with guns such as AK47s. Some of their bodies were discovered in Zuleyli valley, January 2016.

The muhktar of Tal Banat, Salih Qassim, was the first man executed. Nine of those executed were: Hassan Masy, Abass Jeat, Salih Qasim, Alyas Abdullah Mase, Zeblo Haji, Fares Darwesh, Asead Azawy, Malo Azawy, and Saeed Abo Gathep,

Further south, in the village of Kocho, the residents were not as fortunate as Paymon's family who got away. After Daesh took control of Mosul on June 9, 2014, fear gripped the residents of Shingal even though Peshmerga set up bases in every village, promising to protect the residents to their last breath. In Kocho, Peshmerga were living in the school and the residents were bringing them food daily. They were so grateful for their presence.

The villages closest to the east end of the mountain were most vulnerable to an attack from Mosul and Tal Afar. Kocho, far to the southeast with a population of 1735 Yezidis, was surrounded by 15 Arab villages and one Kurdish village.

In July, before the August 3 attack on Shingal, a shepherd from Kocho named Dilshad Suleyman Qassim was captured by Daesh. Basman Elias, from Kocho, called an Arab with Daesh and requested they release Dilshad, because he was just a poor shepherd. The man's reply to Basman was that Daesh would force all Yezidis to convert to Islam and Yezidis would do it. He also told Basman that Daesh will "marry" their Yezidi women.

Basman alerted everyone in Kocho. Because of this dire warning, twenty big families left Kocho before August 3. Some went to their houses in Shingal city, twenty-eight kilometers northwest. Others went to their relatives in other villages. Basman sent his wife, Viyan Havind, and their children, along with his siblings and parents, to Viyan's family's house in Old Tal Qassab for one night, then to their house in Sinjar. Basman remained in his house in Kocho to protect it.

Yezidi men from neighboring Hatamia and Tal Qassab took their guns (those who had not been disarmed by Peshmerga and Asayish) and went to Kocho to protect it. Basman's own uncle, Nawzad Salah Qassab, along with many other Yezidis, condemned them by saying, "It is a shame for them to run away without seeing Daesh."

Men from Hatamia threatened to steal everything from the empty Kocho houses.

Sometime after these families left Kocho, but before the August 3 attack, Nayef Al Jaso, the muhktar or manager of Kocho, went to Sinjar city where he was held overnight by PDK security forces, then released in the morning. When he returned to Kocho, he immediately called the twenty families from Kocho and instructed them to return to their homes in Kocho. He said it was a shame for them to run away. All but two or three of the families obeyed his orders and returned. Those families who did not return left Iraq.

Basman, upon the instructions of Nayef Al Jaso, called his family in Sinjar and said, "Come back." His wife, Viyan Havind, and his mother, pleaded with Basman to go to the safety of Kurdistan instead. But an order was an order. The whole family returned home.

These families who fled Kocho were publicly "shamed" for having left, especially when Peshmerga was there to protect them. After the shaming from Yezidis in Kocho and the neighboring villages, they vowed never to leave Kocho again. They would defend it even if Daesh attacked them and killed them. The men from Hatamia promised the men from Kocho that they would not leave without them. They, too, would stay and fight until death against Daesh.

One man who did not stay was Nayef Al Jaso, the manager of Kocho. While the Kocho families were returning to their homes, Nayef Al Jaso and his wife flew to Istanbul July 28.

Although many Yezidis in Shingal ridiculed those from Kocho for refusing to leave on August 3 or later, survivors from Kocho testify that they were besieged by Daesh for eleven days and unable to escape in spite of multiple attempts.

On August 15, Daesh captured all the residents remaining in Kocho. The men were separated from the women and asked to convert to Islam. When they refused, they were taken to different sites at the perimeter of the village and executed. The women and children were abducted. Eighty older women were taken to the Solagh Institute and shot the next day.

Viyan and her children were held captive by Daesh in Tal Afar for eleven months. Viyan's mother-in-law was shot dead in Solagh. Viyan's husband, Basman, remains missing along with Basman's uncle, Nawzad, and the other men who were in Kocho on the day of the attack. Viyan's father-in-law, Elias, was one of nineteen men who survived the mass executions in Kocho.

Four years after the attack, without the bodies as proof, the rescued women continued to say their husbands were missing. They asked for the mass grave sites to be excavated and the bones tested to identify their loved ones so they might have closure.

The most famous Yezidi singer, Daxil Osman, lived in Siba Sheikh Khudir. He was loved and respected by everyone because of his singing at wedding parties throughout the region. Daxil had been studying history as well as daily events and feared that Daesh would attack Shingal. One month before the attack, he shared his prediction with his friends and family and invited them to go with him to the safety of Kurdistan. None joined him. He was harshly criticized by his fans for leaving for Kurdistan instead of staying in Shingal and encouraging people to defend themselves against Daesh. On August 1, Daxil returned to Duguri under the pressure of shame. There was nothing he could do when his village of Siba Sheikh Khudir was attacked and twenty of his cousins were killed while providing cover for their families to escape.

Tal Banat Escape and Zuleyli Valley Massacre
Paymon Jallal Abad (born 1991), June 4, 2016

In June and July of 2014, before the genocide against Yezidis, Daesh shot at our village of Tal Banat on three occasions from a distance of one kilometer. Each time they fired three or four shots from the Tal Afar side on the southeast of Tal Banat. Tal Afar is west of Mosul. It is the city where Daesh held many of the kidnapped women and children after August 3.

One of our neighbors, who now lives in Germany, was a PUK journalist working in PUK party headquarters in Tal Banat. After each shooting incident, we asked him "Why didn't the PUK Peshmerga shoot back?"

He said, "We could see Daesh, but we did not have orders to shoot."

On August 2, 2014, Daesh bombarded Tal Banat with mortar rounds at 3 PM. My husband, Baderkhan, was away at his job as an interpreter with an oil company. I was at my mother's house in Tal Banat. I went home to my house after they bombed three times. We ate dinner but could not sleep.

At 12:30 AM on August 3, we went to my uncle Abdullah Ali Omar's house. Abdullah told us to go home, pack up, and be ready. He was really worried. He told me and the wife of my husband's uncle to hide everything to do with the US Army. We packed everything in a big white bag that had been used for government-issued sugar. We buried it in the ground. The bag contained photos of my husband with US military forces, his Global Linguistics Solutions (GLS) employee badge used as an interpreter, and his certificates.

The reason my husband had left his GLS badge at home was because previously he had succeeded in passing through a Daesh checkpoint. After that, he never carried his GLS employee badge with him, for fear of being captured by Daesh, because he had worked for the Americans.

Between 1 and 1:30 AM on August 3, Daesh began fighting Peshmerga. We could hear heavy weapons until 5 AM coming from the direction of Ain Ghazal village which is south of Tal Qassab and west of Tal Banat. Ain Ghazal was once Yezidi but had become Arab. Peshmerga had a lookout point four kilometers from Tal Banat overlooking Ain Ghazal.

We ate breakfast after 5 AM. Then we gathered together in the street with our neighbors and their daughters. At 7 AM Jallal Barakat Khudaida, who had been working at the Peshmerga checkpoint overlooking Ain Ghazal, returned to Tal Banat and said, "We have no more ammunition to fight back."

At this time, some people were escaping from Tal Banat by walking directly north to the mountain, because most people did not own cars. My husband's uncle, Abdullah Ali Omar, asked a man escaping what was going on. The man told him that Daesh had entered Tal Banat from the west with the cooperation of

Kheillo village. Kheillo is a village of 2,000 Sunni Arab Muslims. It is only a five minute walk from the western edge of Tal Banat to Kheillo.

At this time, prior to the attack, there were at least 100 Peshmerga soldiers based in every Yezidi town and village. We always felt the Peshmerga were there to control us, not to protect us since there were no Peshmerga stationed in the neighboring Arab villages in Shingal.

The paved road from Tal Banat heading west to Sinjar was closed because people from the neighboring Arab village of Kheillo were shooting at Tal Banat. This was the only paved escape route, so people with cars drove on the dirt road directly to the mountain while others walked.

Daesh finally entered Tal Banat between 9 and 9:30 AM, August 3, and we escaped at the same time. We took nothing with us, not even water or a bite to eat. We thought we would be gone only a few hours. We drove north to Solagh on a dirt road in my father's Chevrolet Optra. We were ten people in the car: me, my father, my two mothers, my small son and my five brothers. My husband was away at his job in the oil field.

In Solagh village we stayed only ten minutes from 10:20 to 10:30 AM because a man told us not to stay because Daesh was close. From Solagh we drove to Zuleyli and stopped there. Soon my uncle Abdullah arrived from Tal Banat. He gave us seven loaves of bread, but no water. Once inside Zuleyli, Uncle Abdullah drove to Qine Merhkan and we followed. Then my uncle Faisal Abbas Mato arrived to Zuleyli and called my father, Jallal, and told us to go back to the first stop in Zuleyli. We did. From there we left the cars and walked into Zuleyli valley.

We sat in the hot sun in the valley. One family living near to Zuleyli gave us one bottle of unclean water. We were only there ten minutes when a Daesh four-door, white Toyota pickup showed up with six men. They surrounded us with AK guns and hand grenades. The leader talked to my uncle, Saeed, and told women to cover their heads. They asked us to give them our weapons and possessions. They told us to fly white flags. They said, "You are our friends and neighbors. No one will hurt you. We will return and take you back to your village of Tal Banat."

When they were collecting our things, one Daesh accidently shot his own foot. So immediately all the Daesh jumped in their pickup trucks and left with the injured man, ten minutes after arriving. They did not stay long enough to take all our belongings, only our weapons, laptops, and some phones. We hid our gold jewelry.

At 6 PM we moved to a house owned by Yezidis. My Uncle Saeed told us to go there. The owners were gone. We stayed two hours, made a fire, and baked bread. We were about 200 people gathered there from Tal Banat. The children slept but the adults did not sleep. We could see three cars stopped on the main road between Tal Afar and Sinjar. On August 4, at 5 AM, the cars left.

When the three cars left, most of the 200 people also left, but my family along with the families of Saeed and Faisal stayed. Saeed's father was in his 70s or 80s. In our culture, we have to follow the decision of the eldest leader which was Saeed. Saeed said we should stay, so we stayed until we got a call from a young boy who was a friend of Saeed's son in college in Mosul.

This friend told Saeed to escape and not to trust Daesh, because they were taking women and girls.

Before Daesh left in their 4 x 4 pickup trucks, the Daesh head man and Saeed exchanged phone numbers. The Daesh man said he would go talk to his boss to decide what to do with our Yezidi group. He said we should wait there until he called. So, Saeed called the Daesh man and asked what they were going to do with us. He told Saeed that his boss said he had to see us to decide. Saeed felt there was a problem, but he said we would wait.

I was scared and crying. I begged my mother to leave and not to wait for my uncle Saeed. So Saeed called the friend in Mosul again and asked if he was sure about Daesh taking women and girls. He said, "Yes, I am sure."

Even after that phone call, Saeed did not agree to leave, so my family left with our father, Jallal, and with Saeed's family and Faisal. Saeed stayed behind with his father who is about seventy. Also, about seventy other older men stayed behind with the muhktar (leader) of Faisal's tribe. Then my father, Jallal, returned to them.

We all crossed over the mountain to the north side and walked to Pire Awra Shrine, about four kilometers west of Sherfadeen Shrine. We arrived at noon on August 4, twenty-seven hours after fleeing our home in Tal Banat.

Saeed's son who was with us, called his father. Saeed told him to wait five minutes and he would call back. Five minutes later my father, Jallal, who had returned to be with Saeed, called my mother and asked that she send someone back to them in Zuleyli Valley with water because Saeed's father was almost dead from dehydration. So my Uncle Faisal sent his son Marwan to take some water. Marwan delivered the water to them in Zuleyli. Then Saeed, Marwan, and my father, Jallal, returned to us at Pire Awra Shrine.

They left about seventy older men in Zuleyli valley, including Saeed's father. Two hours later Daesh returned. They separated the men from the women and children. Daesh told the men if they would convert to Islam, they would not kill them. The men did not agree to convert.

One man named Hussein from Tal Banat, whose family was captured, cried when he told us that Daesh shot two of his friends in front of his eyes at the edge of Zuleyli Valley. The first man Daesh shot was the muhktar. Hussein said, "They made us kneel down and they tied our hands behind our backs with rope."

Then Daesh shot approximately 140 men with guns such as AK47s. Their bones were found on top of the ground in 2016 in Zuleyli. Bodies were removed and buried at holy sites on Mount Shingal, including Sherfadeen. Hussein is living in Zahko now.

My family stayed at Pire Awra Shrine for five days. For three days we had only dirty water to drink. Some religious people who lived near there went to Khanasor and brought us some lentils, chick peas, and wheat. On their return to Pire Awra Shrine from Khanasor, one man got shot twice; once above his heart and once in his hip. His brother's wife got shot once in her right shoulder and once close to her groin.

They made it back to Pire Awra Shrine with their bullet wounds. Saeed's son who was a doctor removed the bullet from the woman's shoulder but could not help the man who died two days later. We buried him. The woman was still alive when we left her, but I do not know if she survived.

On the sixth day of resting at Pire Awra Shrine we left. This was the eighth day of our ordeal. We walked west to Sherfadeen Shrine where we slept one night, and then the next day continued walking toward the Syrian border. My husband picked us up before we reached the border. We saw Kurdish YPG men and YPJ women fighters all the way from Sherfadeen Shrine to Syria. They were helping the Yezidis. We did not see any Peshmerga anywhere.

We estimate that 500 or more Yezidis are missing or dead from our village of Tal Banat. As of today, it is still under Daesh control. There is nothing for us to ever return to. It is the land of death.

Tal Banat was liberated from Daesh control on May 21, 2017, by Hashd al-Sha'abi militia (Popular Mobilization Unit - PMU) from Baghdad and Yezidis. Many houses were damaged from air strikes and bombardments.

Family of Yezidi Party Leader Walks 100 Kilometers off Shingal Mountain
Hamdiya Hamed Abbas, August 13, 2015

We walked 100 kilometers without water to escape Daesh. I thought my daughter would die. I am Hamdiya Hamed Abbas, mother of four girls. I was born in 1979 and was 36 when Daesh attacked us in Tal Banat. My husband is Waad Hamad Mato, the party leader of the political Ezidi Progress Party in Shingal. Waad was born in 1967. Previous to 2014, Waad was held prisoner for two years in Kurdistan for his activities to organize a Yezidi political party.

Tal Banat, where we lived, is a small Yezidi village on the southeast side of Shingal Mountain. Tal Afar, where they took the kidnapped women and girls after the attack, is forty-five kilometers east of our village of Tal Banat. Mosul is further east of Tal Afar and south of Erbil in Kurdistan.

Because Daesh took control of Mosul and Tal Afar on June 10, 2014, it was not possible for people to escape by driving east to these cities. Our only escape route by car was to drive west to Tal Qassab then Sinjar city. From Sinjar one can drive a paved road up onto Shingal Mountain and over the ridge to Sunoni on the north side. The safety of Kurdistan is another two-and-a-half hours.

On the day of the attack, Daesh blocked the road from Tal Banat to Tal Qassab. My husband had our car at his office in Sinjar so we could not get to each other. I and my girls and my sister and her four children rode with our neighbors in their Deer pickup truck. We piled 27 people into the truck. Our only route of escape was an unpaved dirt road going straight north from Tal Banat to the east end of Shingal Mountain which is twenty-two kilometers away.

We drove straight north for one hour, bouncing in the back of the pickup truck. We stopped the car in Zuleyli and walked twenty minutes to the rocky edge of the mountain where there was some shade. Six Daesh men came to visit us in two cars. They, also, walked twenty minutes to get to us. Two of them stood guard over us with guns. One was wearing a vest and said he was a suicide bomber.

They told us to return to Tal Banat. They promised they would not hurt us. They told the girls and women to cover our heads with our scarves. Daesh took the weapons from the men. They took the phones and gold from everyone, but let us keep our cash. The people who were gone to get drinking water were able to keep their gold and phones. Daesh left on foot after thirty minutes. We slept there in the shadow of the mountain for one night.

On the morning of August 4, we climbed up on Shingal Mountain. My family had only three small bottles of water. When we left home so fast, we took no food. We did not know when we left that we would never be going home again. We did not know then that our life in Tal Banat was finished.

My husband talked by phone to his brother who was in a different location on the mountain. He said Daesh had captured him on August 6. Daesh published a video online showing them breaking into his party headquarters compound, lowering his party flag and raising the black flag of Daesh.

According to Saeed Batush, second in leadership of the Ezidi Progress Party, on August 6, my husband told Saeed by phone that he was being held prisoner with hundreds of others in the new municipal building in Sinjar. He told Saeed he managed to escape over the wall to a waiting car. On August 7, he talked by phone to Saeed and said he was driving in a car in Shekhan which was not under Daesh control. He expected to arrive in Lalish in twenty minutes. No one ever heard from him again. We believe my husband is dead in spite of rumors that he is being held by PDK as a prisoner in Kurdistan.

Meanwhile, my family was trapped at the base of the mountain. The harvest was over and the wheat was in fifty-kilo bags. Two men from our town sacrificed themselves and walked to a station to get bags of wheat and carry them back to us. They distributed some wheat to each family. Then Daesh killed the two men while they were getting more wheat. We had only this wheat to eat.

We had heard by phone that there was a strong Peshmerga defense force coming to defend us and we would not have to climb on the mountain to escape. But this never happened. We heard a rumor that President Barzani's son, Masour Barzani, who is chief commander of the Peshmerga, was with the Peshmerga forces. No Peshmerga forces came to rescue us, so we climbed onto the mountain. We were seventy-five kilometers from the safety of the Syrian border. On the mountain we saw YPG and Yezidi fighters.

We slept seven nights on Shingal Mountain. After Vian Dakhil, our Yezidi parliamentarian, pleaded on TV to help us, some helicopters dropped food and water, but we were trapped on the east end of Shingal Mountain. Daesh was all around, and so no helicopters came to drop anything for us, because Daesh would shoot at them.

Really and truly, we thought we were going to die. If we stayed on the mountain we would starve. If we returned to town, we would be killed by Daesh. Our only choice was to keep walking west toward Syria on top of the rocky mountain, one step at a time. I was thinking of what would happen to my four children if I did not survive, so I kept putting one foot in front of another. I gave what food there was to my children. I barely ate enough to keep myself alive.

We were all crying along the way, because the children were starting to die. My youngest girl, Gulizar, who was not yet six, became so dehydrated that I thought she would die, so I told the others to go ahead without me. I would stay with my child until she died, but no one left us. After four hours, Gulizar woke up. Everyone took turns carrying Gulizar all the way to the Syrian border. Along the way, we saw children who had died.

On August 7, after four nights on the mountain, we came to a shepherd. He knew his sheep would die without water, and so he gave us permission to take some sheep. That was when Daesh attacked us and we had to leave before we could eat our dinner from the sheep. We were so hungry we could not think clearly. We were mentally tired and could barely walk.

When I saw other families, the father was with them, but our father was not. I thought my husband had also fled to safety from his office in Shingal. We had to make it to him. His brother, Thabit, did not tell me the truth that Daesh had captured my husband. He wanted to give me hope so we would not give up. Thabit was at Sel Mira shrine, a Yezidi holy place on the mountain. We had to get to him, but it was such a long way to walk. We thought we would all die before we could get there. We felt so helpless.

When we heard the planes overhead, we thought the Americans were coming to rescue us, but we were wrong. At Sherfadeen Shrine, another Yezidi holy place, we heard that cars were coming to get us. When we got there, we saw there were no cars, so we had to keep walking.

On August 9, we walked off the mountain after the YPG opened a safe corridor for us to get to Syria. They put us in cars and drove us to Khanke in Kurdistan. We stayed here first, but were afraid that Daesh would attack us again, so we went to Zakho, near the border of Turkey. After forty days we returned to Khanke. We lived in the open on the bare ground for one month until getting this tent to live in.

For one year, until July 2015, we did not have water to wash. There is one toilet we share with four families. We have to walk a long way to get water and carry it back to our tent. My sister lives in the next tent with her four children. Her husband is also missing.

We are given food supplies like rice and flour every month by the Barzani Charity Foundation, sponsored by the Kurdistan government. Through Yazda, a German organization gives each person 30,000 dinar ($27 USD) each month. They give it to the camp management who distribute it to each family. There are 3,000 tents in Khanke camp with about 18,000 or more Yezidis living here.

My girls were all top students. They loved school and can speak English. Now their education is stopped. We do not know what we can do.

In July 2017, the UNHCR team in Duhok interviewed Hamdiya and her daughters. Canada had promised to take 1200 traumatized IDPs. I strongly recommended Hamdiya's family. When they got the call saying they had not been chosen, Gulbahar, the eldest, called me. She was sobbing and could hardly talk. Since the girls had not been abducted and raped, they were not considered to be a traumatized, vulnerable family. There was no country with an asylum program for more than 200,000 traumatized Ezidis who had not been raped.

By the end of 2017, facing a fourth winter in a tent, and with no hope on the horizon, Gulbahar told me she cried every night and wondered why she was alive. The situation for Yezidis was growing more desperate. I continued to search for a country to grant asylum to Hamdiya's family.

When French President Macron promised Nobel Peace Prize winner Nadia Murad that France would accept 100 Yezidi families, I got Hamdiya's family on the list. On December 20, 2018, Hamdiya and her four daughters arrived in France. Her sister's family was given asylum in Canada, dividing their families. Their husbands are missing, presumed dead.

Iraq - A Failing State

From the first ten minutes that I drove through the city of Erbil in 2015, I saw what had been the plan for an independent Kurdistan. There were high-rise, steel and glass condo buildings going up everywhere. Condos in gated communities were priced at a million dollars and up. The skyline was dotted with towering cranes. There were water fountains, chic restaurant-bars for non-Muslims to drink, air conditioned western-style shopping malls promoting credit cards, and a modern beltway around the city. There was one empty road with five lanes in either direction.

The new development in Erbil was a replica of northern Virginia, outside Washington, D.C.'s beltway. Erbil was intended to boom with Kurdistan's independence and direct oil sales via Turkey. Those condos were intended for western oil executives, many who bought their shares in oil companies when they were in Iraq as contractors obscenely ripping off the US taxpayers from 2003 to 2011.

Kurdistan tried to sell oil directly into Turkey, bypassing Baghdad revenue-sharing, so in January 2014, Baghdad stopped sending money to Erbil for monthly civil servant salaries. It was a stalemate.

After Daesh declared its caliphate in Iraq in June 2014, development stopped. The condos were not selling. The shopping malls were empty. The economy was stalled. Kurdistan was failing along with the Baghdad central government. Most of the population, including Kurds, Arabs, and non-Muslims, felt their future was bleak. Like water running out of a sieve, thousands per day were leaving Iraq by any means.

The secret Sykes-Picot agreement of 1916 that created Iraq out of three distinct ethnic groups plus non-Muslim minorities had never succeeded. Sectarian government based on tribal allegiances could not be replaced with secularism. Since at least 1986, the plan was to divide Iraq into three countries: Shia, Sunni, Kurd. The problem with that plan was that it did not include self-governance for Yezidis in Shingal and other non-Muslim minorities.

Yezidi interpreters who had worked for the US Army stated that Shingal was the reason that the Americans failed to divide the country as planned. Shingal lay between Kurdistan in the north and Sunnis in central Iraq. No one had made a plan to accommodate 400,000 Yezidis living there. Kurdistan pressed forward with its Kurdification plan by refusing to recognize Yezidis as a distinct ethno-religious minority. The Kurdistan Regional Government, under President Masoud Barzani, insisted with an uncompromising, pathological zealotry that Yezidis were Kurds.

A June 2016 survey about the proposed referendum on Kurdistan independence was taken by 40,000 residents in Kurdistan and Shingal. The results listed three minority groups, but did not once acknowledge the existence of Yezidis as an ethnic or religious minority. The KRG government web page with population demographics in 2016 failed to acknowledge the existence of Yezidis even though 300,000 displaced Yezidis were living in IDP camps in Kurdistan after the attack.

The majority Kurdish party, PDK in Erbil and Dohuk, and the minority Kurdish parties, PUK and Goran in Sulaymaniyah, insisted that Yezidis were Kurds. The PYD Kurdish political party from Rojava, Syria, with its YPG and YPJ armed militias, also, insisted the Yezidis were Kurds. The Yezidis had to be Kurds so that Shingal could be claimed as Kurdish territory and annexed to Kurdistan.

As Kurdish parliamentarian Shoresh Haji stated "I hope that the Kurdish leadership will not miss this golden opportunity to bring Kurdish lands in the disputed territories back under Kurdish control".

Inside Kurdistan, Yezidis dared not insist publicly they are Yezidis and not Kurds, for fear of losing their shelter and food, not to mention risking physical violence against them. Fear gripped every Yezidi, of every station in life, living in Kurdistan or with family in Kurdistan. Only those Yezidis whose jobs relied on PDK patronage said they were Kurdish. In 2017, professors in the University of Duhok pressured students to join the PDK political party of Barzani.

By June 2014, Daesh, a Sunni militant force, had control of Mosul and Fallujah, the two largest Sunni cities in Iraq. On June 7-9, Daesh entered Mosul and was joined by residents. On June 10, the Iraqi Army and Iraqi Police stationed in and around Mosul withdrew without any major battle. Differing sources put Iraqi security forces at 15,000; 50,000; or 75,000. Yezidis accused Masoud Barzani, the president of Kurdistan, and Atheel Al Najaifi, the civilian governor of Mosul, of helping Daesh take control of Mosul by offering no resistance.

Sunnis defended Al Najaifi by explaining that as a civilian leader he had no authority over the security forces. The Shia Prime Minister al-Maliki was minister of defense, minister of interior and more. As such, he ruled essentially as a dictator. No military commander in Mosul would have acted with force against Daesh without direct orders from al-Maliki which never came. Without orders to defend Mosul, the Iraqi Army and Police withdrew. In January 2017, the Baghdad central government issued an arrest warrant for Al Najaifi on charges of allowing Turkish troops to enter Iraq. Then Al Najaifi moved to Kurdistan.

There were very few Sunnis in any of the Iraqi security forces. Sunnis in Mosul had refused to join the army or police because they were sectarian Shia forces rather than secular forces. So the Shia soldiers changed into traditional Arab clothing of long shirts to their feet so they could go home to southern Iraq dressed as civilians without being attacked.   The division between Shias and Sunnis was progressing.

On June 29, 2014, Daesh announced the establishment of a new caliphate. Abu Bakr al-Baghdadi proclaimed himself as its caliph, and the group formally changed its name to the Islamic State. Four days later, Abu Bakr al-Baghdadi called upon all Muslims in the world to unite behind him to capture Rome in order to "own the world."

Many imams in Islamic countries challenged al-Baghdadi's legitimacy stating that the leader of the caliphate had to be elected by all the imam's. This is similar to how the Catholic Pope is elected by archbishops from around the world.

The self-proclaimed Islamic State (Daesh) leader, Abu Bakr al-Baghdadi, in a July 2014 speech at the Great Mosque of al-Nuri in Mosul, vowed that "this blessed advance will not stop until we hit the last nail in the coffin of the Sykes–Picot conspiracy".   Arab assimilation of Yezidis had failed under Saddam Hussein. The next tactic was to eliminate them from the face of the earth.

The Yezidi Genocide Was a Plan

The Yezidi genocide happened because of fighting over oil, land, and religion. The western countries wanted control over oil from the Middle East. Kurdistan wanted an independent country for the Kurds with expanded borders to include Shingal, the Nineveh plain, and oil-rich Kirkuk. Sunni Arab extremists, acting under the label of Daesh, wanted their own Islamic country, under fundamentalist Shariah law, which they referred to as the Islamic State and al-Sham. They, too, wanted Shingal, the Nineveh plain, and Kirkuk.

The Yezidi genocide happened because all of these objectives intersected. It was the revised plan to do what US presence from 2003 to 2011 had failed to do in nine years: divide Iraq along ethnic and religious lines. Every person one asked in Iraq agreed that it was a failed state.

Shingal was designated a disputed territory. The new constitution that the Americans left Iraq with in 2005 included Article 140 which called for a referendum by 2007, postponed to October 2016, to decide the future of the disputed territories which included Kirkuk as well as Shingal and the Nineveh plain. The deadlines came and went without a referendum.

An attack upon Yezidis would result in depopulating Shingal. The genocide was a land grab. Viyan Havind, one of 5,270 kidnapped women and children summed it up best: "It was not about religion. It was all about stealing our property and raping our women."

The multi-national oil companies and western countries wanted Kurdistan's oil. It would be easier to buy it directly from an independent Kurdistan loyal to America. Kurdistan built an oil pipeline to the deep water port of Ceyhan, Turkey. It began sending oil to Ceyhan in December 2013, making the US and Europe dependent on maintaining relations with Turkey.

Iran had its own strategy. It was having a hard time selling its crude oil due to the American-imposed blockade. If Iran could control Baghdad and the disputed territories of Kirkuk and Shingal in Iraq, it could build a pipeline from Iran through Iraq to Tartus, Syria, where Russia had its deep water port in the Mediterranean. This would provide an oil source to compete with Ceyhan, Turkey. This route was referred to as the Shia Crescent. Iran, supported by Russia, coveted it. For Iran to simply invade Iraq and grab the land would be an act of war which the Americans would never allow.

Although Daesh was a Sunni terrorist organization, Iran, a predominately Shia country, saw the benefit of covertly supporting Daesh to disrupt and divide Iraq. While Iran was allegedly secretly financing Daesh, it convinced Baghdad to let its Shia PMU (Hashd al-Sha'abi) militias enter Iraq. Once Daesh was defeated with help of these Shia militias, Iran could eventually control Shingal. . .the old war strategy of divide and conquer. So Iran was willing to support the Yezidis to retake Shingal. No other country offered financial or military support to Yezidis.

Baghdad wanted to control Kirkuk for its oil. Iran wanted to control Baghdad as a satellite Iranian city so it could build a pipeline to the Mediterranean. Kurdistan, also, wanted to expand its borders to control Kirkuk to support an independent country. The fundamentalist Sunni Arabs wanted their Islamic caliphate.

In addition to wanting to import Iraq's oil, the US saw the opportunity to export arms, its largest product, to the Middle East. Perpetual war was making the US arms manufacturers and their shareholders wealthy while Muslim countries destroyed one another.

It was not just one thing that motivated the genocide. Each group had its own goal, The genocide resulted from the convergence of greed for land, oil, power, and religious dominance. Extremist Sunni Islamic ideology was the tool that was used to implement the plan to divide Iraq.

Stage 1: Negotiate a Secret Agreement to Sell Out Shingal

According to a PKK commander of the newly organized YPJ for women, on May 13, 2014, a publicized, but closed-door meeting took place in Amman, Jordan. It was attended by mostly Sunnis from Turkey, Jordan, Qatar, and Saudi Arabia. One representative from the PDK Kurdistan government was allegedly in attendance. A secret decision was allegedly made to divide Iraq. There was wide speculation that an agreement had been made to give Shingal to the Kurds in Kurdistan in exchange for Kirkuk for the Sunni Arabs. Sunni leaders in the meeting promised to support the Sunni tribes in Mosul and Ramadi.

Were other countries involved in the agreement to betray Shingal in order to divide Iraq? One may speculate. It is popular opinion in Iraq that the United States, although not directly responsible for the genocide, watched and refused to stop it on the first day and for more than three years thereafter.

The United States' strongest allies in the Middle East are Turkey, Saudi Arabia, and Israel. For decades the US has refrained from condemning human rights abuses by any of these countries. Saudi Arabia has a predominately Sunni population. Women must cover themselves head-to-toe in black and cannot go out without being accompanied by a male relative. Saudi women did not get the right to vote until December 2015. In 2018 they got the right to drive. Saudi Arabia publicly lashes and beheads people for infractions of Shariah law. Drinking a glass of wine in the privacy of one's own home would be such an infraction or blogging against a government policy. How could Saudi Arabia be one of the closest allies of the United States?

In 2016, the US State Department approved the sale of $1.15 billion dollars in tanks and other heavy equipment to Saudi Arabia. This was with full knowledge that Saudi Arabia is headquarters to Islam's fundamentalist Wahhabism that suppresses all forms of human rights, especially for females. The women and girls of Kocho reported that when they were captured and distributed, a Saudi prince got first choice to take the most beautiful girls as sex slaves.

By June 2017 the United States arms deals with Saudi Arabia totaled more than $100 billion. A White House official for the Trump administration said, "It's good for the American economy."

The US is the world's largest arms' manufacturer. Turkey is its fourth largest customer. Made-in-America tanks, war planes, guns and heavy armament were used against Turkey's own citizens. In spite of Turkey's three decades of displacement and massacres amounting to genocide against Kurds in its southeast, the US policy continued to support Turkey to destroy the PKK militants and turn a blind eye to Turkey's escalating human rights abuses against Kurds.

US Congresswoman Tulsi Gabbard, an Iraq war veteran and an Army Captain, stated, "There's a double standard here. For years now, our government, working with countries like Saudi Arabia, Turkey and Qatar, have been, through the CIA, quietly arming and supporting these groups that are directly working with groups like Qaida and ISIS. All in this effort to overthrow the Syrian government."

Colonel Richard Kemp, Head of U.K. International Terrorism Intelligence (from 2001–2006) stated, "We don't approve of what Saudi Arabia does. We don't like what they do, but they are a necessary evil in combating other regimes. And, of course, ultimately, they have a lot of oil."

An Iraqi Air Force pilot stated that the United States, United Kingdom, Saudi Arabia, Turkey, Qatar, and France were involved in the deal to betray Shingal. It was part of a bigger plan to destroy Syria. This theory is supported by many Yezidis. The same pilot was flying generals and VIPs into the Ramadi airport for meetings on a regular basis when Daesh had control of Ramadi. His plane never came under attack.

Stage 2: Announce the Caliphate

On June 9, 2014, Daesh took total control of Mosul, a predominately Sunni Arab city. Mosul became Daesh headquarters in Iraq. On June 29, 2014, Daesh announced its Islamic Caliphate with Abu Bakr al-Baghdadi as its leader. They declared jihad upon non-Muslims which Islam refers to as "kuffirs" or infidels. In July 2014, Daesh announced no more Christians remained in Mosul. Daesh also declared jihad against Shias, stating they were not the real Muslims.

Stage 3: Finance the Daesh Jihad

Sunni Arab jihadists seized hundreds of government-owned Toyota pickup trucks, humvees and heavy equipment left behind for the Iraqi army when the Americans withdrew from Iraq in 2011. They raided an estimated $429 million US dollars from Mosul's central bank and millions more from forty local banks. They captured oil fields and sold oil on the black market, tumbling oil prices from $100 a barrel to $35.

Once Daesh secured Mosul, its next task was to push its control westward to connect with Raqqa, its capital in Syria which it already controlled. The border between Iraq and Syria would be removed. In Arabic, "Daesh" is the acronym for the Islamic State of Iraq and al-Sham (Syria, Jordan, and Lebanon).

Raqqa, in northeast Syria, is 256 miles directly west of Mosul. Highway 47 connects the two cities in a straight line. It goes directly through the Nineveh plain and Shingal, through the main city of Sinjar on the south side of Shingal Mountain, and on to the Syrian border.   This would be the demarcation line between Kurdistan and the new Islamic caliphate.

Shingal was geographically inconvenient, a fly in the ointment. It had to be depopulated.

Daesh now controlled Mosul as its headquarters in Iraq for its Islamic State caliphate. It had hundreds of modern four-wheel drive pickups, tanks, and missile launchers.

Stage 4: Disarm Shingal Before Attacking

On June 9-10, 2014, the Iraqi security forces abandoned Mosul and went home. Peshmerga forces stopped those who went north to Kurdistan or west to Shingal and confiscated their arms. In the following three days, those who made it home to Shingal were visited at home by Peshmerga who confiscated any remaining government-issued weapons and government vehicles.

After the fall of Mosul, Daesh forces surrounded Tal Afar, to the west. Although the Iraqi air force gave aerial coverage, it was not enough to save the Iraqi military from attack. So on July 14, 2014, the Iraqi border patrol for Iraq, under commander Abu Waleed Al Qurashi, withdrew all its forces from Shingal. Al Qurashi, on July 14, was escorted by forty Iraqi Border Patrol vehicles as he drove from his headquarters in Tal Afar to Feysh Khabur contingency operating base (COB) at the border of Kurdistan. The Border Patrol turned in their guns and were sent home. Abu Waleed Al Qurashi drove to Erbil and then flew to Baghdad. The Iraqi military was officially gone from Shingal and Kurdistan, leaving only Kurdistan Peshmerga forces to defend Shingal.

From July 14 to 17, 2014, Serbast Bapiri, commander of KDP Peshmerga 17th branch in Shingal, ordered all security forces to turn in their Iraqi security ID badges in the PDK headquarters in Sinjar. They were told they were officially in

Peshmerga and would be issued weapons. It was official that Iraqi security forces under Baghdad command were no longer protecting Shingal.

Erbil sent Peshmerga to the Yezidi villages and cities in Shingal where they established bases in the schools to protect the residents. Local residents fed them. Some Yezidis say Peshmerga presence was to control them, not protect them, since no Peshmerga bases were established in the neighboring Arab villages. In June and July when Yezidis from the villages southeast of Sinjar tried to leave for Kurdistan, Peshmerga checkpoints at the entrance to Sinjar blocked them and turned them back to their villages, saying "Why are we protecting you, if you are going to leave?" They were trapped.

Stage 5: Peshmerga Withdrawal

Kurdistan is a small region. It is less than 300 miles (483 kilometers) from one end to another. It is easy to know people all over the country. Yezidis lived among Arabs in Shingal and went to work, shopping, or on business to Duhok and Erbil, predominately populated by Kurds. So all Yezidis knew Arabs and Kurds.

At least one week in advance of the attack on Shingal, Arabs began warning their Yezidi friends to leave Shingal. Many Yezidis got calls from Arab friends at 10:30 PM on August 2, 2014, warning them to run, because Daesh were on their way to attack. They were driving their private cars and those white Toyota pickup trucks they had captured in Mosul in June.

Eleven thousand Peshmerga forces withdrew from Shingal between 4 AM and 9:30 AM on August 3, leaving the Yezidis defenseless against the barbaric attack by Daesh that started just after midnight and lasted for a dozen hours. This betrayal of the Peshmerga, who had pledged to defend Shingal until their last breath, is the singular reason why Yezidis lost trust in Kurds and the Kurdistan government.   It was a betrayal that could never be forgotten or forgiven. The retreat left the Yezidis defenseless and allowed the massacre to happen.

Stage 6: Murder and Kidnapping

Religious terrorism was the means to an end. The genocide in Shingal was implemented strictly according to the book. What book was that? The Quran. There was a verse used from the Quran to justify every action.   All human actions are described as either acceptable (halal) or unacceptable (haram). Taking women as slaves and raping them is halal according to the Quran. "And all married women (are forbidden) unto you save those (captives) whom your right hands possess." Since married women are forbidden, Daesh killed their husbands first.

According to the Quran it is halal (acceptable) to kill those who are non-Muslim and do not have a religious "book". Since Christians have the Bible and

Jews have the Torah, they are considered "people of the book" and were not to be killed or raped. But since Yezidis do not have a religious book, it is considered halal to rape women and girls as young as nine so long as they are not pregnant. So with the battle cry of "Allah-u-Akbar," Daesh swept through the villages and cities of Shingal killing Yezidi men and kidnapping Yezidi women and children.

They entered Shingal from Mosul and Tal Afar in the east and fired shots from Ain Gazal, south of Tal Qassab, between 1 and 1:30 AM. Others came from Baaj on the western border with Syria and attacked Gir Zerik at 2:10 AM. They attacked Siba Sheikh Khudir from 2:30 AM until 5:30 AM. They attacked Tal Ezeer at 10:30 AM. By sunrise, Daesh had entered most villages on both the south and north sides of the mountain. They also came from Zumar and Rabia on the north side of the mountain.

From hundreds of witness testimonies, it was clear that the jihadists operated under a command structure. Many Yezidis reported that their captors called their commander for instructions on how to proceed or suddenly left when they got a phone call to go somewhere else. The jihadist foot soldiers were organized and following orders.

In every village or escape point where Daesh captured Yezidis, they separated them according to predetermined criteria. There were no coincidences or arbitrariness. Daesh took the cash, gold jewelry, guns, and phones from everyone they captured. Daesh threatened to kill anyone who kept a concealed phone. A woman who was being held at gun point in one group on the mountain said that a Daesh militant told her the plan was that the Kurdistan government was going to pay a ransom for the release of all the captured Yezidis. This was on August 3, even before the captives were transferred.

According to the Kurdistan Directorate General of Ezidi Affairs, Daesh killed or abducted at least 6417 Yezidis. They were divided and subdivided into very specific categories. Their names and ages were identified and they were distributed over the next month as follows:

- males over 15 who refused to convert to Islam were killed on the spot or driven away and are still missing
- boys ages 5 - 15 were sent to jihadist schools and military training camps in Tal Afar and Syria
- disabled and women over 40 were killed or used as laborers, some freed later
- visibly pregnant women were killed or not captured since they could not be used as sex slaves
- single girls over age 9 were taken to Mosul and Raqqa and given or sold into sexual slavery

- married women along with their children under age 2 or 3 were taken to Tal Afar and raped
- children between 2 and 8 were taken from their mothers, housed in schools, and sold to Arabs
- families with a husband present lived freely in Qaser Al Mehrab and Qasal Kao in Tal Afar

By 1 PM on August 3, 2014, all villages had been attacked and Yezidis who could escape were heading to Kurdistan by car or to Syria or Mount Shingal by foot. The first assault was a classic military "shock and awe" assault. The savagery of the attack was enough to send the entire Yezidi population fleeing, except for those villages surrounded by Arab villages such as Kocho and Hatamia. They were trapped. Many Arabs who lived in Shingal stayed and joined forces with Daesh. Just like in Mosul, Sunni Arab residents themselves raised the black flag and announced their loyalty to Daesh.

This stage was finished. Shingal was empty of Yezidis. But unlike the bloodless take-over in Mosul, the taking of Shingal was barbaric and bloody. Yezidis expressed shock at the brutality with which Daesh had attacked. Peshmerga Commander Qassim Shesho stated, "We never expected something this savage to happen."

Stage 7: Jihad Recruitment

Yezidi girls who escaped sex slavery in the hands of Daesh said the Daesh leaders came from Saudi Arabia. They did not bring their families with them. Whereas, men who joined Daesh from over eighty other countries, often moved their families with them to Iraq or Syria.

Daesh actively recruited through a sophisticated internet media campaign. They had an enticing employment package with benefits. Unemployed, disenfranchised, and religious psychopaths from over eighty countries joined. They were promised a salary, a house that had once belonged to a Shia family, a girl or woman for sex, drugs to stay high, food, and religious Islamic schooling for their children.

Daesh released propaganda videos showing men converting to Islam, young boys in military uniform reciting the Quran and receiving weapons training, and "infidels" being beheaded. These videos enticed whole families to fly to Turkey then easily enter Syria or Iraq and enroll themselves and their kids in jihadi training. An estimated 30,000 foreign fighters joined Daesh and underwent extremist Islamic brainwashing. In June 2016, Daesh fighters were captured in Fallujah hiding in an underground tunnel. They numbered 166 Saudis, 5 Chechen, 16 Afghanis, 9 Egyptians, 14 Turkish, and only 6 Iraqis.

Hundreds who became disillusioned and attempted to leave were publicly beheaded. When Daesh needed more recruits, it forcibly conscripted one male from each family living in Mosul. Fathers often volunteered to save their sons.

Stage 8: Looting and House Demolition

In the first month after Daesh took control of Shingal, it ransacked every house in search of hidden gold and cash. It sold the TVs and appliances in bazaars. In mid-September 2014, Daesh exploded hundreds of Yezidi houses that had been specifically targeted based on the owners' ties to Americans or their resistance to the Ba'ath party under Saddam Hussein. Houses of interpreters who had risked their lives for Americans from 2003 - 2011 were especially targeted.

Stage 9: Conversion, Rape, and Shame

In August 2014, Daesh killed or abducted at least 6417 Yezidis. The men were killed. The women were used in sexual slavery. Yezidis may not marry outside of their religion nor convert to another religion. A woman may not have sex before marriage. If a Yezidi does either of these things, sex or conversion, he or she will be shunned. Such behavior would bring shame and dishonor to her entire family

Daesh knew of the Yezidi culture, with behavior closely controlled by fear of punishment for bringing shame to one's family. Killing their men and raping their women and girls was intended to annihilate the Yezidi culture. Yezidi girls and women were bought and sold and raped by multiple men. Two Yezidi girls told of being the only females living in a building with forty-eight men who continuously raped them whenever they wanted which was all day, every day.

Daesh thought with these techniques the captured Yezidis could never return to their families. By using the concept of shame, Daesh planned to annihilate the Yezidi culture.

Stage 10: Daesh Push to Raqqa

Kurdish and Yezidi independent militias, including PKK, YPG, YPJ, and YBS, along with Peshmerga forces retook control of Sinjar city on the south side of Shingal Mountain, on November 12, 2015. They were ready to push eastward to recapture the Yezidi villages, but the International (air) Coalition to fight Daesh, led by the United States, ordered them to stop their advance. That order was reinforced by a coalition airstrike a few hundred meters in front of them on the route to Tal Afar. For two-and-a-half years they manned the front line circling Shingal Mountain and played a waiting game. They said they were "waiting for the Americans to decide the end of the movie."

The Coalition also refused to allow Peshmerga to advance west of the end of Shingal Mountain. The last twelve kilometers of Highway 47 going to Syria were protected from air strikes. This was Daesh's main supply route between Raqqa and Mosul. That route could have been bombed and closed for more than three years, but mysteriously, the Americans allowed the road to remain open to Daesh. Russia accused the US of protecting Daesh to sell its illegal oil into Turkey.

A Clusterfuck

The term Mongolian Cluster Fuck was coined in the 1960s by poet Ed Sanders. It means "a chaotic situation where everything seems to go wrong. It is often caused by incompetence, communication failure, or a complex environment." No term other than "clusterfuck" could better describe what unfolded in Iraq, Syria, and the world after Daesh declared its caliphate. The chaos of the war in Syria spilled into Iraq and beyond.

No one expected the brutality with which Daesh implemented its Islamic State caliphate. The world could not stomach the beheadings, mass executions, and sex slavery of the Yezidi girls. The savagery of the Sunni extremists backfired. Daesh and its so-called caliphate had to be destroyed.

Enemies teamed up with their enemies. Allies became enemies. Governments and militias fought their ally's allies. Enemies partnered with their enemy's allies.

An air coalition was formed. Countries that performed air strikes in Iraq included the United States, Australia, Belgium, Canada, Denmark, France, Jordan, the Netherlands and the United Kingdom. Coalition nations that conducted strikes in Syria included the United States, Australia, Bahrain, Canada, Denmark, France, Jordan, the Netherlands, Saudi Arabia, Turkey, the United Arab Emirates and the United Kingdom.

The Iraqi central government in Baghdad allowed Shia ground militias from Iran, its sworn enemy, to enter Iraq and join the Iraqi Army's fight against Daesh. These forces were called Hashd al-Sha'abi or Popular Mobilization Units (PMU). Iraq partnered with its previous enemy of Iran. Kurdistan allowed Turkey to establish military bases in Bahzani and Bashiqa in Nineveh province.

Russia and Turkey formed a partnership after Turkey shot down a Russian war plane. Two months later, Russia was teaming up with Iran. The US backed Turkey's war to destroy the PKK, but saw Russia as its enemy. The US supported Free Syrian Army (FSA) militias fighting in Syria to overthrow President Bashar Al-Assad, while Russia bombed those same militias saying they supported Daesh. Turkey and the US wanted President Bashar out of Syria. Russia wanted Bashar to remain in power. It was hard to follow the chaos from one week to the next.

Turkey, Saudi Arabia, the United States, and Qatar were accused, with supporting evidence, of financing and supporting Daesh. Some add France and the United Kingdom to this list.

Masoud Barzani, the Kurdish President of Kurdistan, partnered with President Erdogan in Turkey who was destroying Kurds by the thousands in a military and bombing campaign against civilians and PKK in southeast Turkey and the Qandil Mountains in Kurdistan, Iraq.

The PKK were fighting for Kurdish rights and helping in the return of kidnapped Yezidis, but the KRG demanded they withdraw from Shingal. The Yezidi Peshmerga commanders in Shingal refused to use violence to force the PKK to withdraw.

The PKK created and trained the YBS, an independent militia of Yezidis. KRG and Turkey created the "Rojava Peshmerga," allegedly made up of Kurdish refugees from Syria. But witnesses say the Rojava Peshmerga were Arabs and Sunni Turkmen from Iraq supported by Turkey and KRG. Turkmen speak Turkish and live in Tal Afar where the Yezidis were held captive. The Yezidis called the Rojava Peshmerga the Daesh Peshmerga. On March 3, 2017, the Rojava Peshmerga confronted the Yezidi YBS forces in Shingal resulting in the deaths of five Yezidis. On April 25, 2017, Turkey conducted airstrikes in Syria and Shingal, killing Yezidi and Kurdish Peshmerga and civilians.

Yezidis could neither forgive nor forget the betrayal of the Kurdish Peshmerga withdrawal that allowed the genocide to occur. An intense mistrust and hatred toward Kurds grew and gained momentum among Yezidis. The plan for Kurdistan to annex Shingal was fiercely challenged. Yezidis argued for self-governance and self-defense enforced by international protection. Yezidi Peshmerga commanders in uniform, working for the Kurdistan government, stated privately they were Yezidis and wanted an independent territory for Yezidis.

Oil prices plummeted. There was a world glut. Kurdistan's oil was no longer essential in the world market. Oil companies pulled out of Kurdistan. The million-dollar condos in Erbil remained empty.

The Kurds and the Yezidi leaders were desperate to block Yezidis from leaving Iraq. Canada agreed to resettle 1200 Yezidi and Syrian Kurdish survivors in 2017, but the Kurdistan government quickly took a stand against Canada's "interference". The office for issuing Iraqi nationality cards, called jensias, was closed in February, preventing Yezidis from getting their IDs and passports. Yezidis with conflicting visions lobbied both for and against asylum.

From May 21-28, 2017, the Baghdad-backed Hashd al-Sha'abi forces liberated the Yezidi villages south of Mount Shingal. Yezidi commander Nayef Jaso, muhktar of Kocho, led his unit in leaving Peshmerga and retaking Kocho and other villages. President Masoud Barzani was furious over having the Peshmerga ordered by the US-led Coalition not to participate in liberating the villages. The stand-off between Baghdad Hashd al-Sha'abi and KRG Peshmerga forces intensified. Armed internal conflict was threatened.

Many Yezidis disagreed with the religious and political "leaders" who supported the PDK party and Kurdistan. They opposed annexation of Shingal to Kurdistan and pushed for a self-administered Yezidi region within Iraq and international protection.

On September 25, 2017, 92.7% of the people of Kurdistan voted to become an independent country. Baghdad, the United States, and European countries refused to recognize the result. The disputed territory of Shingal and Nineveh continued unresolved. The promise of Article 140 in the Iraqi constitution, which ordered a referendum for the disputed territories to decide their future, was not fulfilled. The only question on the referendum was "Do you want Kurdistan to be an independent country?" The question, "Do you want Shingal to become part of Kurdistan?" was missing.

Daesh Claims Mosul as Capital of Caliphate

And fight with them until there is no more fitna (disorder, unbelief) and religion should be only for Allah. Quran verse 8:39

In January 2014, Daesh took control of Fallujah, a predominately Sunni city in Anbar province, in the south of Iraq. On June 6, 2014, at 2:30 in the morning, a Daesh convoy of pickup trucks entered the western part of Mosul. Street fighting was reported to have occurred at 3:30 AM.

One resident who escaped Mosul, described this: "The reports of over 1,000 militants is not true. There was a protest of 300 Mosul residents in a poor neighborhood. They were protesting against poor government services such as uncollected garbage in the streets and lack of electricity. The neighborhood demonstrators started noticing about 200 bearded men among them. That's all there were who took over the city. Then people began to join the crowd."

Sleeper cells living in the city rallied to them. There were incidents of battles and suicide bombs on June 7 and 8. On June 9, at 4:30 PM, there was an explosion near forty police officers stationed near Mosul Hotel. The battalion's commander, Colonel Dhiyab Ahmed al-Assi al-Obeidi was wounded.

That night, Iraqi Army generals Aboud Qanbar and Ali Ghaidan withdrew across the river, leaving Lieutenant General Mahdi Gharawi, the operational commander of Nineveh province, at his command post without any orders. The next morning Ghaidan and Qanbar were in Kurdistan. President Al-Maliki did not give an order to fight Daesh, so within a few hours, Iraqi Army soldiers and police disappeared. Many of the Sunni members of the Iraqi Army stationed in Mosul lived there. They had only to go home to their houses in Mosul. Others changed out of their uniforms into their traditional Arab dress and left Mosul.

On the morning of June 10, 2014, Gharawi and twenty-six of his men fought their way across a bridge to eastern Mosul where they came under heavy fire. Three soldiers were killed and their five trucks were burned. It was every man for himself, as Gharawi said.

The militants seized facilities including Mosul International Airport. By June 10, Daesh was in control of Mosul, a predominately Sunni city of two million people. Sixty-one militants, forty-one government troops and seven civilians were reported killed.

Daesh announced a new government on their website, because they banned TVs. They immediately began garbage removal and restored electricity. The security checkpoints were gone. Many Sunni residents welcomed the "new government" in hopes of better treatment and services than they were receiving under the Shia-controlled central government in Baghdad.

When the jihadists entered the city, they reportedly marked Christian houses with an "N" for "Nazarene", and gave their occupants a choice: convert, pay the *jizya*, a tax on non-Muslims, or face possible death. A half-million residents, both Sunni and Shia Muslim and non-Muslim, fled north to the safety of Kurdistan in the first three days before Daesh established their own checkpoints around the city. The drive to Erbil which normally takes forty-five minutes took twelve hours. On the fourth day, those who had not escaped were trapped until its 2017 liberation, having to obey strict Shariah laws.

Daesh confiscated the houses of those who fled. One year later, Daesh delivered written notices to the occupants of their homes, that the registered owners had twenty-four hours to return to Mosul and occupy their own houses or forfeit them.

Daesh did not suddenly appear from somewhere else. Residents just raised the black flag of jihad to announce their participation. The first time I saw this flag, I thought it was a cartoon. Who would choose a black flag for a new country? And why? Black is the color of death. The goal was to terrorize. The white Arabic letters spelled "There is no god but Allah. Mohammed is the messenger of God." This is a declaration of Islamic faith known as the *shahada*. Recitation of it in front of witnesses is all that is required to convert to Islam.

La ilaha illa'llah twice and *allahu la ilaha illa hu.*

Daesh were Iraqi Sunni Arabs, former members of Saddam Hussein's Ba'ath party. Mosul was their stronghold. After Saddam's regime was toppled by the Americans in 2003, Paul Bremer was appointed as the American Coalition Provisional Authority (CPA) of Iraq.

Bremer fired all government managers from the Ba'ath party and disbanded the Iraqi Army, both of which were composed mostly of Sunni Arabs. Shias in Baghdad took over power in Iraq, and Sunnis became second-class citizens. This caused unemployment, poverty, and malcontent among Sunnis which is cited as one of the main causes of the rise of Daesh.

For residents who decided not to flee Mosul in that three-day window of opportunity, the darkness of extremist Islam descended. Daesh ordered all men to grow beards. They publically beheaded resisters, threw gay men to their death from buildings, hanged men from utility poles and left their flesh to rot, and burned soldiers in cages to terrorize others into submitting to their tyranny. They released 2,400 prisoners. After separating the Sunni inmates, they executed the remaining 670 prisoners. Daesh videos showed them drowning Sunnis in cages because they worked for the Iraqi government or military.

Western clothing was destroyed in the stores and replaced with the black garments of Saudi Arabia. All females had to cover themselves head to toe, including a veil over their eyes, black socks and black gloves. Not one square inch of skin could show. They could not go out unaccompanied by a man.

The curriculum in schools was replaced by Islamic studies from the Quran. Art, music, mathematics and more were banned.   Text books were burned. Smoking and drinking alcohol were banned. Doctors and nurses were ordered to report to work in the hospitals. Those who failed to show up for work were killed in their homes.

A $500 fine was levied against anyone with a satellite dish. Only a few spots remained at the edge of the city where a resident could walk and get a phone signal from the front line with Peshmerga. Residents were without news from or communication with the outside world.

Daesh militants were Iraqi citizens.   So the notion that a foreign invading army stormed the city is erroneous. Between 200 and 1500 armed terrorists took control of a city of two million people. It is estimated that the Iraqi Army outnumbered Daesh militants fifteen to one. All Iraqi security forces simply melted into thin air. Sunni Arabs rose up against the Shia central government and took control of Mosul.

On June 12, 2014, Daesh killed at least 1,566 Shia Iraqi Air Force cadets in an attack on Camp Speicher in Tikrit. At the time of the attack, there were between 4,000 and 11,000 unarmed cadets in the camp. Daesh fighters singled out Shia and non-Muslim cadets from Sunni ones and murdered them. The Iraqi government blamed the massacre on both Daesh and members from the Arab Socialist Ba'ath Party in Iraq.

On June 29, 2014, Abu Bakr al-Baghdadi declared himself the caliphate (supreme leader) of the Islamic State. They declared jihad upon Shia Muslims and non-Muslims which Islam refers to as "kuffirs" or infidels. Daesh stated that Shias were not real Muslims. They vowed to kill or convert all Yezidis.

By the time Daesh attacked Mosul in June 2014, there was not one Yezidi family left in Mosul. All Yezidis had already fled in 2007 after Al-Qaeda executed 23 Ezidi men in Mosul. Al-Qaeda was the Sunni militant group said to be the predecessor group to Daesh. The Ezidis were on their way home to Bashiqa from work in a textile factory in Mosul when their bus was hijacked by Al-Qaeda militants. Al-Qaeda checked the religion on everyone's ID and ordered non-Yezidis to get off the bus. They drove the bus to an empty lot, lined the Yezidis up against a wall, and executed them. Al-Qaeda said the executions were in retaliation for the "honor killing" by stoning of the seventeen-year-old Yezidi girl, Du'a Khalil Aswad, in Bashiqa on April 7, 2007.

In July 2014, Daesh announced no more Christians remained in Mosul.

By the time Mosul was liberated between January and July 2017, the city was destroyed from fierce street-to-street battles and coalition aerial bombing. One report estimated 40,000 people were killed during the liberation. There was little to return to without massive international rebuilding funds.

Daesh Attacked Sunni Arabs in Alzewiah

Omar al-Jubouri (not his real name), May 8, 2017

I was working with the US Army when I got shot and lost one kidney. Daesh destroyed my life. Even before the genocide in Shingal against the Yezidis, Daesh attacked the Sunni people of Alzewiah, a village 120 kilometers south of Mosul. Alzewiah is between the Baiji oil refinery and Sharqat. Our village is not like other villages in Iraq. It is open to other cultures. Our jobs are welders and operators in the oil fields and refineries. That is why we speak English, because we were working with American and British oil companies.

Twice in June 2014, a Daesh representative came to negotiate with our town manager or mayor, referred to as the "muhktar". Abu Bakr al-Baghdadi, the leader of Daesh, wanted permission to enter our city. Our muhktar refused and said we were ready to defend ourselves.

On July 6 a negotiator came again. Again our muhktar did not agree. Our muhktar talked to Prime Minister al-Maliki in Baghdad and asked him for help. Maliki promised that the Iraqi Army would defend us. We called for help for two days, but help never came.

At 9 AM, July 7, the Daesh negotiator said they would enter our city by force. Al-Baghdadi had given the order to attack Alzewiah and kill everyone, including women and children. Daesh is mostly Sunni Arabs, so he made an example of the Sunnis so that no Sunni would dare to oppose him. We prepared for battle. I was in the Iraqi police, so I had a weapon.

Alzewiah had a population of 13,000 Sunni Arabs. I am sure not one person in Alzewiah supported Daesh. Before Daesh attacked us in 2014, they were called Al Qaida. Between 2008 and 2012, many people from Alzewiah were abducted or killed by Al Qaida, especially old men.

The Sunni Arab villages surrounding Alzewiah supported Daesh and so did many of the people in Mosul. We were isolated in a dangerous situation. People in the surrounding areas warned our muhktar that Daesh was planning to attack and abduct all our women. From the mosque, our muhktar made a call to warn everyone and tell the women to leave the city. Most went to Erbil on July 8, leaving the men to defend our city.

Daesh attacked us at 12:35 PM on July 7. I fought against Daesh with my younger brother. Again our muhktar called Prime Minister al-Maliki and begged for help, "We are fighting Daesh. We are in danger!" They did not care about us. Some people called me from Mosul and asked me "Why? Why? Why are you fighting against the Islamic State?" Many people in Mosul welcomed Daesh. They called us Jewish for not supporting the Islamic State.

The battle in Alzewiah lasted two days until we ran out of bullets. We were begging Baghdad to send us more ammunition. We did not need soldiers; only ammunition and field equipment.

We killed 300 of the Daesh militants. Daesh killed 100 residents including women and babies. They abducted 200. Rumors say they were taken to Raqqa, Syria, but I am certain Daesh killed them.

My younger brother was burned to death in the battle. Only half of our town managed to escape with the clothes on their backs. I was with my family in the mountains. I called friends who came with their car and rescued us.

Alzewiah is all Sunni, but we are educated, not extremists. I myself have two university degrees. We know the goal of Daesh is to create an Islamic State caliphate. We don't like extremism. My family was rich. Daesh destroyed our house because I used to work as an interpreter with the Americans. I had a big library. I read about history, Europe, Muslims, and Jews.

I don't differentiate between people, Shia, Sunni, Kurd, Yezidi, or anyone. I love all people in the world except Daesh who destroy civilization. In European countries, parents teach their children to enjoy life. Young children learn to play the violin. In Iraq and Syria, Daesh militants teach young children how to shoot guns and hate people. The Islamic State is not Islam.

In 2012, when my American friends encouraged me to go live in America, I told them "I love my country. My country flows in my blood. I will not leave."

Since 2014, my life is destroyed. I had dreams, but Daesh destroyed them. Daesh destroyed my house, my library, our family's store, my life. Daesh destroyed everything. They killed my brother. Daesh thiefed my life. When I think of what happened, I get confused and have attacks of crying and fainting. I cannot sleep at night. I sent my CV to 200 organizations, but no one will hire me. I lose hope.

I joined the Shia Popular Mobilization Units (PMU, also called Hashd al-Sha'abi) from Iran who were fighting Daesh. My mother stayed with me in our camp high up, looking down on a plain. We were between Alzewiah and Baiji. On March 24, 2016, we could not believe our eyes. Six Apache helicopters from the American coalition forces landed right in the middle of Daesh territory. Two F16s were flying overhead to provide air cover. Five cars from Daesh arrived. Everyone got out and met one another for one hour. I was 500 meters away. More than 200 people witnessed this meeting.

My friends in the militia wanted to shoot the Apaches, but I warned them not to, because the F16s would kill us. After one hour, the Apaches took off and flew right over us, then turned north toward Erbil.

My sixty-two-year-old mother watched the meeting with me. She said, "I can't believe my eyes. My son sacrificed his life fighting Daesh and now the American coalition is supporting Daesh. Is this what my son died for?"

I swear the American air coalition sees Daesh and could stop them, but does not. I swear on my dead brother, killed by Daesh, I see the US coalition is helping Daesh. I was losing my mind when I saw those Apaches land in Daesh territory. The next day Daesh attacked us with new M16s, maybe because we were witnesses to the secret meeting. My friend thinks the coalition supplied them with arms during that meeting. I did not see it myself.

I left the Shia PMU when I saw that they had no humanity. They would kill anyone and destroy houses, just like Daesh. Being Sunni, my family is caught in the middle of everyone fighting each other. In 2016, Hezbollah beat my father severely and accused him of working for Daesh. How can we support Daesh when Daesh killed my brother? Sometimes my father loses his mind because of the physical and psychological pain.

I am talking to you from Sharqat, south of Mosul, on January 26, 2017. It is dark and cold because we have no electricity now. We are three-and-a-half kilometers from Daesh. Daesh has been attacking for hours. Do you hear the bombs? They do it every day. I can see their cars on the other side of the river. Now the American coalition is flying overhead. They just fired one missile and left. I do not understand why the coalition does not want to stop Daesh. We were hopeful when the American coalition began, but I see with my eyes the coalition is helping Daesh.

On May 8, 2017, I photographed two coalition Chinook helicopters flying over Sharqat. I swear I see with my own eyes that they are landing regularly inside of Daesh territory. Daesh continues daily attacks on us in Sharqat. Last week they captured my father and held him for two days and beat him. We are not safe anywhere. Please tell me, what do the Americans want from us? Why won't they stop Daesh from attacking us? Tomorrow I may be killed.

Helicopter Crash and Culture of Shame
Mirza Dunnayi, Dec. 31, 2016

I was in Erbil, the capital of Kurdistan, when Daesh attacked. Everyone was shocked at how fast Daesh controlled every town and city in Shingal on August 3, 2014. We were getting phone calls that approximately 40,000 Yezidis had climbed onto Shingal Mountain in 45C heat. In August it is bone dry. Daesh attacked Shingal from the south side of the mountain coming from Mosul in the east and Baaj in the south near the Syrian border. About 300,000 people escaped by car to Kurdistan, but within one day, Daesh also attacked on the north side of the mountain, coming from the Arab villages in Rabia and from the Syrian border near Zumar. By the second day, the mountain was encircled and there were no escape routes.

I knew there was no time to waste. Without water, people would begin dying on the mountain within hours. I contacted the President and Prime Minister who ordered the Iraqi Air Force to fly helicopters to deliver food and water to those trapped on the mountain.

A few days after the attack, we flew from Erbil to the military base in Feysh Khabur near Zakho. In the first days, there was no organization. People spontaneously drove up and dropped off boxes of food and water to the command post. Private citizens, NGOs, political parties, and the Kurdistan government made donations.

By car the drive to the mountain top takes three hours. By helicopter it takes fifteen minutes. The helicopter was able to make three or four trips per day to deliver water and food. I was on twelve of those flights helping to deliver the aid. The displaced Yezidis had gathered in about forty locations on the 100 kilometers mountain range.

When they saw our helicopter, hundreds would come running, but many people received no help. Over 300 children died from dehydration and starvation and their bodies had to be left on the mountain. Many elderly died, too.

Each time the helicopter landed, it was chaotic and dangerous because everyone wanted to be airlifted to safety. We could carry thirty people back to Kurdistan on each flight.

On the morning of August 12, Vian Dakhil, the Yezidi parliamentarian from Nineveh province who had begged for help on the floor of parliament, called me and asked if she could join me on the helicopter. Of course, I agreed, because any publicity we could get out to the world would help. We landed for ten minutes to deliver the supplies. Vian got out and took some photos with the displaced Yezidis.

We were mobbed. When we tried to take off, too many desperate people climbed on board. The pilot was telling us it was overloaded and ordered some people to get off. They refused, and we could not control the frantic people, so he began to lift off while people were clinging to the side of the helicopter. The helicopter was overloaded and it tipped when we were only ten meters in the air.

The pilot might have recovered if it had not been for our precarious location, only twenty-five meters from a 1000-meter vertical drop into a rocky valley. The blade hit the rocky cliff wall and the plane crashed in the valley. There were forty-seven people in the helicopter. I was underneath all the bodies. I could not breathe under their weight. I was suffocating. I went from rushing adrenalin to a dark stillness.

The brain is a mysterious wonder. We can process multiple memories and thoughts all within a few seconds, faster than a computer chip. It was not a life review that flashed through my head, but my final regrets.

I asked God, why should I be punished when I did all good things for my community? Why did I have to die today, on my son's sixth birthday, so he would never be able to celebrate it? Why couldn't I have died yesterday or tomorrow? I was glad that my parents had preceded me in death by a few months, so that they would not have to be heart-broken by their son's death.

My worst regret was for people I did not even know. I had left $40,000 dollars in my apartment in Erbil without telling a soul. The previous week four Yezidis had been killed in a road accident by a truck driver from Iran. In the Muslim culture, it is customary for the responsible party to offer a cash settlement to the bereaved family. In the Yezidi culture, however, it is not permissible to accept money for someone's death. He offered them money, but they refused it.

Someone suggested to the truck driver that he offer to pay for the funeral expenses. So he offered this. This family instructed him to deliver the money to me. Neither the bereaved families nor the truck driver knew me, but they trusted me enough from seeing me on the TV news to deliver $40,000 in cash to my hand. The money was in my apartment without any note of explanation.

We rush through life thinking statistics apply to someone else . . . the bolt of lightning, the Mack truck, the fatal crash. We are recklessly unprepared for our final moment.

Those poor families who had just lost everything after the car accident, then Daesh's attack, now would never get that financial help. I moaned, "arghhh" with bitter regret. How terrible of me to deprive them, and then the world went black.

In the moment I stopped breathing, I saw a white light in front of my eyes, I thought, Oh, God, I will not die! I will not die! So I opened my eyes. There were voices around me. I was disoriented. I heard someone say, "It is Mirza Dunnayi. Let's get him out."

I refused to let anyone move me. I asked first if Vian was safe. She was alive, but the pilot, Major General Majid Abdul-Salam al-Tamimi was dead. His leg was trapped and they could not remove him. I thought, "No, God, why did it have to be him to die? Why did the only Muslim among us have to die?" He was a martyr who sacrificed his life for humanity.

I refused to be removed from the helicopter until he was removed. I did not want him to be left behind. It was work to pull the glass and metal away to free his body. I was the last person to be removed.

A helicopter evacuated us to Feysh Khabur, Zakho, then to Erbil hospital. After three days in a hotel, I flew to Germany for treatment. I had a broken leg, two broken ribs, and severe pain from internal compression injuries. I was in a wheelchair for two months, but the Yezidi emergency raged on, and I could not sit it out.

On September 1, 2014, while confined to my wheelchair, I addressed a UN Human Rights Conference in Geneva and begged for international help to save the Yezidis. I returned to Kurdistan in my wheelchair and visited many displaced persons in the camps.

By that time three Yezidi girls managed to escape from Daesh. They reported that Daesh was raping them and selling the girls in slave markets. Others who were captured had managed to hide phones and call their families. The dreadful news spread fast that Daesh was raping all the women and girls as young as nine.

In the orthodox Muslim culture, especially in the Middle East, a woman is required to be a virgin when she gets married. Her virginity represents the honor of her entire extended family. Thus, young single women are closely monitored by their family. If a woman loses her virginity, regardless of whether it is through mutual consent or through rape, she brings shame to her entire family.

The fear of shame is deeply embedded in the culture. This concept of shame is not limited to loss of virginity. The western culture of dating is forbidden. A girl may also be considered to have brought shame to her family merely for being suspected of having a non-Yezidi boyfriend or for wearing immodest clothing.

In an honor killing, the victim's own family kills the woman to defend their family "honor". In approximately half of all honor killings in Muslim countries, torture and a slow painful death occur. Even though the Yezidis are not Muslim and do not use the Quran, they also share this same Muslim culture of shame. If a single woman is not a virgin, she is ostracized.

Within the Yezidi community, there are three hereditary clans or castes: the Pirs, the Sheikhs, and the Murids. Pirs and Sheikhs are the priesthood. About 93% of Yezidis are Murids. Not only are Yezidis not permitted to marry non-Yezidis, but they also must marry only within their own caste. Within each caste there are levels. Yezidis may also not marry outside of their level. There are 41 levels within the Pirs. Outsiders may not convert to become Yezidi. One is born a Yezidi.

On April 7, 2007 in Iraq, a seventeen-year-old Yezidi girl named Du'a Khalil Aswad was publicly stoned to death in the town square of Bashiqa, a Yezidi town. She was accused of having a Muslim boyfriend. The brutal honor killing lasted thirty minutes and was filmed and shown on the internet. It was said that she had a Sunni Muslim boyfriend. No one was ever charged with the murder although there were hundreds of witnesses.

This murder received both local and worldwide condemnation. In Erbil, Kurds demonstrated for an end to honor killings, but the culture of shame, itself, did not change.

Using Du'a's killing as a pretext for retaliation, Sunni Muslims carried out simultaneous attacks on August 14, 2007, in the Yezidi towns of Tal Ezeer (Qataniya) and Jazeera (Siba Sheikh Khudir). Terrorists detonated four trucks full of explosives in the streets of the crowded markets. Over 400 Yezidis were killed and 1,500 injured, many permanently disabled. It left forty orphans. This attack against the Yezidis was the largest attack in Iraq's history since 2003.

About half-an-hour prior to the explosions, the Kurdistan Regional Government (KRG) removed all security forces from entry inspection check points into the two Yezidis villages. The KRG also withdrew all its militias from the two villages and ordered them to Sinjar city, saying they are having an important political meeting.

Several days after the explosions, one of the terrorists, Talal Ali Kasem, was arrested by Iraq's central government. The KRG convinced the central government to hand him over to them. He admitted that he and his partners packed all four trucks with explosive materials to exterminate the Yezidis in these two villages, because he said the Yezidis are infidels.

KRG transferred Talal Ali Kasem to Duhok then to Syria where he stayed in Syria for one-and-half-years, and then returned to Iraq as a free man.

In response to this attack against Yezidis in 2007, I formed the German organization AirBridge. Using private donations, we airlifted seventy injured children to Germany for medical treatment. We treat hurt children from all parts of Iraq, including Sunni, Shia, Yezidi, and Kurd. We look for one donor for each child.

After Shingal was attacked by Daesh in 2014, I listened to the catastrophic situation of the women and girls who had been sold, raped, and used as sex slaves. When I returned to Germany for two weeks of medical treatment, I did political lobbying in Germany to help the girls.

Daesh's strategy was to use rape and shame to destroy the Yezidi culture, based on the belief that the women, once raped, would be ostracized by their own Yezidi families and community. In addition to using rape, any Yezidi who was forcibly converted to Islam would also be permanently ostracized from the Yezidi community. This is why Daesh insisted the captured Yezidis convert. Daesh believed that once a Yezidi converted, he or she would not attempt to escape.

In order to save the Yezidi culture and religion, we had to take decisive action. The Yezidi religion is led by Baba Sheikh, the Yezidi equivalent of the Pope. His headquarters is in Lalish, Shekhan, Kurdistan. The Yezidi Spiritual Council serves as both spiritual and political leaders. I sit on a twelve-member advisory board to the Council.

We immediately met with Baba Sheikh who pronounced an edict to save our community from total ruin. Every woman and girl returning from Daesh captivity would be welcomed back into the Yezidi religion and community, without question, regardless of whether she had been raped or forced to convert to Islam. The kidnapped women were to be treated as martyrs who had sacrificed for Yezidi people. They were to be accorded the highest honor. We say "on my eyes" to honor them. This edict applied, also, to men and children who were forced to convert to Islam.

Upon returning from the hands of Daesh, the Yezidis go immediately to Lalish for a ceremonial baptism by Baba Sheikh in the sacred spring waters within the Yezidi temple. There is no need to forgive them, since they were victims and are without guilt. They are welcomed home with tearful embraces, love, and honor.

From Lalish, these traumatized women and girls, with their little children, went directly to tents or caravans in IDP camps for Yezidis. I knew I had to help them. Baden-Württemberg, Germany, agreed to take 1000 survivors for resettlement and therapy. Dr. Michael Blume led the project in Stuttgart. I set up a registration office in Duhok, Kurdistan, and interviewed 1200 survivors. Our first plane load flew to Germany in May 2015. Our last group went to Germany in February 2016. I have another waiting list of 1800 names, but no country will offer them asylum.

How Shingal Was Disarmed

Mirza Baker Pisso, May 18, 2016

I am Mirza Baker Pisso, born in 1973.   In 2007, I moved my family from our village of Gir Zerik to Sinjar. That is where we were living when Shingal was attacked by Daesh on August 3, 2014. Gir Zerik, a Yezidi village on the southwest side of Shingal Mountain, was the first to be attacked.

We Yezidis had no weapons with which to defend ourselves, thus, the genocide occurred. Prior to the attack, I had a job as a driver for the Iraqi Army since 2007. During those years, sometimes I worked with the US Army. I was stationed in Mosul for five years.

On June 9, 2014, Mosul was taken in one day by Daesh with little or no shots being fired. Half-a-million residents fled to the safety of Kurdistan in northern Iraq. Those who had waited more than four days to escape were trapped inside of Daesh-controlled Mosul.

All 50,000 government security forces including police (IPS), Iraqi soldiers, Border Police (IBP), and Iraqi National Guard (ING) removed their uniforms and fled from Mosul and disputed territories taking their government-issued weapons, Hummers, and cars with them to their homes. The displaced Sunni Arabs, and also Christians, fled north to Kurdistan.

The Yezidis went back home to Shingal, a disputed territory between Baghdad and Kurdistan. When they were fleeing, their guns were taken from them at the checkpoints by Kurdistan Peshmerga and Asayish (Kurdistan security police). The same day they arrived home in Shingal, the Peshmerga forces came to their houses and took their remaining weapons and government vehicles from them.

In 2014, Abu Waleed Al Qurashi was an Iraqi Army commander stationed in Tal Afar, where the women and children were taken after the August 3rd attack. Abu Waleed was the commander over all Iraqi borders. I was one of his drivers.

Twenty days before Shingal was attacked (making it approximately July 14, 2014), an Iraqi military convoy of forty vehicles escorted Abu Waleed to Feysh Khabur CAB command post on the border of Syria. I was driving Major Rasheed, and I saw Abu Waleed with my own eyes in another car. At the Faysh Khabur CAB Army base, they took our weapons from us. They recorded our names and the serial numbers of our guns. We returned home, and Abu Waleed drove to Erbil, then flew to Baghdad. The Iraqi Army Border Control commander was gone from Kurdistan.

Prior to the attack of Shingal, there had been 400 Iraqi Army soldiers at the Army base in Shingal, of whom more than 200 were Yezidis. After Abu Waleed was gone, all the Iraqi Army officers went home. Then all the soldiers went home. No orders were given. People just went home. So I went home too, to Sinjar city.

On July 14, leaflets were handed to people in Qara Qosh, Karamlees, and Barttela instructing them to turn their light arms or heavy machine guns and ammunition for these weapons into the Security Committee in Al-Hamdania district in Kurdistan.

Sarbast Bapiri is the manager in Sinjar for the PDK party. Two days after Abu Waleed left Kurdistan, Bapiri gave orders for every soldier and police to report to the PDK headquarters in Sinjar with our ID badges. They took our badges or, if we did not have the badge, they accepted a copy. They recorded each person's name, badge number, and phone number.

It took three days to process everyone. There were three lines. One for Iraqi police, one for Iraqi Army, and one for Iraqi border patrol. I stood in the Army line from 8 AM until 4 PM. More than six officers were writing down the names and processing each person.

Sarbast Bapiri announced the Iraqi government was finished in Kurdistan. He promised to give us weapons and pay us the same as Peshmerga. On the fourth day, after everyone had registered, Bapiri announced that there were 20,000 Peshmerga in Shingal. He told us that we would be defending Sinjar and all the villages. He told us all to go home and have a sleep and not to worry, because Shingal was safe because Peshmerga was defending us. During that time, Peshmerga remained on duty in Shingal. In that first week, after the announcement, civilians, also, went to ask for weapons to defend Shingal.

We waited, but no one gave us weapons. All of our weapons were in the hands of the Peshmerga.

Forewarnings of the Attack

Religious superstition was one of several tactics used to manipulate Yezidis. In June and July, 2014, before Daesh attacked Shingal, a woman from Tal Qassab visited many of the Yezidi villages. She told them she had a dream in which Tawus Melak, the angel Yezidis pray to, had appeared. The woman said Tawus Melak had slapped her in her face and blinded her.

In her dream, Tawus Melak instructed her to tell all Yezidis they should not leave their villages, because they will be protected from danger by him. Some people believed her and refused to leave their village. My friend who told me this said even his own mother and the neighbor lady believed the woman.

* * * * *

After Daesh attacked Mosul on June 9, the Shia population fled from Mosul and Tal Afar to Shingal and Kurdistan. Yezidis in Shingal took them into their own homes and also gave them help living in unfinished buildings and schools.

In July, Shias in the south of Iraq were calling all the displaced Tal Afar Shias in Shingal and warning them they had to leave immediately for the south of Iraq, because Shingal would not be safe. This was more evidence that even Shias knew Shingal would be attacked. They warned all of the Yezidis who were feeding them to leave Shingal.

Over two or three weeks, all Shias left either in their own cars, or Shias came from the south to pick them up in cars and long flat-bed trucks. There was a visible exodus of thousands of Shias at about the same time as the Iraqi Army Border Patrol also pulled out of Shingal in mid-July. By August 3, all the Shia from Tal Afar were gone. While leaving, fifty Shias from Tal Afar were killed and 350 injured by Sunnis in Rabia, where the wheat trucks unload wheat in August. Those who escaped went to Kurdistan, then Erbil, then to Baghdad and the south of Iraq.

Prior to the Yezidis giving hospitality to the fleeing Shias, relationships between Shias and Yezidis had not been good. After the attack on Shingal, relationships shifted and became positive out of Shias' gratitude to Yezidis. In a perverted compliment, one Shia man explained, "Yezidis were even better than Daesh with us." Both Kurds and Shias were vying for Yezidis' loyalty in order to claim the disputed territory of Shingal.

* * * * *

Thamir (not his real name) reported as normal to his job in the field with an oil company the week before August 3, 2014. The chief security officer at his company unexpectedly gave him five days leave and told him to go get his family in Tal Banat and leave Shingal. He went to Tal Banat, but his wife thought it was safe and quiet and did not want to leave, so in spite of the warning, they stayed.

Thamir returned to his job. His security officer was alarmed that he had not taken his family to the safety of Kurdistan.   Then at 11:30 at night on August 2, an Arab friend called Thamir from Baaj, twenty-six kilometers southwest of Sinjar.   He said his father and uncle had just come from a Daesh meeting and it was decided that Arab Sunnis would join Daesh to kill all Yezidis. They said that Thamir was a good man, had been good to their family financially, and they had to warn him.

Thamir immediately called a PDK leader in Sinjar city named Nayef and told him of this phone call. Nayef said, "Don't worry. Peshmerga will protect us."

Next Thamir called the Peshmerga commander for Shingal, Sarbast Bapiri. Bapiri told him he had just talked to Mansour Barzani, head of the Peshmerga and son of President Masoud Barzani. (Thamir says this was a lie.)   Bapiri said that Peshmerga reinforcements were in nearby Rabia and they would arrive to Shingal by noon. Bapiri instructed him, "Don't run."

The PDK leader, Nayef, and the Peshmerga leader of the 17th KDP section in Shingal, Sarbast Bapiri, left Shingal with their families. Peshmerga reinforcements never arrived. To the contrary, Peshmerga were leaving Shingal without warning the Yezidis.

On the evening of August 2, a Yezidi doctor of the city hospital overheard a Kurdish Muslim employee talking on the phone. The doctor confronted him since the phone call seemed to be about Shingal and Daesh terrorists. The employee explained that he had spoken to a friend who had joined Daesh. The friend assured him that Daesh would stay in Shingal the next day, "without having a shot fired".

Mirza Baker Pisso, a Yezidi, also, received a call at his home in Sinjar late at night on August 2. An Arab friend called him from Baaj. The Arab caller told Mirza to leave the room so they could speak privately. He told Mirza to take his family and leave immediately for Kurdistan because Daesh was going to attack Shingal. He told Mirza to tell all Yezidis to take their families and leave.

He said, "Tomorrow Daesh will be praying in Abdulrahman Mosque in Sinjar." He told Mirza the plan was that Daesh was going to take the women and girls and the children. "This is going to happen tonight," he warned. He told Mirza that many Daesh were already in their vehicles on their way from Syria, Baaj, Tal Afar, and Mosul to attack Shingal.

Mirza called all of his friends in different villages: Tal Ezeer, Gir Zerik, Siba Sheikh Khudir, Tal Qassab, Tal Banat. He told them, "Tonight Daesh will attack you." No one believed him! All Mirza's friends responded that they would be safe because they had many Peshmerga protecting them.

Next he called a friend in the Asayish. Then he called a lieutenant in Peshmerga stationed right in Sinjar city. The lieutenant told Mirza, "We have a lot of Peshmerga. We don't care."

Mirza turned his attention to his father, Bakir Pisso Khalaf Mirza, and his wife's father, Shamo Kalos, still living in Gir Zerik, the village where Mirza was born. Gir Zerik was a few kilometers southwest of Sinjar city, on the road to Baaj, an Arab town. Daesh would arrive there first. Baaj is less than sixty kilometers from Sinjar city; only a thirty minute drive to Gir Zerik and forty-five minutes to Sinjar on the way to the mountain.

Their Arab neighbors of years were about to attack Mirza's father and father-in-law's homes. It is little wonder that the Yezidis found it hard to believe.

The Peshmerga Retreat

After Daesh took control of Mosul June 10, 2014, PDK Peshmerga forces were sent by Kurdistan to the Yezidi villages and cities to protect Shingal. If the village did not already have a base, they were housed in the local school building and fed by the local families.

Said Kestayi, commander-in-chief of the Peshmerga in Shingal, stated that 8,000 Peshmerga in Shingal were under his command. According to Commander Sarbast Bapiri, there were 11,000 Peshmerga fighters and 200 commanders who were deployed and armed in Shingal and its vicinity (Zumar). One reporter put the number at only 3,000.

In the weeks prior to the attack on Shingal of August 3, 2014, Yezidis were stuck in their villages on the southeast side of Shingal Mountain. Many of those who tried to leave via the paved road from Sinjar over the mountain to Sunoni were turned back by Peshmerga or Kurdistan police at the security check point entering Sinjar. They were told, "Why are we protecting you if you are going to leave? Go back home."

In the pre-dawn hours of August 3, as the Daesh attack began at 1 AM with shooting from the Arab village of Ain Ghazal, Peshmerga began withdrawing from Shingal without warning the Yezidis. To the contrary, Peshmerga told the Yezidis not to flee because reinforcements were on their way.

One Yezidi Peshmerga commander called Commander Sarbast Bapiri at 11 PM, August 2, when he got a warning of the impending attack from Baaj. Bapiri told him Peshmerga forces were in Rabia and were on their way. Rabia is an Arab town on the north side of Shingal mountain near to the borders of Syria and Kurdistan. No Peshmerga ever arrived. Those Yezidis who had managed to flee Shingal in their car were shot at by snipers while driving through Rabia. No Peshmerga were in Rabia to defend them en route to Kurdistan.

As Gir Zerik and Siba Sheikh Khudir, on the south side of the mountain, were under attack by mortar and heavy arms from 2:10 AM to 7 AM, Yezidi civilians who took up arms were calling for help every fifteen minutes throughout the night.

Amin Yusif Haji, who was fighting in Gir Zerik with 200 other civilians, states, "We were being told that Peshmerga were on their way to Shingal or they have just arrived at Karsi on the north side of the mountain. Once we called, they were telling us that planes have taken off, coming to help, or a convoy of Peshmerga vehicles is on its way to us, but nothing at all appeared."

By 7 AM no Peshmerga had arrived and the citizens fled Gir Zerik, leaving their elderly and handicapped behind. Daesh killed them in their houses in a door-to-door search on August 3rd and 4th.

Haci Qeyrani, defending Siba Sheikh Khudir stated, "We were in close communication with the 17th Division of the KDP Peshmerga and informed them about the events. We called them several times. They told us that reinforcements were on the way, saying that they would arrive any moment. They told us to hold our positions and put up resistance until the Peshmerga arrive. We fought for about four hours and not a single unit came for our support."

The Yezidis in Siba Sheikh Khudir and Gir Zerik also telephoned the "Black Unit" of Sheikh Alo Doski, which is stationed only a few kilometers away, to provide support. After June 2014, Sheikh Doski established under the permission of the KDP a special unit called Heza Resh (Black Unit) which consisted of around 700 fighters, 300 of whom were from Siba Sheikh Khudir where they had served in the Iraqi army.

The commander of the "Black Unit" later stated that he had not received the order to dispatch his men, although the Yezidis had informed the 17th KDP division and Peshmerga commanders.

In reality, an eyewitness, Ahmed Khalil, in Siba Sheikh Khudir stated that all 200 Peshmerga in town gathered at 1 AM at the police station on the hill above his house on the north edge of town. He watched them as they left town at 2 AM. The Daesh attack began at 2:30AM. While residents were calling for help, Peshmerga were already heading toward Rabia en route to Kurdistan.

At 3 AM in Kocho, the family of Faisal Ali Aman left home in their four cars and large farm trucks. The Peshmerga refused to let them leave unless they took the 75 or 80 soldiers housed in the school. So they loaded them up and dropped them off in Tal Qassab where other Peshmerga were waiting for them with vehicles.

In Kocho, a teenager, and his mother were sleeping on their roof in the hot August night. At 4 AM, in the first light of dawn, he witnessed about twenty Peshmerga leaving Kocho in their jeep and a large car, heading in the direction of Sinjar. By 7 AM, all of the people in Kocho tried to leave town in their cars. The remaining Peshmerga soldiers at the check point just outside of Kocho blocked them, so they returned home.

Immediately after that, Peshmerga left. When 100 cars of Kocho residents left right on the heels of the Peshmerga retreat, half of them were captured by Daesh and massacred. The family of Khudir Khalaf Ali and his wife, Naam Khero Ayshon, was one of those families. Seven members of their family were captured by Daesh when they reached Sinjar city. The rest of the family escaped to Syria and then to Zakho. The grandmother was released by Daesh on April 25, 2015. The others have not been heard from.

By 7:30 AM all of the remaining Peshmerga left Kocho. They said they were going to fight at the neighboring village of Tal Banat. They said, "Don't worry. We will guard you."

But there was no battle at Tal Banat where 80 Peshmerga were stationed that night at their headquarters at the edge of town. The first half of the Peshmerga group left Tal Banat at 6 AM. The second half left at 7 AM. The very last Peshmerga, a Yezidi named Sultan Hassan Rasho, left at 7:30 AM. Most of the Yezidis who were in Peshmerga went home to their families.

Many of the men from Kocho had been volunteering to help the Peshmerga. Some Peshmerga left in Yezidis' cars at 7:30. Yezidis took the Peshmerga to save them, because the Peshmerga forces did not have enough cars for all of them to leave. When the road to Sinjar was blocked, they returned and escaped on the road going around the east end of the mountain, the direction from which Daesh was arriving. Kocho remained besieged until it was attacked August 15.

By 8:30 AM, August 3, all residents of the entire Shingal region knew they were under attack. Those who tried to enter Sinjar city from the direction of Gir Zerik or Kocho villages or to drive from Sinjar on the paved road over the mountain to Kurdistan were blocked.

Peshmerga had a headquarters on the west side of Tal Ezeer which they left by 6AM. One road connects Gir Zerik, Tal Ezeer, and Siba Sheik Khudir. Peshmerga abandoned their three checkpoints on this road between Gir Zerik and Siba Sheik Khudir, allowing Daesh to drive to attack Siba Sheik Khudir at 2:30AM.

Barakat Mahmoud Khero was prevented by a Peshmerga check point from entering Sinjar at 8:30AM to pick up his daughter and take her to their farm six kilometers north of Tal Ezeer. Barakat was killed in a mass execution at 11AM along with 11 other family members at his farm at the junction to Tal Ezeer on the south side of the mountain. The victims were unarmed. No Peshmerga were there to defend them. At least 57 people were killed in the vicinity.

According to multiple witnesses, Peshmerga soldiers blocked civilian cars and ordered them to turn around so that Peshmerga forces could reach the mountain and retreat. Because of this, Yezidis were turned back into the arms of Daesh and hundreds, maybe thousands, were killed or captured as a result of Peshmerga forcing civilians to turn back so that Peshmerga could reach the mountain first.

Salwa Khalaf Rasho, from Sinjar, swears under repeated questioning that Commander Sarbast Bapiri himself stopped her family's car and told them to clear out of the way for the Peshmerga to use both lanes. When they turned back, eighteen-year-old Salwa was captured by Daesh and physically abused for eight months.

There is video evidence of Peshmerga trucks, heavy equipment with Doshkas (cannons), and pickups full of soldiers driving up the mountain road while civilian cars are blocked on the morning of August 3. Many photos exist of Peshmerga trucks full of soldiers overtaking civilian cars on the road to Kurdistan. A young female TV journalist named Barfin, with microphone in her hand, questioned truck loads of Peshmerga. "Why are you leaving?" she asked. The answer was, "We were given orders."

Qassim Hussein Edo Aldahi, born 1956, was a PUK Peshmerga living in Khanasor. He worked in a political party position, not as a soldier. The Peshmerga forces, while officially the military defense force for Kurdistan, functioned as separate military units loyal to their respective political parties. The PDK Peshmerga belonged to President Barzani's ruling party with its stronghold in Erbil and Duhok. The PUK Peshmerga were strongest in Sulaymaniyah.

There were 100 PDK Peshmerga soldiers based in the city of Khanasor on the northwest side of the mountain. They were all Yezidis, born and living in Khanasor. They were assigned to man the checkpoints. Qassim Hussein and his wife, Nadifa Ibrahim Hassan, were awake all night listening to heavy gunfire from the Syrian border, three kilometers to the north. Qassim's house is on the road leaving town. So he asked Peshmerga in at least ten vehicles why they were leaving. Their answer was, "We have orders."

According to Qassim Hussein Edo, all checkpoints were empty by 6 AM. While the Kurdish PDK Peshmerga from other areas withdrew north to Kurdistan, those 100 PDK Yezidi Peshmerga went south up the mountain to Karsi where they arrived at 8 AM. Qassim did not leave Khanasor until 11:30 AM with twenty-eight family members. When Qassim arrived in Karsi at noon, he saw and talked to the Yezidi Peshmerga from Khanasor, all of whom he knew.

No Daesh arrived to Khanasor until that afternoon. The extended family of Haji Hamid Talo remained in Khanasor hoping they would be safe. Daesh captured or killed 77 members of his family. By 2018, 41 remained missing.

Mosul Council member Dawood Jindy, a Yezidi from Borek, stated that all 80 Peshmerga stationed at Borek, on the north side of Shingal Mountain, left at 6 AM.

By the morning of August 3, Yezidis living in nearby Zorava village knew that the Peshmerga in their village would flee, also. Some Yezidis had volunteered to defend Zorava and were working with the Peshmerga. Other Yezidis were officially employed by Peshmerga. A dozen other Yezidis who had no guns came to the Peshmerga base and asked for the Peshmerga to return their government weapons to them to defend against Daesh since the Peshmerga would be leaving the town. There were seven or eight trucks of guns.

An argument ensued, and a Yezidi witness says one Peshmerga sprayed the group with bullets killing Ali Elias Yousif and his two nephews, Yousif Khalaf

Elias and Ayet Naif Murad who died in hospital. All three killed were Yezidi Peshmerga employees. Jamil Khalaf Elias was injured.

The same day Daesh was also attacking the north side of Shingal Mountain, arriving from Rabia to the north and from Tal Afar to the east. Why didn't General Aziz Waysi, commander of the Peshmerga elite Zeravani unit stationed at Zumar, near Rabia on the border with Kurdistan and Syria, block Daesh? Rabia, near Zumar, was soon controlled by Daesh and was joined by local Arab residents who attacked all of the Yezidi villages on the north side of the mountain.

The entire Shingal region was attacked from all sides. By 1 PM, August 3, it was all over for the Yezidis. At least 40,000 Yezidis who had not been able to escape in their cars to Kurdistan or on foot to Syria fled to the top of Shingal Mountain where they were trapped for nine days. 30,000 gathered in Karsi because it had a water source. Hundreds, mostly children and elderly, died of dehydration on the mountain. At least 270 Yezidis who were escaping to the mountain were captured and executed at the Hardan junction. Hundreds others were massacred between Sunoni and Khanasor, Hamadan, Zuleyli, Qine, and other locations.

In the daylight of August 3, 2014, Chief of Staff of the Iraqi Joint Forces, General Babakir Shawkat Zibari, and his aid, Major Serbast Bozani, landed on Shingal Mountain in a helicopter. Six days passed before US President Obama ordered airstrikes against Daesh on August 9, 2014, to prevent an "imminent genocide" . . . death by dehydration . . . and liberate the Yezidis trapped on the mountain. They walked to Syria through a corridor opened and protected by the PKK guerillas. Peshmerga did not take part in the rescue.

In September 2014, I was in southeast Turkey, meeting hundreds of Yezidis streaming over the border from Iraq. Every person I listened to started by excitedly explaining that the Peshmerga had abandoned them, resulting in a massacre. The PKK had saved them off the mountain and helped them get to Syria, then Kurdistan, then all the way to Turkey. There is so much eye witness testimony, photographs, and video as evidence of the fact that Peshmerga retreated before the Yezidis, without warning them, that this fact is irrefutable.

Who gave the order for Peshmerga to retreat, thus allowing the genocide to happen? Did soldiers abandon their posts without an order? Was it Sarbast Bapiri, Peshmerga commander in Shingal, who gave the order to withdraw? Was it Masoud Barzani, president of Kurdistan? Was it the United States military? Was it a pre-arranged betrayal? How high did the betrayal go? The eye witness statements in this book attempt to shed light on this question.

The leaders responsible for security in Shingal at that time were:

- Masoud Barzani, President of Kurdistan

- Said Kestayi, commander-in-chief of the Peshmerga in Shingal

- Sarbast Bapiri, head of the 17th Kurdistan Peshmerga section in Shingal

- Shawkat Kaniki, head of Asayish intelligence security service

- Aziz Waysi, supreme commander of the 1st Division of Peshmerga's elite Zeravani unit stationed at Zumar

Every Yezidi who was attacked in Shingal blamed President Masoud Barzani for the Peshmerga withdrawal. The rumor alleges that on the night of August 2, Barzani ordered Bapiri to withdraw his forces by the early morning of August 3. The Peshmerga did withdraw, but was an order actually given?

The Peshmerga general and spokesman for the Peshmerga Ministry, General Halgord Hikmat, in an interview with SpiegelOnline stated, "Our soldiers just ran away. It's a shame and apparently a reason which is why they invent such allegations [referring to the alleged tactical retreat]. There was categorically no order to withdraw from any front. There was negligence." *Was he covering up the truth?*

President Barzani promised an investigation into the Peshmerga negligence to defend Shingal. In a letter sent to the Kurdish daily al-Ra'i al-Am, Barzani said: "After the catastrophe visited upon the Yezidis, all the political, security and military officials responsible have been relieved of their positions. What happened in Sinjar did not happen to the Yezidis alone; it is an injury that has hurt us all. Those officials should not have withdrawn; they should have sacrificed themselves in defense of the region."

Two hundred commanders were interviewed, but no results were made public. The official story is that Peshmerga withdrew because they did not have enough ammunition or heavy arms to defend Shingal, even with 11,000 soldiers.

According to Dahar Yusuf from Siba Sheikh Khudir, Peshmerga moved all their heavy equipment from Siba to Sinjar on July 29, four days before the attack. They said there might be some conflict in Sinjar, so they were going there to protect the city. None of the villages had heavy weapons for defense.

Nawaf Isa Ali, former correspondent for the state-backed Kurdistan24 TV in Sinjar, Iraq, stated:

"I can say that the Peshmerga fled before the residents did. They believed that they were a direct target and that the Daesh fighters would definitely kill them if they fell into their hands. Said Kestayi and Sarbast Bapiri decided that the retreat should happen. I was with Sarbast Bapiri, Said Kestayi, Shawkat Kaniki, and several other people, including Qassim Shesho, when the decision was made to retreat. We were in the KDP [PDK] party office in Sinjar. There was no time to coordinate with the next level of authority. The decision to retreat was made within two minutes. [at

approximately 6:45 to 7 AM] There was no time to discuss or to contact Erbil.

"Sarbast Bapiri, Said Kestayi, and Shawkat Kaniki fled to the Syrian border with between eight hundred and one thousand fighters. Qassim Shesho did not agree with the decision to retreat. He asked for the heavy weapons that were available. He wanted to stay in Sinjar and fight. He said that he would at least try to protect the holy Yezidi city of Sherfadin [on north side of mountain].

"When the Daesh captured Tal Afar and Mosul, the 11th Division of the Iraqi army was stationed at the border to Shingal. It had heavy weapons. Sarbast Bapiri, Said Kestayi, and Shawkat Kaniki had all the weapons brought from Shingal. We know that some were transported to Iraqi Kurdistan and another large portion was sold on the black market. They committed treason against the population and abused their positions for their own personal gain."

Yezidi Commander Qassim Shesho acknowledged that Peshmerga fled before the civilians could evacuate. He stated, "If the Peshmerga had left the weapons, which the Iraqi army abandoned, for the Yezidis, the Yezidis would have been able to defend themselves. This catastrophe, this genocide would have never happened."

When I asked Commander Qassim Shesho, "If it were true that Peshmerga had been forewarned of the attack on August 2, then why weren't the Yezidis also warned?" his answer was, "That's what has me confused. We never thought this could happen in this era with the internet and video on our phones."

Qassim Shesho's Peshmerga pickup truck broke down. Witnesses passed him at approximately 9:30 AM being towed and pushed by other Peshmerga on the paved road going up the mountain from Sinjar. His wife and children were with him. Very shortly thereafter the road was blocked by Peshmerga to civilian cars. Shesho went to Sherfadin on the north side, just below the house in which he was born, where he took up command in the following weeks of a re-constituted Peshmerga force of 8,000 Yezidi volunteers. These Yezidis joined Peshmerga after the Kurdish PDK Peshmerga abandoned Shingal. Their numbers may be inflated. One Yezidi Peshmerga returned to his family in Tal Qassab Kevan and said he was ordered to retreat.

I spent two years lying awake at night thinking about Qassim Shesho's answer. Were the Peshmerga commanders warned of the attack? Had they been told that the plan to take control of Shingal would be bloodless like how Mosul was taken? Is that why Qassim was confused about the savageness of the attack?

When Qassim Shesho and his nephew, Haider Shesho, commander of the independent Yezidi forces, were both asked who ordered the withdrawal of

Peshmerga forces in the early morning hours of August 3, both replied that it may have been an international conspiracy. Yezidis were at the mercy of powerful countries with their own agendas.

One version of the international conspiracy theory was that Iran was secretly financing Daesh to invade Iraq. Without the excuse of war, Iran could not simply invade Iraq and grab the land. However, with the extremist religious agenda of Daesh, Iran saw its opportunity to complete its Shia Crescent from Iran through Shingal to Syria to the Mediterranean. By taking advantage of the war in Syria and letting Daesh invade Iraq, Iraq could be divided by Daesh.

One theory is that Iran made huge payoffs to Iraqi commanders to abandon their posts and give Mosul to Daesh. By 2017, it was widely agreed in Iraq that Baghdad was under the control of Iran. After Daesh controlled Mosul, Tal Afar, and Shingal, Iranian-backed militias called Popular Mobilization Forces (referred to as PMF, PMU, or Hashd al-Sha'abi) could come into Iraq and, alongside of Yezidis, take back control of Shingal . . . and then Iran would control Shingal. Iran could build its oil pipeline to the Mediterranean. Peshmerga were ordered by the US not to interfere with what happened in Shingal. . .neither to defend it nor liberate it from Daesh.

But of what benefit to the US would it be for Iran to gain control of Shingal and build its pipeline? ExxonMobil, the world's sixth largest company by revenue, would be a customer of Iran's crude oil.

In 2011, Rex Tillerson, CEO of ExxonMobil , had signed an agreement with the Kurdistan Regional Government to allow for oil drilling on Yezidi lands. In 2013, ExxonMobil employed local security forces which fired upon Yezidi activists, killing two of them. ExxonMobil turned a blind eye to any claim that Yezidis had for their ancestral land. It is estimated that between 2011 and 2013 over 5,000 Yezidis were forced from their lands in Iraq so that ExxonMobil could conduct oil drilling.

In 2014, Tillerson, who had made business deals on behalf of ExxonMobil with President Vladimir Putin of Russia, opposed sanctions against Russia. He had previously been the director of the joint United States-Russia oil company Exxon Neftegas. Russia controlled the deep water port of Tartus, Syria, on the Mediterranean. This strategy was a Russian-Iranian-Iraqi alliance.

In 2017, Rex Tillerson was appointed by President Trump as US Secretary of State. ExxonMobil already had a vested interest in supporting Kurdistan, with whom it had signed an agreement to drill in the disputed territories in Iraq. Its former CEO was now in a position to drive official US government policy in Iraq.

David Shumock is an American special forces vet who served thirteen years in Afghanistan and retired from the US military after twenty years. After the genocide, he volunteered with the Peshmerga 2nd Division Special Forces Quick Reaction Brigade guarding the frontline south of Sinjar city. Shumock was the only trained medic in Peshmerga in Shingal after the Daesh attack. He gave urban warfare instruction to all the units in Shingal.

When I asked Shumock who ordered the Peshmerga to withdraw on August 3, he answered, "Everyone knows the Americans ordered Peshmerga to leave. Peshmerga soldiers were trapped between Arabs in Sinjar city to the north who had already raised the black flag of Daesh even before Daesh had arrived from Baaj to the south of us. If Peshmerga had not retreated, they would have been killed, because they had no heavy weapons with which to defend themselves. Then every Yezidi would have been killed. By retreating, the Peshmerga lived to fight Daesh later. Peshmerga saved the Yezidis."

My jaw dropped open at this official defense for a "tactical retreat".

"What about the 6,000 Yezidis who were killed?" I asked.

"Collateral damage," he replied. "It comes with every war."

Several Peshmerga soldiers who found asylum in Germany also stated that in the early hours of August 3, Peshmerga forces were ordered by Americans to leave Shingal. This is unverified.

After Yezidis got their families safely to Kurdistan, thousands of them returned to Shingal to join Haider Shesho's Ezidkhan Protection Unit (HBS) or Peshmerga under Qassim Shesho in Sherfadin. Others joined YPG (male) or YPJ (female) militias, formed under the PYD political party in Rojava, northeast Syria. The PKK created and trained an independent Yezidi militia named YBS. President Barzani declared that only the flag of Kurdistan would fly in Shingal, but into 2017 the various flags continued to fly as each group vied for control of Shingal after Daesh would be defeated.

One week before the genocide, Haider Shesho told AraNews about the necessity of arming Yezidi volunteers. The 17th politburo of the KDP (also known as PDK) under Sarbast Bapiri, however, declined to arm the Yezidis, stating that the unit was "a pure Yezidi but not a Kurdish one," adding that the Peshmerga had already taken adequate precautions to defend the Yezidis.

On April 6, 2015, Haider Shesho was arrested by the Kurdistan Regional Government after having approached the Iranian-backed PMU for weapons.

The arrest of Haider sparked Yezidi protests in Europe and Kurdistan. With pressure from the German consulate, Haider (who holds German citizenship) was released after nine days. After that, he wore the flag of both Kurdistan and Yezidis on his uniform. Qassim Shesho wore absolutely no insignia on his khaki shirt. When asked why, he replied, "I do not wear any flag for any country. I never have and I never will."

Yet, Qassim Shesho's Peshmerga were supported by President Masoud Barzani's PDK party which controlled Kurdistan, Iraq. Barzani aligned himself with President Erdogan of Turkey who was waging a war of terror and bombing against PKK and Kurds in southeast Turkey under the guise of fighting terrorism.

Haider went to Baghdad central government and many countries of the world seeking support for his independent Yezidi force.

In 2016, when I asked Qassim Shesho if his 8,000 Yezidi Peshmerga could ever be combined with Haider's 3,000 Yezidi volunteers, he stated that could never happen, because "each group is supported with food and arms by different foreign countries. We are not free to decide for ourselves."

Haider Shesho, unable to raise financial support for his soldiers, joined his unit to Peshmerga on March 7, 2017. Haider stated, "Yezidis need time to resume trust in Peshmerga after the fall of Shingal to Daesh in August 2014, when the group committed countless atrocities against the Yezidis. Lacking sufficient weapons, ammunition and military training to combat Daesh, Peshmerga was not able to protect Shingal in August 2014 when the jihadists attacked."

In September 2017, Haider Shesho joined his forces with PMU. Shortly after, they were officially put under the Iraqi Ministry of Defense. It was widely reported that Major General Qassim Soleimani, the commander of QUDS (Islamic Revolutionary Guard) in Iran, was in Baghdad controlling Hashd al Sha'abi in Iraq.

After the Peshmerga forces were pushed out of Kirkuk by Hashd al Sha'abi (PMU) and the Iraqi Army, October 16, 2017, Peshmerga were pushed back by the Iraqi Army from Shingal to Kurdistan. They were no longer permitted to enter Shingal. Yezidi Commander Qassim Shesho took off his uniform and retreated to Sherfadeen, his childhood home. Other Yezidis began organizing and vying for political and military leadership of Shingal.

Gir Zerik First Yezidi Village To Be Attacked
Ibrahim Khalaf (fictitious name), October 11, 2016

I fought from the first shot until the last shot in the battle of Gir Zerik. Daesh drove two Toyota pickup trucks to Gir Zerik and parked at the edge of town. At 2:10 AM on August 3, 2014, a Yezidi leader known as Khudaida Golod ordered all the Yezidi men to open fire on these two pickup trucks. We used our small weapons. I had a Kalashnikov. Three Peshmerga joined us in the attack with their BKC weapons. We Yezidis had three or four BKCs and two RPGs.

Within five minutes the trucks were burned with the people inside and it was silent. Ten minutes later about 200 or 250 Daesh forces arrived in many pickup trucks and hummers, filling the night air with their shouting of "Allahu Akbar".

At 2:40 AM, they attacked us with heavy arms including six RPGs and two Doshkas. We could count the RPGs from the six white streams of rockets flying toward us in the black night sky. Daesh was firing from a small house and water well called a "siba" about 350 meters from the perimeter of Gir Zerik. We were fighting from behind a dirt berm that had been dug previously for our protection.

At 3 AM, Dilshod Sheik Ibrahim killed the Daesh gunner. At 4 AM Peshmerga left town, leaving behind their two BKCs and two Doshkas with only fifty bullets. Hazim Haider bravely fired the Doshka. Only Yezidi civilians remained to fight Daesh. I myself had three hand grenades that I threw.

The people in Gir Zerik did not have enough cars to escape, so at 6 AM our Yezidi neighbors from Rambousi, three kilometers to the north, drove every car and pickup truck to Gir Zerik to rescue us. When Daesh saw the headlights coming, they might have thought Peshmerga reinforcements were coming, so there was a lull in the battle. Rambousi cars loaded up the families and took them. When Daesh saw that it was not Peshmerga, the battle resumed. At 7 AM the fighting stopped because we ran out of ammunition. I could see about 180 bodies of Daesh beyond our dirt berm. I went to my house, but my family was already gone. Everyone had headed north to the mountain.

I and my three friends were the last to leave. We piled into a car and went to Hoshi, a neighboring Arab village. From Hoshi we ran to Rambousi with a population of both Yezidis and Kurdish Muslims, By the time we arrived at 8 AM, not one Yezidi was left in Rambousi, but the Kurdish Muslims remained.

I called my uncle and he told me to save myself. There was an Opel car leaving town. Even though it was full, we managed to squeeze ourselves in and make it to Sinjar. From Sinjar I walked up the mountain at 8:30 AM. By 9:30 AM the road up the mountain was closed by Peshmerga to civilian traffic so that Peshmerga forces could withdraw with their trucks and equipment.

About seventy old men stayed behind in Gir Zerik and remained fighting Daesh in the streets of Gir Zerik. I heard shots until 10 AM.

"Your Old Men Are Killed" - The Battle of Gir Zerik

Amin Yusef Haji Darwesh Kalos, July 1, 2016

I am Amin, the son of Yusef Haji Kalos, born in 1974. I am from the village of Gir Zerik at the foot of Shingal Mountain, ten kilometers southwest of Sinjar. My village had both Yezidis and Kurdish Muslims living in it. We were the first place in Shingal to be attacked by Daesh.

I was looking at my mobile phone at 2:15 AM on August 3, 2014, when I heard the first three shots in Gir Zerik. They shouted "Allahu Akbar."

I and ten other men went to fight Daesh on the perimeter. Hassan Baker Khuder Khalif Al Mato and Mehsin Khuder Khalif Al Mato were in battle with me. There were about 400 or 500 meters between us and Daesh.

They sent two pick-up trucks to us to tell us to surrender, "You do not need to fight." Then we burned them all. More than 200 gunmen were shooting them apart with BKCs. My brother fired two magazines of ammo. They were so close as if they were telling themselves they had won.

We burned them in less than five minutes. I think we burned eight or nine trucks. I swear that they had no experience to fight, so at 3:00 AM Daesh withdrew and escaped. Afterwards, an Arab called me on August 6 and told me that 284 men of Daesh got killed in the battle of Gir Zerik.

At dawn, Gir Zerik's mullah, named Suliman Khudir Hussein, called for prayer three times. We were astonished, because we had never heard a mullah call for prayer three consecutive times. Maybe he was telling them we could be defeated, because we had no support, so after his call to prayer, Daesh returned to fight against us again. The conflict became more violent, more forceful.

Unfortunately, we ran out of ammunition. If we had gotten support, Daesh would not have been able to control Gir Zerik. We kept calling for help every 15 minutes. We were being told that Peshmerga were on their way to Shingal or they have just arrived at Karsi on the north side of the mountain. Once we called, they were telling us that planes had taken off, coming to help, or a convoy of Peshmerga vehicles is on its way to us, but nothing at all appeared.

My family called me up and told me to come back to the house, because my mother had died. So I withdrew and went home, but my brothers stayed there in battle, Ziad, Aydo, and Hussein, the sons of Yusef Haji Darwesh. I found my mother alive. She had fainted from fear.

I told my family to leave, and I would stay with my brothers, but my father refused to get in the car. I put him in the car, but he got out of the car again. I begged him to leave, but he said he would not go without me.

My father, Yusef Haji Darwesh (born 1946), and his two brothers, Elias Haji Darwesh (born 1936) and Bapir Haji Darwesh (born 1970) adamantly refused to leave.

The conflict lasted until 7:00 AM when we ran out of ammunition. We fought until the last bullet we had in our weapons. At 7:10 Daesh came with armor-plated vehicles. A friend named Hassan shot at one with his BKC with fifty or sixty bullets, but the bullets did not affect it.

Then Daesh aimed their Doshka at us and shot. We got down and lay in the drainage ditch. I felt the bullets fly above our heads, and I got covered in dirt.

We saw the Daesh cars were so close. I phoned my brother to come back and could hardly convince him, because he owned a BKC with sixty bullets. He was thinking that he had a lot with which to attack.

I said, "What are you going to do with one BKC and sixty bullets?" A BKC was pointless, so he returned.

A missile came from 500 meters away and landed in a pool of water. How dangerous it was! If there had not been that pool, it would have destroyed all of us.

Our Doshka was out of order because the missiles were not exploding. There was an old Peshmerga soldier who fired four shots with his Doshka to their car, but all of them missed. He could not hit it. Either his shot was passing beside it or it hit in front of it. He tried unsuccessfully to hit it.

Honestly, those Peshmerga who were in our village fought against Daesh, and even two of them were killed, and two others were injured after a missile hit their base.

We were afraid of a big explosion, so while they were busy with each other, I told my friends to run, otherwise, they were going to kill us all. We went and crouched down behind a house until they all drove away.

I told my friends to escape. "Staying here is pointless."

We were at our houses when a missile went vvvrrooooooooooo. It hit and its shrapnel was green and red. Five minutes later, we heard another missile launching, then another one. We did not know exactly where the missiles were landing.

The village was attacked by 250 missiles until morning arrived. One hit the gate of my house, and I was there. It hit it and the only thing that helped me to survive was the wall. The missiles that hit our village destroyed the world. Daesh destroyed the world.

I told my family to leave and be safe, and I put them in the cars. I told them I am going to stay with the three old men, but the family told me that they were not going to leave unless I joined them. They got out of the cars and refused to go. After that I decided to go with them, because I simply had to have them leave.

I got the family into three cars. My brothers' and father's family managed to get into two cars. We put my mother in the car with my brother. I told them to drive and I would follow them. I put my family in another car and we drove north a few kilometers to Rambousi village.

I had to leave my father and his two brothers behind, because they would not leave. They were ages 78, 68, and 44. It was a terrible choice to have to make.

The distance between us and Daesh was only 400 meters. We drove on an unpaved dirt road towards Rambousi, because Daesh had control of the main road. We arrived to the north side of town, even though we came from the south, because there was no other choice.

The inhabitants of Rambousi left their families and came to give us a helping hand. While the families of Rambousi were themselves being captured, they were selflessly rescuing other people's families. Daesh was attacking Gir Zerik, Rambousi, and Siba Sheik Khudir at the same time.

In Rambousi I went to the house of one of my relatives who were farmers. I told them to leave, because even the Peshmerga soldiers were leaving. "What are you going to wait for? "

They agreed and told me, "Since Peshmerga are leaving, we, also, are going to leave."

We drove toward Sinjar, but came first to a checkpoint of Domise village. We told the guards to let us pass, but they blocked us, telling us sooner or later Peshmerga forces will arrive.

I told them, "We have been fighting since 2:15 AM. If Peshmerga really had wanted to come to help, they would have been here a long time ago."

So we entered by force and hit one of the Peshmerga soldier's car so we could pass. We arrived at Sinjar where it was a deserted city. There were no Peshmerga to be seen. All the people were moving towards the mountain. I stopped beside Sinjar's town hall waiting for forces or something to come. Somebody there told me to escape, I asked, "Why?"

He said, "Daesh has control of Sinjar, so escape."

We decided to move. My mother and brother were in a car going towards Gabari. He called me, and I told them to wait in Gabari. I told the ones who were in Gabari to stay in Gabari. They said they would climb the mountain. I said, "OK."

We continued driving and arrived at the top of the mountain, beside the mountain's electrical post. The road was filled with cars. We could see two members of Daesh coming up. Daesh was not yet in Sinjar. "Who are these three people?" we wondered. "Aren't they the Muslims who live in Sinjar?" They were from the Kichala, Meteoti, and Khatouni Muslim tribes in Shingal who tortured Yezidis more than Daesh did. Daesh who came from different countries were not as aggressive and violent as these three tribes.

PKK shot one of them with a Doshka. Another one escaped, and later went to Kurdistan. Around 10 AM, Daesh closed the road coming from Sinjar.

We drove to Karsi on the north side of Shingal mountain. Our families stopped for lunch in an acquaintance's house. Then we decided to drive to Kurdistan. To get to Kurdistan we had to drive through Sunoni which was thought to be a safe place. Peshmerga were scattered from Sunoni along the road to Rabia which is an Arab town near the Kurdistan border

However, before we arrived to Sunoni, Daesh were shooting people to make them turn back. Daesh had also arrived from the north side of the mountain. So we turned back and we again drove to the top of the mountain where we were trapped for nine days with barely any food or water.

The next day on August 4, at 2 PM, my brother Ziad finally was able to reach our neighbor Muneef Hassan Mahmood by phone. He and his family had been our Muslim neighbors in the village for more than 100 years. Muneef was still in Gir Zerik village.

My brother Ziad told Muneef, "We still have three of our old men there in the village, including our father." He asked if Muneef would be able to go search for them.

Muneef answered, "Your old men are killed."

So we asked Muneef to please take their cadavers into a room of our house, because we had a good relation with Muneef when we were in Gir Zerik village, but he refused to take them.

I asked "Why?"

He said they were scared. He told us, "Come down from the mountain, because Daesh has declared an amnesty, and they are not going to hurt anyone." This was Muneef, our trusted neighbor, talking.

I asked him if he himself had seen the dead bodies of my father and uncles by his own eyes. Muneef said, "No."

I asked him, "So how did you hear this news?"

He said, "From my family and children."

I told my brother Ziad to stop talking to him because it's pointless. I told my brother that he is telling us this so that we go down into the village and get captured by Daesh. Muneef is an intelligence man for Daesh, because if he were not, he would not have stayed in the village after Daesh took control of it.

What kind of amnesty did Daesh declare if they are killing old men and children? We are all military men. I am a policeman, my brothers are in the army, another brother is also police. They were definitely going to kill us if they captured us, so I told my brother to hang up.

Ziad next phoned our cousin, Ahmad, the son of my Uncle Bapir, and told him what had happened. Ahmad told Ziad that at 11 AM on August 3, Ahmad's sister called their father Bapir, who had decided to stay in the village with my father, to find out how Daesh was dealing with people in the village.

My Uncle Bapir told her that they are in trouble with Daesh and that asking about them is useless.

She asked him, "Why?"

He told her that his brother, Yusef, who is my father, is shot fatally, and he himself is at home, also, and has no idea about when he is going to be arrested and killed. He said they could kill him at any moment. He said that he is looking at Yusef's dead body through a door that is ajar.

Ahmad's sister asked their father Bapir if he had any idea about the people involved in the murders. Bapir swore to God that Nouri Silo Hitka and Muneef Hassan Mahmood both were sitting in the front seat of a Daesh car. They had teamed up with Daesh and were leading them in searching houses one by one. They gave Daesh the addresses of those who were remaining in their houses, and Daesh killed them all.

After that they came to Duhok, Kurdistan. I gave their names to Asayish security police two or three times, but it was useless. One of them was arrested for two days, and then they released him.

The only thing we wish is to get our revenge for those Kurdish traitors who betrayed and tortured us. Some people from the Kurdish Muslim Serhoki tribe living in Gir Zerik were fighting against us. They joined with Daesh and killed all the people who stayed behind.

Some of them escaped with us. My neighbor escaped with me. Khalid Enjo escaped with me, and he was my neighbor.

Nouri Silo Hitka, Ahmad Silo Hitka, Muneef Hassan Mahmood and his brothers and nephews, and Hazim, Hashim and Jassim who are the sons of Muhammad Hassan Mahmood. They all stayed in Gir Zerik. Suliman Khudir Hussein, who was the mullah of the mosque, stayed in the mosque and did not escape. Adnan Hassan Mahmood was also a mullah and did not escape. Sadoon Hami Jujan did not escape.

Why didn't they escape? Because they were supporting Daesh.

They stayed four or five days in the village, even as many as twenty to thirty days. After that they came back to Kurdistan and pretended as if they had escaped with us. Our children died because of the shortage of water and food, and they came with their air conditioned cars. If Daesh did not allow them to come, would they have been able to arrive here in Kurdistan from the middle of Sinjar which was controlled by Daesh? Daesh allowed them to leave.

We cannot go back to our villages. We were forty-six persons from my father's family and his brothers' families and nephews. Now, my family is living in a tent, and the life is very tough. What we wish for is for genocide to be acknowledged and there be international protection for us. We need a place just for Yezidis to live in safety.

There is no hope to live among those who killed us. Do you think we can live with Daesh? Do you think we can live with the Muslims who killed us? I cannot look at them again. If someone killed my father, can I be his neighbor again? Can I see someone who killed my father pass by me? No, I cannot. I do not see it is an appropriate decision for me to live with them again.

My hope is when the genocide is acknowledged, when there is international protection for Yezidis, we would not be scared anymore, but without international protection it would be hopeless. Nobody can live without international protection, because Daesh may come in another shape and with a different name. Without international protection, what happened before will be repeated.

The Martyrs of Siba Sheikh Khudir

Daxil Osman, September 5, 2017

I am a professional Yezidi singer whose music is widely played on the radio and at parties. I have sung at hundreds of Yezidi wedding parties. I sang in Kocho for the wedding party of Nayef Jaso's son before Daesh attacked. I loved joking and bringing smiles to peoples' faces. Because I am famous among Yezidis, my friends and fans also expected me to be their leader when Daesh attacked. I was unprepared for this role, because I am an entertainer, not a military commander or politician.

On June 3, 2014, forty young Yezidi men in the Iraqi Army were killed in Terifahwee. Two of them were my cousins, Hadi Ami Shero and Hussein Abbas Hammoka. One of them was my uncle. The hostages asked me for money to pay for their freedom. They were my relatives.

I was rich at that time, because I was earning good money singing at the wedding parties. I paid $70,000 dollars to free seven hostages, a hundred million Iraqi dinars, without getting reimbursed. I knew how much their children were suffering and waiting for their fathers.

A month before the attack on Shingal, I realized something was going to happen, because I was reading history and following the news. I told my inner group of friends and family that I feel Daesh will attack Shingal and they will behead people and rape women. I told them, "I am going to Kurdistan. If you want to come, it's up to you."

I came before August 3 to Kurdistan, but my community blamed me and said, "It is a big shame for someone like Daxil Osman who is famous to leave us. He has to encourage us to fight Daesh, instead of going to the safe zone of Kurdistan."

Everyone told me to return to Shingal. Only my mother told me, "Do not come back to Shingal." People were ridiculing me. Because of that pressure of shame, I returned to Shingal two days before the attack. I understood that the people were right, because if all my community died, why would Daxil Osman live? I had to be among my people and encourage them and help them and raise my voice to the world. I went back with my pickup truck full of food, ice, and water. I was distributing it to the Peshmerga by Rabia, then I turned to the south side of Shingal Mountain to Hayala and other villages where I also distributed food, water, and ice to Peshmerga.

The young people for whom I had played and sang at their wedding parties and the friends who I had before Daesh attacked were calling me and asking about my condition, especially Ahmed Jaso, leader of the al-Mandkany clan, and my nephew Nuri from Kocho. The night of August 2, I was making plans to get together with Nuri Sor, Mr. Nawzad, Nejmon, and other friends in Kocho. They later got killed by Daesh. Hozni and Said, the brothers of Nadia Murad, and some other friends are alive now. I told this group of friends, "I will come to Kocho for encouragement. Do not tell the ladies I am coming. Let it be a surprise."

I did not know that Daesh was preparing to attack Shingal. I could not get to Kocho, because the battle started. At 2:45 in the morning of August 3, my mother called me from Siba Sheikh Khudir. I was in Duguri. My mother is a strong woman. When her crying was choking her words on the phone, I knew something was terribly wrong.

She said, "The Muslims are attacking us from all sides, and they are walking over the dead bodies." She said all the village had been seized by Daesh, and our Arab neighbors from the al-Khatouni tribe who lived in Siba Sheikh Khudir and who speak Kurdish had joined with Daesh. My mother told me, "My son, just rescue yourself. This is another genocide." She was sobbing.

My mother told me they captured all my cousins. My uncle Hassan and Haji and their families had been captured by Daesh. Arabs shot my uncle and his wife. I heard the rockets and bombs. I could hear the crying and the sound of the battle. My mother told me the first rounds of the battle started when they attacked Gir Zerik. Before that, they shot some rockets at Tal Banat and some other places.

I called my brothers and asked "What are you going to do?"

They yelled, "We are in the battle fighting them now. The Arabs have taken control of the police station at the top of the hill. We are defending ourselves by God and Tawus Melak. Until we get killed, we will not let them kill our children."

I called my son-in-law. In a panic, he told me they are shooting people randomly with rockets from a Doshka 23. It is an unmerciful rocket launcher. The rounds are about ten inches long.

I called one of my closest friends, Khudir Allo, before he sacrificed his soul. He is a good human being for taking care of people. He told me, "It is just like what we were talking about before." Before this day, we were always predicting this kind of battle, because we knew that Christians and Yezidis cannot live among Iraqis, especially Arabs, and especially those from Mosul.

One of our muhktars (mayor), named Mahlo, and fifteen of my cousins with about twenty Yezidi fighters stayed to distract Daesh and keep them busy until the families could flee to Shingal Mountain. Daesh slaughtered all of them in Siba Sheikh Khudir. They beheaded some of them. They cut off some of their noses and other parts of their bodies. It breaks me down to watch the video of their blackened, decaying bodies gathered haphazardly together on the bare dirt as if they had been tossed out like garbage.

I told my mother to rescue herself and to flee. I could hear the cars and the screaming of the children. Our villages of Siba Sheikh Khudir, Tal Ezeer, and

Gir Zerik are about ten kilometers from Shingal Mountain. Whoever had his own car could manage to get his family and some neighbors out.

Who did not have cars, like old people and kids and handicapped could not go to the mountain. They crawled going to the mountain. Just imagine how they had to go ten kilometers to get to the mountain. Many people were riding on top of the cars or holding on to the side because of their fear of Daesh, and so, many were falling down off the cars and Daesh captured them. Many had arranged themselves in the car like how you stack logs on a truck, lying one on top of another.

I told my mother to come and leave the village. She cried, "I cannot come and leave my daughters here inside the village under Daesh." My sisters were married, so they were living in different houses.

My mother left Siba Sheikh Khudir between 5 and 6 in the morning. She refused to come directly to the mountain. She said, "I'm going to your home in Skeenia." She said she had to go first to where she grew up and where my father is buried. She did not want to leave her homeland. I knew after what happened in Gir Zerik, we would not have life there ever again. I had only one solution to convince my mother to come directly to the mountain, and not to go to Skeenia.

The people of Iraq have many weapons. I had a pistol, because when I was going to wedding parties, I was afraid of Arab gangs killing me while going from the south side to the north side of the mountain. I had a permit, because the Iraqi government knew I was always getting threatened by Arabs.

I told my mother, "I swear by God on my father's grave, I'm going to kill myself with my pistol if you do not come." After I said that, she screamed and I knew she would come. I told my mother and brother to take the Shiloh road around the west end of Shingal Mountain. She said it was very dangerous because Arabs were there. I told her she had to risk it anyway. My mother and my brothers and some of my sisters came at 8 in the morning. They were covered with dust. I had several houses. I had a house with three floors in Skeenia village. Daesh exploded my house later.

When I met my mother and saw her crying, I told her, "Don't worry, we will get away to safety."

My mother told me, "I am not crying about this. I want you to know what is happening to the Yezidi community. Daesh has destroyed us."

When I saw my mother crying for our Yezidi people, I knew what happened to all Yezidi mothers. I knew my mother was alive, but I knew some Yezidis would never see their mothers alive. I knew I had my brothers and sisters, but other Yezidis would lose their brothers and sisters. I did not want to be alive.

I was frantic. I went to the market and bought a lot of mobile phone credits. I knew I would need that, because I knew that my people would need communication. They would need me to ask about their condition and raise their voice to the world. I left Duguri. Some people were blaming me and saying "Daxil Osman is a coward. He wants to flee and leave his people behind. They said, 'Ah, the son of Ezdikhan, you are trying to escape again?'"

I told those guys, "You will see what happens to you. I am going to rescue myself."

There is an old man from my uncle's tribe. He told them, "I know Daxil Osman is not lying. His words are precious, so we have to listen to him. What he says is going to happen." All those people laughed at him.

On the way to Kurdistan, we had to pass through Arab villages in Rabia. Snipers were shooting at the cars from inside the hospital. They would have killed us if they could have. Also, Arabs came from the neighboring villages of Rabia to join Daesh. When I saw the Arabs were so happy because of what happened to Yezidis, and they were laughing at us, I blamed God, "Why did you create Yezidis?"

Six of my family members are still in the hands of Daesh. There is nothing I can do now in Shingal. Daesh destroyed me mentally, physically, and financially. I gave all my money to help Yezidis in the camps. Like the other Yezidis, I lost everything and moved into one of the camps near Zakho.

In August 2017, Daxil Osman went to Germany and returned to his profession of singing for wedding parties to maintain the Yezidi culture and support his family. His family remained stuck in their tent in Kurdistan.

Sheikh Khairi's Civilian Defense of Siba Sheikh Khudir

Dahar Yusuf, interviewed by Tore Rørbæk, August 2017

The attack upon Siba Sheikh Khudir began fifteen minutes after Gir Zerik. The news by telephone was very bad, so we were expecting to be attacked. We could hear the gunfire and mortars from Gir Zerik. I was in the house of the great Yezidi leader, Sheikh Khairi Khudir, with other Yezidi civilians like myself from Siba Sheikh Khudir village. Sheikh Khairi was commander and founder of the Yazidi militia Malik Al-Tawus Troop, which later became the Sinjar Resistance Units (YBS). He was born in Siba, and had returned from Germany where he had lived many years.

The Iraqi Border Patrol had left Shingal on July 14. The Peshmerga left Siba Sheikh Khudir July 29, saying they had to go to defend Sinjar city. All Peshmerga's big weapons were in Sinjar. We were exposed on all sides with no defenses except ourselves using weapons we had purchased.

I had exchanged my car with an Arab for a BKC and a Doshka, a heavy machine gun. I had not yet delivered my car keys and registration in exchange for the Doshka, but I had the BKC. Sheikh Khairi had warned me not to take my car keys and get the Doshka, because the Arab man would steal my keys and kill me. So all I got for my car was the BKC.

We loaded three trucks with armed men and headed to Gir Zerik to support our neighbors. We had only three or four BKCs. I had my BKC. Before we could go anywhere, we saw Daesh's car lights coming from Gir Zerik, and so we stayed in Siba Sheikh Khudir where the clashes began within minutes.

First, Daesh fired smoke mortars at Siba, so we could barely see. Then they randomly fired mortars and many other types of weapons at Siba. They were also firing an Anti-aircraft (AA) gun which was demolishing houses. We could not see anything for a while, because of the thick concrete dust of the houses made of mud bricks, that were destroyed by the AA-gun. Daesh had both armored vehicles and normal cars. We were no match to armored cars. We had only one RPG. Our only objective was to hold them back long enough to save our families.

Our AK47s did not have enough impact to shoot armored cars, but fortunately the land was rocky with valleys making it difficult for Daesh to traverse and enter the village. There were berms we had dug in Siba to block the road and for us to lie behind and fight, but Daesh fighters were shooting from all sides. We pulled back and hid between the houses under protection of the night.

Daesh were fighting from the flat open area. Bullets were flying everywhere, over the berm into the houses. We could hear the cries and screams of babies and women. It was terrifying. The fighting in Siba lasted more than four hours, from approximately 2:30 until 6:30 AM. We called for reinforcements, but no one ever came. We never saw any Peshmerga even though Sinjar is only 25 minutes away.

Daesh were well-trained. Their numbers were growing because men were coming out of Al Wardiyah village to the east and joining them in the attack. Some were probably former military officers over fifty years old who may have participated in the Iran-Iraq war under Saddam Hussein. Daesh attacked from three directions, but not from the mountainside. We ordered our families to go on foot to the mountain. We had just enough ammo to provide cover for them to escape.

Over 150 Yezidis were killed in Siba Sheikh Khudir. It was a massacre. Seven were martyred in Sheikh Khairi's family. The last of us left Siba Sheikh Khudir at 7 AM. We went to Skeenia village close to the mountain. Eight Daesh men arrived in their cars. Then they entered Skeenia and told people they would not hurt us. They asked us to convert to Islam.

They had a BKC on their car, but I did not meet them with my weapon. We hid our weapons in the valley. We met with Daesh, but they were not kind with us. We discussed among ourselves why we did not just attack and kill them because they were only eight people. Sheikh Khairi was a very experienced military leader. He said no, because if we did that, more men would come and attack all 10,000 women and children gathered there. Once they left, we started walking up the mountain.

Sheikh Khairi stayed in Skeenia. He had us position some BKC weapons on the mountain. Daesh was never able to establish a position on the mountain, because it is hard and rocky. They could not drive up the mountain. They would have to get out of their cars and walk. Daesh tried many times to come up the mountain, but could not succeed, because we fought them. Every time they would try to attack, we would shoot them. So the 50,000 Yezidis who fled to the mountain were safe.

Sheikh Khairi was killed by a Daesh mortar attack in Skeenia (or above it) on October 22, 2014. He died a hero defending Yezidis and their homeland.

Raping Women Is Halal

A reported number of 5,270 Yezidi women and children were abducted by Daesh in 2014. Daesh planned and prepared in advance for their abduction. The sexual enslavement of the females was done strictly according to Shariah law prescribed by Islamic teaching in the Quran and Hadith. Some actions of sparing prisoners from rape or murder actually seemed like small gestures of humanity which might erroneously lead one to think not every Daesh fighter was cruel and heartless. Maybe he was secretly defying orders.

A variety of surprisingly different treatments were reported by the survivors of Daesh captivity. As their testimonies accumulated, it became clear that these were not random deviations from the rules by a sympathetic Daesh fighter. A clear pattern emerged that Daesh was following carefully prescribed Islamic dictates for treatment of their prisoners. It is obvious that they were carefully instructed in the rules before they attacked on August 3. Violating an Islamic rule caused them more concern than raping a school girl or shooting her father.

The Yezidi culture and religion is tight-knit, family-oriented, and closed to outsiders. Yezidis may not marry outside of their religion nor convert to another religion. A woman may not have sex before marriage. If a Yezidi does either of these things, sex or conversion, he or she will be shunned and, in the past, might even have been killed. Such behavior would bring shame and dishonor to the entire family

This practice is similar to fundamentalist Islam. Daesh knew of the Yezidi culture, with behavior closely controlled by fear of punishment for bringing shame to one's family. So Daesh forced all captives to convert to Islam or be killed. Islam calls this choice free will. Muslims worldwide protest that Islam never coerces anyone to convert, citing the Quran [verse 2:256]: "There shall be no compulsion in [acceptance of] the religion."

Daesh asked Yezidis three times to convert or be killed. Males who refused to convert were killed. Females were enslaved and raped. Daesh thought these techniques would prevent the captured Yezidis from ever returning to their families. Even if they did return, there would be no virgins. In both Muslim and Yezidi cultures, the man expects his bride to be a virgin. If he discovers she is not, he can return her to her family.

Indeed, in previous genocides against Yezidis, captives had been unwelcomed to return to their families or communities. By using the concept of shame, Daesh planned to destroy the Yezidi culture.

According to Islam, it is *halal*, or permissible, to have sex with a female slave over age nine who is *kuffir* meaning someone who has no religious book. The phrase *"those your right hand possesses"* in the Quran [verse is 4:24] is interpreted to mean female slaves. The captured Yezidi females were singled out to be sold as slaves. Raping them was considered the owner's right and religious duty. Other non-Muslims, such as Christian, Assyrians, and Jews were not used as sex slaves, although there were instances of Christian women being raped. They had the chance to escape or pay a tax called *jizya*.

Shariah law also allowed that if a slave became blind or handicapped, he would also become free. One might surmise that this law was intended to relieve Islamic slave-holders of the responsibility of caring for those whom they had enslaved after they were no longer useful. In early 2015, Daesh released more than 400 infirm and handicapped Yezidis. They returned weak and malnourished.

Upon being captured, females were immediately separated and taken to Baaj near the Syrian border or to Mosul, east of Shingal. In Mosul, they were sent in large groups to the Galaxy Wedding Hall, the Badoosh prison compound, or the Directory of Youth building. In Tal Afar, Solagh, Sinjar city, and Baaj, they were herded into schools and municipal buildings.

Most females under age forty did not escape being raped. Each one had to stand in a row, step forward and turn around for inspection. Their names, ages, hometowns, marital status, and number of children were recorded. In some places they were photographed. During this viewing, some were immediately taken into a room and raped. During their stay in these places, men would regularly come and rape them.

Sales were conducted in slave markets and the contracts of sale were registered with the Islamic State court. Some girls said photos of girls for sale were posted on walls in the court house. Daesh referred to the abducted girls with the Arabic word *sabaya* meaning slave.

"When they put us in the building, they said we had arrived at the 'Sabaya Market,'" said one nineteen-year-old victim. "I understood we were now in a slave market."

According to Islam, a man cannot have intercourse with a slave woman if she is pregnant with another man's child. Most females were forced to take birth control pills which they welcomed so as not to become pregnant by their rapist. Some were given monthly 150 mg injections of the birth control Depo-Provera. Daesh performed both abortions and tubal ligations on some women. If there were no birth control, the man would follow the Shariah instruction for intercourse with a slave and practice *al-azl,* pulling out before orgasm. When a woman was sold to another man, her owner had to guarantee that she was not pregnant.

Some captives were forced to answer intimate questions, including reporting the exact date of her last menstrual cycle. An owner must wait for a female captive to have her menstruating cycle, in order to "make sure there is nothing in her womb," before having intercourse with her. The elapse of one menstrual period is referred to as the *Istibraa.* Sometimes the owner's mother would take her to the hospital for a pregnancy test to avoid waiting. These rules of when a man could have intercourse with a slave girl are carefully detailed in the Quran and Hadith.

These rules explain why a pregnant woman was allowed to accompany her mother-in-law and nearly eighty older women in Solagh Institute, when they were led outside, shot, and covered with dirt by an excavator on August 16, 2014. Since Islam prevents sex with a pregnant slave, she was considered useless. Allegedly, Islam also considers it haram (not allowed) for a man to shoot a woman, so they chose a twelve-year-old boy to be the executioner of the old women.

At the same massacre, Asim Amin, grandson of Ahmed Al Jaso from Kocho, saved his mother from being taken out with the older women and shot, because she refused to be separated from him because Asim was diabetic and needed injections. Daesh sent Asim and his mother back inside in adherence to Shariah law dictates. They were later released with other disabled captives.

What kind of twisted sense of humanity under Islamic law allowed the diabetic boy to be released with his mother, while the pregnant woman was shot with her mother-in-law? The only code that Daesh fighters followed was the unquestioning obedience to the rules of Shariah law concerning prisoners taken during jihad. They were not to concern themselves with the morality of their actions, because Shariah law comes from Allah whose wisdom is never to be questioned.

In other cases, Daesh did not abduct pregnant women such as in the case of Mayan Sino Barakat, age 28 and visibly pregnant. She was left behind when Daesh killed seven men, including her husband, and abducted 28 females from the Barakat Mahmoud Khero farm north of Tal Ezeer.

Not all females escaped pregnancy while in captivity. At least one nine-year-old girl was pregnant when she returned to freedom. The doctor said she would die if she delivered the baby. Although abortion is illegal in Iraq, most survivors who returned pregnant received abortions. Upon returning to Kurdistan, they went first to file a police report at the genocide office in Duhok. Before giving their report, they were sent to the hospital for examination. The Ministry of Health required them to undergo a virginity test with three doctors if they were single and reporting their rape(s). Depending on their condition, they could stay up to ten days. So most pregnancies were not recorded in the police reports.

Some girls who got pregnant resigned themselves to their fate with Daesh, saying, "This is my life now. What can I do?" Some chose suicide.

One woman refused the opportunity to escape with the driver sent by her husband to smuggle her out, because she thought she might be pregnant. At the last moment, she again had a change of heart and asked the girl who replaced her to send the driver back if she succeeded in escaping. When the driver returned for her the following week, he was caught and executed.

Many girls and women reported that her captor would kneel next to her and pray over her before and after raping her. This was called *ibadah*, a term from Islamic scripture meaning to worship and serve Allah. In their twisted logic, raping the Yezidi girl was considered service to Allah. From an August 2015 New York Times report:

In the moments before he raped the twelve-year-old girl, the Islamic State fighter took the time to explain that what he was about to do was not a sin. Because the preteen girl practiced a religion other than Islam, the Quran not only gave him the right to rape her—it condoned and encouraged it.

He bound her hands and gagged her. Then he knelt beside the bed and prostrated himself in prayer before getting on top of her. When it was over, he knelt to pray again, bookending the rape with acts of religious devotion....' I kept telling him it hurts – please stop.'

Al-Binali, from a prominent Bahraini family, was reportedly head of the Research and Fatwa Department of the Islamic State and its chief religious advisor. They published online, in December 2014, "Questions and Answers on Taking Captives and Slaves," which explained Shariah law for having sex with slaves. It explained that slaves belong to the estate of the fighter who bought them and therefore can be sold or willed to another man and disposed of just like any other property after his death.

This rule on ownership explains why Ayshan Barakat Mahmoud was imprisoned along with her captor, Abu Rasul, for two months when he was found guilty of embezzling from the Daesh government. The Daesh Shariah court imprisoned Rasul and seized all his money and property. Since she was his slave, she was locked up, too. He sold her from prison.

Ayshan's cousin, Sameera Mirza Mahmoud, was bought by a Daesh man from Australia along with five other Yezidi girls. They lived with his wife and five children. They cooked, cleaned, and took care of his family. According to Ayshan, he did not rape the young women, but did explain that his commander had ordered him to sell three of them, because according to their Islamic rules, he was not permitted to own more than two slaves. "We have rules we have to follow," he explained. She escaped before being sold again.

According to Shariah law, a man cannot have sex with a slave woman whose husband is alive, so their husbands were killed after refusing to convert to Islam. If, however, a Yezidi woman was captured along with her husband, and the husband was not killed, Daesh would sometimes let them live together with their own children.

Islam dictates that a slave owner is forbidden from having sex with his female slave if she is married and her husband is inside of the conquerors' Islamic territory. But if the husband is outside of Islamic territory, she can be used for sex, because it is assumed she will never see her husband again. So before distributing the captured girls to Daesh soldiers, they separated them from their men and transported them to Mosul, the headquarters of Daesh in Iraq.

This Shariah law explains why Ivana Waleed was spared from being raped for five months and was instead allowed to live with her male cousin, Moneer. Ivana knew that her cousin Moneer also had been captured, so she lied and told the Daesh leader who wanted to marry her that she was already married. She was in Mosul; her cousin in Tal Afar. Daesh sent her to join Moneer. They lived free in the village of Qaser Al Mehrab in Tal Afar along with other married couples and families. A total of 234 Yezidis lived there surrounded by Daesh patrols. Daesh used families as laborers.

In Raqqa, the Daesh husband of an abducted Yezidi woman came in one day, grabbed his suicide vest and parted with the words, "You might not see me again." The Daesh Shariah court gave the widow, who had pretended to convert to Islam, a widow's pension and her freedom within Raqqa for a period of four months and ten days. This is called *uddah*, a period after the death of a woman's husband in which she is not allowed to marry to ensure a future husband or slave owner that she is not pregnant. When her real husband sent someone to rescue her, he was captured and beheaded in front of her by order of the Daesh Shariah court. Her life sentence was commuted and she was threatened with beheading if she tried again to escape.

Many online websites justify the Islamic Shariah laws that condone sex with a slave girl. Islam refers to the enslaved rape victims as maidens and portrays the brutal practice of sexual enslavement as almost as good as legal marriage. These sites helped entice recruits worldwide. The English language website of islamqa.org has a database of 52,000 questions and answers on Islam. It is an eye-opener to search for "sex slave" and read the pages of "scholarly" Islamic garbage glorifying, instructing, and justifying the raping of women. In a twisted denial of reality, it states that sexual slavery would cure the abducted girl's psychological grief:

"Islam ensured that the slave girl's duties were not restricted merely to domestic chores but also gave her master permission to copulate with her. This concession created an atmosphere of love and harmony between the slave girl and her master. Islam thereby raised the status of the war captive-maidens close to that of wives. It was a psychological cure to her grief-stricken heart, being deprived of her family and thrown into the hands of a strange society."

The famous "Stockholm Syndrome" in which a prisoner eventually falls in love with her jailer-rapist did not apply to any survivors interviewed. Teenager Haifa Barakat Mahmud was locked in solitary confinement in a house for one-

and-a-half years. Her Daesh captor came every night to rape her after finishing work in the hospital. When asked if she became friends with him out of need for human companionship, she answered, "No. Even though I had not one living soul to talk to, I never considered becoming friends with him. I did not want to utter one word to him. I disliked him so intensely for what he was doing to me. He did what he came for and left."

Every waking aspect of Muslim behavior is dictated by the complex rules of Shariah law. According to Islam, if something is prescribed as halal (allowed) or as haram (forbidden), there need be no further discussion. No independent judgment as to its morality enters into it.

Over 5,000 documents allegedly recovered from Daesh in Tabqa, Raqqa Province, Syria reveal monthly benefits were awarded to Daesh based on the number of slaves they held, up to $50 USD per woman and $35 USD for children. Multiple documents, including health certificates, would mention the number of female slaves extremists owned for administrative purposes.

Massacres in Solagh

Mirza Baker Pisso, May 18, 2016:

My wife Nisra's father, Shamo Kalos, stayed in Gir Zerik fighting Daesh from 2:15 AM until 7 AM on August 3. Shamo is a civilian. Both civilians and Peshmerga were fighting Daesh. The civilians were on the first line of defense, and about eighteen or twenty were killed. Peshmerga were fighting from their base and homes.

I got the call from Shamo at 7 AM that the Peshmerga had left Gir Zerik, so Shamo left right behind the Peshmerga. There were not many cars in Gir Zerik with which to escape, so Shamo and my father, Baker Pisso, went north to Rambousi where people had trucks and took some of them to Sinjar.

The elderly who stayed behind in Gir Zerik were all killed.

When my father and Shamo reached our house, they decided to stay in Sinjar, thinking they would be safe there. My family and many other Yezidi families went by cars to Solagh, just outside of the city, at the base of the mountain. My eldest son, Mazank (born 1979) with his two friends stayed below the cars with their guns to defend the families. At 10 AM Daesh arrived and shot about sixty people, including my son and his friends.

I was not close enough to see Mazan killed, but someone told me later. The rest of us left our cars and walked to Galia Haji in the mountain.

Three days later, on August 6, Daesh took my father, Baker Pisso, and my father-in-law, Shamo Kalos, from our house in Sinjar to Tal Afar which is about thirty kilometers east on the way to Mosul. In Tal Afar, Shamo escaped and walked west to Gohlat village near the mountain. Daesh recaptured him three days later. They drove over him with a car, breaking his arms and legs. Afterwards, they shot him to death.

At midnight, Daesh returned Shamo's body to Tal Afar and put him in the room with my father, Baker Pisso, and other Yezidi prisoners. They told Baker, "This is what will happen to anyone else who tries to escape." My father buried Shamo's body in Qaser Al Mehrab in Tal Afar.

My father was held prisoner in Tal Afar for nine months and 17 days. Daesh made two mass releases of elderly and handicapped Yezidis. After the first release of 217 people, Tal Afar city received electricity 24 hours a day, while the rest of Kurdistan continued to suffer from hours-long power outages multiple times per day. Tal Afar always had electricity. My father and others confirmed this when they were released three months later, in April 2015, with the second group.

Three of my brothers live with my father who is suffering badly and had surgery for kidney stones. I reported the murders of my son and father-in-law to the genocide office in Duhok, Kurdistan.

Nassim Qassim Alias, September 19, 2016:

I am from Solagh, a few kilometers east of Sinjar. When Daesh came, I and my family were on my poultry farm between Solagh and the cement factory. Everyone in Solagh was escaping to the mountain. I got in my car with my wife and four children, but when my family got to the mountain, we had to stop because the road was very crowded on the mountain.

Daesh came and captured all my family. They drove us in my car and took us back to my brother's house in Sinjar. Immediately they took my teenage son, Ardawan, and my brother's family to Tal Afar. After three days, my whole family walked fifteen kilometers during the night to Hatamia village.

After the initial attack on August 3, Hatamia and Kocho villages were surrounded by Daesh guards. On August 7, Daesh took my mother from Hatamia to Kocho and put her in a house with another old woman, the mother of Adrees Bashar Silo. My mother could not walk.

On August 15, when Daesh attacked Kocho, they drove the old women to Solagh Institute. Adrees is one of the nineteen men in Kocho who survived from his gunshot wounds when Daesh executed the men. Daesh took Nadia Murad's mother, Shamee, along with my mother to Solagh Institute in my car. All the old women who could not walk were taken to Solagh Institute directly while everyone else in Kocho was ordered to report to the school.

On November 12-13, 2015, PKK, YPG, YPJ, Peshmerga forces, and independent Yezidi forces, with the air support of the US-led coalition, drove Daesh out of Sinjar. The next day the mass grave of seventy-eight women was found near Solagh Institute. One ID was found on the ground. It belonged to Shamee, the mother of Nadia Murad and Saeed Murad Pissee, who survived one of the mass executions in Kocho. I think my mother was in that mass grave site.

Viyan Havind Khalaf from Kocho, October 31, 2016:

After Daesh took all the men and teenage boys out of the school in Kocho on August 15, 2014, they transferred the married women with our children and the older women to Solagh Institute. I was transferred in a group with five women with our children. The Daesh manager who took us to Solagh was called Abu Saood. He was from Saudi Arabia. He chose all the single girls, more than 100, and sent them to Mosul. They kept the rest of us overnight.

In the morning, they wrenched all the older women over age forty away from their daughters and daughters-in-law. These were the elders whom they thought were too old for raping. I was sitting next to my mother-in-law, clinging to her.

I asked, "Where are you taking her? Take me with her." I followed her outside with about eighty older women. She was holding my baby. They asked if the baby were mine. I could not speak. If I said the baby was mine, my mother-in-law would be taken away. If I said the baby was hers, I would be sent away with the single girls. My mother-in-law spoke for me and said the baby was mine. They told me to go back inside with my baby.

Another woman was pregnant and begged to stay with her mother, so they let her. I saw one of the men give a gun to a boy around age fifteen. Daesh teaches it is haram (forbidden) for a Muslim to kill a woman by a bullet. When I walked back to the building, I heard about seven shots and the women moaning. It was not enough shots to kill everyone. Others told me an excavator came, pushed them into a hole and buried them. Some were still alive. Afterwards, one of the Daesh men told me my mother-in-law was in the ground.

Abu Saood came inside and told me I had to convert to Islam and marry him. I told him I did not want to become Muslim, but if he would bring my husband to me, I would become Muslim and go with him. He said, "We killed all your men."

Khatoon Ahmed Jaso from Kocho, May 2017:

I am one of the abducted daughters of Ahmed Al Jaso, the leader of the al-Mandkany tribe of Kocho. He was killed along with my husband and all the other men of Kocho. On August 15, 2014, I was taken with my son, Asim, and the other older women to Solagh Institute. They took me and my mother outside with the other women. I kept Asim with me. They ordered me to send him back inside, but I refused. They tried to pull him from me, but I fought and would not let go. I explained to Daesh that Asim is diabetic and needs injections six times per day, so they sent us both back inside. That is what saved us from being killed.

Daesh Process of Selecting the Girls
Salwa Khalaf Rasho, March 14, 2016
testimony to U.K. parliament

My name is Salwa Khalaf Rasho. This is my story of eight months of enslavement, rape, and physical and social torture in the hands of the Daesh monsters. I was born in 1998 and was in the ninth grade. I was leading a simple and modest life with my family until the day when Daesh attacked Shingal on August 3, 2014. I liked my city, Sinjar, very much. I grew up under the principal of co-existence with all societies within the community, regardless of one's religion or sect, because the values of my religion do not allow to hate others and discriminate against them.

Therefore, Sinjar was well-known as the city of tolerance and ethnic diversity. What happened was shocking and unexpected, because we saw Daesh as our brothers. With this, I mean the Arab tribes of the villages that belong to Shingal. Suddenly, they became monsters and wolves. They collaborated with Daesh when Yezidi women and children were enslaved and men were killed.

There were about 9,000 Peshmerga in my city who were armed with various types of weapons. They said to us, "We will protect and defend Shingal, and Daesh will only enter Shingal over our dead bodies. We will defend Shingal until the last bullet."

Unfortunately, they ran away without any resistance and without warning or giving notice to the civilians so we could escape from falling into the arms of Daesh monsters. They left us women and children to our cold-blooded fate. I and the people with me tried to flee into the mountains like the others.

At 8:30 in the morning, we fled from our house in the direction of Shingal Mountain, but a check point of Peshmerga soldiers stopped us and blocked our way. Therefore, we had to look for an alternative route. We found another way. In order to leave Sinjar and reach the mountain, this other way was further. When we reached this other way, a convoy of Peshmerga together with its commander, Sarbast Bapiri, and his soldiers pointed their guns at us and threatened us and said, "Clear out of the way so the Peshmerga convoy can flee first and reach the mountain."

When the convoy went, we could go a few hundred meters toward the mountain, until one car broke down and blocked the road. Therefore, the cars were stuck in a traffic jam. We waited. During this time, Daesh terrorists reached us and surrounded us. Most of them were Arabic and Kurdish Sunnis from the region. They said, "Don't be afraid of us. Go back to your houses. We are not here because of you. We will not injure you."

They forced us to get out of our cars and return to the city. Because of my disabled cousin, they allowed me to get into the car with my grandmother and another cousin. The rest of the family had to walk back, but they were able to escape and reach the mountain.

When we reached Sinjar, they put us in a hall as prisoners. There were a lot of families. When we drove in Sinjar, we saw a lot of dead bodies. The bodies of a young girl and young man are still in my mind. In this hall, they separated women and children from men. When we were captured, there was a young girl from Gir Zerik village who had just had surgery. (Gir Zerik had been attacked at 2:10 AM.) She was begging for food and water, but the terrorists denied her. They did not give her anything. After a few hours she died from exhaustion and thirst.

At 5 in the evening, they separated women and young girls and put us in buses and drove us to Mosul. There were about 120 women and girls with me in the same bus. Along the way Daesh terrorists were groping us and humiliating us. They were laughing at us. At 2 AM, we reached Mosul, and they put us all in a sporting hall in the district of Hay Al Zirahi. We were about 700 women, girls, and children.

After that an imam came and prayed and said we are now Muslim. "Forget your families. We will marry you. You are starting a new life."

After that, they registered our names and ages and separated us into two groups: married and unmarried girls and women. They did this until 3 AM in the morning. They took away our mobile phones, but my cousin hid hers. We knew what was going to happen to us: raping, violence, pain and humiliation. Therefore, we tried to kill ourselves and tried to find a rope or something in order to hang ourselves, but we did not find anything. We also tried to cut an electric cable, but we did not succeed.

We stayed for six days in this hall. After that, they brought us to a new hall, and we stayed there for three days. In this hall, older women and children were also separated from younger women and girls.

After that, I and other girls were brought to a big house near to Al Noor mosque. In this house there were about 700 girls from age 9 to 35. We stayed only one day in this building. After that an emir and officers of Daesh came and chose the most beautiful girls for themselves. Each of them took three or four girls. The girls who did not want to go with them were hit and tortured. After that, they separated siblings and transferred them to Syria as gifts for the officers there. This process took two days.

After this process, just 150 were left. About seventy girls were transferred to Syria. Me and my cousin and the rest of the girls were transported to Baaj, Iraq. After that, in Baaj, three Saudis came and bought thirteen girls. The same day Jilan, a seventeen-year-old girl from Tel Azeer committed suicide. After she learned that Daesh killed her family, she cut her wrists. In revenge, the Daesh terrorists took their dead bodies and threw them to the dogs.

After this, we were taken to Al Medina School. There we stayed for one week. After that, I and thirty-two other girls were taken to Tal Banat. We stayed there one week, also. Then we were taken to Kocho. There we saw some hands that had been cut off. These hands were near the village school. After that, I and six other girls were taken to Rambousi. There Daesh terrorists forced us to "marry" them. They threatened to take us to the slave market in Syria if we refused. They showed us some photos of Yezidi girls with bonded hands at the slave market and said to us, "This will be your fate, also."

So we said, "Just give us one day, and we will give you our answer." That night we decided to flee. Rambousi village is close to Shingal Mountain. We divided ourselves into two groups. The first group was supposed to flee first and the second one fifteen minutes later. The first group fled. After that, another girl and I fled, but we were captured when we tried to escape. When Daesh asked us about the other girls, we said, "Some of your friends came and took them away."

I was locked in a dark room and they denied me food and water. They came into the room twice a day and hit me and harassed me until I fell down and lost consciousness. This punishment came from Emir Abu Meriam. When he tried to go from Tal Afar to Sinjar, his car was bombed by coalition air strikes and he was killed.

After that, Abu Karam was his replacement. His full name was Ali Newaf Khalaf Al Jubouri. His punishment to me was that he blindfolded me and took me to a location where there was a young man whom he said was a Christian journalist. He beheaded him in front of me, and said to me they will do the same to my family if I try to escape.

After that, Abu Karam took me as his slave and took me to his house. He had two wives. At first, they were very bad to me, and, therefore, I tried to kill myself. After the women knew about my attempted suicide, they commiserated with me. When we were in a discussion, I found out that one of the women was the daughter of my father's friend. They told me if I do my housework good and look after the children good, they would be better to me, and they would not allow me to be sold.

In order to gain their trust, I did all my housework and improved my relationship with them. After two months, the family moved to Mosul. When the fights intensified, Abu Karam went to fight, and I was left alone with his wives in the house.

On March 18, 2015, I was able to get a mobile phone and send a message to my father. I told him where I was. After that, he contacted a friend in Mosul and told him about my situation. This friend told my father he would try to help me if he could reach me. My father sent him my address. The next day, when the whole family was having an afternoon nap, at 3 PM, I wore a burqa and left the house.

I stopped a taxi, and the driver took me to the address of my father's friend. I stayed there for one week. He found a smuggler with whom I could flee. He took me to Khanke near Duhok, Kurdistan. After that, I lived with my family in a tent in Berseve camp for displaced Yezidis near Zakho. This was, also, a horrible situation, but with God's and Germany's help and kindness, I and 1100 other Yezidi girls, women, and children went to Germany in a therapy program.

I and the other women and girls of various ages were in so many terrible and difficult situations. They raped us and forced us to do things they wanted. After some days of this, they sold us to others for only ten dollars. There are still several thousand Yezidi women and girls who are in the same situation and are sold, raped, humiliated, and tortured every day. There are still several hundred Yezidi children in Daesh training camps being drilled and brainwashed to be Daesh terrorists.

About 300,000 Yezidi people are currently living in tents. Their situation is bad after having lost everything. I ask the U.K. government, in the name of humanity, to take action on our recommendations to save the Yezidi community and rescue the kidnapped women and children.

Gohbal: How Arabs Stole Yezidi Land
Hamad Ajaj Murad Barakat, July 13, 2016

I am Hamad Ajaj Murad Barakat. I was born in 1978 in Gohbal. Gohbal is in the district of Sunoni, Shingal, on the north side of the mountain. I am Yezidi. The village of Gohbal in Arabic is called Al-Andulis. Gohbal is its Kurdish name. I was the town manager of Gohbal when Daesh attacked us. After the attack, I became a Peshmerga commander at the Domiz front line. It is on the south side of the mountain next to the Hamadan massacre site where Daesh killed over eighty Yezidis in an open field.

The founder of Gohbal was Sheikh Khalaf, the brother of my great-grandfather. He was a well-known religious man as well as the chief of his tribe. Before he came to Gohbal, he was living in Bashiqa and Bahzan, Yezidi villages. His father, Sheikh Nasser, moved to Karsi. After he died, his son Sheikh Khalaf founded Gohbal village in 1962. By that time Khalaf was already around eighty years old. He died in 1968.

Sheikh Khalaf and his brother, Sheikh Barakat, bought this land from the Iraqi government. It is 56,000 dunams (13,838 acres). I have the original, official documents with signatures and stamp. The ownership of this land is registered under Sheikh Khalaf's and Barakat's names. Some of this land was west of Gohbal, and some of it was in Gohbal proper.

Khalaf gathered the inhabitants for Gohbal from Bazili, Zumar, and elsewhere. After founding Gohbal, Sheikh Khalaf distributed 5,000 dunams (1,235 acres) to Gohbal's poor inhabitants and kept the rest for himself.

Next, some Jihish Arabs came and became Sheikh Khalaf's farmers. They were planting for him. Jihish (also spelled Jaish, Jaeesh) are a Sunni Arab Muslim tribe.

The Ajeel, who are part of a Muslim tribe called Shammar, warned Sheikh Khalaf to kick the Jihish farmers off his land or they would be like a nail in his back, meaning they would make a problem for him and his people. Sheikh Khalaf told them the Jihish are poor, and since he owned four vacant houses, he let them live here.

After they lived here for a while, their population increased, and they grew powerful. Then they betrayed Sheikh Khalaf who had been kind to them, and began to fight against him. They burned his house and stole his land.

They were Jihish Sunni Arabs and, because the government, also, was Sunni, it supported them in stealing our land. The government's position was, "How can Kurdish people be the owners of this land? Impossible."

So the government distributed the land to Arabs. They divided the land into sixty dunams (fifteen acres), making 400 parcels of land. After that, they divided it among themselves.

Apart from this, the government took 416 dunams (103 acres) and claimed that it was for the Ministry of Finance, then they gave it to their people. I asked for that land in 2014. The government said that Baghdad should deal with this problem.

Sheikh Khalaf and Barakat were allowed to keep only four thousand dunams (988 acres) where Gohbal is.

Ninety-five percent of the land was given to the Jihish tribe. They were farming it for themselves in front of our eyes. Furthermore, we could not protest. We had to accept living among them. We were even forced to thank them for that, but still they were not satisfied.

This was our land and Jihish Arabs took it through the backing of a dictatorial regime. After Saddam Hussein's regime was finished by the American occupation, we asked the new government two or three times to get our land back, and it refused. The government said when the decision on Article 140 is made, you will get it, and if it is not done, you are not going to get it back.

Article 140 of the Iraqi constitution requires a referendum be held for the disputed territories to decide if they want to belong to the Kurdistan or Baghdad government. The referendum was supposed to be held by October 2016, but the deadline came and went.

We have asked the government many times for our land, but the Arabs are the ones who have the authority. The speaker of the Council of Representatives of Iraq was Osama Al Najaifi. He is not going to take the land from Sunni and give it to us. Abdullah Al Humidi (from Ajeel's tribe) knows that this land belongs to us, and that Shallan village is our border. Jihish's tribe was living between us in Gohbal and Shammer's tribe.

After Daesh invaded Mosul, our Jihish Arab neighbors were more confident, laughing and comfortable, telling us, "You guys are going to run away one day." We did not expect them to do what they did. After Daesh controlled many areas, the Jihish tribe supported them.

Before Daesh controlled Shingal, our Jihish neighbors were visiting each Yezidi house and telling us, "Daesh is not interested in you. They will come only to destroy Nouri Al-Maliki's government. Daesh is not going to hurt anyone. "

Both before and after Daesh controlled Mosul, there were threats against us. When Shia were escaping from Tal Afar, they came to our villages, and we showed compassion to them, so in return the Jihish Sunni Arabs destroyed our properties.

They forced many people out of their houses, burned their houses, and destroyed their water wells with explosives. My house on my farm, north of Gohbal and south of Rabia, was one of them that was burned. They destroyed my brother's well, my cousin's well, and another one of my relatives. We quit living there until the present moment.

Before the attack on Shingal, our Yezidi drivers were taking passengers to Duhok when Jihish killed many of them and burned their cars. Jihish killed one man, injured another, and burned a car from my village of Gohbal.

The chief of Jihish's village came to our houses and denied responsibility. They refused to name the killers. Okay, please explain to me, if you are not the guilty ones, when someone kills a driver and burns a car publically in your village, is it logical to say that you do not know him?

Jihish taunted us, "If you want to get your revenge on us, go ahead. We dare you to do what you can." They have been torturing us since the moment they seized our lands decades ago until August 3, 2014.

Now what we want from the world, regardless of any specific country . . . Kurdistan, America, the United States Congress, or each human being . . . we want to tell them that we are innocent people. If they are going to let Arabs live with us again, we want to say that we are not going to live here. Yezidis and Arabs can never co-exist.

After Daesh invaded Shingal, they came and said, "Don't leave your places" and "No one is going to hurt you. " Afterwards they massacred Hardan's people. The people of the villages of Zorava, Gohbal, Borek, Dohala, Duguri, and Sunoni had to run. Many were captured and killed.

Daesh blocked the roads of the two villages, Hardan and Khanasor, so we could not drive to Sunoni then Kurdistan for safety. We had to run to the mountain. Not everyone escaped. Daesh arrested some people, and more than 250 people from Gohbal were taken captive because of these Jihish Arabs. Jihish and other surrounding Arab villages slaughtered Yezidis from Hardan in the east to Khanasor in the west.

They came to exterminate us. The things they did not manage to do to us were only because they were not able to. They destroyed the houses in Gohbal. If you want, I can show them to you. Thirty houses out of every one hundred houses are burned. The bullets of their Doshka cannons left holes in my house in Gohbal and are still there.

After Al-Maliki's regime failed, Jihish seized all the border's weapons and cars. They took any government vehicle they saw. There was a governmental Hummer parked on a hill, and Jihish just took it. Why did they take that Hummer? Why didn't I take it? Because I did not have the authority to take a Hummer. But they took the Hummer and we know the man who took it, even the name of his father.

I personally know the Jihish who burned the police station. Some of them are now in Badoosh, and they are called Abu Salim tribe. Fifteen families are living in Rabia. I have no idea about where the rest of them live. The most important thing is that one of them is a member of a provincial council and he is supporting Jihish in his role as a member of that authority.

There is no hope for us ever to live together again with Arabs even if they were innocent, because these innocent groups are going to be aggressive again in the future. It is not due only to the problem of the land. The matter is bigger. It is a problem of religion.

We would not ask now for that land if only they had not kidnapped our women and girls by force, did not burn our houses, and did not kill our men. So what we want now is not to allow the Arabs to return to our village, because we cannot live among them if they come back.

The matter is I cannot trust those who bought our honor; our women and our sisters. When they come back, nobody is going to remain here. I promise you when Jihish come back here, you are not going to see two Yezidi families in Gohbal.

Okay, if they were not supporting Daesh, why did they escape with Daesh? If they were actually innocent people, they would have escaped with *us* when we escaped. None of those Arabs denied on TV that they did not participate with Daesh in killing us.

All the Arabs who lived in our area were Jihish from the Abu Salim tribe. Jihish were living between us and the Shammer tribe. There are always good and evil people in every place, so I can neither tell you every Shammer man was evil nor everyone was good.

Regardless of their tribe, we are not going to accept living among them, even if one of those Arab families who escaped with us promised us to be good and loyal. In such a case, we still will not accept them, because they may later marry someone from a family that supports Daesh.

Even if I would accept them, our people will not accept them. As the manager of Gohbal, I represent more than 500 families. If I personally said I want Jihish to come to live with us again, in such a case, there is a possibility that the people of the villages of Borek, Dohala, and Duguri may not accept my decision.

All Yezidi people are furious with Arabs. When a family lost their daughter, or their son was killed, or their house burned, or the mother is killed, in these cases, how can I defend Jihish?

I have nothing to say to the Iraqi government, but from the Kurdistan government, I want them to understand that we cannot live with Arabs anymore, and if they are going to let Arabs come back, we want them to find somewhere else for us to live. We had religious temples here and they exploded everything, so nothing is left here for us.

Even if America surrounds us with their big weapons and gives us a helping hand, we will not be satisfied and will not stay in our villages when there are Arabs living close to us or among us. It is out of the question to deal with Arabs any more.   We will thank any human being and organization when they do something for us.

The Agrarian Reform Law of 1958 broke up large estates and distributed land to peasant families. By the end of 1964, the number of landowners whose excess land was expropriated in all of Iraq was 1,621 persons of whom nearly 200 lived in Mosul province, also referred to as Nineveh.   The total area expropriated in all of Iraq amounted to 7 million donums (4.5 million acres). Approximately 20% of the expropriated land was in Mosul province and mostly in the Shingal region. Yezidis were heavily impacted. Most of the expropriated land was redistributed to Arabs.

To compensate for low agricultural production, the state leased out land. Large state-owned farms replaced the feudal system, weakening the power of tribal sheikhs. The government expropriated more land under the Iraqi Agrarian Reform Law No. 117 of 1970 . The Ba'ath party, under the rule of Saddam Hussein, drove out at least 70,000 Kurds from Mosul's western half, thus making western Mosul all Sunni Arab.

In 1974, the government ordered the destruction of the mostly Yezidi villages in Shingal and the forced settlement into new towns that were constructed 6 to 25 km away from Shingal Mountain. In 1975, there were 37 Yezidi villages destroyed and five neighborhoods in Sinjar city Arabized. The same year, 413 Muslim Kurd and Yezidi farmers were dispossessed of their lands by the government or had their agricultural contracts cancelled and replaced by Arab settlers.

In Sheikhan in 1975, 147 out of a total of 182 villages suffered forced displacement, and 64 villages were handed over to Arab settlers in the years following. Property deeds of land belonging to displaced Muslim Kurds and Yezidis were invalidated. In the Iraqi censuses in 1977 and 1987, Yezidis were forced to register as Arabs.

When Daesh attacked Shingal in 2014, they exploded more than 1,000 Yezidi houses. The displaced Yezidis have no deeds to their properties to use in a legal pursuit for fair compensation.

Aug. 2 Arabs from Rabia Attacked Gohbal Family

Hammo Ali Shero, July 10, 2016

I am Hammo Ali Shero from Gohbal in the Sunoni sub-district of Shingal. I am Yezidi. Gohbal is between the neighboring Arab village of Rabia to the north and Shingal mountain to the south. This is disputed territory between Iraq and Kurdistan. You have to drive north through Rabia and other Arab villages to get to the safety of Kurdistan.

We were on our farm on the north side of Gohbal. On August 2, 2014, Daesh came from Rabia and shot at us and arrested all the women and kids. They blew up the first farm where there is a water pump, so we ran south to the second farm near to Gohbal. We call it Sheikh Khalaf area. Later that day, Daesh released the women and kids. We were afraid and trapped.

On August 3, when Daesh attacked Shingal, someone called and told me the border to Syria was open, so I took my family and drove directly to Syria. I saw a lot of Daesh trucks over there.

My mother and my uncle's wife and five men from our family refused to leave our farm. They said, "We will stay here on the farm and fight." Daesh came and took all seven of them on August 5.

My mother and uncle's wife returned from Daesh after nearly one year. The other five men are missing. We do not know what happened to them. I have asked many people and no one has seen or heard anything about them since that day. This is a big family of women and children, and there is no man to care for them except me. My son, Hawas, is missing, and I have his children to care for. My brother, Nouri, is also missing, and I have his whole family to care for, also. We get paid about $300 dollars once every three months in Peshmerga.

Before there was Daesh, they were called Al Qaida. In 2006, my father visited an old friend in Mosul to get some things for his farm and Al Qaida killed my father and uncle. There is only me now to care for everyone.

As soon as I got my family to safety in Kurdistan, I returned and joined Peshmerga on Mount Shingal to fight Daesh. When we discovered the Hamadan grave site on the south side of the mountain, in December 2014, I discovered one of my relatives from Kocho had been killed there. He was Yusif Suleyman Ammon. I found his ID card in his pocket along with his shirt with the hole from a bullet. We found one more ID card of a man named Hrero. He was a Faqir from the north side of the mountain.

Yusif had run from Kocho and tried to get to the mountain, but when he got near the highway, Daesh captured him and brought him to that valley where they killed around eighty men on August 3 or 4. The grass did not grow back in that place where the men were massacred. We counted fifty-eight bodies and clothes, but we think the rain took a lot of bodies.

How Tal Afar Got Electricity
Preskee Ismail Atto, July 10, 2016

I am Preskee Ismail Atto. I am seventy-eight. I was born in 1939.

After my son, Hammo Ali Shero, drove the family to Syria on August 3, 2014, Daesh came to the farm near Gohbal and captured all of us who had stayed behind. They tied the hands of our sons, and then they took us to a farm with a lot of trees in Rabia.

Then they took us to one building, the police station I think. In the middle of the night, they took the women to Tal Afar city. They took us to one house that belonged to the Shia, near to the silo in Tal Afar city. We stayed there for eight days.

After that we said, "Why don't you take us to some Yezidi females?" After that they took us to one school. It was full of Yezidi families.

From the school they took us to the village of Qaser Al Mehrab on the south side of Tal Afar city. Each house had one Yezidi family in it. These were Shia Arab houses, but the owners had fled when Daesh took Mosul and Tal Afar. We were twenty persons. There was no empty house for us, so we just slept outside in the shade in one spot in the morning and another spot in the afternoon.

Daesh men came to Qaser Al Mehrab village and took all the nice, young girls to use for sex. They kept the old men and old women in Qaser Al Mehrab. They used it for the Daesh men who were fighting and having sex with those girls. All the men and women stayed in the village, but they took the girls away from the village. Maybe they took some to Raqqa.

From Qaser Al Mehrab they transferred us to a wedding hall in a forest in Mosul. The area is called Ghabat. We stayed there twenty-two days. Then they brought us back to Tal Afar city and put each family in a Shia's house, because the Shia houses were empty.

One day they came and wrote down our names and said they would release us. On January 18, 2015, they released the first group of more than 200 elderly. After they were released, our kitchen got electricity 24 hours a day, because we used it for making bread. Everywhere in Kurdistan the government cut the electricity many times a day, but we never had any power outages in Tal Afar.

Three months later, on April 8, 2015, I was released with a group of 217 other elderly Yezidis. Daesh never explained why we were being released. They just released us. First they took us to Hawijah, near Kirkuk, and from there we came to Kurdistan. It was not Daesh who brought us to Kurdistan. We came in one big bus belonging to an Arab sheik.

They brought us to some pass, but the border was blocked, so they brought us back again and we stayed there one night. The next day when we came near to the border, a bulldozer broke the berm, and then we passed the border to Kurdistan.

After we passed the border, they unloaded us, and we used other buses belonging to Kurdistan to go to Erbil. Not any Daesh came near to Kurdistan with us; only the sheik of that tribe and then a normal driver who brought us to Kurdistan . . . not any Daesh. From Erbil we took other buses to Lalish holy temple. From Lalish, we came in our own trucks to our homes where we are displaced in Kurdistan.

Our situation now is very bad, not just because of our poor living situation, but because our family is still under Daesh control. Five men from my family are missing, and we don't know anything about them.

On April 26, 2015, six children, two women, and two men from one Yezidi family managed to escape from Tal Afar during clashes between Daesh gunmen and Kurdish fighters. The same day Daesh separated Yezidi men and boys over fourteen from girls and women. Up until this time, Daesh had believed if Yezidis had converted, no one would return to Shingal, but many were escaping anyway.

According to Mirza Dinnayi, on April 26, 300 to 500 males were taken to the village of Cino near Tal Afar. It was speculated that the next day, they were taken to Alo Antar, a Valley on the north side of Tal Afar and executed.

Mosul Governor, Atheel al-Nujaifi, confirmed this massacre on April 27, 2015. A mass grave in this location was discovered January 5, 2018.

Jihish tribe leader Omar Hussein Ibrahim was responsible for the enslavement of hundreds of Yezidi women and operated as a commander for Daesh in the area of Sunoni and Gohbal. Hussein Ibrahim was killed in the Peshmerga offensive in December 2015.

Preskee Ismail Atto and her remaining son, Hammo Ali Shero, and the surviving widows and grandchildren of her family were granted asylum in Australia.

Recording the Dead on Christmas Eve

On Christmas Eve, December 24, 2014, I visited Faisal Mahmoud Khero and his wife in Germany where he related the horrifying story of how his three brothers and their families were massacred on their family farm known as Siba Mahmoud Khero, six kilometers north of Tal Ezeer. After Daesh attacked and controlled Gir Zerik and Siba Sheikh Khudir by 7 AM, August 3, 2014, they continued north and east to other Yezidi villages and to Sinjar city at the foot of Shingal Mountain.

I traveled to meet Faisal from southeast Turkey where for three months I had been documenting the Daesh atrocities of beheadings, mass executions, kidnappings, torture, and rape against Yezidis.

I was invited first to be a guest speaker at the Ezidisch Akademie in Hanover. My initial introduction to the director, Hatab Omar, was derailed before we could sit for a cup of coffee. He told me to remove my checkered red, green, and yellow Kurdish scarf, saying it was a PKK terrorist scarf. I protested that it was simply representative of Kurdish colors.

Having come this distance to speak to his membership, I tried to smooth over our disagreement by shifting the conversation to the topic of my presentation about the Yezidi genocide. I explained that all the Yezidis I had met had told me that PKK had rescued them off Shingal Mountain and helped them all the way over the mountains to Turkey. Hatab forbade me to mention PKK in my presentation because the Akademie gets government funding which he would not jeopardize. I refused to be censored. Within ten minutes we were at loggerheads. We agreed to cancel my presentation. This portended future attempts to silence Yezidis from telling the truth to the world, because mentioning the PKK as saviors conflicted with political agendas of countries that listed the PKK as a terrorist organization.

The next day I traveled to Bielefeld to meet Faisal. He came to meet my train with his life-long friend Ali Sedo, a Yezidi historian. In Faisal's home we sat at the table with our computers, listing the names and ages of the dead and abducted as business-like as if we were doing end-of year inventory.

Faisal gave me permission to publish the names and photos of the abducted girls in the hope of having them returned from Daesh. On that sad winter day, I harbored little hope of their rescue. I never thought that in a few years I would be hugging them upon their return, listening to their stories, getting passports for all their surviving family members, and lobbying Germany to grant them asylum.

I questioned Faisal about that terrible day like an interrogator to verify all the details. "Was the road paved or dirt?" "Were they shot inside the house or outside?" I cringed inside with each question, searching for words to soften the brutality.

All eyes remained dry through the four-hour telling of the story. A massacre on the scale of genocide petrifies your heart, dries your eyes, freezes the muscles on your face. Would I ever smile again?

When we finished, I went to bed and smothered my sobs in my pillow, although I wanted to go outside in the cold night and wail until my scream reached the edge of the universe.

One female and eleven adult males of the Mahmoud Khero family were massacred by Daesh on their family farm at 11 AM, August 3. Twenty-eight females and four children were abducted. What follows is but one family's terrifying, but representative experience as recounted by the uncle Faisal, the grandmother, two teenage boys, and three sisters who escaped from Daesh captivity and repeated sexual assaults after two and three years.

The massacre and abduction at the Barakat Mahmoud Khero farm is representative of what happened throughout the villages of Shingal. Daesh killed or abducted at least 6417 Yezidis. Many families lost as many as seventy-five family members. All families were ripped asunder and separated between camps and countries.

Mahmoud Khero Family Massacre at Tal Ezeer Farm
Faisal Mahmoud Khero, December 24, 2014

I am Faisal Mahmoud Khero, a Yezidi from Shingal, Iraq. Twelve members of my family were mercilessly executed on our farm and twenty-eight females, four children, and a ten-day-old infant boy were abducted on August 3, 2014, after Daesh attacked the nearby villages of Gir Zerik and Siba Sheikh Khudir.

My father died in 2012 at age eighty-five.   My seventy-five-year-old mother, Ghazal Qassim, remained on our family farm with her grown children and grandchildren. It is between Tal Ezeer and Jiddalah on the south side of Shingal Mountain at the western end. It is called Siba Mahmoud Khero. The Arabic word "siba" means a deep well that is pumping water. My mother and family of my brother, Barakat, were living on the farm, six kilometers north at Highway 47 and the junction to Tal Ezeer.

My parents were farmers in Shingal and owned their own well and pumping station to irrigate their fields and water their animals. They owned fifty acres (eighty Iraqi donum). They were growing barley and wheat for cereal and alfalfa for the animals. They had a modern sprinkler irrigation system. They also grew vegetables in their greenhouse. They owned 152 sheep. They owned two cars and two pickup trucks for their farm.

This is where I grew up, but I fled with my wife and daughter to Germany in 2009 where we are refugees. This is not the first time Yezidis have come under attack, but it is the worst, because now our homeland of Shingal is finished. There is nothing to return to. Our hope is lost.

Some of our family lived in the town of Tal Ezeer. They had already come to the family farm at the outskirts of town to be together with all our relatives. They thought this was safer than staying in Tal Ezeer village. It was also nearer to Shingal Mountain. Approximately 100 of my relatives and neighbors gathered inside the house on our property.

When Daesh was advancing, my family could hear random shooting. Yezidis began fleeing toward the mountain on foot. They stopped at our pumping station for water. It was a hot, dusty August day. August is the dry season, and there is no rain.

By late morning, Daesh reached my family's farm. They arrived in twelve cars on the paved highway and turned off the highway to our home.   The massacre and abduction lasted for half-an-hour.

When the men refused to convert to Islam, Daesh shot and killed all but one of them. My three brothers, Barakat (age 45), Murad (39), and Mirza Mahmoud Khero (35), were killed. Barakat's son, Farman (24), was wounded and his other son, Farhan (22), was killed. Six male cousins and one female cousin were also killed.   My brothers' daughters were abducted: Muhbat (25), Ayshan (21), Hadiah (19), Haifa (17), Nazdar (17), and Sameera (15).

I talked to my mother and Farman on the phone when it was over. They were together in the neighbor's house. Farman told me he would bleed to death from his bullet wounds if he did not reach a hospital.

I called my Arab friend in Baaj (who speaks Kurdish) and he agreed to take Farman to the hospital. I talked to Farman in the hospital at 2 PM. I heard the ambulance and the voice of a man speaking Arabic in the background. He was saying they had to take Farman to Tal Afar. I also heard the sound of bombardments. Then the call went silent. We do not know what happened to Farman, but we fear he is dead.

In 2014, I was in frequent phone communication with my niece, Ayshan. She was held prisoner by Daesh in Mosul. She knew the house number (945/5/132/R) where she was being held, but not the street name, so it was impossible to locate her. Daesh told her that her only solution was for her family to come to Mosul and convert to Islam.

Zeri Khudir Ismael Returns To Lalish
by Amy Beam

Faisal opened his phone, leaned over, and showed me a photo he had received of one of his nieces who was kidnapped. It had been circulated on the internet. It was a close-up head shot of a dead woman on the floor. He told me she had committed suicide. He passed the phone to me so I could study it. She had two long cuts on her neck. One cut extended a quarter-way around her neck at the jugular vein like a choker necklace. One seven-inch vertical cut ran down the side of her throat. It was crudely stitched closed.

"I don't think she killed herself," I told Faisal. "Who can cut themselves twice in the neck? The jugular vein would spurt blood all over. That is like a person committing suicide by shooting two bullets into her head."

I did not have the courage to tell Faisal I had seen two photos of naked women being held horizontally with their heads pulled back by their long blond hair, the aorta and esophagus sliced open at a right angle, and their blood gushing out. In one photo the blood was being caught in a stainless steel bowl. One cut came from under the left ear around to the Adam's apple. The other cut went seven inches down the esophagus. The cuts corresponded to the two cuts on Faisal's niece. There were rumors that Yezidis were being forced to give blood to use for injured Daesh fighters.

I passed the phone back. Faisal studied the photo, then picked up his pen and on his list of abducted women, he crossed out "suicide" and wrote "killed" next to the name of Zeri Khudir Ismael.

Zeri's body was recovered three years later.   On September 24, 2017, Yezidis buried Zeri in a ceremony on the sacred grounds of Lalish.   The story goes that she committed suicide rather than let Daesh touch her body.   A sentimental comfort, but probably not true.

Sultan Witnessed His Family's Massacre in Tal Ezeer

Sultan Barakat Mahmoud Khero, October 2017

My name is Sultan. I am one of the few male survivors of the massacre of the Mahmoud Khero families of Tal Ezeer. My father was Barakat Mahmoud Khero. My family of twelve people lived in a nice home on our farm at the intersection to Tal Ezeer, just north of Tal Ezeer on the south side of Shingal Mountain. It had a beautiful green garden and a water wheel.

I was only thirteen when Daesh attacked us in our home. Daesh separated me and six other boys from the men's room and sent us to the room with the women and children. After they took the girls away, they locked fifty of us in the kitchen. They had a different plan for us, but one of the Daesh men got a phone call after shooting the men, and they immediately left without taking us. I think that is the only reason we did not get captured and sent for Daesh military training.

Before Daesh attacked, my cousin, Jameel Chetto, called my father at 7 AM on the morning of August 3, 2014, and told him to go with his car to bring six families of our relatives from town to our farm just north of Tal Ezeer. We had heard that Daesh had already attacked the neighboring village of Gir Zerik. During the night we could hear the gunfire and mortars.

My father brought Jameel Chetto's families from Tal Ezeer to our farmhouse. By 8:30 AM, seven families of about fifty people had gathered in our house. My two uncles, Mirza Mahmoud Khero and Murad Mahmoud Khero, also came with their families to our house. They were another fifteen people.

By 9:30, my father, Barakat, brought his two sisters and their six children to our farm house. Then he immediately drove to Sinjar city to get another one of my older sisters. The Peshmerga check point was still there. Peshmerga did not let him enter Sinjar city so he returned home at 9:50 AM without my sister.

By now there were about 140 or 150 people gathered around our house. People were coming to our house from Tal Ezeer and stopping for water on their way to the mountain. My family and I were helping them. Tal Ezeer is between Gir Zerik and Siba Sheikh Khuder where Yezidis defended themselves and fought Daesh during the night, but many of them were killed.

In Tal Ezeer we did not fight Daesh. We did not see any Peshmerga anywhere to defend us. We knew we did not have good weapons to fight Daesh who had heavy equipment and trucks. Maybe they captured them from the Iraqi Army or Syria. They had enough power to attack a country, not only the Yezidis. Yezidi people are brave and good, but we did not have those kinds of heavy weapons with which to defend ourselves.

We were preparing to flee to the mountain when a convoy of men arrived in four-door Maleezi trucks. They were shooting randomly toward the Yezidi people. When the shooting started, many people ran to our house. I saw many people killed with my own eyes.

Ghuro Jerdo got off a truck full of people escaping to the mountain and hid in the generator building with his sniper gun. Ghuro shot two rounds toward the last Daesh truck. He hit a man in his arm. When he did that, Daesh turned back and came to our house. Daesh shot about 500 rounds from their Doshkas and other guns toward our house before they arrived. They also fired one mortar rocket at us, but it did not explode. When they got to our house at 10 AM, Daesh shot Ghuro Jerdo and then beheaded him.

Around 10:30 AM Daesh entered our house. They separated the men from the women and put us in two different rooms. Three Daesh went to the men's room where I was. Four others went to the women's room. We were twenty-one men and boys in the men's room, plus my sister, Asia Barakat Mahmoud Khero, sitting on our father's lap. She was only eight. One Daesh man who was speaking Kurdish said "Kids, get out."

They took Asia to the women's room. They also kicked out me and my brother, Pasha, plus four other boys from the men's room. That left fifteen men in the men's room. They sent us to the women's room, where they selected all the girls and women between ages ten and thirty. They loaded them into our three family vehicles plus Daesh pickup trucks. They took twenty-four females from my own family plus another eight females from my village.

When they were taking the girls and women out, I heard them asking each other, "Who can drive the cars?" which means the Daesh terrorists did not know each other if they had to ask this question. They bombed one of our vehicles that was not starting so we would have no transportation.

After they drove away, the Daesh men who stayed behind came back into the house. They put me and six boys plus the older women and little children in the kitchen, and tied the door shut. We were about fifty people locked in the room. I was looking out the holes in the door to the men's room and listening. They asked the men, "What is your religion?"

The men answered, "We belong to the Yezidi religion."

Daesh said, "Oh, yes, you guys are infidels. So your killing is halal," meaning, according to Islam it is alright to kill them.

After that, they took the men's car keys, phones, watches, rings, and weapons.

Once again they asked the men about their religion. They said "Will you convert to Islam?"

The men said "We are Yezidis. We will never convert to Islam."

So they ordered the men outside to an execution line. After two or three people were kneeling in the line to be executed, my father, Barakat Mahmoud

Khero, yelled for everyone to run, because he knew they were going to make a mass execution.

When the men ran randomly, Daesh killed seven of my family and relatives, including my father, Barakat Mahmoud Khero, and my brother, Farhan, plus my two uncles, Murad, and Mirza. They also killed five others on our farm. My brother Farman was wounded in the knee and the thigh. Those who escaped ran to the mountain along with most of the people who had been put into the kitchen with me.

After Daesh left, I remained behind with two nephews, my grandmother, Ghazal, and my brother Farman's wife, Mayan Senow Barakat. Daesh did not take Mayan because she was pregnant. Farman sent me and my mother to the neighbor's house to get help for him.

When I got to the neighbor's house, I fainted from fear, so I could not return home. About seventy people were gathered there. My grandmother talked with my uncle Faisal in Germany after the attack and told him what had happened. She asked for a solution for Farman. Uncle Faisal called his Muslim friends from the al-Khatouni tribe living in Baaj. They came from Baaj and took Farman to Sinjar hospital.

At 7 pm we all ran to the mountain. I had to leave my grandmother behind, because she could not walk fast. I stayed with them in the Jaddala area for four days. My grandmother and Farman's wife stayed three days in the neighbor's house before climbing the mountain and joining us. We made our way off the mountain to Kurdistan.

I live with my mother, grandmother, and rescued sisters now in a tent in Kurdistan. It is unbearably hot in the summer and freezing cold in the winter. When it rains our tent leaks. We are thirteen people. We are miserable living like this with all our fathers and husbands killed. We hope to join my Uncle Faisal in Germany if the German government will keep its promise to him to bring his family who survived the massacre.

On November 13, 2015, Kurdish forces freed Sinjar city and the village of Tal Ezeer. On November 15, they located 35 bodies at a massacre grave site of my family and relatives at our farm by the intersection of Tal Ezeer. In June 2017, the field of bones was intentionally burned, destroying the evidence.

My grandmother is old. She refuses to leave, so I will stay in Iraq with her. I want my sisters to go to Germany where they will be safe.

Jaed Watched the Massacre from the Kitchen Window
Jaed Murad Muhmoud Khero, September 29, 2017

On August 3, 2014, at 2 AM I was sleeping at home in Tal Ezeer. I was fifteen. My father, Murad Mahmoud Khero, spoke with someone from the village of Gir Zerik. He told my father that the Arabs were advancing to our village with their heavy weapons. We hoped they would not attack us because we had only very light weapons. Tal Ezeer is between Siba Sheikh Khudir village to the west and Gir Zerik to the east. Baaj is twenty kilometers south near the border of Syria. It takes thirty minutes to drive there.

People in Tal Ezeer were numb with fear. I was terrified. The sounds of gun shots and mortars between the men of the villages and the Arab attackers grew louder for five hours. By 8:00 AM my father told me we would leave the house and escape to the mountain. First we would go to my Uncle Barakat's farm which is six kilometers north of town, near the mountain. We arrived at my uncle's farm at Tal Ezeer junction at 9 AM and drank water from his well.

Gathered near his farm were about 200 people from Tal Ezeer and Siba Sheikh Khudir villages. Daesh members approached the farm and fired a Doshka into the crowd. My father took us inside the house to escape the gunfire. There were about 110 men, women and children on the farm. About seventy-seven men, women, and children were killed in that location.

I was with my father and my uncles and the sons of my uncles in one of the rooms. They were shooting at us through the windows. Then they entered the house. I was terrified. They looked like monkeys with their long beards. On one man's Kalashnikov gun was inscribed, "Allah". They told us to give them our mobile phones, keys, cars, and money. Some were speaking Kurmanji Kurdish spoken in the Duhok region and others were speaking Sorani Kurdish which is spoken in the Erbil and Sulaymaniyah region. This means they were Kurds. Still others spoke Arabic, Dutch, and Russian.

They ordered the boys under age 16 to leave the men's room. My cousins and I left the room.

Their leader said to us, "We will kill you. You are kuffir," meaning non-believers. He came to us and was going to kill us. One of them said to him, "These are young children. Let them go to their mothers. It is pointless to kill them." So they took five boys, including me, to the room of women and girls. An Arab entered the room and had three gasoline cans in his hand to burn the room.

The Chechen man came to him and said, "Do not burn them, because we will take them." He opened the door of the room and told us who he would choose. He sent us boys and women over forty to the kitchen. He said they would take the younger women and girls for sex. My sister was crying. We were terrified. He raised a weapon in front of my mother and said, "If you do not go, I will kill you." So my mother and I went to the kitchen leaving the girls fifteen to twenty-five-years-old behind. I was trembling inside.

There was a window in the kitchen. I looked out and watched them take my sister, Nazdar, and cousins outside to my father's car and drive away. The girls walked between two rows of men to prevent them from running away. Altogether they took twenty-eight females and one infant.

Then they took my father, my brother, my uncles, and the sons of my uncles outside. They forced most of them inside the enclosed yard for our sheep. It has a four-foot wall around the yard next to the building for our sheep. They asked them if they would become Muslims or be killed. My father and uncle said to them, "We are Yezidis."

I watched through the window as they began shooting them. They were killing my family. I saw them shoot my father in the head.

I ran to the door of the room. I was frantic to go to my father, but unfortunately I could not get out because the door of the room was tied shut with a rope. I was helpless to do anything. We watched out the window as Daesh ran to the cars, including our family's cars, and left.

I went to the door again and pounded on it until it opened. I rushed to my father next to the sheep shed. Part of his head was blown off. I found my uncle Barakat under the tree by the corner of the house. Barakat was still conscious with his eyes open. He looked at me, but could not talk. His forehead was blown open. I stayed with him until he died two minutes later. Farman was still alive underneath Barakat's body with two bullet wounds in his leg. They killed one woman and eleven men, including my father, two uncles, and cousins.

They are my father, Murad Mahmoud Khero (1975), Barakat Mahmoud Khero (1969), Mirza Mahmoud Khero (1979), Farhan Barakat Mahmoud Khero (1992), Farman Barakat Mahmoud Khero (1990), Atto Chatto Kharo (1951), Khalil Chatto Kharo (1968), Sabri Atto Chatto (1981), Sami Jendu Khudaida (1993), Eido Sabri Atto (1990), Salem Sabri Atto, (1995), Ayshan Sharaf Ajool, (1974, female).

I could not find my brother Talal nor my cousin Farhan. I could not search for them, because of the dangerous sheep dogs. The haystack behind the building for the sheep was on fire, so we thought Talal may have burned to death.

The road was close to the farm house. Daesh cars were passing by. We knew that if we stayed at this farm they will take us, so we joined with others walking toward the mountain. There was nothing else we could do. We could not believe all the men in my family were executed. We were dazed with grief.

We stayed in the mountain for ten days. There was very little water and food. I did not eat for seven days. The road between the west end of Shingal Mountain in Iraq and Syria was opened on August 9, thanks to the PKK. We walked from

Shingal to Syria where we were transferred by cars to the camps in the Kurdistan region of Iraq. We are now living in tents in the camps.

On August 11, someone said to me, "Is your brother named Talal?"

I said "Yes."

He told me Talal is alive. When the shooting began, Talal ran into the building where we kept our sheep, then climbed out the small, back window facing the gulley. When Daesh saw him hiding behind the haystack, they shot from the road, setting the hay on fire. Talal escaped into the gulley.

It has been years since the attack and nothing has changed for us. My cousin Farman, who was wounded, is still missing. My sister, Nazdar, is still missing. She was seventeen when they took her. Five of the kidnapped females are still missing. We have no word from any of them.

Every day I wish that I were dead with my family. When Mirza Dunnayi interviewed us for the program in Germany, he refused to take me or my little sisters, because he said the program was only for traumatized women and girls who had been kidnapped and raped by Daesh. Mirza ruined my life. We are stuck here in this tent. I will die if I do not get away from here.

Note by Amy Beam

After Jaed told me his story, with his mother and siblings filling in details, I spent twenty minutes coaxing them to leave their tent with me for the evening. Everyone was depressed with the memory of that day and had no mood for going out. They felt it would be wrong to be happy while their sister was still missing. At last Jaed and his three younger sisters agreed. Talal stayed home with his mom.

First we went to the shopping mall where the youngest picked out a toy. The older kids refused any gifts. Next we rode the escalator for the first time in their lives. Then we went to the local Dream City with carnival rides under the stars. The manager made the rides free for us and promised to do the same for other IDPs or refugees I would bring. They had never been on a Ferris wheel nor merry-go-round. Their eyes were wide with wonder, clinging to one another and peering down on the night lights of Duhok. Their spontaneous giggles were genuine.

For three hours, they got to forget their suffering. Afterwards, twelve-year-old Rukan said it had been the happiest day in her life since August 3, 2014. If only more volunteers would take the Yezidis out of their tents for a day of relief and enjoyment. The soul needs emotional nourishment to recover, not just food and shelter.

In 2019, Jaed, his mother, and three sisters were granted asylum in Australia.

Grandmother Betrayed by al-Khatouni Arabs

Ghazal Qassim, October 2017

I was 75 when Daesh murdered three of my sons, Barakat, Mirza, and Murad Mahmoud Khero, along with my adult grandsons on my farm north of Tal Ezeer. They took all the girls and young mothers and left me behind with about sixty or seventy women and children.

Our men's bloody bodies were scattered all over the yard where they were shot while trying to run away. I found my grandson, Farman Barakat Mahmoud, still alive. He was shot in the thigh and the knee. He told me that they had been told to convert to Islam but all had refused.

Farman's wife, Mayan Sino Barakat, was pregnant. We made a stretcher with two poles, rope, and a blanket and carried him to the neighbor's farmhouse 300 meters away. The neighbor cleaned his wounds, and wrapped them to try to stop the bleeding. Then Mayan left with everyone else on foot for the mountain around noon. Only the neighbor woman stayed with me. We knew Farman would bleed to death if we did not get him to the hospital.

My son, Faisal, called me from Germany. I told him what had happened.

Faisal called his Arab friends from the Alwaza family of the al-Khatouni tribe who lived in Baaj. We have been close friends for years. They are like family. It was Arabs from Baaj who had attacked Gir Zerik and Siba Sheikh Khudir to the south of our farm, but Faisal trusted his friends. Faisal asked them to get Farman and take him to the hospital. There was no one else to call for help, because Daesh had control of the area.

They promised Faisal they would take Farman to the hospital and take care of him. After that, they would take Farman to one of their houses to recover. They came to me the same day and said they were sorry for my sons who were dead. I cried. Then they asked where Farman was. I took them inside the house to him, and they took him in their car.

When Farman got to Sinjar hospital, he called me. He told me, "Mom, I will call you. I'm okay now, but if Daesh takes me or anything happens or I die, I won't be able to call you."

After one or two hours, Faisal called Farman. Farman said, "I don't know where I am now. Maybe I will bleed to death. Maybe I will disappear, I don't know. There's fighting." Faisal could hear the noise in the background, then Farman went silent although the phone call was still connected. Faisal waited five minutes before ending the call. After that, Faisal tried to call Farman again for the next month, but no one answered the phone.

Faisal called his Arab friend who told him that Daesh had taken Farman from them. We do not know the truth. Faisal called his friend a few more times and offered him money if they would return Farman, either dead or alive, just so we would know what happened to him. The al-Khatouni tribe said, "If we can get him back, we will return him, but if we can't, then he's gone."

After that, Faisal's ties with them ended. The al-Khatouni tribe joined with Daesh to attack and kill the Yezidis. They speak Kurdish. People say that tribe is really Kurdish who became Arabs during Saddam Hussein's Arabization program for Shingal. That is why they still speak Kurdish. We are very afraid of this al-Khatouni tribe. They joined with Daesh in the attack upon Yezidis. They also stole our 152 sheep worth at least $45,000 dollars.

I live in these two tents in a camp near Duhok with my daughter, daughter-in-law, and seven grandchildren. The first year our tents flooded. This is now our fourth winter in tents. I want the children to go to Germany to live with their Uncle Faisal in a safe place and have a chance for a better future.

As for myself, I will never leave Iraq. This is where I was born and grew up with my father and grandfather, so I love here. This is where my husband is buried. For me, I cannot start over somewhere else. I and my family want to go back to Shingal to live, but we cannot go back. We don't have anything. No money, no houses, no men, nothing. Daesh damaged or exploded the houses.

I cannot return to Shingal, because it is dangerous and there are no services like water and electricity. I cannot risk my grandchildren's lives. I have no choice but to stay in this tent. The only thing we can hope for now is just to be safe. I have witnessed other genocides against the Yezidis, but for me, this is the last Yezidi genocide. We are finished.

Hadiah Barakat, the Lucky Kidnapped Yezidi Sister

Hadiah Barakat Mahmoud Khero, October 2017

I was living with my family in paradise. I have five brothers and seven sisters. Our livelihood was growing wheat and barley and raising sheep and goats. We had a nice house and gardens. I was nineteen and in love with my boyfriend. I loved my family and my life. I was so very happy. It all came to an end on August 3, 2014, at 10:30 AM. I lost everything in that hour . . . my family, my friends, my home, my education, and my future. I had plans for my future, but they were destroyed on that day.

I do not know how many total were captured at our house, because so many strangers from Tal Ezeer came to our farmhouse in the country. They sent all the women to a different room and kept the men in another room. That first hour they took our money, our gold, and our phones. Then they separated the girls like me. They loaded us into their four-door trucks. They had BKC guns and one Doshka on the trucks. They also took my family's two Deer trucks and one Opel Vectra car. They drove us south to Baaj. I think those people were Sunni Arabs from Mosul, because when we went to Mosul we saw them living in Mosul. I did not know any of the men who captured us, but one man was giving us orders in Kurdish.

The man who captured me in Tal Ezeer is a Sunni Arab who grew up in Siba Sheikh Khudir. He speaks Kurdish like the Yezidis. They called him Abu Diab. So you can say my own neighbor joined Daesh and kidnapped me. That is why we can never return to live in Shingal among Sunni Arabs.

On the way to Baaj, we were afraid and crying because we had nowhere to hide. They asked us to convert to Islam on the way. They said they will take us to their families and we all would be Muslims. We did not know they were killing our men, including my father, brother, and uncles. When we got to Baaj there were many other kidnapped Yezidi women, men, and children in different places. They asked us to be Muslims, so we agreed, because we were crying and afraid of what would happen if we refused. They gave us food and water, and then they took us in four big buses to Mosul. There were a lot of women with us.

They gathered many of us in the Galaxy Wedding Hall in Mosul for two weeks. Then they moved us to a school. I stayed there for two weeks. They took me with my sisters, Ayshan and Haifa, and my cousins, Nazdar and Nadia, to Khindi military camp. There, I was separated from my sisters. They gave each of us to a Daesh family. The man who chose me as his slave is named Hussein Ali Hussein.

Hussein took me to his house in Al Abour neighborhood in Mosul. He beat me then raped me for the first three days. I was held prisoner by him in Mosul for two-and-a-half years. I was lucky I was with the same man for all that time.

He never sold me or loaned me to a friend for sex. Why do people say they are lucky when something terrible happens to them?

Yes, I was lucky that I was sexually enslaved by only one man, not like my sister, Ayshan who was sold and raped by eleven different men in Raqqa, Syria. I was lucky. Ayshan was unlucky. The same thing happened to about 5,000 Yezidi women and girls. Everyone of us was tortured and raped. So the old concept of shame from being raped was removed from us, because every single one of us was raped and beaten. Daesh wanted to destroy the Yezidi community.

I was lucky I was beaten only once for refusing to have sex. I was a nineteen-year-old virgin. Of course I fought him. After that terrible beating, I submitted. He broke my spirit. I had no way to avoid the rapes. Being raped was less painful than being both raped *and* beaten. I could have one or both, but I could not escape being raped. I was lucky he only raped me. He did not beat me again or tie me up or gag me.

When I was in pain from his continual raping, I was lucky he took me to the hospital three times to be treated. He got me medical treatment so he could keep using me as his sex slave.

I was lucky I never got pregnant. He always withdrew before climaxing inside of me. His wife was pregnant when Daesh captured me in my family's home. So he was lucky he had me for sex. His wife was lucky he left her alone with their two little kids under age three. I ask you, what kind of a woman allows her husband to keep another human being as a prisoner in their house?

I was locked in their house and raped for two-and-a-half years by Hussein Ali Hussein. Never once was I able to put my hand on a phone to call for help to escape. During my entire captivity they never took their eyes off of me. I was locked inside the house whenever they went out. So that is the kind of luck I am talking about. Tell me, do you think I was lucky?

After a month we moved to Al Somar neighborhood. Many Daesh families came to visit us in his home. Men came with their families from different countries to join Daesh. Some were originally from Mosul, but others were from Turkey, Russia, Algeria, Syria, and Saudi Arabia. They spoke Turkish, Kurdish, and Arabic. I heard dialects from Syria, Algeria, and Mosul. The families were coming through Turkey to join Daesh. That means Turkey was supporting Daesh.

Life was very hard in Mosul. Daesh was not letting people have satellite dishes to hear the news. They were fined if Daesh caught them with a dish. Daesh houses, however, could have satellite dishes, so we had TV. They always turned to a religious channel teaching the Quran when I was in the room. After I left the room, they would change the TV channel to news.

Hussein's family considered me as one of their family, but I was not free like them. I could not leave the house unless one of them was with me. When they left the house they locked the doors on me so I could not get out. When I went out with them, I had to cover myself in black clothes from head to toe, including my hands and feet.

They kept me cut off from the world. For me it is missing time. I did not know about the execution lines in which they killed the Yezidi men. It was a long time before Hussein told me that they had killed my father, two uncles, and my brother Farhan at our farm on the day I was captured. It was crushing news, but before I was separated from my older sister, Ayshan, she told me not to attempt suicide. I was always remembering her advice. I never lost hope. I had faith in God and Tawus Melak that I would be free one day.

When we first arrived in Mosul, the phone signal was good for three months. Then the signal was cut because there was no phone company to maintain the cell phone towers. It was not until the start of the liberation of Mosul in October 2016 that the Iraqi Army brought a phone signal to the area, but my captors never once let me use a phone.

In August 2016, Hussein was killed while fighting against the Iraqi Army in Mosul. When the Iraqi Army, ninth division was fighting to liberate Mosul, I went with his wife and three children who surrendered on January 3, 2017.

Two days later I got to my mother's tent here in a camp in Kurdistan. Twenty-three out of twenty-nine who were kidnapped from my family are now free. Money was paid to free most of them. We still hope for the safe return of five others. They include my sister, Haifa, and my cousins Nazdar and Nadia. Zeri is dead. Also missing are my three relatives, Suad Dawood Chetto, Tawaf Dawood Chetto, and Asia Kamal Chetto Khoro. My oldest brother, Farman Barakat Mahmud is missing. He was shot in the leg on the day of the attack.

Even though I am free now, I am in pain because my sister and cousins are still in the hands of Daesh. I cannot ever forget what happened in the past. I really *do* want to forget it. I wish I could have my memory erased just like a computer hard drive. I want to get out of this country and get to my one surviving uncle, Faisal Mahmoud Khero, in Germany where I can feel comfortable and safe. Now we are suffering from bad conditions living in the tents. We lost everything. People, money, cars, houses, everything. In spite of that, I have not lost hope.

We really appreciate everyone who helped us, Amy L. Beam, and Stan from Prescott, Arizona, who has donated thousands of dollars for Yezidi survivors. Stan donated a thousand dollars to my family to get our documents, IDs and passports. We really are grateful to Stan for his humanity.

Ayshan Barakat, the Unlucky Kidnapped Sister

Ayshan Barakat Mahmoud, August 2017

My father, Barakat Mahmoud Khero, was the muhktar (manager) of our tribe. I was his assistant. I was twenty-one. My home and my family were everything in my life. I did not expect the attack and that those who attacked us would separate us, because everyone was a friend with our family and welcomed in our home.

Daesh transferred me and my sisters from Baaj to Mosul. I stayed one month at the Galaxy Wedding Hall and then a school before they separated me from my sisters, Hadiah and Haifa, and other women. They gave each one of us to a Daesh fighter for free. I was taken by eleven different men in twenty-seven months. All of them sexually assaulted me and treated me brutally.

The first one was Muhandas. His real name is Rasul Abdullah Ali. His wife's name is Amina Hassan Ali. They were Muslims from Mosul. Abdullah and Annis were Rasul's sons. Both joined Daesh.

Muhandas tied me up, gagged me and blindfolded me because I refused to have sex with him. They beat me because I did not give in to them. After beating me, they were raping me. I went one time to the hospital, because my condition from being beaten was very bad.

I asked Muhandas' wife to keep him away from me, but she refused and said having sex with me is halal in their religion. She took me to the doctor once for a pregnancy test. Even though I converted to Islam, they were both treating me brutally. Even his wife hit me and tortured me. Twice I tried to escape, but got caught and returned and was brutally beaten with sticks, so I gave up trying to run away, because I knew it was impossible. Instead, I tried to commit suicide. One day I was baking and I tried to kill myself with electricity but the electric oven was broken.

The only way to escape was to have a phone. Abu Muhandes gave me a phone to call my family, but he did not leave me alone, so I could not make a plan. I was treated like a slave. They did not let me know about anything. I did not even know that Shingal had been liberated. Sometimes I was living in the man's house and sometimes in their headquarters. In Mosul they were happy with Daesh and their living situation. I was not locked in the houses, but I was not allowed to leave the house by myself. When I was in their headquarters, I was locked inside. When I went out, I was forced to wear black clothes with a veil covering my eyes. At home, sometimes I was forced to wear sexy clothes and makeup for them.

In Mosul in the beginning we had TV. Then they prohibited having TVs, but we had a secret TV and satellite dish. Rasul's own daughters would watch TV secretly. When their brother saw his sisters were watching TV, he took the

satellite dish from the roof and dropped it down to the street and crashed it.   He
said, "It is haram. You cannot watch TV."

There were men who had joined Daesh from Algeria, Yemen, Tunisia,
America, Saudi Arabia, Syria, Iraq, Turkey, Egypt, Africa, and Chechnya. I met
an American man who was speaking English and Arabic. His fake name was
Abu Osama. Another man was German. My friend was forcibly married to him.
His fake name was Abu Yahya.

I saw two advisers to the leader of the Islamic State, Abu Bakr Al Baghdadi.
One was named Abu Mattess Al Baghdadi and he had taken my sister, Haifa
Barakat Mahmoud. I met him and my sister in Mosul. Abu Mansour was the
other assistant. Both were trafficking Yezidi women in Mosul.

I stayed more than one year with Abu Rasul. Then, because of his financial
crimes against the Islamic State, Daesh imprisoned Rasul and confiscated all his
money and property. They also imprisoned me for two months because I was his
property. I think the Daesh Shariah court may have sentenced him to death.

From prison Rasul sold me to Abu Abaida who moved me to Raqqa, Syria,
where he was selling Yezidi women to be used for sex for a few days or weeks
and then returned. My life was one of indescribable suffering, because they were
treating us as slaves, raping, and torturing us. There was no TV in Syria, so I did
not know what was happening in the outside world, but they terrorized me by
showing me the videos of Daesh executing people.

Many times I was lined up and put on display for men to choose me. They
also took photos and videos of me when we were lined up.   One time a man took
me to a room, raped me and directly returned me.   One time two men raped me
together in the same room. Like all of the kidnapped Yezidi girls, I was held
down and forced to do what they wanted. I did not get pregnant because I was
stealing birth control pills from Daesh. In Syria I was moved to Mayadin, Raqqa,
Der Azier, Tapqa, and Aleppo (Halep).

Abu Abaida sold me three times to Abu Khatab Al Iraqi for 15 days and
again for one month when he tortured me and beat me with a stick. The third
time Abu Khatab bought me, he then sold me to Abu Michhal for one week. Abu
Michhal sold me to Abu Ruwaha. After ten days, Abu Ruwaha sold me to Abu
Jihad. After two months, Abu Jihad sold me to Abu Khalid. After three days,
Abu Khalid sold me to Abu Mazan. After four days, Abu Mazan sold me to Abu
Salih. After ten days, Abu Salih sold me to Abu Ahmed. I stayed there one
month before escaping.

Abu Ahmed let me call my younger brother, Sultan, on the internet using a
Daesh phone. Two smugglers from Iraq had communication with Arab friends in
Syria. They bought my freedom. I returned from Daesh October 21, 2016. I
arrived to Kurdistan October 23, after spending two nights with PKK.

My family paid $15,000 dollars for my freedom. Nechervan Barzani's Yezidi Affairs Office in Duhok paid us back $10,000 and we borrowed $5,000 from friends. We still owe them the money. I really want to get the money to reimburse the people who loaned us $5,000 for my freedom.

Also, I want a good future for my family, my siblings, my mother and my grandmother. Thirteen of us are living in a tent in a camp in Kurdistan. I have severe psychological problems because of the sexual abuse and murders of the men in my family. I want to leave Iraq and be reunited with my one surviving uncle in Germany, Faisal Muhmoud Khero.   Five female relatives are still in the hands of Daesh. My brother Farman, who was wounded, is missing.

I was back in Kurdistan for ten months before I could get my Iraqi nationality card, called a jensia, so that I could get my passport. The government office would not give the jensia card to my mother because she has no living husband or male relatives to verify who she is. Daesh killed them all. Even though she went before a judge who gave her a document making her the legal head of our family and stating her husband was killed, the jensia office refused to accept this. So we were trapped in Iraq without IDs.

After Amy Beam escalated the jensia problem to Mosul Governor Nofal, in September 2017, my family and I got our jensias. In November, we got passports for twelve people in my family, more than three years after my family was attacked and thirteen months after I was freed.

Haifa, the Last Sister To Return
Haifa Barakat Mahmoud Khero, October 2017

I am Haifa Barakat Muhmoud Khero from Tal Ezeer. I was born in 1997. I was seventeen when Daesh took me and twenty when I escaped in August 2017. My family owned two houses; one in the center of Tal Ezeer and one on the farm. I knew we did not have a lot of money, but we were very happy. I attended school and when summer came, we would go live on the farm.

We were outside of the farmhouse on August 3, 2014, when we heard gunfire. All of our family and relatives crowded inside. My body was frozen with fear. Men came into my house with guns and took me and my sisters. I counted 34 girls that they took. Six were in my family. Twenty-eight were my relatives. There were also three children plus the baby.

They took us to Baaj for ten days. I felt shocked. It was like the end of the world for me. Then they took us to Mosul and put us in Galaxy Wedding Hall. We stayed ten or fifteen days there with our families. Then Daesh came and separated us into groups of 20 girls and took everyone to another place in Qaser Al Mehrab, a village outside of Tal Afar city. Then men came and each one selected one of us and took us away.

It was very hard for me when I was separated from my sisters. We were clinging to each other hoping to stay together. I thought maybe I would die and not see them again. I went with a Daesh man who sexually assaulted me and hurt me every day. He would wake up in the morning, go to work, and come back in the evening. In that house were another two girls and another two men. The same thing happened to them. When all three men were gone, they locked the house and put a guard there.

After fifteen days, the first man sold me to a forty-year-old man. In the beginning we were very cheap for selling, like eighteen dollars, but after many months the price was $10,000 dollars. That old man only came to me to have sex. He did not speak to me or anything. If I refused, he hurt me. He did not sleep in that house.

Then the old man sent me as a gift to another man, without selling me. He put me in a car and sent me to a Kurdish man living in Syria in a village called Shadadi. I never saw any other Yezidi women or children there. That man told me his name was Diyar. He had joined Daesh. He and his wife were Kurdish from Sulaymaniyah. They have two children named Aman and Anis aged three and six. The family spoke Kurdish. I lived one-and-a-half years with Diyar's family.

Sometimes Diyar was good to me, and sometimes he would hurt me. He was using me for sex. His wife was very bad with me and to her husband, too. So

Diyar gave me to another person who called himself Abu Ali, and Abu Ali gave another girl to Diyar in exchange for me.

Abu Ali was not his real name. He was a Turkman from Tal Afar who spoke only Arabic. He was living and working between Tal Afar and Mosul. His wife and children lived in Mosul. He kept all his documents in his house in Mosul, so I could never discover his real name.

Abu Ali kept me as his secret prisoner for one-and-a-half years in Hawija. He was thirty-two. He worked during the day as a security guard. In the evening he went to his second job as a doctor's assistant in the Hawija hospital. He kept me locked up across the street in a house that had belonged to a Shia family. When Daesh took control of Hawija, the Shias ran from Hawija to Duhok and Iran. Daesh took every Shia house for themselves. Even though I was in a very nice house, for me it was still prison.

After six months, we moved to another house which was also near the hospital so he could get the internet signal from the hospital, because there was no mobile phone signal in Hawija. Living in Hawija was very bad for me. Sometimes when Abu Ali came home, he was angry and he beat me. Sometimes he beat me for no reason. I don't know why.

In Hawija I was always alone for one-and-a-half years. There was no TV, no radio, no phone, nothing. Sometimes I washed dishes or did housework to pass the hours. I was always thinking about my family, nothing else. I missed them so much, it hurt. All the time I was alone, I was thinking how awful and impossible my situation was.

Even though I cried every day and night, from the first day that Daesh took me until I was free, every day I had hope. Every day I told myself I must come back. I *will* come back. Before I was separated from my sisters, my older sister, Ayshan, made me promise never to give up hope or attempt suicide, so her words gave me strength. I lost track of time. Three winters passed.

One day, two Yezidi girls came to the house and spoke with me and then they left. They were also being held in Hawija in the Zap area. Halla Mahlo was with Abu Haithem. She was twenty years old from Hardan. Baska Saeed, aged eighteen, was from Sunoni. As far as I know, they are still in Hawija.

After Abu Ali's evening job in the hospital across the street, he would come to use me for sex. He brought me birth control pills so I never got pregnant. After he did what he wanted to me, then he would use the internet signal from the hospital. Then he would leave. He never stayed long. Even though I had not one living soul to talk to, I never considered becoming friends with him. I did not want to utter one word to him. I disliked him so intensely for what he was doing to me. Solitary confinement, in addition to the rape, is a very cruel form of torture.

Added to my mental and physical suffering was the not knowing about my family. For three years I never knew what happened to them, if they were dead or alive. I wondered if my sisters were still being held prisoner. I begged Abu Ali to let me use the internet on his phone to call my family and find out about my sisters. He refused.

I never knew about the war or that Daesh was controlling Hawija, the city where I was being held. I did not know anything that was happening in Iraq or the world. I was truly in prison with all the doors locked.

In August 2017, Hawija was liberated. I could hear the Coalition planes overhead for five or six days. One morning I heard many people outside the house. I had not seen Abu Ali for three days. Normally, he came every night. On this morning, the doors in that house were unlocked. I do not know who unlocked them.

I went outside and saw many families without any men. There was no Daesh left in the city. I walked with those families from morning until evening until we saw the Peshmerga. I knew they were Peshmerga, because they were speaking Kurdish and they were wearing Peshmerga uniforms with Kurdistan flags on them.

I am grieving to discover my father, brothers, and uncles were killed, but I am so happy to see my mother, grandmother, sisters, and younger brothers. I feel I am a newborn person. I feel my life has been given back to me. We are living in this tent with my grandmother. In this country, I have no future. I want many things, but the important thing is I want my family to be together, happy, and safe. We need your help, Amy, to get our passports and help us get German visas. We want to join my Uncle Faisal in Altenburg or my cousin, Sameera and her little brothers, in Oldenberg. All our men are gone. Our families are separated. We do not know what to do and there is no help for us.

PKK and the Doshka Mythology: Who Saved Yezidis on the Mountain?

On top of Shingal Mountain, just before the paved road from Sinjar reaches the summit, there is a Peshmerga flat-bed truck with a Doshka mounted on it. It looks like a long, double-barreled missile-launcher. A ten-foot-photo of Kurdistan President Masoud Barzani gazes down at it. It is preserved as a memorial in the same position it was on the day of the attack.

The first time I heard about this Doshka was in June 2015. I spent a day with a YPJ commander in their headquarters on the north side of the mountain, just above the village of Karsi. About twenty young female volunteers were across the hall in a room, listening to their teacher explain passages from Abdullah Ocalan's writings. Ocalan, known as "Apo" is the imprisoned leader of the PKK which has been struggling for Kurdish rights against the Turkish government since 1988.

The YPG is the military arm of the PYD Kurdish political party in Rojava, fighting for Kurdish rights from Syria's regime. The YPJ is the women's military wing. The YPG and YPJ were the first to respond to the attack on Shingal August 3, 2014, after Peshmerga retreated. It was the YPG/YPJ who opened a corridor for the Yezidis to escape off the mountain after nine days of being under siege in 45C heat without food or water. The YPG/YPJ gave water, medical attention, and transportation to those too weak to walk to the safety of the Syrian border.

A half-dozen Yezidi women were among the volunteers I met in 2015. Some of them joined without parental permission or even a goodbye note; others had their parents' blessing. Some had been orphaned by Daesh. They had a fire burning in their hearts to defeat Daesh and free more than 3000 of their sisters who were being raped daily. The Yezidi culture is not a stellar model for women's equality. Women stay home, cook, clean, and have babies. They work from morning until night inside their own home. For these young Yezidi women to take up arms in defense of Shingal was a jolt to the status quo. Overnight, the YPJ became international heroines.

I sat cross-legged on a mat with the YPJ commander who had served twenty-three years in the PKK, based in Qandil Mountain. She was confident and knew her history. This is her story of how Daesh was prevented from taking control of the mountain and killing all the Yezidis:

On May 13, 2014, there was a meeting held in Jordan. It was attended by mostly Sunnis from Syria, Turkey, Jordan, Iraq, and Saudi Arabia. One representative from the PDK Kurdistan government was allegedly in attendance. The meeting was reported in the news, but the discussions and results were not reported. The decision was made to divide Iraq into three sections: Kurdish,

Sunni, and Shia. Sunni leaders in the meeting said they had to support the Sunni tribes in Mosul and Ramadi.

They also wanted to remove the border between Iraq and Syria. In Arabic, the acronym Daesh (pronounced Da-ish) stands for Islamic State of Iraq and al-Sham (Syria, Jordan, and Lebanon).

Less than four weeks later, on June 9, 2014, Mosul was taken with a mere 200 Daesh fighters. There was no battle. The Iraqi army did nothing to defend it. Fifty thousand military and security forces from Mosul to the Syrian border took off their uniforms and went home without a fight.

The YPJ commander continued her account. Two months before Shingal was attacked, Abdullah Ocalan allegedly sent a message from his prison cell on Imrali Island, Turkey, to the PKK leadership in Qandil mountains. This was during the brief period of peace talks in Turkey when the Kurdish elected officials were allowed shuttle diplomacy between Ocalan and PKK leadership in the Qandil mountains.

The message was a command: "Go immediately to defend Shingal." After that, Turkey broke the peace process and Ocalan was denied visitors for two years.

On previous occasions, when PKK left the Qandil mountains and entered into Iraq in civilian clothes, they would get their fake ID cards made within three days. After Ocalan's warning, they could not get their IDs and were prevented from coming to defend Shingal. There were, however, thirteen undercover PKK militants already inside of Kurdistan. On August 3, when they headed to Shingal, seven of them were arrested by KRG Peshmerga and not heard from again. The other six made it to the top of Shingal mountain on August 3.

As the Peshmerga were fleeing that morning in their four-wheel drives with their guns and Doshka's, the PKK ordered the Peshmerga, at gun point, to leave behind one truck with a Doshka. That is the famous Doshka that sits as a memorial under Barzani's gaze.

By approximately 9:30 AM, the road leading out of Sinjar and snaking up the mountain was blocked to civilians by the Peshmerga who were using both lanes to retreat. By 10:30 or 11 AM the road was empty of vehicles and Daesh had taken control at the bottom of the mountain.

The six PKK kept up a series of phone calls, hoping to fool Daesh into thinking there was a large contingent of PKK fighters on the mountain. This belief was borne out by some Yezidis I interviewed who had escaped to the mountain. They had all heard talk that PKK was all over defending the mountain, but none of my witnesses had seen them on August 3.

That night, the PKK prepared for a fight until death as a Daesh vehicle drove up the mountain road from Sinjar. They would only have one chance to fire. Either Daesh would die, or they would die. They watched the headlights approaching in the dark, waiting until the first Daesh vehicle was right upon them before firing the Doshka and killing Daesh.

Daesh retreated to the base of the mountain. Daesh tried two more attempts the next day to gain control of the mountain road, but were repelled by PKK and gave up the effort.

After August 3, when the Yezidis were stranded on the mountain, YPG and YPJ came from the Syrian border at the west end of the mountain and opened a corridor for escape. They say they did this before the coalition airstrikes. The coalition claims success at opening the corridor with air strikes. On August 12, Yezidis began walking off the mountain to Syria.

In June 2016, I stopped to photograph the Doshka monument just below the electricity tower on top of the mountain overlooking Sinjar. Hassan Derbo, the non-military manager, invited me inside for tea and lunch. I was on my way to meet with his brother, Peshmerga Commander Qassim Derbo, at the headquarters in Sinjar. Hassan shared a great deal of helpful information with me about the dire situation of the displaced Yezidis living in tents. As I got up to leave, I asked as an after-thought, "Oh, by the way, what's the story about that gun on the truck outside?" This was the reason I had stopped for tea. I turned around and sat down again.

This is Hassan Derbo's story about repelling Daesh with the Peshmerga Doshka.

Hassan Derbo lived in Sinjar with his family. He was at home at 8:30 AM on August 3. He said he and his brothers seized the Doshka at 10 AM and used it to fire upon Daesh coming up the road. I wondered how he could have fired at Daesh if Yezidis were still in their cars fleeing. Wouldn't he have hit the Yezidis' cars?

By 10 AM, he explained, the road had just been closed by Daesh at the bottom of the hill. This corresponds with other witness testimonies. I asked how he got to the top of the mountain if the road was closed. He explained he had grown up in Sinjar and knew the trails on the mountain. He and his family walked. At 8:30 they set out from home up a path on the mountain. They reached the site of the Doshka at 11 AM. His two brothers, Qassim and Hussein, had already reached the Doshka at 10 AM.

According to Hassan, they found it abandoned with the keys in the ignition and the engine still running! I asked if the wreckage of the Daesh vehicles was still on the mountain after being hit by the Doshka. Hassan explained that they did not actually fire the Doshka. They used their own guns to shoot at the Daesh cars coming up the road. The bullets just pinged off their cars, and the cars turned around and went back down the hill to Sinjar.

Hassan showed me the copper plaque they had engraved to preserve the event for future generations. It is in English, not the local languages of Arabic or Kurdish, for consumption by foreign journalists

In the name of God and Tawus Melak

> *The heroes of Sinjar Mountain {Qassim Drbo Jelki and his brothers Hassan and Husain} with a blessed twin 23mm cannon stopped the enemy and defeated them on the 3rd of August 2014. They did not let ISIS reach the thousands of Yezidi people who fled from Sinjar up the Mountain. Their heroic actions and the actions of others who followed their example saved thousands from being captured or killed.*
>
> *-This is a memorial for these Heroes,*
> *completed on the 1st of October 2015.*

A certificate for a "Star of Valor" is signed by the *Free Burma Rangers*. The signature is illegible and mysteriously there is no name on the certificate, although the director and founder is David Eubank. The certificate was dressed up with a gold star dangling on a black ribbon.

I had the chance to meet the *Free Burma Rangers* (FBR), a pleasant expat American missionary family that moved to Burma thirty years before. They were in Sinjar on a mission to distribute aid packages and teach English using comic book Bible stories. They also had a volunteer dentist with them. They were teaching first aid, but they only had two weeks in the country. They gave me an aid package which contained t-shirts and caps with their logo "Free Burma Rangers". In 2017, they renamed themselves "Free Kurd Rangers." I met them in a house where I had the opportunity to overhear one woman reading the Bible story of the virgin Mary to a nineteen-year-old Yezidi man.

Like so many other NGOs that flocked to Kurdistan to "save lives" of the non-Muslim Yezidis, they were trying to convert Yezidis to Jesus, as if Yezidis had not had quite enough of being pressured to convert by Daesh. The Yezidis have their own religion which is different from Islam or Christianity or Judaism, in spite of that boiler-plate phrase copied by mainstream journalists who say the Yezidi religion is similar to Islam, Christianity, and Judaism.

The Kurdistan government was so sensitive to allowing religious freedom that they tolerated this foreign missionary movement thinly disguised as teaching English. The most genuine assistance to the IDPs came from the local Kurdish and Yezidi organizations. As for large international charities, there was an amazing absence, mostly because of bureaucratic government obstacles.

The real truth about the Doshka is that it broke down the morning of August 3, 2014, nearly at the top of the mountain near the electric power station. The

Peshmerga soldiers driving it wanted to push it over the cliff to prevent Daesh from capturing and using it. But two PKK named Hadar (female) and Rohat (male), joined with a Yezidi mechanic named Ibrahim Murad Howin, convinced them to leave it, so they could repair it. Ibrahim fixed both the broken down truck and the malfunctioning Doshka. They used it to fire that night upon Daesh to prevent them from gaining control of the mountain top. They were joined by Peshmerga commander Qassim Derbo, Khudir Tala, Marwan Ali, and Daoud Salam. They had among them 8 AK47s, 1 BKC, 1 GC automatic rifle, and one pistol.

Three Daesh fighters from Sunoni in a Toyota 4x4 drove up the mountain road from Sinjar city and were shot and killed before noon. A Daesh convoy of ten trucks came behind them. They got almost to the old police station just below the Doshka before being repelled. After that, Daesh abandoned the mountain road.

The PKK left the Doshka with Qassim Derbo who used it for the next fifteen months to fire upon the Daesh oil trucks passing through Sinjar city en route to Syria. There were originally a Doshka 23 and a Doshka 12.5 on the Peshmerga truck. A flag of the imprisoned PKK leader, APO was flown on the truck. The Doshka 12.5 was moved to Karsi to defend the 30,000 Yezidis who had run there.

Peshmerga General Qassim Derbo later replaced the truck with a concrete replica painted to look real. The APO flag was replaced with the PDK party flag and a Kurdistan flag. Later, the PDK flag was removed. Kurdistan President Masoud Barzani had vowed that the only flag that would fly in Shingal would be the Kurdistan flag. He wanted PKK to leave Shingal.

After the Peshmerga were forced out of Shingal by the Iraqi Army on October 17, 2017, The Kurdistan flags and poster of Barzani were removed. An Iraqi flag was painted on the side of the concrete model of the military truck with the imitation Doshka 23, creating yet another myth about this Doshka and who saved the Yezidis on the mountain. Only the Iraqi flags were flown at the guard post. Shingal continued to be a disputed territory.

Ibrahim Murad Howin, who had repaired the Doshka, and his teenage daughter, Yusra, stayed on the mountain to fight Daesh for six years. They both joined YBS when it was formed by Yezidis in 2014 to defend Shingal. Yusra became a sniper and trainer. She participated in the fierce battle to drive Daesh out of Sinjar in November 2015. She climbed the wheat silo and removed the black Daesh flag. Ibrahim, with the help of his entire family, delivered spring water daily from 2014 until 2020 to the 2300 displaced Yezidi families living in tents on the mountain.

Khanasor Mass Grave and Sherfadeen Funeral Show

Khanasor was a city of 75,000 on the north side of the mountain at the western end, only three kilometers from the Syrian border. Daesh was attacking the villages and Sinjar city on the south side of the mountain. During the night residents Qassim Hussein Edo and his wife, Nadifa Ibrahim Hassan, heard loud guns from the Syrian border to the northwest. Peshmerga left at 6AM. They fled to Karsi on the mountain at 11:30 AM.

Some Yezidi residents chose to stay behind in Khanasor. They did not believe Daesh would come to kill them. Many owned land, nice homes, cars, and businesses, so they took their chances and remained to protect their property in Khanasor.

Assaf Khalaf Tallo went to Karsi leaving his wife and children behind with her father, Haji Hamo Tallo, the muhktar of the Al Assaf family. Daesh put checkpoints on the road in and out of Khanasor, but did not enter Khanasor until August 6. At 10 PM, Haji Hamo Tallo made it to Karsi to share the tragic news that forty-six of his family had been captured by Daesh in Khanasor, including his daughter who was Assaf's wife. Three years later, only three people had been freed: Assaf's daughter, son, and daughter-in-law. PKK returned the daughter from Syria without money. Another list of seventy-four missing was also circulated.

On August 7, 2014, Daesh executed most of those captured from Khanasor. On February 4, 2015, six months after the initial attack on Shingal, Peshmerga opened a mass grave between Khanasor and Sunoni. It contained twenty-seven bodies from five families. All were identified by family members by their clothing, keys, medicine, or IDs. Kamal Haji Sado from Khanasor identified his father from his ID and his uncle next to him from his clothes. Another man identified his uncle from the keys that fit his safe.

Two other graves were discovered between Khanasor and Sunoni containing another thirty-eight bodies which remained unidentified. On August 15, 2015, these sixty-five Yezidi bodies were transferred to Sherfadeen shrine in Shingal for a mass funeral on the one-year anniversary of the attack on Kocho. The ceremony was attended by KRG Prime Minister Nechervan Barzani, hundreds of Peshmerga, a band, and TV crews. They made a big event out of it with dignitaries sitting next to the grieving widows. After they showed the funeral ceremony on TV, no other grave sites were examined.

An American team and also a French team visited the Hardan grave site in 2015 and advised Peshmerga not to touch the bones and to protect the sites with fences, which they did. The foreign teams promised to return to properly remove the bodies for forensic examination, but after more than two years, no team returned. The bones are disappearing.

The Erbil and Baghdad governments ignored families' requests to identify the bones in mass graves. Although the Duhok Ministry of Health collected hair and blood samples from all bereaved family members, Iraq does not possess equipment nor capability to conduct DNA testing of bones.

The bereaved family members, especially the widows, cannot bring closure or move forward with their lives until the bones are identified. Until then, they say their husband is missing. It is a wound that cannot heal in the heart of every Yezidi. According to Nuri Gurmiz, whose uncle was buried at Sherfadeen, "All is a lost cause. It is pointless and we know it."

On March 16, 2019, the United Nations Investigation Team for Accountability for Daesh Crimes (UNITAD) began exhuming bodies from the mass graves in Kocho. Remains were sent to Baghdad for forensic testing. The UN plan is to exhume all the mass graves which could take years.

Kurds Saved Us, Arabs Betrayed Us

Barakat Ali, September 2, 2016

I am from Khanasor on the north side of Shingal. When Daesh invaded Shingal on August 3, 2014, first they attacked the south side of Shingal mountain which is a Yezidi area also. Yezidis defended themselves with their small weapons. When they finished their ammunition, Daesh came with very heavy weapons. We realized we could not stand up against them, because we were civilians. We did not have enough weapons and ammunition to support ourselves against the very big terrorist groups.

There were two choices for people to run away. We could run to the mountain or drive to Kurdistan. Many people, especially without cars, walked to Karsi in the mountain. In the mountain they were with no life support services: no water, no food, nothing. It was a very hot day. The temperature in Iraq in August is about 44 to 50 C. It is too hard for people to live in this heat. It was Shingal Mountain that stopped Daesh from killing the last of the Yezidis. Enough of us died anyway on that mountain. More than 300 children and many elderly died from thirst in those nine days that we were besieged.

My family decided to come directly to Kurdistan, but it was a very difficult decision. There were many obstacles in front of us. The biggest one was Rabia which is an area with Arab people living there. Many of them were already involved with Daesh. We knew they were going to kill us if they could.

Fortunately, when we came there and passed many of the Arab villages, they did not have the confidence to attack us, because we were many people coming together and we had some small rifles with us. We got shot from their side three times, but fortunately, they did not injure one of us.

Normally, it takes a maximum of three hours from Khanasor to Duhok, not just to the bridge. When we came that day from Khanasor to the bridge it took twelve hours. The road was full with all the cars going in one direction.

We spent one night in a gas station in Zakho. We thought it would take one or two or maybe even three days to get back to Shingal. I want to thank everybody in Duhok and Zakho and all around Kurdistan. People really helped Yezidis at that time. They opened their houses for Yezidis. They gave us a lot of respect and they were feeling very sorry and sad for us. They gave us food and water. They provided anything we needed in that day.

In the morning we decided to go to our Muslim Kurdish friend in Duhok. He had no room in his house, because his house was not so big, and he had a very big family. He said, "I'm not going to let you guys leave us. You are going to stay with me."

So he gave us his ice cream factory to live in. He opened two rooms for us to live in. We were forty-five people living in those two rooms with ice cream coolers. He provided food and water on that first day for us. We were so tired. We did not take anything from home like food or water or anything. Just the clothes we were wearing.

I did not even have time to take my IDs and documents from home. I am threatened, because Daesh saw my photos with Americans in my home. I was wearing an American uniform in my photos. They took my photos and IDs, so they can identify me. They know I was working with Americans as an interpreter.

When we came here to Duhok, we lived in that factory. I want to thank him for his hospitality. But we knew he could not run his business in that factory since forty-five people were living in two rooms. So we decided to get out of his factory. He begged us "Please don't leave here." He said, "Just go out and look for a good location for yourself before you leave."

My brother and I went one day and looked at a Yezidi village with many friends in that village. The friends said we were welcome to come, but it was hard, also, in that village, because it is only twenty kilometers from Mosul under Daesh control. We were almost at the front line with Daesh, but we had no other choice, so we went there. We stayed in an unfinished house. NGO charities who came to see our situation made doors and windows in the house, so it was good enough to live there.

I applied for Special Immigrant Visa (SIV), the program especially for interpreters who served the American army in the past years. I was an interpreter from 2006 to 2010. I picked Nebraska, because many Yezidis are already there.

I had that opportunity to apply to immigrate to America before Daesh came to invade our land. I liked staying in my homeland. I did not want to leave my homeland and go anywhere else. Even if they gave me a paradise, I am not going to leave my homeland before Daesh came. After August 3, 2014, when Daesh took control of our area, I was disappointed. I feel a sorrow so deep that it cannot be cured. It is very hard to get back to Shingal again, because Arab villages surround us.

Those Arabs were our friends before Daesh came. We had very strong relationships with them and friendships. We were inviting each other to our wedding parties and dancing together and eating together like very serious friends. After Daesh attacked Shingal, the dancing stopped. I am a well-known singer and tambour player in Shingal, but after that, there were no more wedding parties. I did not want to show up on TV, because I felt that would be a shame on me to show up on TV singing as a happy man.

All Yezidis had Arab friends before August 3, 2014, before the genocide happened. But after that, we just cut those relationships. Since the attack, not one of my Arab friends has called me to ask how I am.

After Daesh came, our Arab neighbors became involved with Daesh. They themselves became Daesh. I am not going to say all of them, but many of them. Maybe 75% of Arabs around us are involved. They became like Daesh. They attacked us like Daesh. After that, trust was broken.

So I do not know who we can trust to live with in Shingal. It is very hard for us to make that decision. That is why maybe 50% or more of Yezidi people wish to get out of Iraq. We have no support. We have no idea what to do . . . there is no way for Yezidis to stay in Shingal and be safe.

There is only one thing that will convince Yezidis to return to Shingal, and that is to have international protection. Except for that, nothing will be acceptable to make Yezidis live comfortably in Shingal.

We have no trust with any Iraqi government to protect us after August 3. What we need from the powerful countries like the United States and the United Nations is for those countries to take care of Shingal and get some air bases in Shingal to prove to Yezidi people that some people are taking care of Yezidis and taking care of our safety.

I am pretty sure at that time when we get that, many Yezidis living outside of the country will miss their homeland. They will come back; they will miss their wedding parties, their dancing, they will miss their culture. They will come back to Shingal again.

Hardan Massacre Was Witnessed from Gurmiz
Shamdeen Qassim, July 10, 2015

I am Shamdeen Qassim from Gurmiz village. I and a lot of my family witnessed when Daesh killed 75 to 100 men and boys from Hardan village on August 3 and 4, 2014. There were about 150 Yezidis living in Gurmiz, all my family. We all have the same grandfather.

Gurmiz is on the northeast side of Shingal mountain in the Sunoni sub-district. To get to Gurmiz, the road is already ascending to the mountain which is in our back yard. We overlook Hardan village seven kilometers to the north. The main paved road that goes around the base of the mountain is between Gurmiz and Hardan. At the intersection on the main road, the cross road goes north about six kilometers to Hardan on the flat plain. Gurmiz is 700 meters south of that intersection.

Because Gurmiz is elevated, we can see the intersection clearly and beyond that we can see Hardan with a population of 1900. Hardan people tried to escape from Daesh by running to the mountain, but at the Hardan intersection of the main road some Arab Sunni from the Meteoti, Jihish, Shammer, and Khatouni tribes stopped the Yezidis from Hardan until some forces came from Tal Afar city, called Talafari. The people who came from Tal Afar were Daesh. They were all Sunni Arabs.

They made two groups of Yezidis. They loaded all the females and small children in the trucks and tractors and took them to Tal Afar city. They were all crying. The men and boys were in the other group. They were tied with their hands behind their backs for more than four or five hours. We could see them very well. It was at that intersection that the killing took place. Only a small number escaped being killed or captured. There are still 510 people missing from Hardan.

I was in my village of Gurmiz. No one from my village got killed or captured, because on the first day we protected ourselves. We watched with binoculars from an observation point in front of our village, but we could also see with our own eyes. It is 700 meters from our village to the Hardan intersection. We were 100 meters in front of our village and about 600 meters to the intersection where the massacre occurred. Because we were in a high position, it was very easy to see. We had a clear view.

They shot them at two different times on August 3. The first time they shot people was in the afternoon at 4 pm. Between seventy and eighty men and boys were killed over there. I am a witness. I saw it with my eyes. We could see their guns. There were about sixteen trucks full of Daesh men. They came from all sides and shot them there at the intersection. It lasted about five or ten minutes.

There were other witnesses with me at the lookout point who also saw this. The witnesses are me, Shamdeen Qassim Gurmiz, Abdu Gurmiz Abdu, Babir Gurmiz Abdu, Khalid Fersan Gurmiz, Ameen Qassim Gurmiz, Salam Qassim Gurmiz, Alkan Qassim Gurmiz, Suliman Qassim Gurmiz. We saw the mass executions when they killed the people from Hardan.

Around 10 PM at night they shot more people. We could see the fire from the guns when they were shooting. I think they brought more Yezidis there. Right after that, they shot the first house in our village with a BKC, just one shot. It is destroyed. The roof collapsed.

We took all the family to the mountain. Only eight men stayed in our valley to fight Daesh.

At dawn on August 4th, they brought six more people by car from the direction of Tal Afar, and they burned their bodies at the intersection. They were lying on the ground, so I could not tell if they were dead or alive when they burned them. After that, around 9 or 10 in the morning, they brought the water truck and washed the dirt and blood away. After that they brought the bulldozer to shovel up the bodies and dump them at the side of the road. Then Daesh made a check point at the intersection.

We put all our families . . . the families of my uncle, my father, my brother . . . . in the valley and they stayed there. Just eight men stayed behind them. Daesh returned to fight against us, then we fought them for about six or seven days. In the mountain we went to Sherfadeen area and called for help. Our cars came from Kurdistan and they took us to Kurdistan. I built this house we are in from mud. Me and my wife and five kids live in these two rooms and one bathroom.

No one has had any news from those people from Hardan. They think they are all dead. There are at least three mass grave sites near the Hardan intersection. Peshmerga fenced them off. No one is allowed to open them right now.

All the people who say "hello" and show their faces like our friends are our enemies, Daesh. I know a lot of those Arabs who joined with Daesh. They were our neighbors. One of their villages is only one kilometer from my village. Another village is four kilometers away.

Since 2008, I was the manager for the workers for cleaning the municipality, and all those Arab kids I took to Suleymania. I know all these people very well. We were in school together, because I studied over there. And we were also shepherds together. I managed more than 1,000 workers, and I took them to Suleymania. They were all Arab Sunni from around my village. Some of their villages are Awaynat, Gholat, Eyashot, Girshabak, Zaer, Rabia, Halloom, Eyadia.

There were many Daesh in Shorey village, but they did not run. They are still there. In Shorey they kidnapped three Yezidi girls from Hardan and raped them. One of the girls escaped. The other two were taken to Daesh territory. Maybe to Baaj or Baiji. The Arabs who raped them still live in Shorey village.

Everyone was Daesh, but afterwards, who shaved his beard said he was not Daesh. I think it is hard to fix this problem. We know that not all Arabs fought with the Daesh, but they supported Daesh. They were friends with Daesh. They gave them money, they hid them and helped them. One who was fighting with Daesh for a long time and fighting us is now living in Kurdistan and Turkey. We have information about him.

I gave Asayish (Kurdistan security police) a lot of names. They did nothing. They captured some of them. Then they said come, "What do you have to tell us about them?" We said, "They are Daesh."

They said, "We have to follow the rules. The judge has to decide."

Some of them went to court in Kurdistan. I heard that one was sentenced in Duhok to prison for ten years, but that man killed more than three or four men. They are supposed to burn him. This is not a good judge.

I have no work or source of income. Every three or four months the government gives us ten kilos of rice and ten kilos of sugar and some cooking oil. It is a very bad situation.

When Daesh is defeated, I will go back to Shingal, because it is our home, and I want to go there, but our request is we need international protection, like from the U.N. We don't like to have to have this, but we do not know if Daesh will come again.

Nuri Gurmiz

I am Nuri from Gurmiz, the Yezidi village overlooking the intersection where eighty or more people from Hardan and Girshabek were killed. Hardan had a population of 1500. We watched through our binoculars. The mountain begins in our back yard. We had the high ground and our guns, so we were able to defend ourselves.

The moment the Daesh militants arrived from Tal Afar, our Arab neighbors teamed up with them. The neighbors arrested ninety percent of the people from Hardan and brought many people here telling them to convert to Islam or face a certain death. Our Arab neighbors killed them. Even the majority who converted were killed. Later some of the elderly were freed when the government bought them.

Daesh immediately buried the bodies at the Hardan massacre with excavators. The rain washed a lot of dirt away. When I first saw this site, you could see skulls and spines; now they have disappeared. Daesh also buried bodies with an excavator at many other massacre sites. At some sites, bodies were left on the ground to rot in the sun, be eaten by dogs, or washed away by rain and flooding culverts. The physical evidence of the genocide is disappearing.

If America is looking for evidence, however, we have more than two or three places. Shingal is strewn with over thirty-five mass graves from August 2014. We have more than a thousand pieces of evidence. If you are looking for witnesses to massacres, we have witnesses. If you are looking for who were hostages, we have hostages. If you are looking for girls who got pregnant by Daesh, we have a nine-year-old girl. I know her personally. In this case, the doctor says there is no solution. If she gives birth, she will die.

If America is not supporting Daesh, why didn't they come and save us? We are one religion on this earth. We also are created by God like you. So why is the Islamic State trying to eradicate Yezidis from the face of this earth? Where are our human rights? We are helpless. Nobody helps us.

Nuseria and Kocho Escape, Hamadan Massacre
Sardar Duraie Ali Al Hababi, July 29, 2016

I am Sardar Duraie Ali Al Hababi from the village of Nuseria. It is on the south side of Shingal Mountain, two kilometers east of Domise. I have 200 relatives from Nuseria. My uncle, Hussein Ali Duqo Al Hababi, was the sheik of Nuseria. A sheik is the head of a tribe. His position is above a mukhtar. Hussein was too ashamed to run away. My cousin is Osman Ibrahim Al Hababi. Together Hussein and Osman devised a plan for 247 people trapped in Nuseria to escape.

After Peshmerga left Kocho at 7:30 AM, August 3, 2014, about 100 people fled right behind them. Daesh captured half of them in their cars and shot them in Hamadan. Khalaf, a teacher from Kocho, was one of forty people who managed to escape and make it to Nuseria, a village eight kilometers from Kocho.

Before the attack, Nuseria's population was over 400. After August 3, there were 247 Yezidis trapped in Nuseria. Family members living nearby and in Sinjar gathered in Nuseria. Throughout Shingal, family members were desperately calling one another and trying to gather together.

On August 3, Daesh brought two women named Bassima Qassim and Turko from Gir Zerik to Nuseria. Gir Zerik had been the first Yezidi village to be attacked at 2:10 AM, August 3. The battle raged on until 7 AM when the men ran out of ammunition and fled to the mountain leaving the old men and disabled behind. Bassima, who had been pregnant when Daesh shot her, lost her baby. Turko's son was killed in the battle for Gir Zerik.

On August 4, Osman Ibrahim's family tried to escape in two cars from Sinjar to the mountain, but Daesh captured them and asked where they were going. They lied and said they were going to join their family in Nuseria, so Daesh let them go to Nuseria. Osman arrived safely with his sister, Wadha Ibrahim, to Nuseria. Wadha had just had surgery and was at home in Sinjar recuperating when Daesh entered Sinjar.

Osman's other sister, Zahara, was in a separate car with her family. A Daesh vehicle intentionally rammed Zahara's car. She and her son, Anwar, were killed in the car accident. The other family members were injured and taken by Daesh to Sinjar hospital. They spent one night in hospital, then Daesh kicked them out and sent them to Nuseria on August 5. Nurses in Nuseria cared for them.

Both Kocho and Nuseria were besieged by Daesh guards between August 3 and August 15. There was a mounting sense of impending doom and urgency to escape. On August 7, Ahmed Al Jaso, the clan leader from Kocho, went to neighboring Hatamia and met with the Hatamia manager, Hussein Barjas. A photo of the meeting also includes another Yezidi man and the manager of the nearby Arab village of Piskee. The Hatamia manager told Ahmed Al Jaso they wanted to escape, because the Daesh emir, Abu Hamza, told them they would have to convert to Islam on August 10. They did not want to be used as Daesh propaganda and be shown on TV converting to Islam. Ahmed Al Jaso, mukhtar of Kocho, refused to join Hatamia in an escape attempt because Kocho was surrounded by Arab villages. They were afraid of being caught and killed since others from Kocho had already been killed attempting to escape on August 3.

At 7 PM on August 8, under cover of dark, the village of 600 people of Hatamia escaped in two separate groups. Everyone turned off their phones, and left the lights burning in their houses and their cars parked outside. They silently snuck through the Daesh guards who were sleeping at their observation points around the village. All of them made it to the mountain. By August 10, they were safe in Kurdistan. Kocho remained besieged.

It was impossible to escape during the day, because the wheat fields had been harvested and one could see for miles across the flat, barren plains. In Nuseria, the manager Hussein Ali Daqo and Osman Ibrahim divided the 247 people into small groups so they would have a better chance to escape without being seen. They began escaping on August 10.

Right after sunset, at 8 PM, on August 9, everyone gathered in Nuseria. The Kocho people who had escaped to Nuseria said they could not run with the people from Nuseria, because it would be nighttime and they did not know the roads they would choose. So Kocho people decided to go on a different road to Hamadan, then Solagh, then to the mountain.

The people from Kocho went the wrong way and got trapped in a Daesh observation point. Daesh attacked them and killed five of them near Hamadan, injured four or five of them, and captured some. The rest fled to Shingal Mountain, including one named Salih from Kocho. Salih is missing. Khalaf, the teacher from Kocho, escaped.

On August 12, 2014, the remaining people in Nuseria tried to escape. Rasho Hadi was a nurse. While he and his family tried to flee to Shingal Mountain, Daesh saw them and shot and killed Rasho and his father, Hadi. Rasho's mother was old and died from exhaustion.

Hussein and Osman and their families were among those who tried to flee that day. Daesh caught them and returned them to Nuseria. Daesh talked to them for one-and-a-half hours explaining to them how to convert to Islam. They said Islam was the right religion. If they did not convert, they would be killed. Daesh called Haji, their leader, for advice. After the call, Daesh told them they had to turn in their weapons and promise not to escape. If they tried to escape, they would be killed. So Nuseria people promised Daesh to stay in their village. Daesh left.

Every day Hussein Ali Daqo was communicating by phone with the leader of the Kocho tribe, Ahmed Al Jaso. The last call between them was August 15, at

11 AM. Hussein asked Ahmed Jaso, leader of Kocho, "What will be the last solution for us in Nuseria? What is your final advice?"

Ahmed Jaso said that Daesh told people in Kocho to stay in their village and in one hour Daesh would come with vehicles for them and move them to a safe area. Daesh promised not to hurt them, saying they would be treated the same as Daesh treats Christian people (meaning they would not kill them). Kocho people were ordered to give all their weapons to Daesh, which they did.

At 11 AM, Ahmed Al Jaso told Hussein that they should come to Kocho at 2 PM and be prepared to go together with the people of Kocho to the mountain. Hussein agreed, but when he tried again to call Ahmed after 11 AM, he could not make contact with anyone in Kocho.

Soon after, Hussein got news from the TV that people in Kocho had been massacred. When Hussein Ali Daqo and Osman Berheem Osman heard this news, everyone remaining in Nuseria made a desperate effort to escape.

The two women who had come from Gir Zerik, Bassima and Turko, along with Osman's sister, Wadha Berheem Osman, offered an unknown Muslim man 500,000 Iraqi dinar (about $450 dollars) to drive them to the safety of Kurdistan. His name was Yassir. Because he was Muslim and had a beard, he was able to pass successfully through the Daesh check points with them.   When Yasser returned to Shingal, Daesh executed him for helping Yezidis.

Twenty-seven old men and women who could not walk, stayed in Nuseria village. Daesh moved them to Kocho, then to Tal Afar, then to Mosul, then Kirkuk.   They were held for six months, then released from Kirkuk to a Peshmerga check point. A one-year-old girl named Sheilan Farouk Hamma, whom Daesh took from her mother, was not released.

Hussein Ali Duqo Al Hababi and Osman Ibrahim Al Hababi with their families succeeded in fleeing to safety in Kurdistan. They went to the Yezidi Affairs Office in Duhok to report their captivity. The office refused to give them a report confirming that their families were really captured by Daesh, then escaped. So the people from Nuseria cannot get their passports or their rights. The women and kids with them were bitterly disappointed to be trapped in Iraq.

Safwan, Kocho Teenager, Escapes Execution Lines
Safwan Abbas Rasho, July 15, 2015

I am one of nineteen survivors of mass executions in Kocho. I am seventeen years old. I was five when the Americans invaded my country and fourteen when they left. I have known only war for most of my life, but in 2014, I was enjoying peace for the first time and attending high school. My brother and father were not often at home. Normally there was just me and my mother and two little brothers, Safiyan, age thirteen, and Kamiran, age eleven, living at home. . . . until Daesh came to Iraq.

My older brother, Darvan, was lucky to be at home that Monday, June 9, 2014, when Daesh invaded the city of Mosul. The only reason he was home in Kocho instead of finishing university in Mosul, one hundred fifty kilometers away, was because of what happened the year before in February 2013.

Three bus drivers who regularly drove Yezidi students back and forth every day from Bashiqa and Bahzani to Mosul University were waiting to carry the students home when Daesh terrorists killed them in the street. Two drivers were Yezidi and one was Muslim. They were from the Yezidi village of Bashiqa.

A Yezidi can be identified by his ID card. Everyone's ID card states one's religion, like Islam or Yezidi. For this reason, for years, Yezidis will not drive between cities after dark because we have to drive through Arab villages. Kocho is surrounded by Arab villages on all sides. To get from Sunoni on the north side of the mountain to Duhok or Erbil, you have to drive through Arab villages and then go through the security check points at the Kurdistan border. We do not feel safe if we are stopped and they check our ID cards. We have already had 73 genocides committed against us.

After those bus drivers were killed, thousands of Yezidi students who were living in Bashiqa or other villages and commuting each day to Mosul University quit school. They either returned to their homes in Shingal or transferred to a university in Kurdistan. My brother, Darvan who was twenty, came home to Kocho.

My father was in the Iraqi Army stationed on the Syrian border. After Daesh took control of Mosul on June 9, 2014, he took off his uniform that day, like every other soldier in Iraq, and came home. He felt it was too dangerous to be a soldier. We hoped we would be safe in Kocho. After Daesh took over Mosul, all the schools closed.

About seventy Peshmerga soldiers from Kurdistan came to Kocho and set up their station in the school at the entrance to our village. They told us, "Don't be worried, we will protect you." We were so happy to have Peshmerga protecting us. My mother and all the other women in Kocho cooked food at home every day and took it to feed the Peshmerga.

On August 3, sometime after midnight, we heard shooting coming from the direction of Tal Ezeer, Siba Sheikh Khuder, and Gir Zerik to the west of us, north of Baaj and south of Sinjar city.

Others in Kocho went up to their roof tops which are flat. In the summer we often sleep on the roof because it is so hot. In the daytime the temperature is 45C. Some people reported seeing car headlights in the dark at 2 AM, less than one kilometer away. They were driving from an Arabic village heading north to fight in Tal Banat which is a Yezidi village close to Kocho. The road passes near to Kocho.

Two hours later, at 4 AM, we heard gun shots near Kocho which woke me up, so we, also, went to our roof to look out. It is light by 4 AM and we can see neighboring villages in the distance. The villages are separated by miles of flat farm land, without trees. The crops were harvested and the landscape was dry and brown from drought. We saw cars heading south on the road from Tal Banat to the neighboring Arab village.

My mother, Fahima, was on our roof with me. She saw seven pickup trucks piled high with RBG guns in the back going to the closest Arab village. They were about a half-kilometer away on the road that passes by the east side of Kocho. Two kilometers away, we saw about thirty cars heading south from Tal Banat to the different Arab villages that surround Kocho. They were normal cars. They were not flying the black Daesh flag.

I guess they were our neighbors. Understand that Daesh did not come from somewhere far away. After Daesh took Mosul in June, then the people living in Baaj joined Daesh. Baaj is only eight kilometers from Kocho. On August 3, our own Arab neighbors living in the villages that surround Kocho joined with Daesh to attack Shingal. We felt a terrible sense of foreboding.

We saw and heard Peshmerga in a military jeep shoot five times at the cars that were coming from Tal Banat and going to the Arab villages. Immediately after that, about twenty Peshmerga left Kocho in the jeep and a large car. They all headed in the direction of Sinjar city. That was 4 AM.

We stayed in Kocho because we thought the remaining Peshmerga would protect us, but by 7 AM, all of the people in Kocho tried to leave town in their cars. The Peshmerga soldiers blocked us, so we went back home. By 7:30 AM all of the remaining Peshmerga left town. They said they were going to fight at the neighboring village of Tal Banat. They said, "Don't worry. We will guard you."

Many of the men from Kocho had been volunteering to help the Peshmerga. So some Yezidis left with Peshmerga in their cars at 7:30. They took the Peshmerga to save them, because the Peshmerga forces did not have enough cars for all of them to leave. When the road to Sinjar was blocked, they returned and escaped on the road going to the east end of the mountain. I heard that on the north side of the mountain, the Peshmerga from Kocho joined up with other Peshmerga.

As soon as the last of the Peshmerga left town, all the people from Kocho got in their cars again and headed northwest toward Sinjar city, because we thought Peshmerga was going to fight in Tal Banat to the northeast. We drove in the other direction. As soon as we left, we heard that the road from Kocho to Sinjar was blocked. We drove only five minutes before Peshmerga stopped us outside of town and made us return a second time.

The road to Tal Banat, the only other escape route, was also blocked. So we turned back to Kocho. By 10 AM everyone was back inside their house. We stayed in our houses with nothing to do because the electricity was cut for Kocho. We had no news because we had no radio, no TV, no internet, and no electricity to charge our phones.

The people who had followed right behind Peshmerga called us and told us that Daesh had arrested more than 100 people as they neared Sinjar city. Fifty-three of them were my relatives. Daesh took most of their phones, but some people hid theirs.

It was not until an hour after Peshmerga left and friends called us that we knew Peshmerga had been lying. They did not go to Tal Banat to protect the Yezidis there. My cousin, Madran Abdullah Khalaf, left Kocho after we got the news that 100 people were arrested by Daesh. He was the first person from Kocho to be killed. He was shot in his car when arriving to Sinjar city. His family was arrested.

Those of us who did not get away were trapped.

Later that same day at 4 PM on August 3, Daesh came to Kocho. The Daesh leader came in a jeep and introduced himself as Abu Hamza. We did not know him.

About twenty men in three pickup trucks came with him as his protection. They drank tea with Ahmed Al Jaso, the leader of our al-Mandkany clan. The senior men from Kocho were there, too.

Abu Hamza told us to fly a white flag on our house and they would not hurt us. They told us to lead our lives as normal like we did in the past. They told the men to go home and get their guns and turn them over to Daesh. Some men did follow their orders and gave their guns to Daesh. Some kept their guns. At 4:30 PM, Daesh left.

We put a white scarf on our house.

After Daesh took over Mosul back in June 9, we could see Daesh cars coming daily from Syria, passing one kilometer from Kocho and going to the Arabic villages around us. They were trading oil and guns.

In early July, a lot of Arabs from neighboring villages, including a village clan leader, had come shopping in Kocho. This was an unusual thing to go to the market in a different village. Apparently, Daesh had sent their spies to Kocho in order to plan the attack.

In July, Daesh stole one sheep and arrested a Yezidi shepherd named Dilshad Sulaiman Qassim from Kocho who was tending his flock near the Arabic town of Baaj, southwest of Kocho. A Peshmerga soldier saw them.

On August 5, Abu Hamza told us we had to convert to Islam. He gave us three days to decide. During the next three days, many families tried to leave Kocho in their cars, but when they saw Daesh, they turned back.

On August 8, Abu Hamza and his body guards returned to Kocho and returned the kidnapped shepherd, Dilshad, as a sign of friendship. He is one of the 19 survivors, like me. I was in that meeting along with all the other men in Kocho. Hamza was a little man; short and thin. He walked with a limp because of an injured leg. He had a small beard on his chin and looked to be between thirty and forty years old.

Hamza told us we would not have to convert to Islam. He said Daesh is the new government now.

Ahmed Al Jaso said everyone in Kocho would give Daesh our sheep, and gold and money if they would just let us escape to the mountain with our ID cards. Hamza said he would have to go to Mosul to ask the Daesh leader for permission. He pretended like he was trying to help us.

August 15, 2014, was the day of the attack. Abu Hamza returned to Kocho with about 100 new pickup Toyota trucks. Two were red and the others were white. They were all the same model and could carry up to six men, but I could see only a driver in each truck. The back of each truck was piled with RBG guns, and one man was sitting with the guns. I saw them from my house when they arrived.

They met with Ahmed Al Jaso and told him that Daesh was going to let us go to the mountain. They instructed Ahmed Al Jaso to tell everyone to go home and prepare, then return to the school. We brought our gold, cash, IDs and some water. A few people brought a blanket and sweet cake for a snack.

One Daesh man stood by the door as we entered and took everyone's phone. About five or ten women risked their lives and hid their phones. After giving up our phones at the door, Daesh separated me from my mother and little brothers. I was sent with the men and boys over age fourteen into the meeting hall on the ground floor. They sent my mother and brothers upstairs with all the women and children.

I saw Abu Hamza in the school standing next to Al Jaso instructing him what to tell us. They said that since we had refused to convert to Islam, they were taking our gold and cash from us. They told Al Jaso to tell all of us that they would search us afterwards and if anyone kept anything, we would be killed.

There were about ten empty, black suitcases on the floor; the kind with hard sides used for ammunition. They were empty inside and were about 1.5m x 2m x .5m. It was around 11 AM when everyone put their money and gold in them. I had $2 dollars hidden in my shoe which I did not give them. My father had $200 and my brother Darvan had $100. We also gave them our gold, worth $2,000 dollars.

The richest man in Kocho was our clan leader, Ahmed Al Jaso Qassim. My family was not as rich as him, but we were well-off. We had 400,000,000 dinar ($365,000 USD) in assets. We had four cars: one Deer pickup, one KIA car, and 2 Omega cars. We had a new house only three years old worth 70,000,000 dinar ($60,000 USD). We owned four cows, one hundred sheep and a sheep dog, and many chickens. The sheep were in our building for animals which is connected to our house. Each sheep is worth at least $150 dollars. We lived on agriculture and trading animals. Daesh told us they would take us to the mountain. Then they separated me from my father and brother, and ordered me to go outside. My father said, "Go, I will follow and see you," but I never saw him again.

They took me outside to my family's own KIA car parked outside the school. I got in along with others. Others climbed into our Deer pickup truck. We were about thirty Yezidis. Daesh drove us to a place at the southeast edge of Kocho. Each car had a man with a gun. There were three car loads of approximately fifteen Daesh men waiting for us. They shot some guns to scare us and stood us in two lines. Then they told us to get down on our knees.

The Daesh drivers and armed men left in our cars. Eight Daesh men stayed behind. One Daesh recorded a video of us. One Daesh said to shoot ("Ermy"). They were standing about four or five meters away from us. About nine people survived the first round of shooting. Then one Daesh person immediately came and shot those who had survived.

Daesh did not know I survived. I didn't move. Three bullets had grazed my skin, but did not penetrate my body: one bullet across my arm, one bullet across my neck, and one bullet in my shirt on the front of my chest. I fell down with the others. I opened my eyes and saw one person. Daesh said, "Let's go to kill another line."

They returned with about fifteen more Yezidis in a pickup truck and killed them near to us. I opened my eyes and saw it. After they killed them, they drove toward the east. When they were gone, I got up and left with two other survivors, Faris Shahab Kuti and Kitche Amo Silo.

We walked for ten minutes toward another village. We had to stop to rest because we were injured. Then we walked another thirty minutes to an Arab village to the north of Kocho. At 1:30 PM, we hid in a little valley where three other survivors from another execution line in Kocho joined us five minutes later.

They were Saad Murad Melham Hamad, Sameh Pissee Murad, and Nafid Hadi Hussein.

We stayed there until it grew dark around 9 PM. Then the six of us all left together. Two people could not walk, so the other four of us carried them. Saad had a bullet in his knee. Kitche was in such a terrible disoriented psychological condition from seeing his brother shot, that we had to carry him, too. We came to another Yezidi village which was empty, but Daesh was nearby. We avoided houses with a light on and went inside a dark house and got some water.

We continued walking north toward Hamadan village, a Yezidi village next to Shingal Mountain. We got lost and ended up in Solagh, another Yezidi village, instead of Hamadan. There were sheep near Solagh so we looked for their water but could not find any. We were all wounded and exhausted. Finding water and escaping was all we could think of.

We then walked to a valley and saw the dead bodies of two men who had been shot. By 11 PM we got to an empty house next to the mountain. We went to search for water, but saw the lights from a lot of cars, so we ran away without finding water. Next we walked to Qine village where we knew there was a water project. There we got three two-liter bottles of water for the six of us. By midnight we arrived at Mehrka and climbed the mountain. It was so hard carrying two men. At 3 AM we rested in the mountain for thirty minutes then kept walking to the top.

We arrived by sunrise to a sacred Yezidi place called Peri Awra. There was one person there who gave us one bottle of water for the six of us. We asked for directions to another sacred place called Sherfadeen. We walked for another three hours in the heat, but had to stop because we were too weak and thirsty to continue. We found a car and drank the water from the car's window washer. I saw one Yezidi man with a gun and asked him where to find water.

At 11 AM we arrived to another sacred place called Yusifa u Bakra where we finally drank water, but the water was bad. We drank it anyway. We gave a man there six cigarettes in exchange for tea, but he brought us only some stale bread. Then we continued walking and carrying the two men to Sherfadeen where we arrived at 1 PM. We stayed four days.

Then one Arab and one Yezidi drove us in a pickup truck with one person who had died from dehydration and lack of food. There were fifteen of us, plus the dead man. They drove us to Syria and then to my uncle in Zakho, Iraq, near the border of Turkey. I went to live with the Yezidi family of Engineer Mahdi in Duhok for a month. They became like my family. They never left me alone.

Then I moved to Qadia camp. My mother and little brothers returned from Daesh after six months. We are hoping my mother's sister will be returned soon. Someone who is holding her in Syria has contacted us for ransom money. My mother's brother, Hosne, is with us now, but his wife and two-year-old son are still kidnapped. We have not heard from them. He will go to Syria and ask if anyone knows where they are.

I have not heard from my father, Abbas Rasho, and my older brother, Darvan, since I left them in the school last year. I will not have peace of mind until Daesh is defeated and the bodies are found. Now we say they are missing. When I made my report to the Genocide Office in Duhok, they sent me to the hospital to give a blood sample. The Ministry of Health is keeping blood samples of everyone who was kidnapped, so they can do DNA matching on the bodies when the mass graves are opened.

Dec. 23, 2015

I live in Germany now with my mother and younger brothers. I want to thank the good people of Germany for helping us and welcoming us. I am so happy to be in a good school. Danke.

The Sex Slave Market in Syria

Farida Abbas Rasho, January 4, 2016

I was fourteen when Daesh attacked Kocho, August 15, 2014. My father and brother, Darvan, were killed that day by Daesh. My younger brother, Safwan, escaped after being put in an execution line. Raqqa, Syria, was where Daesh took the Yezidi girls to be sold and raped repeatedly. I attempted suicide seven times in three months before I escaped from Raqqa.

When Daesh reached our village on August 3, they asked us not to leave our houses, assuring us we would be safe. For the first three days they did nothing to us and only surrounded our village. They approached our clan leader, Ahmed Al Jaso, on the fourth day and asked him to convert to Islam. Not only did he refuse, but all the villagers did, also.

On August 15, thirteen vehicles approached our village. Not rickety pick-ups, but new, white Toyota pickups, mounted with heavy-duty military equipment on their rear beds. In each of them sat men dressed in black. I ran downstairs to my father and cried in a panic, "They're coming, they're coming! They're coming to kill us!"

They ordered all villagers to gather in the central plaza and then separated us: elders, women and children on one side and men on the other. They took all the females to the second floor of Kocho school and the men to the first floor. I was separated from my father and eldest brothers, Safwan and Darvan. My mother, two younger brothers, and I were sent to the second floor.

When they separated us from our father in the school, the last thing I saw of him was a terribly sad look he gave me. I have stored this memory forever in my mind. I watched from an upstairs window, as all the men were herded out in groups and driven off in different directions. We did not know what happened to them.

After the men were gone, we were pushed into a bus and driven to Solagh Institute. We were terrified and crying. Some pounded the windows or hit their heads against the glass. In Solagh, they forcibly separated me from my mother, Fahima, and little brothers, Sifiyan and Kamiran. We girls were put in big buses and transported to a large house in Mosul. Nearly two dozen armed men stood guard.

The TV was broadcasting news of a massacre of the men in my town of Kocho. I thought of my father and brothers and collapsed in a fit of hysteria, much like an epileptic seizure. When I came to, my captors threatened to kill me if it happened again.

"You're all alone in this world," one fighter told us. "You've just got us now. We're your new masters. You are now our property."

They frequently reassured each other that they were justified in enslaving us because, as non-Muslims, we were not their equals. They said they were the master race.

The next morning, I and 46 other Yezidi girls were driven in a convoy ten hours to Raqqa, Syria, under Daesh control. We were held in a single-story warehouse surrounded by barbed wire. There was only one window with bars.

The next morning, dozens of new Daesh fighters came into the room. There were men from Iraq, Syria, Egypt, Saudi Arabia, and Tunisia. One of the guards yelled, "All you new ones, stand together in a group!"

We all ignored him. Some of us turned and faced the wall. For this, we were dragged to the center of the room and brutally beaten.

"Are all of these girls really still virgins?" one man asked.

"Fresh goods," replied another.

One approached me and stroked my face. Then he opened my mouth to inspect my teeth. I bit down.

"You bitch!" he cried. He beat me until I convulsed in another seizure. The sight of it caused him to lose interest which meant I would be sold in the slave market.

We had a basin and a little water, but we refused to wash ourselves. The filthier and more repulsive we were, the less likely we were to be sold.

Daesh members were coming every night in groups and choosing girls for themselves. Anyone who refused to go with them was beaten and forced to go with them anyway. One night they took me with another girl from my village, Jilan Ibrahim, to a house in which there were already two other girls.

I tried to commit suicide that night with a small piece of glass from the window, with which I tried to cut the veins in my hands. I lost consciousness. When I woke up, I was in a doctor's house, to which they had transported me along with Jilan. I stayed in the doctor's house for five days. After that they took Jilan and me with four other girls to a house at the edge of Raqqa.

One day, while the men were sleeping, Jilan and I took their guns and we were going to shoot them. But they took the gun from me before I was able to shoot and another pushed Jilan, so she was unable to kill anyone. After that they began to punish us even more severely.

Jilan was so beautiful that a Daesh man said he would marry her. They tried to separate Jilan and me but we insisted we were sisters. Another time, we were all gathered and they told us that if anyone escaped, they would bring our mothers and punish them instead of us and kill our family.

I stole a cell phone from that house, but there was no network there. We tried to escape twice from there, but did not succeed. Later, they took us to a region called Shadadia which is part of Deir ez-Zor, where we stayed for ten days. Daesh members were beating and raping us continually and treating us like animals. Because of the severe beatings, I was unable to walk.

After those ten savage days, we were transported to inside Deir ez-Zor. This house was near a Koniku gas factory and we were there for over two months. Although I was not able to walk or move, they did not stop beating or raping me. I pretended that I was a married woman, but they were dealing with me as if I were not. They were speaking in Arabic among themselves and were saying that if any of the girls could speak Arabic, they would take her to Libya.

That is why I did not speak Arabic for the entire time even though they beat me and told me they knew I could speak Arabic. I managed to deceive them and never spoke one word of Arabic.

Some days later they brought another girl from Kocho village. She knew me and out of fear, she told them I knew how to speak and write Arabic. At that time, they treated me in a very harsh way. They put iron handcuffs on my hands and feet and raped me and beat me with a whip. Again I attempted suicide by hanging myself, but was found in time.

This time the man who owned me, Zeyad, beat me with electrical cord and a metal clothes hanger on my head causing internal bleeding. Blood seeped into my eyes, and I could not see out of one of them for two months. My dear friend Jilan lost the sight of both eyes for two months.

Zeyad sold me to a new band of Daesh soldiers, stationed in a military camp taken from the Free Syrian Army out in the desert. Their commander sent me to a local hospital controlled by Daesh. My hospital door was locked from the outside. I spent 45 days in bed, recovering from Zeyad's near-fatal beating.

Upon my release, I was given to a soldier who rolled out his mat and kneeled down to pray before raping me. Raping a Yezidi girl was their sick form of worship.

At the Koniku gas factory, we were forced to memorize the Quran or risk beatings. I met a twelve-year-old girl named Besma, who had been brutally beaten after attempting to stab her rapist. She was most desperate to get out, preferring to risk dying rather than remain.

There were lots of caravans in the Koniku factory. We were living in two caravans and Daesh members in others. We had stolen a SIM card and cell phone from Daesh. I called my uncle, Khalaf Abbas, from Kocho village. He had moved to New Zealand years before, but returned to Iraq to free more than twenty of his female relatives who had been abducted.

We described to Khalaf where we were. With his connections he was able to call people for help, but he was informed it was too difficult to get us because we were surrounded by Daesh. We were on our own. No one was coming to our rescue. Every day I was plotting on how we could escape.

There was a metal fence around our caravans. One black night there were only three Daesh guards. Five other girls and I were able to reach the yard and escape through a small hole in the fence. The sound of the rain covered the noise of our footsteps as we ran.

We were miserable, exhausted, and soaking wet. Eventually we reached an empty, secluded house. We attempted to get in, but an iron piece fell down and made a loud sound. We ran again out of fear and then came upon another empty house and sheltered there for the night. We traveled the next day and hid when cars passed by us. We came upon another house with a family who offered to hide us if we paid money.

We called Khalaf again, who gave us the number of a man from Hasaka. He negotiated with the people in that house who agreed to hide us. The man in that house recognized us and told us that we were living in Koniku gas factory. I asked if he was with Daesh, but he replied that he only worked in that factory. Another man arrived and gave the house owner money and took us by truck to Hasaka, where we stayed for several days. Later, they took us to a region where Iraq, Syria, and Turkey meet.

Finally, we were delivered to Peshmerga in Kurdistan, Iraq. When I arrived at the camp which would be my new home, none of my family was there except my teenaged brother, Safwan, who had escaped from a mass execution line in Kocho. I learned my mother, Fahima, and two younger brothers, Sifyan and Kamiran, were still being held captive by Daesh. It was a horrific time for me until they were rescued after nine months of being held prisoners.

When I was offered a chance to go to Germany, my mother insisted I go. "There's no fresh start here, and we will never make peace with the Muslims," my mother said.

Soon after, my mother and two brothers joined me in Germany. There still is no news about the fate of my father, Abbas, or older brother, Darvan, but we know that Daesh killed the men in Kocho.

I decided that my life will go on, in spite of all the terrors. I will not give my tormentors the victory of having destroyed it.

The Girl Who Escaped Daesh: This Is My Story, by Farida Khalaf with Andrea C. Hoffman (Atria Books), 2016

Rape, Suicide, and Hysteria

A euphemism is widely used to describe the kidnapping and rape of the Yezidi women. When raped, they say they were "taken" or "married." Yezidis do not use the word "rape" to describe what happened to them. But make no mistake; the Yezidi girls and women did not willingly "marry" their Daesh captors. There were no white dresses and wedding bells.

The women and girls did not submit willingly. They were abducted, beaten unconscious, bloodied, bruised, drugged, tied, gagged, and savagely raped repeatedly. This is Daesh's idea of "marriage." When the girls and women became too much trouble because of their resistance, they were sold and resold.

Over one hundred girls and women chose suicide over torture and rape at the hands of Daesh. Some experienced unbearable torture and repeated gang raping. One girl who managed to call her father told him she had been raped eighteen times in one day and she would commit suicide as soon as she had the opportunity.

Many were beaten with cables, wires and clothes hangers. Two girls were beaten on the head so severely they bled internally into their eyes and could not see for two months.

One girl was suspended from a ceiling fan and spun around.

Little girls, as young as nine, had their vaginas cut because they were too small for a male to penetrate.

Some were locked in tiny rooms with no toilets or windows for more than one month.

There were many whose husbands and children had been killed. They were sick, depressed, and without hope.

The "lucky" women were those who were taken by only one Daesh man and not sold or shared from man to man. But for others, they lived in buildings where Daesh fighters regularly came to choose a girl for sex for a day or a week, then return her. The girls would be ordered to wash up, put on pretty dresses and makeup and line up for the men to inspect and choose. Those who refused were beaten. There was an unverified rumor that a group of women who refused to wash up were dragged into the courtyard by their hair and shot as an example to the other women.

Jilan, age nineteen, was part of a group of twenty-one girls, including two as young as ten and twelve, held captive in a single room. The girls were given clothes "that looked like dance costumes" and ordered to go wash up and change. In the bathroom, Jilan cut her wrists and hanged herself. Her family had already been killed.

Amnesty International interviewed a twenty-seven-year-old woman who said that she and her sister had tried to strangle themselves with scarves after their

Daesh captor threatened that if they did not marry him and his brother, he would sell them.

Sara, a beautiful girl, poured kerosene over her body and burned herself rather than be used as a sex slave.

Commonly, women were gagged, tied, and drugged.

Captives were also subjected to brutal psychological torture, especially to be a deterrent to escaping. Ahlam was forced to watch as they broke the bones of two Yezidi men who were caught trying to escape. The gunmen tied the men to a truck and drove them through the streets. Another woman was forced to watch a foreign journalist beheaded.

Luna, a girl who escaped, told Amnesty International, "There was a twenty-year-old Yezidi girl who committed suicide after a militant showed her a video in which she was lying unconscious, after being fed sleeping pills, while some militants took turns raping her. I knew one Yezidi girl in Raqqa who could not stand all these numerous tortures, so she shot herself with a pistol."

Eighteen-year-old Barfi Kheder Ibrahim, a Yezidi girl from Duguri, Shingal, was not as fortunate. She committed suicide in Syria in a particularly desperate act to escape captivity and rape. Barfi died as a result of a car accident while being held by Daesh terrorists. It was not an ordinary car accident.

On August 3, 2014, Barfi, her mother, two teenage sisters, and eleven-year-old brother were abducted from their home in Duguri on the north side of Shingal Mountain. After more than three months being held by Daesh, Barfi was transferred to Syria to be sold.

All kidnapped Yezidi girls and women had enormous fear of being sold into Syria from Iraq, because in Syria, they had a greater chance of being put in a house and rented out on a daily or weekly basis to be raped repeatedly by multiple men and then returned. Being sent to Syria or having your little children taken away and sent to Syria was a threat frequently used to make women cooperate and submit to rape.

On November 19, 2014, Barfi was taken to a slave market with tens of Yezidi girls in Deir ez-Zor, a city in Syria. In the Deir ez-Zor slave market, a member of Daesh wanted to buy Barfi and then "marry" her, but she refused to accompany him. She told them that she would not "marry" any one of them. However, they forced her to ride in their car. When the car was speeding on the road, Barfi wanted to kill the driver and commit suicide. So she grabbed the steering wheel and beat the driver, causing an accident. The driver died at the scene of the accident. The other Daesh militant in the car was injured.

Barfi died three days later in Deir ez-Zor city. She was able to tell what happened to another kidnapped Yezidi girl who was with her before she died. Barfi's mother, siblings, sister-in-law and two children were returned from Daesh in 2016 after two years in captivity. When that Yezidi girl who was with Barfi managed to escape to Kurdistan, she told Barfi's family how Barfi had died.

Many women in captivity with Daesh attempted suicide multiple times. They tried jumping from the roof of their house, swallowing poison or sleeping pills, hanging, and cutting themselves with a knife or broken glass. Viyan Havind, a mother of two, tried all of these methods and was prevented each time from succeeding.

The Yezidi culture has a deeply rooted requirement that a woman be a virgin when she is married. If she is raped, she is ostracized and may even be murdered in an "honor killing." A rape victim is considered to bring dishonor and shame upon her family. Also, anyone who converts to Islam can never return to the Yezidi religion. Against this cultural fear and belief that they would never be allowed to return to their family or Yezidi community, some committed suicide.

When Viyan managed to steal a phone and call her father, she told him she would be unable to return because she had been raped and forced to convert to Islam. Her father told her, "No, no, no! You must return! You must return. Baba Sheikh has said all the kidnapped women will be welcomed back by the Yezidis. Everything is changed now. We know what Daesh did to you. We know that Daesh forced you to convert to Islam. It does not matter. It's not like before. Tell all the women and girls they will be welcomed back. They must return to their families. We want you to come home. You *must* come home to us."

After eleven months, Viyan escaped with her children to the loving arms of her family. Her husband is missing, presumed killed by Daesh in Kocho.

Those women and girls who escaped captivity remain deeply traumatized. So many experience fits of hysteria that the local hospitals in Kurdistan have a code of "HYS" for their condition of hysteria. A hysteria fit looks much like an epileptic seizure. The woman drops in a dead faint. She is silent and within a minute the seizure begins. She arches her back, and her legs and arms become rigid. Instead of foaming at the mouth, she moans in agony and yells loudly as if reliving the rape. To witness an attack of hysteria leaves one trembling inside.

When I took Iman (not her real name) to get a new Iraqi citizenship card (jensia), the woman with whom she had escaped two weeks before entered the office. When the two women saw each other, they fell into each other's arms. Their reunion triggered Iman's memory of captivity. A minute later, Iman collapsed in a fit of hysteria next to the director's desk. The room was packed with people. Three men pulled her arms and legs, pinning her down, in an attempt to stop her seizure. This was absolutely the worst thing to do, which would reinforce her memory of being forcibly held down and raped.

It is distressing for anyone to witness a fit of hysteria which lasts for ten to twenty minutes. When the woman is completely exhausted, she goes silent and limp like a balloon being pricked. In a minute the woman regains awareness. Fits of hysteria typically come in waves of four or five episodes separated by five minutes of calm.

By the time Iman came around and we walked her outside for fresh air, she had another seizure on the grass. We put her into a car, stretched out on the back seat with her head in Jiyan's lap and drove her to the nearby hospital in Shekhan. "Hysteria attack; Kocho woman," I told the doctor as she met us in the parking lot with a gurney. They knew the diagnosis immediately. In the IDP camps in Kurdistan, hysteria seizures happen every day of the week. In the clinic, Iman had two more seizures which were stopped only by two injections of a heavy tranquilizer.

To ensure that Iman genuinely was not epileptic, the hospital gave her a CT brain scan and x-ray. In an hour we went to visit Lalish, the Yezidi religious center. Iman was shot so full of drugs, she was absolutely euphoric and enjoyed the visit more than any of us.

A fit of hysteria in a traumatized woman is triggered by her memory of being abused and raped. Therefore, traditional psychological therapies of talking about one's traumatic experience is not recommended. Therapy comes through forgetting, not reliving the trauma. A safe environment far removed from the scene of the crime is the best therapy. With this as a goal, 1100 women and children survivors of Daesh captivity were resettled in Badden-Württenberg, Germany, in 2015.

Said, Survivor of Kocho Mass Execution

Said Murad Pissee, August 22, 2015

My name on my Iraqi ID card is Said Murad Pissee. Since the attack on my village of Kocho (or Kojo), I changed my name to Said Kocho. What happened in Kocho must never be forgotten.   Kocho is a story of betrayal more unimaginable than a mother drowning her infant.

Sometimes I lay awake at night and wish I could blot out what happened, but it keeps replaying in my head, disturbing my dreams. I am running, but there is no escape. Six of my brothers are missing. They were killed by Daesh in the execution lines. My sister, Nadia Murad, was kidnapped and brutally abused. She escaped. My mother was killed with the old women. My brother's wife, Muna, and their two-year-old son, Hani, were kidnapped and are still missing. What happened can never be fixed. There is only retribution.

I was twenty-two when Daesh attacked us with our Arab neighbors. I was born in 1992, the youngest of twelve sons. That was after Iraq invaded Kuwait. It was one year after the Uprising against Saddam Hussein's tyranny against the Kurds in April 1991. In the late 1980s, Saddam killed 182,000 Kurds, including the chemical gas attack in Halabja which killed 5,000 Kurds on March 16, 1988. In 1991 the United States created the autonomous region of Kurdistan in northern Iraq, with guarded borders, and enforced a no-fly zone over it.   For that, the Kurds love America.

When the Americans invaded Iraq in 2003, I was eleven. I was fifteen when they hanged Saddam and nineteen when they withdrew. The war was over for the Americans, but not for us. After the Americans left without rebuilding Iraq, fighting broke out between the Shia Arabs controlling Baghdad central government in the south and the Sunni Arabs living in Mosul.

In Shingal, we lived in a constant state of insecurity. Shingal was a disputed territory.   Baghdad claimed it as belonging to the Mosul province, but Kurdistan sent its Kurdish Peshmerga forces to defend us and made the Iraqi army retreat. Officially we belonged to Mosul, but in reality we belonged to Erbil, the capital of Kurdistan in the north.

Kocho had a population of 1,735 Yezidis before Daesh attacked us. It is twenty-two kilometers from Sinjar, our big city. We speak Yezidi, a dialect of Kurdish, but we call Shingal city by its Arabic name, Sinjar. We were forced to speak and write Arabic in school so I cannot write my own language.   Now the schools in Shingal have been taken over by Daesh and our kidnapped children are taught to memorize verses of the Quran.

On August 3, 2014, I was with Yezidi volunteers protecting Kocho when Daesh attacked the rest of Shingal. Daesh came from the east at 2 AM in the night when everyone was sleeping. They arrived in their personal cars and white

Toyota pickup trucks, captured in Mosul on June 9, 2014, when the Iraqi army abandoned Mosul without a fight. By the time people woke up at sunrise on August 3, Daesh was already inside their villages.

Daesh did not come to Kocho that morning. No one called my family, so we did not know what was happening elsewhere.

The Peshmerga were guarding Kocho at the school, but at 7 AM the Peshmerga escaped from Kocho. We asked them where they were going. They said they would return soon with more support which was on its way, but this was a lie. Peshmerga also abandoned Yezidi people from neighboring Siba Sheikh Khudir and Gir Zerik who were being attacked by Daesh that morning.

After the Peshmerga left Kocho, twenty pickup trucks filled with families left right behind the Peshmerga trucks. Daesh caught fifteen trucks and killed the people in them thirty kilometers north of Kocho. The massacre happened in Qine Mehrkan, close to Shingal Mountain. Five trucks got away to the mountain and called and told us what had happened. There were Yezidis on the mountain who watched the attack through binoculars. Daesh shot all the men over age fourteen; twenty-eight in total. They kidnapped thirty-one women and thirty-six children, all from Kocho. Some were only babies nursing at their mother's breast.

After that massacre, no one dared to escape by car from Kocho.

After the twenty trucks left Kocho on August 3, Daesh arrived and told the people of Kocho "If you put a white flag on your house, nothing will happen to you." They said they were not here for the Yezidis, and they left. We raised three white flags, but we did not trust them.

Daesh returned that same afternoon and asked us to give them all our weapons. Some of us gave them our weapons while others did not. We gave them about thirty-five weapons and kept the rest. After we gave them our weapons, they told us, "There is nothing to be afraid of."

Then they installed their observation points (OP) of hundreds of Arab guards around the perimeter of our village. By 3 PM on August 3, Daesh was in total control of all of Kocho. We were trapped, flying our white flags.

There was no one left in Iraq or Europe or America that we did not inform about our desperate situation and begged to be rescued. That included the coalition airplanes flying overhead. Everyone knew about our predicament, but no one answered our cry for help. We spent twelve days like that calling for help.

On August 5th, Daesh returned to Kocho. Emir Abu Hamza al-Khatouni, the Daesh leader, came from Baaj to meet with Ahmed Jaso Qassim, our clan leader for Kocho and four other villages. Baaj is six kilometers southwest of Kocho.

Abu Hamza and Ahmed Jaso drank tea together at the reception hall next to Ahmed's house. Hamza told Ahmed Jaso, "You have three days to decide to convert to Islam or we will kill you."

After Abu Hamza left, Ahmed Jaso met with all the men and told them "You are free to choose." They all decided not convert to Islam. They said "Let them kill us, but we will not convert to Islam."

Hatamia village of 500 Yezidis is four kilometers north of Kocho. It was also surrounded by Arab security guards. Hussein Barjas Uso is the clan leader of Hatamia village. Barjas promised Ahmed Jaso that everyone from both villages would leave together. They made a solemn vow that no village would abandon the other.

Late at night on August 9, Hatamia village residents left without telling Ahmed Jaso. Under cover of dark, they silently snuck between the observation points while the guards were mostly sleeping.

Abu Hamza, the Daesh leader, returned to Kocho for a third meeting, this time in the big building for meetings of tribal leaders. All of the elder men of Kocho attended, too. He asked Ahmed Jaso, "Do you know about Hatamia?" Jaso told him, "No."

Ahhh, we felt betrayed by Hatamia. I will never forgive Hussein Barjas for abandoning us. [Author's note: Unbeknown to Kocho residents, on August 7, Ahmed Jaso met with Hussein Barjas and declined to join Hatamia in their escape due to the high risk of being captured. They also met with Abu Hamza. Ahmed Jaso kept the meetings secret so as not to give away Hatamia's plan. Everyone in Hatamia was instructed to turn their phones off so that no one could communicate with them from Kocho and betray their plan.]

Hamza acted like he came as our friend. In a sign of good will, he returned a shepherd whom Daesh had kidnapped in July near Baaj. This was just a trick to try to gain our trust.

He said "We will not punish you or deny you food or water. We have no problem with you, and we will not force you to become Muslim. Daesh is the new government. Just stay put and go about your normal life like in the past."

Daesh had cut the electricity to Kocho since August 3, so we had no TV, radio or internet. But some people had generators, so we could charge our phones. Friends were calling us and telling us about the murders and beheadings of men and kidnapping of women. We were terrified, but trapped.

Ahmed Jaso offered Abu Hamza for us to give Daesh all our sheep and gold and property in exchange for being driven to the mountain to escape. "Just let us go with our IDs," Jaso asked. Abu Hamza said he would have to ask permission from the Daesh leaders in Mosul. He promised to return with an answer in three days.

At 9 AM on August 15, Daesh brought a truck of food for Kocho to Ahmed Jaso's house. At 11 AM, eighty Daesh trucks came to Kocho. Daesh went to each house and told everyone to drive to the school and bring all our gold and cash. We were instructed to leave the keys in the ignition. Abu Hamza promised they would drive us to the mountain. We didn't believe him.

As we entered the school, they made us put our cell phones in a bag. Some people lied and said they did not have a phone. Daesh said they would search each person later, and if anyone was found with his phone, he would be killed. I gave them my phone.

They took women and children to the upstairs and kept us, the men, downstairs. There were over 400 men. I believe fewer than 500 people had already escaped from the village. Then they took our money and gold. They went to each person with separate bags for gold and money and told us to put it in.

We knew the faces of Daesh. They were not wearing masks. Some wore military uniforms and ordered us with guns. We recognized faces from our neighboring Arab villages of Khanessi, Baaj, Baiji, and Pisqi.

They told us, "Those of you who want to convert to Islam raise your fingers and go back home."

No one raised his hand. We said, "We will not convert to Islam."

After they collected our money and gold, they loaded two pickup trucks at once. They used our own trucks. Each one had a driver and an armed guard. They took three groups of twenty to thirty men before me. I was in the fourth group. Before they took us, they repeated if anyone wanted to convert to Islam they could remain in their house. Again, we said, "We will not convert."

There were about fifty men in my group in four trucks. They threatened us with weapons. As soon as we rode in the vehicles, we realized they would kill us, because we could see many of them still surrounding the village, and because they drove us towards the artesian well on a farm, not to the mountain.

The wells are used to collect and store water for irrigation. August is the dry season and the harvest was over, so the dirt storage pools for the wells were empty. They took us to the farm house of Atto Ahmed Garris, a Yezidi. It is in the green area one kilometer north of Kocho.

They stopped the cars by the storage pool. While some of their men were standing at the edges of the pool, some others were behind us and said, "Get out." We got out of the car. They told us to line up in rows in the empty pool. It was one-and-a-half meters deep. Then they walked around us and videoed us and took photos for ten minutes.

We started to moan and cry and pray to god whom we call *Tawus Melak*. I was not so afraid that they were going to kill us for our religion. I was thinking it is okay for us to die as long as we are keeping our religion, because those who die for their religion are immortal.

When they finished making the video, five Daesh leaders told the fighters to shoot us. Everyone was standing except me. I was lying down and covering my head with my arms. They stood around us and started to shoot at us with BKCs, GCs, and machine guns. Twelve Daesh were shooting at us for ten minutes. Bodies fell on top of me.

We recognized the people who shot us. They did not wear masks, because they did not intend for there to be any survivors. They were from the Meteoti and Khatouni clans. I also saw Kurdish Muslims from Sinjar with them. I know all of them. They lived in the Arab villages that surround Kocho. There were none from Chechnya or Afghanistan among them. The two other survivors know them, too.

When they stopped shooting, I was already hit by five bullets: three by my left knee, one in my left buttock, one in my left shoulder. But one of our men shouted "Ah, my heart and stomach," so they looked for people still alive and shot at us with a pistol aimed at the head. They hit me with one more bullet near the base of my neck. I used to work with the man who shot me in my neck. He lived in the neighboring Arab village.

When they stopped shooting, I didn't move. I heard the engines start and the trucks drive away. When it was silent, Dilshad spoke, "Is anyone still alive?"

I answered, "Yes, I am alive." The other survivor was Ali Abbas Ismail, age thirty-five. Before we could get out of the pool, Dilshad ran away in the direction of Qapusia village toward the mountain. I don't know Dilshad's last name and I don't know what happened to him.

I was under the bodies of other men. I raised my head and heard fighter planes like F-16s above us. Yes, I swear to God. I lifted the head of one man and saw it was my uncle. I did not stay to look at others.

Ali and I ran about 150 meters and hid in a small building housing the generator. There was a small opening just big enough to look out. I watched Daesh return and use an excavator to dig up earth and bury the men in the pool. Ali huddled in the corner, too traumatized to watch them bury the bodies. He had one wound. The bullet had entered him in his side at the back and exited in the front. Eventually, his bleeding stopped.

I kept putting dirt into my wounds to slow the bleeding. I was in terrible pain. We stayed in the generator room from about 12:30 PM until it was dark. All afternoon we could hear the planes flying above and around Kocho.

At 8 PM we started walking six hours until I reached the house of a Kurdish friend. My wounds were bleeding again. We stayed with them for six days without medical treatment. Ali was not as bad as me, but he did not leave my side. Finally, I told them we had to leave because my wounds were getting infected. I knew I would die if I did not get treatment.

My friend gave me a phone and a SIM card. We took one liter of water. We left at 8 PM under cover of dark and headed to the mountain. But we did not walk in a direct line. We had to walk off the road and change directions to avoid being seen. We walked from Qapousi toward Tal Qassab Kevan. We had to cross over the main paved road from Tal Qassab Kevan to Sinjar and continue to Solagh. We had to be careful not to be seen. We saw one passing truck. After walking for ten-and-a-half hours, we arrived at a PKK station on the mountain at 6:30 AM.

The PKK cleaned our wounds and treated them. They gave us food and water. They wanted to hear our story, but we were so exhausted, we could only tell them a short story that Daesh shot everyone and we ran. We rested two hours with the PKK, without being able to sleep from the pain.

I called my uncle who was working with Qassim Simmo, the Asayish (police) leader of Sunoni. When he arrived and saw me, he was shocked. The Asayish ambulance was there at the PKK check point. They drove Ali and me to Syria on a dirt road that the PKK had opened. From there they took us to the hospital in Zakho, Kurdistan, where I had emergency surgery under anesthesia. The doctor removed three bullets. I give thanks to God for surviving.

I went to my aunt's house near Duhok. She and others are living in an unfinished house. I stayed there two months to heal. In November 2014, Qassim Shesho, the Yezidi commander, saved me from my depression. I joined the volunteer Yezidi Peshmerga. I wore the Peshmerga uniform, but did not get paid. I got shot twice while serving under Qassim Derbo. Two Kurdish Peshmerga got shot at the same time. They took those Kurds to Erbil for surgery, but they took me to Syria for surgery.

I rejoined my unit when I got out of the hospital and returned to fighting. Kurdistan did not want an independent Yezidi military force, so 3,000 Yezidi volunteers were officially made part of the Kurdistan Peshmerga under Commander Qassim Shesho's leadership. This meant I could get paid, but we only get paid once every three or four months and then only for one month.

I am not here on Sinjar to leave Daesh alone. I am here to do the same to them, God willing. I will not do harm to their women and girls, but I will not pass any man. I will not do anything to kids either, because our religion does not accept such things. We are Yezidis.

On November 13, 2015, we liberated Sinjar city. The next day we identified a mass grave of eighty women from Kocho, over age forty, near Solagh. Even though the grave is not excavated yet, I know my dear mother's body is in that grave. Her ID card along with two or three others was found near the mass grave. She was sixty. May she rest in peace. We need an international team of forensic experts to excavate the grave site and identify the bodies. Until then, I cannot rest.

On December 16, 2015, my brave sister, Nadia Murad Bassee, told her story to the United Nations Security Council of what Daesh did to her and the Yezidi people. I am so proud of my sister. I give her all my love and respect. I hope the world leaders will listen to her requests on behalf of all the Yezidis. We have suffered a genocide and we need international help.

On May 26, 2017, I joined Hashd al-Sha'abi fighters with Nayef Al Jaso and other Yezidi men from Kocho and we liberated our village from Daesh. Afterwards, Kurdistan Asayish called me in for a meeting. They told me if I do not quit Hashd al-Sha'abi they will kick me and my family out of the camp and out of Kurdistan.

Said's sister-in-law, Muna, and her young son, Hani, returned from Daesh captivity in 2017, to live in an IDP camp in Zakho, Kurdistan. In April 2019, they emigrated to Australia. Her husband, Khairi, is one of Said's brothers who was killed.

Survivor of Qine Valley Massacre

Muhsin Elias Mahjo, September 25, 2020

On the morning of August 3, 2014, when we learned that Daesh was attacking Shingal, many families from Tal Qassab drove north on a rough dirt road to Qine. Qine is really just a few farm houses about 8 kilometers north of Tal Qassab on the southeast side of Shingal Mountain. My uncles, Fadil and Fileet Hachim Kashan, lived there. They survived because they were moving their sheep up onto the mountain when we arrived.

More than 200 or 300 people were resting there when a car of armed men arrived at 2 PM. They had captured my other uncle, Babir Hachim Kashan, who was in the car with them. They ordered Babir to stick his head out of the sunroof and tell all of us to fly a white flag and give them our phones, gold, cash, and weapons. I never saw my uncle again after that.

Right behind that car, another dozen or more vehicles arrived filled with armed men. They were driving Iraqi army and police vehicles seized from Mosul in June. One Hummer had a heavy-duty gun called a Doshka mounted on it. We were trapped because the dirt road ended at my uncles' house. The men were wearing the Daesh clothes of pants ending six inches above their ankles and shirts ending below the knee. Some had big beards. Others wore masks.

After they collected our phones, gold, cash, and weapons, the emir said they were going to take us to Snoni, a major Ezidi city one hour away by car on the north side of the mountain. They separated the women and children from the men and teenage boys and loaded them into the vehicles including our own cars. Then they drove off. Later I learned they took them to Tal Afar which was Daesh headquarters thirty kilometers to the east. My mother and nine sisters were among them.

Their emir ordered us to begin walking toward the mountain. He was about forty and could see out of only one eye. His right eye socket was empty. He didn't cover it. He wanted the whole word to see his wound. I was afraid of him, because I thought this man would be cruel to get revenge for his missing eye.

We walked up into the foothills on a single footpath through the weeds. They followed behind with their guns on us. I was filled with dread. As we were walking, I could see over my shoulder that some of the Daesh men were videoing us with their phones while the others were holding their guns on us. We reached the valley in ten minutes and were ordered to get into three lines of thirty each and sit down cross-legged facing the mountain. They stood at our backs. We knew the fate that was coming. I was only 24 (DoB 1990).

I overcame my fear and protested that two of the boys were too young and they needed to go with their moms. So one of the Arabs punched me in the face with his clenched fist and ordered me to stand up in the center of the first line. We faced the mountain with our backs to about thirty men who stood behind us with their guns pointed while others continued to take videos.

Khalif Mishko, an Ezidi, called out "Run" to all of us, but I was frozen with terror. Everyone was silent. No one moved. One man put his BKC gun on my back at the waist. A momentary thought flashed through my mind that I wanted to grab his BKC. I knew I was about to die. When I heard his gun click three times in rapid succession, I felt like a grenade had exploded inside my chest from fear. Through the dark, I heard the emir order his men to shoot.

The next thing I knew, I was lying on top of the man next to me. I don't remember going down. I lay motionless with my eyes closed, listened to the shooting. When it stopped I heard the emir speaking Turkish from Tal Afar. Others were speaking Arabic from Egypt. They said to shoot anyone who was moving. I could see from the slit in my eyes that they were still videoing with their phones. They went from man to man shooting anyone who was moving. I heard one man call out, "The man in the red t-shirt is alive. Shoot him."

I knew my cousin Khairi was wearing a red t-shirt. I heard them shoot him. I lay there disoriented. Maybe I lost consciousness. By some miracle, I did not have any bullet wounds. My executioner's gun had failed to shoot. Not more than thirty minutes had elapsed from the time we started walking until the shooting was over and the Daesh murderers were gone. When I finally moved, I walked up and down the three rows and checked each and every body to see if anyone were still alive.

All were dead including my father and five brothers. I did not want to leave them. I was numb with unimaginable despair and shock. I could not focus to think what I should do. I stayed there for twenty or thirty minutes in mourning, feeling heavy as stone. Finally, I began to walk up hill where I found Jalal Puko from Tal Qassab. Jalal was badly wounded. He had managed to walk, then crawl through the weeds on his belly about 500 meters before stopping.

I did not know how I could help him, so I had to leave him. I believe Daesh returned and found him and killed him there. I learned much later that seven other men escaped with their bullet wounds before I had opened my eyes.

I had never before been climbing on Shingal Mountain. It is very rocky, rugged, and steep. There was no path. The rocks cut my feet and the sharp prickers scratched my legs. It took me two hours to reach the top where I found a few people. I told myself I did not die from the massacre, but surely I would die from thirst. Then in five minutes I found a bottle of spring water and half a cucumber, so I knew I would live.

I kept walking without a path for three or four more hours. I did not know the way. It was dark when I stumbled into Qine Mirikand where about 3,000 people from Tal Qassab and Tal Banat were gathered. I was caked with dust from my sweat and tears, and my clothes were stained with blood. I collapsed at my friend's feet and mumbled, "They killed everyone. I have lost everything."

My friend replied, "At least you survived, thank God."

I answered, "No, I wish I had died, too."

Qine Mirikand was an old deserted village that had been destroyed in 1975 by Saddam Hussein's men when they forced all Ezidis off the mountain and onto the flat plains. The people from Qine Mirikand were relocated to Tal Qassab.

After nine days trapped on the mountain, we walked to safety in Syria and were driven to Kurdistan, Iraq. My mother, Sara Khudir Hassan, and six of my sisters escaped (without money) one by one in October 2014. They and I came to Germany in 2015 under a special program for survivors. Three of my sisters, Zeriva, Manar, and Yusra, are missing along with my niece, Sahirar Khudir Elias. We have no news of any of them.

In 2020, we heard my sister, Zeriva Elias Mahjo, was living in Al Hol refugee camp in Syria. This camp had 70,000 mostly women and children who were the families of Daesh fighters. Many Ezidis were being held there. Even though Daesh was declared defeated in 2017, we were told that we could get Zeriva back if we paid $20,000 US dollars. We could not possibly raise this money, but I went anyway to see her and discovered she was not Zeriva.

After six years we see no signs that any country wants to help us find and return our missing family members. Even though I live in Germany, I do not have one day of peace, knowing my sisters are missing.

Kocho Survivor Ali Abbas Walked 8 Days with Bullet Wounds in His Back
Ali Abbas Ismail Loko, October 2017

After Daesh took control of Mosul on June 10, 2014, we were trying to live our normal life in our small village of Kocho. Although many towns and villages surrounding us were controlled by Daesh, their fighters did not show any aggressive signs toward us in the beginning. The neighboring Yezidi village of Tal Banat was bombarded for nearly a month, but even this did not make us feel that we were in great danger because we had confidence in Peshmerga.

There were some rumors August 2, 2014, that Sinjar will be attacked by Daesh. So we went to the trenches dug around Kocho to protect Kocho alongside Peshmerga from a possible attack. At 2 AM on August 3, many Daesh troops came from Baaj to attack the nearby villages of Gir Zerik (Adnania), Qatania (Tal Ezeer), and Siba Sheikh Khudir (Jazeera). Meanwhile there were some other Daesh troops heading toward Tal Qassab and Tal Banat from Al Qayrwan.

During the night there were many clashes between the Daesh fighters and Peshmerga with Yezidi fighters using various kinds of weapons. The clashes continued until 5 AM and ended with Daesh controlling Gir Zerik. At 6 AM, Peshmerga retreated because of lack of weapons. Our village was left without any protection. We made many phone calls with our friends and they informed us that Daesh had taken control of Shingal.

As a result of this, many Yezidis escaped from their villages and also from Sinjar city and headed towards the mountain. In only two or three hours all the villages were empty of Yezidis for the first time in ages. At 9 AM, in that bloody black day, we escaped from Kocho, and we managed to reach Sinjar.

There were two of our relatives' families with us who also managed to escape in their cars. We and the two other families were stuck in the middle of Sinjar and we couldn't find a clear and safe way to the mountain because there were many Daesh checkpoints almost everywhere. So we were captured by one of these checkpoints and they asked us to convert to Islam. Then we told them that we want to return to our village Kocho, because we received phone calls from our people in the village and they told us that the Daesh leader, the person in charge of Kocho who was called Abu Hamza Al-Khatouni, had ordered that the people of Kocho are free to return to their homes and no one will harm them.

We put white pieces of cloth on our cars as we were returning to Kocho, so we managed to enter the village again. When we returned to Kocho, we heard that Abu Hamza Al-Khatouni was in the house of the mayor of the village, Ahmad Al Jaso Qassim. Abu Hamza told him that the Kocho people will be safe and he will not let anyone hurt us. He asked the mayor to collect all the weapons in the village. Every house should have a piece of white cloth on its roof. Every person in Kocho will get his own Daesh ID in his next visit.

On his second visit on August 6, 2014, Abu Hamza told the people of Kocho that he will give us four days, ending on August 10, to choose to convert to Islam or be killed. At that time, our village was surrounded by Daesh fighters.

Our clan leader, Ahmad Al Jaso Qassim, made many phone calls to the persons he knew and trusted from Arabs around our village. They were: Mahmoud Al-Khatouni, Mohammad Hamadi Al-Shemarri, Malik Nouri Jadaan Jarralah, Zaid Khalaf Al-Jassim, Hajim Menif Al-Houroosh, Salim Mulah Alou, Sarhan Rashid Al-Tahan and many others. They made a delegation that headed towards Mosul where they met the brother of the Daesh leader in Mosul. After the meeting, they called Ahmed Al Jaso in Kocho and told him that everything was okay. They had managed to extend the deadline to August 13 to review the case.

In the evening of August 11, 2014, Abu Hamza visited Ahmed Al Jaso's house and told him that he had met the Walli (leader) of Mosul. He told him that no one will harm people of Kocho and that they will not be forced to convert to Islam.

The next afternoon, Abu Hamza visited us again and told the mayor that they will allow us to leave our village as they allowed the Christians to leave Mosul on one condition. We had to leave all our properties and houses and they will allow us to leave in peace. Our leader, Ahmed, thanked him. Abu Hamza told us that he will find us a safe path to the mountain and he left us.

On the bloody Friday, August 15, 2014, at about 11 AM we were astonished and terrified when many troop of vehicles carrying large numbers of Daesh fighters entered Kocho from three directions. The fighters began to spread around the village. They warned people through speakers to gather in the high school yard and bring our gold, jewelry, mobile phones and money. Those who owned cars had to bring their cars and leave the doors unlocked and the key in the ignition. My people did not find any other way but to follow their orders, so we gathered and did what we had been told. There were 1172 people.

As we gathered in the school yard, Abu Hamza made a speech and said, "Since August 3, 2014, you have been liberated from the dark age you have been living in. You have been asked to convert to Islam, but you refused that. Today you have two choices: first to convert to Islam, and you will be allowed to keep all your properties in your houses and you live in peace. Second, you have to leave all your properties and leave your houses as we allowed the Christians in Mosul, and you will not be asked to convert to Islam."

Then Abu Hamza said we are free to make our choice. We felt happy when we heard that. The clan leader, Ahmad Jaso, thanked him for not forcing us to convert to Islam in return for our property. Ahmad advised the people to leave everything for them. That was his personal choice, but everyone is free to choose. Then Abu Hamza gave an order to gather every single mobile phone, jewelry, and money. We put them in different containers for each item.

Meanwhile, children and women were separated from the teenage boys and men and moved to the upper floor in the school. Men were moved in cars and KIA pickups, thirty persons in each pickup. We were thinking that they were moving them to a place near the mountain as they had promised. I was in the fourth pickup truck. I was surprised when we turned to a place outside the village, about 350 meters west of the village. The strangest thing was we were able to hear the aircrafts flying in the sky above us.

We were taken to a farm accompanied by armed military vehicles of Daesh. They forced us to walk to a dried pool made out of dirt which is used to contain water for watering the plants. We were forced to go inside that dried pool and ordered to get down on our knees. Then we could hear them yelling "Allah Akbar." I heard them telling each other "take some pictures." Then they shot us. After they had finished the shooting, they were saying, "This is what you get, you misbelievers, for not converting to Islam."

I could not believe at first that I was still alive. I was badly injured with very serious wounds in my shoulder, my head, and my back. Then they said to each other, "Let's shoot them in the head because some may still be alive." They left us about ten minutes later.

I called at the victims and said "Who is alive?" and "Can anyone save himself?" Then I heard two of them, Said Murad Pissee and Dilshad Sulaiman Qassim.

We started to creep out of the pool towards the west where we found another fifteen corpses. I tried to get close to the dead bodies to see if my cousin was among them, but I could not recognize anyone, because I was so terrified and we were in a hurry. Again we could hear the aircrafts flying above us without doing anything. [Author's note: this was a drone according to a secret intelligence report.]

The farm where we had been shot belonged to Ibrahim Ahmed Garris from Kocho. I am sure that 407 men and teenagers were killed in the same way. They were all taken from the school and that only lasted one or two hours.

Women and children were taken to Mosul as spoils of war according to Islam's belief. Women would be sold as sex slaves or even forced to marry the Daesh fighters. Children were sent to training camps to be trained to fight for Daesh. In this brutal and inhumane behavior, they had finished the existence of 1,172 people in just a few hours. God fuck them and their belief. They kill innocent people only because they refuse to convert to Islam. What happened to us in Kocho is only one of the thousands of crimes committed by Daesh against the Yezidis, the peaceful people of Shingal.

The Daesh fighters were taking the people from the school in groups. They were busy with shooting another group. At about one o'clock in the afternoon, we moved 300 meters north of the pool and reached a farm belonging to Simo Elias Khalaf from Kocho. Said Murad Pissee and I stayed in the generator cabin until nightfall. Our third friend, Dilshad, was ahead of us.

It was about 3 PM when we saw a bulldozer moving dirt to cover the bodies. It took fifteen minutes. We think that it buried the dead. The wounded men who could not walk were buried alive.

At night we left the farm towards the west where there was a small valley called Nekhellah. We hid there for an hour, then we headed toward another valley called East-West Valley which connects Kocho with Sinjar center. After we crossed the valley, we walked on the flat plain for half-hour. On the horizon we could see the lights on a cell phone tower. We thought it was Al Qapousi village. The distance was about ten kilometers, and we felt very tired and thirsty. It was about 1 AM when we reached Al Qapousi village. Said told me that he had a friend, Abu Ali (not real name), who lives in the village, and he could help us.

It was late when we entered Abu Ali's house without his permission when he was sleeping with his family in the garden because it was too hot to sleep inside. He was astonished and terrified when he saw us. We told him what happened with us in Kocho and they felt really sorry for that.

Abu Ali brought the medic in their village to the house. He was forced to lie to him, telling him that his old mom is sick. The medic treated our wounds and we thanked him a lot for saving our lives. After two hours, Abu Ali asked us to leave his house because Daesh had told them they will be punished if they help any Yezidis.

So we told him to show us a secure path to the mountain. He guided us towards a valley in the east of Al Qapousi. We walked about 250 meters when we heard the dawn call for prayer from a nearby mosque. Night was over and we could not make it to the safety of the mountain. We decided to go back to Al Qapousi before sunrise. On our way to the village we saw a man who was going to the mosque for prayer. We asked him to help us and he welcomed us. He took us to an old house on the outside of the village and left us there, then he went to the mosque.

When he returned from the mosque, he brought us breakfast. After breakfast, he brought a young man who dressed our wounds and took care of us for two days. After we told him our story, he got angry and said that what Daesh did to us is brutal, inhumane and true Islam does not allow it. He told us that there is someone we can trust who will help us get to Syria. In return we have to pay that person some money because my injuries were very serious. After lunch time, he took us to the abandoned farm of Kamil Khuder Khalaf, a Yezidi.

The farm was between Al Qapousi village and Domiz Complex. Our third friend, Dilshad, was waiting for us in that place. He had made an agreement with someone to take us to Syria. When we came to the place, we were looking for him when we saw in the distance some of Daesh's vehicles. That made the old man leave us in a hurry feeling terrified. It was about two o'clock in the afternoon. There were some shepherds and other people coming to the farm to get vegetables. We did not feel safe, so we hid in the abandoned farm.

We could not find Dilshad, although we had been looking for him for a long time. We could not do anything else but return to Al Qapousi, so we walked to the village. At about 10 PM a man came to Said and they talked for a moment. Then they called me to follow them to the house. He welcomed us and wept for what happened to us and said it was tragic. They washed our feet and hands because we were in a miserable condition and could not do it for ourselves.

After we had dinner, the owner of the house told us that he can have only one of us in his house, so I asked him if he can take me back to the house where we had been. He said ok and made his son take me. When we reached the house, the Muslim owner welcomed me and told me that he is going to keep me in an old abandoned house near his. He told me if Daesh finds me in that house, I should tell them I do not know him. He brought everything I needed to the old house. I stayed there for three days.

At that time he was working on how to get me out of there and take us to Zakho in Kurdistan through Syria. He agreed with a person to take us for $2000, but then that person asked $8000. I could not find anyone who could provide me with that sum of money. This man caring for me felt sorry because he did not have the money. He offered to raise some of the amount by selling his barely, but that did not work either.

On the third day, when it was afternoon, the man helping me told me that my friend Said is in a nearby farm with his brother, Khalid, who also managed to survive from one of the bloody massacres in Kocho. They gave me a mobile phone, some bottles of water and food and drove me to Said. They showed us the path to the mountain. At that time, my wounds began to bleed again, so the driver took off his shirt, tore it into pieces, and bandaged my wounds to stop the bleeding. Then they returned home. We were on our own.

At night we walked through the valley towards Al-Sabbahiya village near the highway which connects Sinjar with Tal Qassab village. When we reached the highway, we felt terrified and tried to cross to the other side to the east of the road. At this time we saw a laser light coming from a Daesh checkpoint near the main road junction in Sinjar. A car was heading toward us from Sinjar. We immediately ran and hid ourselves in an olive farm on the other side. After that, we walked in pitch darkness toward Solagh Valley in the east.

We continued walking through the valley until we came close to the main Highway 47 which connects Sinjar to Mosul. We were very careful in crossing the road to the other side toward the mountain when we heard some dogs barking. We were very worried that Daesh may notice us. At last, we made our way toward Solagh in the north, until we reached a spring of water. We drank as much as we could, washed our hands and faces, and filled up our bottles.

When we got near Solagh, another group of dogs barked at us and followed us. We spent half-an-hour trying to get rid of them. We saw three Daesh vehicles enter Solagh as they suspected that there may be some people around because too many dogs were barking. Finally, we reached the mountain. For the first time, we felt safe and enjoyed the peaceful short moment.

As I was laying down it was about twelve midnight. I was exhausted and had lost all my strength, so I asked my friends to continue without me to save themselves. I spent that night alone sleeping on a rock. In the morning, I continued walking toward Rashka's shrine until I reached the cemetery where I found a small bottle of water. I drank that water and continued on my way until I reached a place where there was a tractor. I managed to remove some water from its radiator. I filtered it with a piece of cloth to make it drinkable. I spent the night without food.

In the morning, I walked on my way through Qaly Haji toward Chel Meran Shrine on the top of the mountain. On the way I saw a shepherd, so I yelled at him and told him that I was wounded and needed help. He sent two Yezidis to help me,. They gave me some water and food and walked with me for a while until we reached a narrow path which is used by sheep and goats. They told me to go on that path until I see people on the top of the mountain.

Before I could reach my destination, the two Yezidi guys brought a donkey to carry me. It was 2 PM on August 23, 2014, when I reached the PKK fighters on the top of the mountain. It had taken me eight days from the time I was shot. The PKK medics cleaned and bandaged my wounds. I thanked them a lot. They told me that Daesh are in Syria, but they could send me to a place under PKK control.

One of my relatives who works for the PDK Asayish (security police) took me to Zakho Hospital through the Syrian border. My cousin was waiting for me at the hospital in Zakho where he performed surgery on me and removed the bullets. I spent fifteen days recovering in the hospital. I thank each one who helped me, and I thank Zakho medical team for their kindness.

My brothers' wives and children are still missing. Also, my two sisters and their children are missing. It has been two-and-a-half years since the attack, and we have heard nothing from any of them. I am in very bad physical and mental health. I am living in a camp and no one is helping me. I need to get out of Iraq to feel safe and get some relief.

Separating the Girls from the Married Women

Ivana Waleed Hussein, August 4, 2015

I was seventeen when Daesh attacked my village in Shingal one year ago on August 3, 2014. I was going to school and living with my family in Tal Qassab Kevan and was very happy. When Daesh attacked us, we ran away to Shingal mountain, but they captured me, my mother, and my little brother Gallop. Also, they captured twenty-five of my close relatives when we were on the mountain.

My village is a border village between a large Arab city named Baaj and other Arab villages on one side and Kurdish villages on the other side. Half of my village of Tal Qassab Kevan was Yezidi and the other half was Sunni Muslims.

The first time I heard Daesh attack us was at 3 AM. The fighting continued to grow stronger, hour by hour. At 7 AM everyone else ran away. Also, Peshmerga ran away, but we did not believe that Shingal was finished.

At 8 AM we saw that everyone was gone, so twenty-five of us left in only two cars and headed toward Shingal mountain which is about twenty minutes by car. When we got outside of Tal Qassab Kevan, we saw Daesh 200m from us. When we ran away, the fighting stopped. Then we knew that Shingal was finished.

When we were going, we heard a bomb in the center of Sinjar in Zeyneb neighborhood where Shia Arabs live. So everyone was afraid and all the cars were leaving. The cars were stopped on the road, trying to move. Some Yezidis called us from Hatamia and from Kocho villages. They told us that Daesh had said to them, "Don't run away. They will never take us. This is normal. We just want to finish off the Kurdistan government, not the people. "

So, they told us, "When Daesh sees you, raise a white flag. Daesh will not hurt you." We had reached the road going out of the city and up the mountain." We stopped and we stayed there, low on the mountain, until 12 noon. At 12 o'clock, Daesh attacked us with four cars and took nearly 500 Yezidis. We were men, women, and children. The first people Daesh took was my own family.

The Arab men told us to divide into two groups: one Yezidi and one Muslim. They took the Yezidis away. We were in that group. Later they told us that they killed the Shia Muslim and let the Sunni Muslim go free. The Daesh said they came from Saudi Arabia. I saw him shoot and kill someone only two or three meters behind me. At first there were only ten Daesh, but more came until there were twenty or thirty.

They divided the kidnapped Yezidis into men and women with their children. They put us in the cars and drove us back to the center of Sinjar. They put us in the new government building for jensias (Iraqi citizenship cards). We were nearly 400 women and children and young unmarried girls. There were no men.

We arrived at 1 in the afternoon and stayed until 8 PM. The first time some Daesh told us that Yezidis have no god and they would make us convert to Islam. They gave us the choice to be Muslim or be killed. Everyone was crying and sad. I said to myself, "Ok, they can kill me, because I will never be a Muslim."

At 2 PM in the afternoon, Daesh took us out of the building and we saw a lot of men. We were together. Nearly twenty Daesh guarding us.

My situation was very difficult. We had no water or food. All the children were crying. It was so bad. It was so hot. I had a phone, so I called my father. I told him that Daesh told us they would kill us if we do not agree to be Muslims. My father was crying.

They asked who was single and they took the young single girls. Daesh chose the nicest ones and took sixty girls away in cars. They did not take me. I was keeping myself hidden. When they took the sixty girls, they came back to take another group of girls at 8 PM. They looked carefully through the entire group and they took the remaining young girls.

I had a black scarf and I covered my face with it like a veil. Three times the Daesh came near me, but did not take me. The fourth time Daesh removed my scarf and took me and my cousin. I was crying. My cousins Manal, Malyeen, and Barivan were with me in the car. A Daesh man took us to Baaj. His name was Abu Saad.

The car broke down, so we had to stop. We tried to run away, but two Daesh men stopped us with Kalashnikov guns. One Daesh man called another Daesh and they sent us a new car. They took us to Baaj where we arrived at 12 midnight. Abu Saad is from Baaj. He is Arabic, Meteowta tribe. His family lives in Syria. He is 38. He said, "I have been working with Daesh since 2007."

He asked us our names and if we would agree to be Muslims. They moved us into a school with two floors. He told me, "You will be a Muslim, and you will be mine."

The school is the Daesh base camp. Daesh had nearly twenty young girls, women and children inside when we arrived. We asked them where they were from. They said from Kocho and from Tal Ezeer. We stayed three days in the school. They locked the door and gave us food and water. One Arab woman came into the school. Her name is Tarfa from Baaj. She told us, "You will be Muslims. We will divide all of you and give you as gifts for the Daesh men."

After five minutes, she taught us to say a Muslim prayer. All the time, I was thinking about my mother and baby brother and wondering where they are. The Arab woman taught us to say, "Ashhadu an la ilaha illallah, wa ashhadu anna Muhammadan rasulullah," which means something like "I swear that Muhammad is the messenger of God." All of us Yezidi kidnapped had to repeat it.

Tarfa told us that if we repeated this Muslim prayer, we would be allowed to be free. I refused to say it. Some others repeated it, but not me. Two cars took us back to Sinjar city. We saw another group of Yezidis in three cars. In this group of five cars, they drove us to Tal Afar and put us in a school. In that school there were nearly 500 kidnapped Yezidis. I was searching for my mother, but I did not see her.

We stayed three days in this school. They gave us food and water, but very little. It was a very bad situation. After three days, they put us in five cars and moved us to Badoush prison in Mosul. This is the same prison where Daesh killed 670 mostly Shia Muslims on June 10, the day after Daesh took control of Mosul.

In Badoush prison, I found my mother, Dallal, and my baby brother, Gallop. There were nearly 3,000 Yezidis there. There were no men there.

My situation was very, very bad. We were so hungry. We had no food or water, so we used the water from the toilet faucet. We could not sleep. We stayed there eight days.

A plane bombed the electric plant, so they moved us to another school in Tal Afar city. I was together with my mother and brother. Daesh separated the members of every family. So I was separated from my mother and brother again. They selected 500 girls and took them, including me.

On August 12, 2014, at 12 midnight, they moved us to Mosul. They put us in an apartment building with four floors. We saw 200 young girls already there when we arrived, so then we were 700. Daesh wrote down each girl's name and age.

Sheikh Abdullah came to us. He was the assistant to Abu Bakir Baghdadi who was the supreme Daesh leader in Iraq of their so-called caliphate. Abu Lite was also there along with Haji Bakir, the manager of Tal Afar. Abu Saad, the manager of Daesh government in Tal Afar, and Abu Waleed, the driver for Abu Lite, were there. They wrote all of our names down. One of the Daesh was inspecting each of the girls. They would read our name and the girl would step forward. They would look at her face, make her turn around and look at her entire body.

If they liked her face, they put her in a different room and made her remove her clothes. If they liked her body, they raped her. I saw them take my friend like this. When my friend returned in tears, I asked her what had happened. She told me a man had raped her.

All of the six Daesh men had a sword. While they were looking at each girl, they were swinging their swords in the air. Sheikh Abdullah, assistant to Abu Bakir Baghdadi, tapped me on my head with his sword and ordered me to sit down. I was too afraid to sit down. I thought to myself, "I will never have sex with him. They can kill me."

He grabbed my arm and pushed me to sit down. He said to me, "I love you.
I want *you*."

They had made two groups. One was for the nicest girls. He put me in that
group. He said to me, "I will marry you."

Immediately, I told him, "I am married. I have a husband."

He asked me, "Who is your husband?"

I said, "My cousin. His name is Moneer." He was with me in Shingal
mountain when we were caught, so I knew he was with Daesh. Sheikh Abdullah
believed me. He told me, "I will find your husband. If I find him, I will take you
to him. If I don't find him, I will take you for myself."

Moneer did not know I said this. I never loved my cousin Moneer. I had a
boyfriend, but I told Daesh this lie. Sheikh Abdullah looked for Moneer. Since
he is the manager, he called Tal Afar and asked another Daesh for Moneer. They
hung up the phone. A few minutes later someone called back and put Moneer on
the phone. Sheikh Abdullah directly handed the phone to me and said, "Here is
Moneer."

I spoke in Kurdish to Moneer, so Daesh would not understand me, and I
explained to him that I had told Daesh he was my husband. I told him that if
Daesh asked him if I am his wife, please say, "Yes."

Sheikh Abdullah told me he would send me back to Tal Afar to my
"husband" Moneer. He kept his word and sent me.

Then Daesh divided the kidnapped Ezidis into individual families. They sent
the families to houses in the village of Qaser Al Mehrab in Tal Afar. My cousin
Moneer and I would be a family. This is a normal Shia village, but it was empty
because the Shia had fled. I was with my mother, little brother, cousin Moneer
and Moneer's family in one house.

We were 234 persons in Qaser Al Mehrab where we stayed five months.
They turned one building into a mosque for us. They took all the men, including
Moneer, to the mosque and made them pray to Allah. They told us, "Everyone
now is Muslim. You will be free in Qaser Al Mehrab."

Daesh made a video of the men being converted to Islam and put it on the
internet. Moneer is in this video.

He told us that if anyone tries to run away, he will be killed. Daesh did kill
men who tried to escape.

Daesh took ninety women and girls with no husbands and sent them to Syria.

We lived in the village like normal. Everyone knew Moneer was not my
husband, but we were just acting.

Daesh tried to take me, but others said, "She has a husband." Sometimes,
they asked, "If she has a husband, why isn't she pregnant?"

My cousin, Viyan, was also kidnapped and living in Tal Afar with the manager of Tal Afar. He let her visit me often. She defended me and told the manager not to let anyone take me, because I had a husband. So Daesh moved me and my family back into Tal Afar in Hiel Hadra. The citizens of Tal Afar were so bad to us.

They were using us as farm laborers. We were taking care of the cows for four months. We heard that someone ran away, so we knew it was possible to run away. We always had a phone and we were talking with our father in Kurdistan and sometimes my uncle in the refugee camp in Turkey. Thirty-four of my relatives made a plan to escape.

My father, who was free, sent me a phone number and told me to call that number. I called it and the man told me to go to Heil Al Wahda, the name of a street. We went there and hid behind the bushes. We were wearing black Muslim clothing. The women's faces and entire bodies were covered.

On April 26, 2015, we escaped with some food and water with us.

Someone gave us the address of an old house to go to. We went there and stayed in the house. The Daesh smuggler told us they would come to get us at 8 PM when it was dark. He came to get us with two cars. They took eighteen people in the two cars, including Moneer. That group took the phone with them, so we were left without a phone.

I was left behind with my mother, my brother, Gallop, and fifteen people. Moneer was gone and I am still in Tal Afar. The smuggler said they would return to get us in two hours. We waited two hours, three hours and finally we waited five days. We had no food or water so we could not live. Some Yezidis in other houses knew we had run away and were hiding. They helped us with food and water.

My mother decided to risk going outside for help. She asked two young men to give us some food. Immediately, the two young men went to the manager of Tal Afar and reported that we were in the house. Daesh came immediately and took us.

Daesh took the men from our group. Haji Bakir, the governor of Tal Afar, took me as his wife (raped me) and sent my mother and brother to Syria.

Three Daesh men "married" me. First, a forty-year-old midget took (raped) me one time. Then Daesh took me to another man for one night. Then the governor Haji Bakir took me to his house and also raped me. I spent two months with him.

Sometimes I would see my cousin Viyan. She and I made a plan to run away. We escaped wearing black Muslim dresses and veils over our faces with her two children, Naam and Diljon. We spent one night running away in one deserted house.

Continued with Viyan Havind's story.

In 2015, I went to Germany with my mother and siblings. We live in an apartment building for refugees. The German program did not allow my father to join us, so we are sad, because after Daesh separated us for a year from our father, now we are still separated from him by the German government. None of the men over age eighteen were allowed to come to Germany with the women and kids who escaped Daesh.

We saved our money and sent it to my father in Iraq. In 2017, he spent four months in Turkey trying unsuccessfully to smuggle to Germany through Bulgaria, but it was impossible. He returned to his camp in Kurdistan, Iraq. We remain separated from my father after nearly four years. This family separation, after how Daesh separated us, is so painful we can never be happy like this.

The Badden-Wurttenburg program for survivors did not allow male family members over age 18 to join their female family members in Germany. In 2018, Ivana's father, Waleed, succeeded in smuggling himself to Hungary where he was fingerprinted. He applied for asylum in Germany to join his family. After waiting five months, his asylum was approved. The family was reunited after four years of separation.

Viyan, Prisoner of Daesh Governor of Tal Afar
Viyan Havind Khalaf, March 19, 2016

I am Viyan Havind from Tal Qassab Kevan. I was married and living with my husband, Basman Alyas, in Kocho. He operated a medical clinic. We had a nice house and two beautiful children. That day on August 15, 2014, when Daesh came to Kocho, we lost everything. We didn't just lose our money and gold and phones and cars. No. We lost our happy lives and the very earth itself. Even we lost our men. They took Basman from me.

A few days before the attack, the Daesh leader Abu Hamza visited with our clan leader. We all knew we were trapped. We knew about what Daesh had done in all the other Shingal towns, so the clan leader of Kocho, Ahmed Jaso al-Mandkany, offered to give all our gold jewelry and sheep to Daesh if they would let us escape to the mountain. This was a very desperate offer. It meant we would give Daesh everything and be destitute in exchange for our lives.

On the day of the attack, they came in 200 cars and pickup trucks from two directions. There were nearly 1,000 men. Abu Hamza, the Daesh leader, talked to our clan leader, Ahmed Jaso, and ordered him to tell everyone to report to the school with our money and gold. He said Daesh would drive us to the mountain.

That morning my father sent our Kurdish Muslim neighbor of twenty-five years to our house. He offered to take us to the mountain, but my husband said "no". Daesh promised that in one hour everything would be settled and they would take everyone to the mountain. Kocho was already surrounded.

I gave our friend all my gold jewelry worth $12,000. He promised to return it to me in Erbil if we got free. I kept one bracelet and my earrings so I would have some gold to give Daesh when we reported to the school. When I got free eleven months later, our friend kept his promise and returned my gold.

In the school, I gave Daesh $100 dollars and my jewelry. My wedding ring was the last thing I gave them. Twice in my dreams I dreamed of two gold wedding bands falling on the floor and rolling away from me.

They asked us to agree to be Muslim. Our men did not agree. We women followed our men's decision. It was not good for us, because Daesh is an enemy of the whole world, so how could we side with Daesh? We would not agree to join this organization, because it was not like a political party like a Kurdish one or like in America.

From the time of our ancestors, in Iraq there were political parties we have joined. Many governments came, and always we were with those who liked humanity. Daesh is not a government party we could join. But unfortunately, even though we did not join the terrorists, no one defended us or took revenge or reclaimed our rights. What a shame. I see today no one cares about us and did not do anything for us yet.

After they separated me from my husband and sent all the women and children to the second floor of the school, they took the men outside and drove away. We heard the sound of bullets. The weather turned dark and a great wind storm broke a window in the school.

Two young boys around age nine were with the men. They escaped and ran back to the school and said, "We saw our fathers and brothers being killed. They lined them up and shot them. We are children, so Daesh said to us, 'We will take you back and make you fighters. We will train you and make you Muslims. Only we are the real Islam. We will teach you the Quran and about Islam. We are not going to kill you.' "

When the boys came back and said the men were killed, we screamed and began weeping and wailing, "They are killing our men!"

We stayed one hour in the school. After they finished taking the men, they took the women and children in cars to Solagh Institute. I tried to escape, but the car door was locked.

The men who captured us had big black beards, but no mustaches. Their cheeks were shaved so that their beards ringed their chin. They wore black, brown, or grey dresses to the knees with pants underneath that were six inches above their ankles. They dressed like Pakistani men.

In Solagh they made us wear black scarves with only our eyes showing. After a few months, when we were moved to Tal Afar, we also had to cover our eyes and wear black gloves and socks when we went out. Every square inch of us had to be covered in black.

In Solagh Institute we were so many. We were the entire population of Kocho. First they asked for girls. Abu Saoud from Mecca, Saudi Arabia, was there. He took thirty-eight single girls between ages twenty and thirty years. I gave my three-year-old daughter to my sister-in-law so they would think she was married. Abu Saoud also took about twenty-five boys between the ages of five and fourteen years.

They muscled in among us and took infants and boys. I saw with my own eyes they took infants who were still nursing at their mother's breast. The mothers said, "I have only this one." It was really true that one mother had only one, because her older children had been killed. They beat her until she was unconscious and took away her infant. I managed to keep my six-month-old baby with me.

I said to myself, as long as they don't take us and violate our honor. I saw thousands of others like us. Not only my husband and I were in this same situation. Even I would say to myself, I did not want to be the only one rescued. Because they tortured Yezidis, I wouldn't want to get preferential treatment.

I myself heard that the Daesh governor referred to as "wallie" would gain his position as wallie when he kills many people and does nasty things like torturing and beheading people who are Yezidis and Shias. Even Christians, but not the same as to Yezidis and Shias.

And then they get promoted to Emir. The Emir would select five or six girls as his wives; young girls who were not yet having their periods. They were nine years old. They said, "Get them, we want to rape them."

I asked myself, how can this happen? I objected by saying, "This is not right according to God's teachings. And it is not acceptable in heaven or on earth to treat girls like this. It is illicit."

They said, "Yes, it's acceptable according to our religion."

Not just one or two said this. Everyone agreed this was lawful in their Islamic religion to take nine-year-old girls.

I became upset. I said to myself, "It is better to be killed, than to be taken in their hands."

In the morning, they wrenched all the older women over age fifty away from their daughters and daughters-in-law. These were the elders whom they thought were too old for raping. I was with my mother-in-law.

I asked, "Where are you taking her? Take me with her." I followed her outside with about eighty older women.

They said, "You have a child. If you are not married, give this child to its mother (my mother-in-law), so we can take you with the single girls." They thought the child was my mother-in-law's, and so I gave her my baby.

They said, "If this child is yours and if you are married, we will take this woman and kill her with the elderly women."

At that moment, I was so distressed, I could not make a choice. I could neither pretend to be single and give away my honor, nor could I let them kill my mother-in-law. I was so distressed that I could not talk, so my mother-in-law answered for me, "This is my daughter-in-law, and this is her child."

They gave me back my son. A friend of mine said, "I would like to go with my mother-in-law."

She was pregnant and in the last month of her pregnancy. She recently got married. They took her with the elders and shot them. I swear by God, I was the last one who returned back to the Solagh Institute from the elderly women being killed. I heard only about seven shots. I was told that before they died, some were buried alive, even without shooting them first. Afterwards, one of the Daesh men told me my mother-in-law was in the ground.

The only people left inside were married women between thirty-one and forty-nine years, some younger girls, and boys under age five. Eight boys had been hiding, but Daesh threatened us with a sword and found them. They took the boys, including my husband's brother, Salih Alyas, who was thirteen.

Their Emir, Abu Saoud from Saudi Arabia, chose me first from among all the women. He was the Daesh leader for all of Shingal. Abu Saoud said to me, "I will take you for myself."

He was tall and fat with a big black beard and black makeup under his eyes. He looked to be about thirty-five. I saw the blood stains of Kocho people on his clothes.

I told him, "No, I cannot agree. I want my husband."

He said, "No, I killed your husband."

I answered, "Despite everything you have done, you killed my husband and destroyed my family, you are going to take away my honor? I'm not coming."

He said, "If you do not marry me, I will take your baby boy."

Still I refused, and so he took my baby away. When he took my baby, I said, "I will hang myself."

He said, "Really, you will hang yourself?

I said, "Yes."

He said, "No, don't bother to hang yourself. I can kill you myself." He waved his sword and said, "I can cut your head off right now."

My friends cried out and tried to protect me from him and pleaded, "Don't kill her. Leave her with us."

He said, "I'm not going to kill you, but you are going to see what is going to happen to you next and how many of us will take you."

He brought my baby back and took a photo of us. He said he would return the next day for me. I asked my friends for clothes and changed so he might not recognize me. I moved to the other side of the room, and a guard saw me. He asked me what I was going to do.

I said I was going to kill myself. He said, "No, don't say that. There is a God."

I said, "If God exists, why are you doing this to us?"

And of course, we know God. And we consider him as the greatest one. No one is greater than him, and we worship God. From first to last, there is only one God. We say it in Kurdish, that God is the greatest, but they don't accept it because we don't say it in Arabic. So they said to us, "You don't believe in God."

I asked, "I am an Iraqi girl. How are these Saudis and Syrians purchasing me? What kind of conscience do you have?"

He said to me, "He's Saudi and he is our Emir. There is nothing I can do."

I said, "Alright. *Allah Kareem* (God is merciful, but your day we will come). I will kill myself."

He said, "Don't kill yourself." He told me he was from Mosul and he said, "I know Yezidis are good people." He helped me by hiding me that night in another room. The next day he took me and my baby with ten women and their children to Tal Afar. I never saw that man again. After leaving Solagh Institute and escaping from the Emir, Abu Saoud, I felt free by comparison.

I stayed eleven months in Tal Afar before I escaped. I was taken, bought and sold and raped by four men. I was always being moved from house to house. It would take me ten years to tell how I suffered. Even my ordeal was not as bad as that of many other girls and women.

They put us in a school in Tal Afar filled with 3,450 Yezidi women and children. We were without our men. They did not serve food or water. We got one sandwich each day and it had ants in it. There was no washing. The babies had diarrhea and dehydration. They were vomiting. They had no clothes, because when we escaped, we had only the clothes on our backs. We stayed there eighteen days.

There were five Yezidi men with us. They would go for the food, because we women were afraid if we went, a Daesh man would take us. Unfortunately, when we would go to wash in groups of three or four women, three of these Yezidi men would demand sex in exchange for giving us food. I had my baby and I refused.

We lacked everything. I saw babies dying all around me every day. Daughters and sons were dying. Mine also was about to die. He needed milk, but I had none for him. I could not hold him anymore. I knew if we stayed there, we would die. I asked the guard to help me. "My baby is sick," but he said he could not help, because the situation outside was bad. So I got an idea.

I told the guard, "If you can't help me, then take my baby. I don't want him anymore." He called his superior.

I said, "Why are you doing this? What have we done? Tell me the reason. We are the same as you, worshipping God. We are Tawus Melak followers. What's wrong with that?"

And now I'm saying, like I used to say when I was with them, if it is true that because of Yezidi religion, I would like every Muslim to hear what I say. I say this not for only one or two Muslims. To those who hear me, I tell the truth, Yezidi people were not killed for religion, because Daesh is not a religion. It was all about violating our honor and stealing our property.

A woman like me, how would my husband give me to another man to be raped? If they know my husband is alive, they would know that he will come to protect his dignity and his honor. So they would kill my husband first, and then take me and my children.

They killed the men and raped the women to destroy our culture. Our men would not accept our honor to be violated. So they decided to kill the men first, then buy and sell the women. They took the daughters as sex slaves and servants.

Our men did not want to convert to Islam and join them. Daesh said they will raise our children and train them in Islam.

Everyone must know, they told us, "Because you are Yezidis, we are doing this to you."

I asked the man in charge, "Why do you treat us like this without conscience? You do not give us food and you have not given milk for my son. Five children have already died from starvation."

He told me, "We are doing this to you to force each one like you to follow one like me and to marry me for the sake of your children. You have to come, and you will kiss my hand and you will tell me, 'Take me for yourself,' or you will see in front of you that your children are tormented to death."

I cried out and put my baby on the table. I said, "Let it be yours. If he dies, it's your fault, not mine." I started to walk away.

He said, "Ok, let me take you to the doctor." I believed him.

"I will take your son to the doctor," He said to me. "My wife is pregnant, so come and be our servant until God decides our fate and for the sake of your son."

That night the driver took me and my baby to the main hospital in Tal Afar, then left. The doctor was in medical school. He was good to us. I was alone in the hospital with two doctors and my child.

That night two Daesh men came and tried to take me away. I cried and resisted them. My baby and I stayed two nights in the hospital until another driver came for us and returned us to Tal Afar school. From there they piled us into empty houses in Tal Afar that had belonged to Shias before they fled. We used anything left inside the houses. We were prisoners. If they could, they would have prevented us from seeing the sun.

If the prisoners were old or handicapped or not beautiful, Daesh did not care about the family, so some people starved to death. When they did give us food, the products they were giving us were from Turkey, even a bottle of water was imported from Turkey. I saw that they were importing and exporting from Turkey.

Periodically, men would come and view us and select us for selling. Some would come from Syria. Others would come from Libya, Kazakistan, America, Belgium, France, Germany, from everywhere. When they showed us, they would tell each Daesh man to come and select one woman for himself.

I kept my baby with me, and he was always crying, so I did not get taken. If there was a young girl available, why would they take a married woman with two children to feed? Then one man told me "Tomorrow we will take you to Raqqa, Syria."

I was afraid because we knew Daesh was taking the single girls to Raqqa and selling them in the slave market for sex. I asked one man to help me stay in Tal Afar. He took me and my baby to a house with a Yezidi family who was also kidnapped.

Daesh lived in the same house with us, but they were not always there. We were free to go out and walk around, but the Yezidi family would not go out with me. They said if anyone saw me, they would take me because I was beautiful. Even though we were free in the village, we were trapped in Tal Afar because of

Daesh security guards around the city.

People from Baaj and Syria would kill Yezidis when they captured them. Those from Mosul would not hold captives, but they would take the most beautiful girls. The cruelest treatment we received happened at the hands of the Sunnis from Tal Afar. After some months, more and more Sunnis returned to live in Tal Afar. Tal Afar Sunnis tortured us.

Winter was coming. It was rainy and cold. I needed clothes. I lived alone with my son in one small upstairs room. I thought I would die with this life. One day when the manager of Tal Afar delivered the food to our house he saw me. He said, "I want you. Will you marry me?"

I refused. Three days later the governor of Tal Afar told me, "If you do not marry the manager of Tal Afar, I will send you and your children to Syria." I knew he could really do this, so I agreed to marry the manager. I said, "I have one condition. I have to have both of my children with me."

The Daesh manager of all the prisoners in Tal Afar was Mohammad Salih, an Arab. When he came to get me, I said I would be his servant, but I did not want to marry him. He had a wife who was pregnant. He agreed and promised that no one could take my children from me. He took me to his house, but did not return my daughter to me. She remained living with my husband's sister. I did not have my daughter with me for eight months.

After two days, Mohammad pressured me to marry him. He said, "You are going to see what I am going to do to you if you do not stay with me in bed and accept me as your husband."

I refused, so he beat me in the head and punched my nose until it bled. I decided to hang myself. I tied my scarf to the railing on the staircase and wrapped the other end around my neck. Mohammad's wife prevented me from jumping and told her husband.

I begged and pleaded with him and told him, "My pain is too deep. You men took my husband and now you want to rape me? I will agree to be your servant and anything else, except do not rape me."

He picked up my son and said, "You can choose between your son or your life. I have a friend who is a doctor in Tal Afar. He does not want a Yezidi woman, but he wants a boy, because his wife is infertile."

He took my son. I followed him and begged him not to take him away and told him instead, "Kill us both."

Mohammad told me, "Then I will take you now for myself instead of your baby."

I became hysterical. When they asked us to convert to Islam, I thought this is overwhelming, but then when they took my husband, this was even more overwhelming. Then when they demanded sex, it was much worse. But then when they asked for my son, I said this is even more overwhelming than taking my honor (rape).

I have nothing but these kids. They took everything from me. I am destroyed, also, on the inside.

He told me, "Come. I want to take you now."

I said to him, "You betrayed me. You are married and have a wife. This is not what we agreed to. We are not the same religion. You do not need to get married again."

I begged him so much. I was enraged. He came towards me and I spit at him. He insulted me and spit back at me. He started beating me. Actually, I wanted him to kill me in order to avoid being raped. He punched me in the face and my nose was bleeding. I wiped the blood off myself.

Mohammad did everything to me, beating and everything. He knocked me down and choked me with his hands. I had the red marks on my neck for one month. Finally, he tied my hands, and he brought a pill for me.

He told me to swallow this pill. "It is for psychological conditions. I also take this pill."

Because I was so depressed, even if the pill was poisonous, I would have swallowed it. I swallowed the pill at midnight. He gagged my mouth, then he raped me with my son in the room. At 6 AM I woke up. I found myself naked lying in bed next to his naked body. I said, "How can your conscience allow you to do this?"

I got up and put my clothes on. Mohammad said, "What are you going to do?"

"I'm going to the kitchen to make breakfast," I said. I could not take it anymore. I was so depressed. He knew it and came with me. I opened the drawer and pulled out a knife to cut my wrist. He grabbed it from me, and we struggled.

I said, when he takes my son, my husband, my family, my sisters, my husband's sisters and brothers who are like my own sisters and brothers . . . His mother is like mine, too. I said after all he does to me, and during the night to have sex with me, I definitely will not accept this. So when I cut myself, he knew that I was going to kill myself.

They took me by force to the doctor for Yezidis, and I got four stitches in my wrist. I have a scar as a reminder.

Even the doctor was sympathetic and cried for me, because he sees women who are like me in the same psychological condition who are doing things to themselves, and he is forced to treat them. So even the doctor was affected and became disturbed.

Another time I drank poison. They found me unconscious. Another time I jumped from the roof. Four times I tried to commit suicide to end my pain.

The manager of Tal Afar is not human. It would not be right to call Daesh human in the media. Their acts are inhumane. They destroy every living thing.

They would kill animals and even a bird flying overhead. They would kill a dog, a mule. I saw with my own eyes in the houses that had belonged to Shia, they closed the gates on the animals in the yard and left them to die.

They destroyed houses. They demolished cities and towns. They destroyed everything. They call themselves Muslims, but then they destroyed mosques. It did not make sense. They said, "We are the real Islam."

If I would tell them that Shia militia, who were fighting Daesh, are also Muslims, they would say, "No, they are not. *We* are the real Islam. We are Sunnis. We are the *real* Sunnis." They say, "We will not do anything to Sunnis, but we kill Yezidis and Shia, and it is halal, meaning permissible by the Quran."

Mohammad was obsessed with me. He told me he loved me and he wanted me to love him. I told him I could not love him ever because I have a husband and because Mohammad is Daesh. After he would rape me, I would be crying and he would cry with me. I was always crying, so he took me to Mosul for three days to his other wife and four children. He wanted her to comfort me.

She hated me, but his mother and two sisters were kind to me. I told them about my family who had escaped to Kurdistan. Mohammad told them to take me to another room to teach me the Quran. Then they secretly let me call my father and brother-in-law in Kurdistan while they listened. My family was so excited to hear I was alive. I asked them to contact Daesh and make a plan to rescue me.

The mother asked me if I would convert to Islam and I agreed to. She asked me if I would forget the Yezidis and I promised I would. She asked if I would agree to be Muslim. I said "yes". I had to memorize verses from the Quran and pray five times per day. I was lying to win their trust. She talked to her son and asked him to let me return to my mother and father, but he refused. Mohammed's mother said she was helpless to help me.

I cried and did not eat. His mother asked me why I was crying. I showed her a photo of me and my sister, Jiyan, and my mother.

For months I kept crying and resisting Mohammad. We fought constantly and he got angry with me.

On April 1, 2015, Mohammad rented me to another Daesh man in exchange for a Kalashnikov gun. This man's Daesh name was Baqir. All Daesh used fake names in front of us, even for their wives and children, so we could not accuse them in court later, but I secretly searched for his ID and discovered Baqir's real name was Haithem Hussein. He was forty-five. Haithem Hussein beat and raped me.

After two weeks, Mohammad came and took me back to his own house. Again, he kept asking me to marry him, but I always refused. He beat me and raped me anyway. After he beat me, he cried with me because I refused to love him. He did not sleep with the other women. He wanted only me.

I was not allowed to have my daughter for eight months, but I visited other Yezidi captives and heard Daesh men talking in Turkish. They thought I do not understand Turkish. They were telling each other if they take my sister-in-law to Syria, they can keep my little girl for themselves. She was only two. This is *my* daughter.

I asked them, "Why are you men taking my daughter?"

They told me, "Because Syria will be taken, and they kill kids in Syria, but they do not kill kids in Iraq. Sunnis take them for themselves and adopt them, because they are so young and frightened they will be like us in the future."

I went to them and asked for my daughter and told them she's mine, not my sister-in-law's.

They would not believe me and would not give her to me. They tested my daughter and son and found that it was true that they were mine.

Mohammed, who was keeping me as his prisoner said, "Since you lied to me and told me this is not your daughter, I know what to do to you for not telling me."

I replied, "I told you she was mine, but you refused to give her to me."

He said, "I did not have to feed all three of you."

He beat me a lot, then he did sell me. I was standing up in the same place where I was sold before. He handed me over to the walli of Tal Afar for $3,200 dollars. At least I had my daughter with me.

In their organization there was a "wallie" and a "caliph" (leader of Islamic State or ISIS). They call Abu Bakir Al-Baghdadi "caliph".

They were applying Mohammed's teachings. They were doing as Mohammed taught them according to his book and applying it with us. So they call the leaders "wallie" and "caliph". The wallie was Tal Afar's governor. His name was Faisal.

Governor Faisal was the same man who had made me go with Mohammed, the manager of Tal Afar, months earlier. He put me into his car with my children. It looked like he was wearing a suicide vest. There were bombs in the back of the car. My children sat on top of them.

He asked me to marry him, but I refused. He grabbed me roughly behind my neck and said, "If you do not marry me, I will let your children play with the bombs. Maybe they will explode. If you want to save your children, you will marry me now."

He took me to a Shia house for thirty minutes and raped me. I was crying. Afterwards, he asked me "What do you want?"

I said I wanted to go to a house where one of my friends was living. Since Faisal was the Daesh governor of Tal Afar, he could do anything he wanted. The owner of the house where he took me was named Abdullah and my friend was his prisoner. I stayed one week with her.

Faisal bought me dresses, pink, purple, and black. He also brought me shampoo, makeup, and perfume. He wanted me to wear the dresses and makeup for him.

I refused by saying, "Give me some time, but not now."

He slapped me hard on my face, until I was crying. He forced me to put on the makeup.

I told him, "What happened to Yezidis will one day happen to you."

He said, "No, for these things we are doing to Yezidis, we will go to paradise. This can never happen to the Muslims, because we have the Quran."

I said, "God will protect us."

Faisal tore off all of my clothes and said, "There is no one who will come and help you."

After one week he moved me to a Sunni house with my children. He locked me in the house from morning until night while he was gone. I asked him to leave the door unlocked, in case of fire, and I promised not to leave. He agreed.

I found an Arab neighbor lady and asked her to bring me a SIM card in exchange for 15,000 dinar ($12) and a bag of clothes in the house. Even though there were three phones in the house, I did not touch any of them. I found an old phone in the trash. The number zero did not work. I had to press it many times to work. I called my brother-in-law who was free and told him I want to run away.

He told me I would have to move to a Yezidi neighborhood, because it was too dangerous to plan an escape in the Arab neighborhood where I was living. So I did not eat for three days. I was praying to Allah all the time so Faisal could see me. He wanted me to really be Muslim. I asked Faisal to move me to a Yezidi house. He agreed. The next week, in June, he moved me to Hai Al-Khathraa next to Tal Afar.

My brother-in-law gave me the name of a trafficker to call to help me escape. When there was no one around, I called the trafficker. Then I went outside with my children to wait for him, but he did not come. When I called again, he said it was too dangerous.

In the second week, Faisal removed my clothes and searched my body. He said, "We know you have a mobile phone. Give it to me. If you do not, I will beat you and rape you and hurt your children."

The SIM card and phone were hidden in my baby's diaper. I gave them to Faisal. He locked me in the bedroom without my children. Later, he gave me the phone and ordered me to call the trafficker to come so they could catch him. I swore that I had only called my brother-in-law. There was no trafficker.

Faisal raped me and did terrible things to me. I would not let him touch me except for when he tied my wrists or gave me a pill. He was not satisfied because of my attitude. I always was telling him, "Kill me," but he said, "Instead of killing you, I will give you away for a dowry."

He brought a second Yezidi woman and said we would join him and travel to Ramadi to fight. We would be his human shields. I did not go. He took a sixteen-year-old girl with him instead.

Before Faisal left, in May, he sold me for a second time to Haithem Hussein (Baqir). This time, instead of in exchange for a gun, Haithem paid $5300 dollars for me. Faisal had bought me from the manager of Tal Afar for $3200. He said he was satisfied with a $2100 profit.

Haithem took me to a house with another Yezidi woman and her four-year-old daughter. We made a plan to escape by going first to the hospital to say we were getting pregnancy tests. We took a taxi, but when we arrived to the hospital, we could find no one to help us escape. We returned to the house and cried.

After Faisal left for Ramadi, a new wallie or governor came to Tal Afar. He was named Haji Toemal. He took me from Haithem and put me in his headquarters. All the windows were closed and painted black. They would not let me see the sunlight. I was cooking and washing and ironing clothes for ten to twenty people. Dirty bastards! I had to so that I would not lose my kids. I had to do everything they wanted.

I said to myself this is going to be fine with me as long as I have my children with me and they do not force me to be someone's wife. I started cleaning and cooking. I washed the dishes.

I said, "I'm going to take a bath," because I was dirty.

After I took a bath, a huge man was waiting in my bedroom and asked, "Did you take a bath for me?"

I said, "No. Who are you?"

He replied, "Do you know the wallie who is in the news? It's me. I am the wallie of this headquarters."

Then I was so frightened and depressed. I thought to myself, definitely, this man has taken me for himself, but none of his guards in the headquarters would be able to rape me, because he would own me. I tried to leave the bedroom, but he grabbed my wrist and said, "Stop! Where are you going?"

I said, "Why?" He said, "I have six wives, and you will be the seventh."

I tried to hide my fear and said, "I will never accept this."

He said, "You have no choice. I will take you."

I asked, "Where are your wives?"

He said, "I have two Muslim wives and four Yezidi wives. Two Yezidi wives have children. The others are fourteen and sixteen years old."

I said to him, "If you have all these wives, why are you going to take me and commit a sin? I will be the servant for you and your wives. That's enough! How long are you going to do this to us? To buy and sell us among yourselves? Why? We are not human? What are we that you are doing this to us? We are ill. We are in a bad psychological condition."

At that time, we asked God for death a thousand times. What is the purpose of our living? I do not feel like I am alive. I am still in pain. My heart is broken. I told him I would not accept this.

He said, "You will *have* to accept it and you will be my seventh wife. Then I will make it nine."

I asked, "Why nine?"

He said, "Because I am holding two more Yezidi girls. I will take all the virgins. It is accepted in our religion."

I said, "I do not know in what religion this is accepted! Let me go to my children."

I wanted to hold my children to myself, so he could not do anything to me.

He took his clothes off immediately in front of my children. He was completely naked and excited. With his long beard and long hair, he looked like a monster. He was under the influence of drugs, like he was drunk. He ordered me to remove my scarf. I refused. My children began crying. He dragged them away from me and shut them out of the bedroom.

He came at me and ripped off my scarf and clothes by force. He slapped me in my face, and I fell down and fainted. He raped me while my children cried and screamed outside the door and asked God why he did not help us.

After Haji raped me, he stroked my cheek and recited the Quran over me. He told me he could not beat me because it is "haram," meaning forbidden by the Quran. Haji Toemal kept me as his prisoner for one month and raped me repeatedly.

A driver brought an eleven-year-old Yezidi girl to be with me. The driver raped her. His name was Hussam.

They sent my sister-in-law to Raqqa where they sent the single women to be sold and used for sex. To this day, she refuses to talk about what happened to her. I only know they locked her in a room for one month with no toilet and no windows. They gave her an injection before raping her. She escaped after me.

They took me to Baaj for ten days and put me in one prison cell with six other single Yezidi girls. Of course, they had all been raped.

On the road to Baaj, I saw dead men hanging from the electric poles. Their flesh was falling off their bodies. I saw dogs eating their flesh. For no reason, just because they refused to join Daesh and fight against others. If you don't join them, they will kill you. They took young boys to Ramadi to wear suicide vests.

Up until now, my kids are still talking to me about the men hung on the electric poles. They know their father is captured and saying, "Mama, is our dad beheaded?" because Daesh beheaded people. "Mama, are they going to release our dad?"

I was returned again to the governor's headquarters in Tal Afar. The governor used me as a human shield against the air strikes. When the planes were striking, he told me, "Be next to me. If you die with me, it does not matter. When the plane sees you with me, they will think it is a family and the plane will not strike us and kill us."

And I am sure they use all Yezidi women as human shields. They would not go to the toilet without us. They would not sleep without two or three of us.

They were telling us, "Go up to the rooftop and show yourself to the planes while we are meeting."

I was with my family for two-and-a-half months in Tal Afar. We were in a headquarters that belonged to them. We were human shields for them all the time.

Before I escaped, I was really sick. The governor was abusing me. It was too much to take. I just wanted to die. I was not eating. I was not drinking. I grew weak. My situation was worsening. I was crying and shouting continuously. They drugged me with narcotic pills. My kids were crazy. We could not sleep. I have seen too much. I am like a dead person now.

The governor asked me, "Why don't you want to be with us? You are not satisfied with Daesh's activities? We will do worse than we did to you. As long as you are not satisfied with us, you know what your fate will be."

I was upset. Just because of my children, I tried to do what they wanted, but my conscience was uncomfortable. They brought a Daesh doctor to me. The doctor told me that I have a psychological problem. I told him, "Yes, you are my psychological problem."

I promised to marry the governor if he wanted, but with official papers to prove we are married so no one else can take me. They did not even marry us with official papers. They said they do not have to.

A Yezidi girl who was with me was afraid that if a man married her without papers, he would marry her to ten men. She asked one of the men and begged him to marry her with official papers. She even said, "I'm willing to be pregnant from you, but do not pass me from one man to another."

The man said, "Why should I marry you with official papers and make you pregnant, when I can sell you to another man? I don't accept official papers."

I begged governor Haji to put me in a house with other Yezidis, so in June he took me to another headquarters. There were no surveillance cameras in the second headquarters like there were in the first place that I lived where there were also many guards. There were three other friends in the new location including my seventeen-year-old cousin, Ivana. I became the fourth. The house belonged to a Shia family.

All three women in the house were also forcibly married to Daesh men. We were eleven people in the house, but the men were not always there. Every day at 10 AM, 1 PM, and 5 PM, the men would come to the house to eat. At night the three men would come to be with the three women. The children slept in the same room with their mothers. I had my own room with my children.

Governor Haji would come to me late at night every two or three nights. He would give me a pill. My children were crying while he raped me. He would stay with me half-an-hour then go home to his Muslim wife in Tal Afar. He also had a Muslim wife in Mosul.

There were 300 children living in the school without their mothers. Twenty-four were infants. A man told me there were another 700 children being held in Mosul. Did they take the mothers and kill them? Did they sell them to be raped? None of us knows.

Do you expect if the mothers were alive they would not come and take care of their own children, even if one of those women were given to ten men from one to another? She would still return to take care of her children during the three hot summer months.

One of my guards came to me and said, "I have bathed five of them, but I cannot continue washing them because they stink. They can stay dirty."

Why did he tell me that? He warned me, "Stop crying and beating yourself, because I heard them saying that they will take your children and put them with the other children. So stop doing that, for the sake of your children."

The other woman in my house asked our guard to get her sister's child in the school. He refused. She left and they brought her back and beat her really hard. The leader said, "Take her and her daughter and kill them."

I heard them say that killing a woman by a bullet is forbidden. He told them to take her and hang her. I pleaded for her life, and I told him that this woman did not try to escape.

Then he said, "She tried to escape, and she cannot stay with us anymore. Send her to Syria since she left the house without our permission."

They issued a warrant to kill me, because they said I helped her.

The guard came to me that evening and swore to me, "If I hear that you try to escape or do something wrong, we will hang you naked on the electricity pole and stone you to death." Like Mosul residents, because they were doing that to Mosul clans, killing their women by stoning when they were making mistakes.

As if what *they* were doing were not mistakes. Everything Daesh was doing was a mistake. They were always waiting for their own friend to make a mistake so they could torture him to death in order to get a promotion. For example, if the man who I was under his control stripped me naked, burned me, and killed me, they would tell him he did a very good job and promote him to be a governor or give him forty fighters to command.

That was what they were doing. Normally, people get promoted by getting certificates or graduating, but Daesh were committing horrible crimes to be promoted.

Twice they forced a Yezidi to go to the mountain with a suicide vest to explode himself on Peshmerga. He did not want to do it. He returned and said his vest had failed to explode. They told him it did not matter if it went off or not, and they shot and killed him.

After the guard warned me, people told me they are cleaning a house for me and will install camera surveillance in it to watch me and keep me forever. I knew I had to escape.

I found a broken phone at a Shia house, and I kept it hidden behind the refrigerator. One of the women had stolen a SIM card from one of the Daesh men's pocket. So we were able to call our fathers and brothers in Kurdistan. Ivana and I found a man willing to risk his life and come for us. The location of our house was well-known because they used it as a Daesh headquarters.

When the house was empty and we had a chance to escape, I went up to the roof to call the man. If I had been caught, I would have said I was adjusting the satellite dish. When the man finally came to help us escape, he was caught. We never learned what happened to him, but we knew many men were killed if they were caught helping women escape.

Ivana and I did not give up. Every day we were afraid of being sent to Raqqa. We had to keep our efforts secret from everyone, even the other Yezidi women. If Daesh thought the other women knew about our plan, they would be severely beaten or tortured to talk after we escaped.

On our next attempt to escape, we succeeded. We were dressed in black, head to toe. Even our eyes were covered as required by Daesh. I put a grey dress on my son. Ivana, my two children, and I used a chair to climb over the six-foot garden wall when Daesh were at work. The others were sleeping in the heat of the day. We walked to a waiting car. The driver took us to an empty house to hide until it was dark.

We walked all night with the driver who was kind to us. He carried my baby on his shoulders. We had to be very careful, because we walked through IED mine fields. If we stepped on a bomb it would kill us. The driver said he must have taken the wrong path. By morning our feet had cuts and blisters. When we got within two kilometers of the front line, Peshmerga shot at us six times. We fell to the ground. The driver gave me his phone, and I called to Duhok. My contact called the Peshmerga commander and told them not to shoot us. The driver took his phone and ran back. Ivana and I walked with my two kids to freedom on July 2, 2015.

The cost to my family for our freedom was $12,000. Sadly, the next week, our driver returned again to rescue more Yezidi women and children from Tal Afar. Daesh caught him and executed him. We heard that two other smugglers were caught that week in July 2015 and beheaded in Mosul.

How will my pain be cured? There is no remedy. Who wants to listen to this? The person who listens to me, may ask, "How can she be healed?"

Nothing can heal my broken heart, not even if they put me in a palace in any country of Europe. I will not say I am comforted. How can I be comforted, if on one side of my family, I am far away from my family, my sisters, my brothers? And from the other side, I lost the sisters and brothers of my husband, Basman, who are like my own? His sisters and brothers are mine. His mother is *my* mother. His father is *my* father. I feel the same pain as they do. During the night I imagine them and cry for them. There is no cure.

Do not say, "You went to Germany and it's finished. You are at ease." No. Wrong! I will not be comforted until I see the enemies are out of my land or until I see the Yezidi children are released, or until I see the men and women are rescued, or until I find their execution sites and bury their bones, so as to avoid denying what happened to us by the infidels and criminals.

I do not want to forget the torture we have been through. I want to tell the world so they know the truth, what the enemy of our religion and the infidels did to us. I do not want to deny what they did to us. Do not cover it up and say, "It was only an attack."

It was an invasion against God's law. It was genocide.

How can they marry a nine-year-old girl to an old man of fifty? *No.* In addition to that, take a one-year-old infant still nursing from his mother's breast and kill his mother? What religion would accept this? I want to know, in what religion is this stated, except Daesh's religion? Daesh did so very much to Yezidis. I tell you, even the earth that Daesh stopped on became spoiled.

We pleaded to the whole world to listen to us that Daesh gave us a deadline in Kocho to convert to Islam, but we refused. We pleaded to Europe, and America and to Yezidis in foreign countries. Imagine what Yezidis did in foreign countries. Some burned themselves or jumped off high buildings to make European countries take action. Why couldn't they rescue us with two planes?

We did not know how many people were killed, but the American plane that flew overhead that day would know how many were killed in Kocho. I saw with my own eyes a convoy of over 200 vehicles entering Kocho. How is it possible the American airplane could not see it and video it? How is it they could not know what Daesh were going to do to us?

They knew that they would not take us to Shingal mountain and let us go to Kurdistan.

Killing us with an air strike would have been better than letting Daesh do this to us. They captured my husband and his family. I would have gone with them too. If they would kidnap and rape me with my kids, *no.* I would prefer what happened in Halabja to happen to us when Saddam Hussein killed 5,000 Kurds in one day by poison gas.

When our own country could not do anything to save us, nor did America, we would prefer America would have bombed and killed us that day along with

Daesh in Kocho, instead of what happened. It was necessary, *necessary* to stop Daesh, because of what happened to Yezidis in Shingal; not only Yezidis in Shingal, but people in all of Iraq. Especially in Kocho village.

The ones who were killed by Daesh, their corpses are still exposed on the land, the rain is washing them away, and dogs probably have eaten them. I do not know anything about my husband, but if he is alive, I would have heard something about him. There is no evidence. Even if they know he is dead, who will tell me? They know I am in pain. No one will tell me.

We need to know how many people are killed in the mass grave sites and how they were killed. It is very important to us to know who is killed, who is rescued, and who is missing. Until I know what happened to my husband, I will never be able to sort out my life. This goes for all the thousands of women whose husbands are missing so we can find some peace. We need the bones identified, because it is too late to stop their death.

The most important thing is that we want our captives rescued so our grief may be soothed. There are thousands of Yezidi girls and women like me weeping who remain with Daesh. Their hearts are broken and eyes are filled with tears and their mouths are filled with blood. The families who are waiting for the captives to be released cannot concentrate. They are busy thinking all the time about them. They are unable to cook or do anything else because of this heavy burden.

We are being sold by Daesh, so how come other countries are unable to buy us back? The ones who sold out the Yezidis, aren't they able to buy us back? For how long will the world allow Daesh to sell us for sex, but the governments refuse to buy our freedom?

I was with the Daesh governor while he was talking on the phone with a Kurdistan intelligence man. The governor asked the man if Kurdistan will buy the Yezidis. The governor said, "We will sell them." The intelligence man will not buy them. I heard this with my own ears. Why? Because Kurdistan government cannot take care of Yezidis or else they would have bought us.

How long will we be in this situation and people say, "Oh, you will get over it."

I will never get over it. What they took from me can never be fixed, but I will *not* abandon my husband's rights.

I will always say it is not too late. I would love to see one day that Yezidis are going to be taken care of, to get Yezidis together, to stand for their rights, to get acknowledgment for their genocide.

A European country is supposed to give Yezidis protection and keep them together in one place instead of scattering them; my mother in one location, my brother somewhere else, Basman's father somewhere else, and today I find myself alone in Germany. My parents and sisters in France, my brothers and uncles scattered all in different cities. The family I have left is all separated. I am alone in Germany in a critical situation.

After what happened to me, at least I should have someone from my family with me. At least my brother could take care of me and help heal my pain, so that I would not think that we cannot be together. And this is worse than losing my husband, being taken by Daesh, and everything. The entire Yezidi population is being destroyed. We will vanish if we are not protected. Yezidis are scattered throughout the world.

The burden of helping the Yezidis could be managed. It could be. Why not? If I had a friend, who had done nothing wrong, why wouldn't I shoulder his burden? Those whom we tell could do something for Yezidis.

We want our enemies out of our homes and our areas to be liberated. We want our homeland taken back from the hands of those infidels and tyrants.

We need assistance from other countries to protect and help Yezidis. We want them to take the remaining Yezidis out from among Muslims and to keep Yezidis together. Yezidis cannot live with Muslims.

Governments could solve this problem. They are able to. America is able to. We appeal to America, especially America, and all European countries. Everyone who was taken by Daesh suffered including Christians, Shia, Yezidis, even Sunnis who would not submit to their will. Yezidis are innocent and never betrayed anyone.

I am not looking for a good living situation for myself and my children. I am not looking for money. I am just asking for my rights, my family's rights, and Yezidis like me. I do not want to lose our rights.

Unfortunately, today I see all the parliaments, councils, and meetings about Daesh, but they cannot cut off the routes of Daesh or help the Yezidis. *Yes!* They can if they want to!

So if you can do something for us, we *want* you to do it. We want you to help us, and we are willing to have your help. Our story will not end, no matter how much we tell it. Whatever we say, we can never finish it.

How long, oh Lord? How long must we endure this?

In 2017, Germany granted asylum to Viyan's single brother, Zuhar. Zuhar smuggled to Spain in 2014 for $17,500 dollars where he was apprehended and fingerprinted. He then moved to his uncle's home in Germany where he lived and worked undocumented for more than two years before applying for asylum to be reunited with his sister and uncle's family. Viyan's parents, two single sisters and another single brother were given asylum in France in 2016. The family remains separated across Iraq, Germany, and France.

Daesh Destroyed Yezidi Houses

There were four stages to the destruction of Yezidi houses in Shingal. The first stage was on the first day of the attack, August 3, 2014. Daesh launched missiles that destroyed houses in villages throughout Shingal. In Gir Zerik over 250 missiles were launched in a five-hour period from 2:40 AM until 7 AM when the Yezidi fighters ran out of ammunition and fled.

The second and third stages were not random destruction. The houses were carefully targeted based on knowledge of the owner or of the contents in the house.

The second stage came two weeks after the initial attack. Daesh's first order of business was to identify by name and age each and every Yezidi they captured. The young women were photographed to be sold.

In those first two weeks of captivity, Yezidis were beaten and interrogated about the location of their house and where they kept their gold inside their house. Yezidis, like most people in the Middle East, put their savings into gold jewelry, not into a bank. Their Daesh captors returned to their houses, broke into their secret closets or safes with drills and angle grinders and stole their gold. The safe of Adiba Khudaida Qassim's family in Khanasor was opened with a grenade.

Yezidi houses were totally ransacked, windows broken, and many were burned on the inside. Appliances were sold in the Daesh open air market places.

After all the valuables were stolen from the Yezidi houses, the third stage of destruction began. Six weeks after the initial attack, Daesh rigged hundreds of carefully selected, beautiful houses with explosives and detonated them. In all of the villages in Shingal, there are hundreds of houses that were exploded while many surrounding houses remained untouched. These houses were often the most expensive in the village.

Daesh targeted the interpreters who had risked their lives working for the US Army between 2003 and 2011. When the interpreters fled, most of them left behind their treasured photos in which they were proudly wearing the uniform of the United States army and standing with their American commanders. Many of them displayed certificates of recognition with their names. When Daesh found these photos, they targeted their houses for demolition.

Many of the owners of destroyed houses had been opponents or political prisoners under Saddam Hussein's dictatorship. Some were already living in exile in Europe. Ali Sado Rasho was one. He is a Yezidi historian who wrote about the previous 73 Yezidi genocides. He fled to Germany in 2009. Ali's house, worth $100,000 dollars, as well as his brother's house, were both exploded on September 23, 2014.

There were twenty-two Yezidi political prisoners held in Abu Ghraeb prison from 1996 to 2002 under Saddam Hussein. Hassan Alyias Hami served seven years as a political prisoner, along with his brother. He was tortured for nine months. On September 22, 2014, his and his brother's new house was exploded in Hrecko, Sunoni. They had spent $130,000 dollars to build it in 2013.

The fourth stage of destruction of the Yezidi houses came in 2016 when Daesh retreated in front of Peshmerga's advance and demolished and torched entire villages. They rigged many houses with IEDs. In 2017 and 2018 when some Yezidis returned to examine their houses, they were killed by explosions when opening the door.

Sinjar is the main city in Shingal. When it was liberated on November 12, 2015, Kurdish and Yezidi forces found all buildings in the historic old city section on the north side of Sinjar city reduced to piles of rubble.

In June 2016, Daesh called Peshmerga and told them that there were only twenty Daesh fighters left in Tal Qassab, and Peshmerga could come and get it if they wanted. Peshmerga did not take the bait. The next week Daesh torched Tal Banat village as they retreated. The week after, on July 3, 2016, Daesh torched the village of Tal Qassab which had had a population of 30,000. Standing six kilometers north of Tal Qassab, at the Domise Peshmerga command post #12, southeast of Sinjar, we watched it as it went up in an inferno of flames and burned all night. Daesh was giving a clear message that Yezidis would have nothing left to return to.

Elias Dakheel Sidoo was another Yezidi interpreter who had risked his life serving with the US Army. His family owned a large, green farm ten kilometers north of Tal Ezeer (Al Qatania). In 2016, Daesh cut down all the trees and demolished his house.

Those families who survived the attack in August 2014 moved into tents and small caravans in IDP camps in Kurdistan. There was nothing left for them to return to. They would never feel psychologically secure again in Shingal or Iraq unless they had international protection.

Even those whose houses remained standing stated they could not envision themselves ever returning. Nadia and Said Murad Pissee were escorted by Nayef Jaso, mayor of Kocho, to their home in Kocho after it was liberated May 26, 2017. Nadia stooped down in her old bedroom and picked up a scrap of paper, all that remained of her former life. Every Yezidi in the world cried with them as brother and sister sobbed into each other's arms.

Week by week, Yezidis returned to inspect the ruins of their home, like attending a burial. They returned to their tents and caravans in Kurdistan, despondent and more certain that they had to leave Iraq.

Both before and after Sinjar city was liberated, the last piece of clothing, furniture, mats, pillows, dishes, pots and pans was stolen. The sinks and plumbing fixtures were removed. The light fixtures, chandeliers, ceiling fans, wall switches, and electrical wiring were ripped out. The rubber encasing of the wires was burned off and the copper sold in Duhok for 3,000 dinar or about $2.50 USD per kilo. Many houses were burned to a black crisp on the interior by putting a propane gas tank inside a stack of tires, pouring fuel over it, and setting it on fire to explode. These houses need high-pressure water hoses to wash the black soot off before repairing the walls and painting. All the glass in the doors and windows is broken. The minimum cost to restore a house to a livable condition would be $10,000 to $20,000 US dollars.

When Adiba Khudaida Qassim from Khanasor was asked in a 2017 PBS TV documentary if she would ever return, she said "no." When asked if she could ever forgive her Arab neighbors, she spoke for many when she quietly answered, "That would be hard."

Political Prisoner from Saddam to Daesh

Hassan Alyias Hami, August 15, 2015

On December 7, 1995, I was arrested in my home along with Abbas Haji Hafko. Three men in plain clothes came to my house. One was named Borek. We did not know them. They said, "We have five minutes work with you, then we will be finished."

We got into their car. They took us two kilometers on the highway to where another car was waiting with five men inside. It was not a police car. The five men arrested us. They were Saddam Hussein's Istikhbarat (like the CIA).

We were in between two men in the car. One of the men said, "I am the assistant manager of Istikhbarat."

They took us to the director of Istikhbarat in his office in the mayor's building. They blindfolded us and tied our hands. They took us to Mosul and put us in an underground room, 2m x 1m. There were six people in the room. We suffered so much. There was not enough room to sit or sleep for everyone, so we paced. There was no light and no toilet. Once per day for three minutes we were allowed to go outside of this room.

At 8 AM the investigator came. He beat us with a wire cable. He said, "We know you won't confess here. We will take you to Baghdad."

At 3 AM, December 9, 1995, they took us to a bus. We were tied and blindfolded. When we arrived in Baghdad, they took off all our clothes. They gave us one pair of pants and one shirt. They said we have to forget our name. They gave each of us a number and said, "From now on this number is your name."

We still remember our numbers. Mine is 1201. My friend Abbas' number is 1203.

They took us to a room 2m x 2m on the third floor. It had one toilet inside. The color of the walls was dark red from dried blood. There were 51 rooms like this. The door was very strong. It was made of iron. There was one small window in the door for passing food. The window was 30cm x 25cm. There was a bright light outside of the window.

After one week they took me to a different room on the first floor to interrogate me. The investigator asked me, "Did you make a group and did you have communication with the Kurdish PDK party and Syrian Istikhbarat?"

I answered, "No."

They took me to a room underground. They handcuffed my hands behind me and blindfolded me. When I was walking into the room, they punched me and I fell down hard on the concrete floor. Because my hands were tied behind my back, I could not break my fall.

They suspended me from the ceiling by my arms. My shoulders were dislocated. My feet were one meter from the floor. For more than one hour they hung me there and beat me with a cable until I lost consciousness. They beat me on the back, arms, and legs with cable, but not on the face or stomach, so I would not die. They insulted me. They were talking about religion because they knew I am a Yezidi.

My friends told me afterwards that two guards brought me back to my cell on a blanket.

Praise God, because I had a friend arrested six months before me in the same cell with me. He tried to help me with my shoulders. Every time they tortured me and returned me to my cell, he stood me against the wall and pushed my shoulders back to improve them.

The water we drank for breakfast and lunch was bad. In the mornings we got one small cup of soup. It was old and was not good, but we had to eat it. Lunch was a small cup of rice. The rice was old, also. The dinner was a small piece of bread and a cup of good water.

Every ten or fifteen days they took us out of the cell and repeated the interrogations and beating with cables and hanging by our arms. They did this for nine months to both me and my friend Abbas. We did not confess anything, but we signed a statement. However, we were blindfolded and did not know what we signed. After the signatures, the interrogations and beatings stopped.

My health was deteriorating because of bruising and swelling and tenderness from the cable beatings. Today my back still hurts. My shoulders are okay.

Twenty days after I signed, my health was very bad so I asked to meet with the investigator. We met. I told him, "Please, just get me out of here and I will sign an agreement that I will stay 100 years in prison." This was because of my suffering and illness and thinking about my family.

He told me, "Maybe the government will kill you if you sign."

I told him, "Only God can take my soul."

On August 28, 1996, I went to court with Abbas and three others. One got sentenced to be executed by hanging. He was an Arab Muslim and a political prisoner. He bombed an office building. Abbas got twenty years. I got sentenced to fifteen years. Another two prisoners who were Shia Arabs got twelve years.

After court, they took us to Abu Ghraeb prison. We felt we were at home compared to the past nine months of beatings and punishment.

My four children were little, and there was no money, so my family worked with my brother in the fields farming, planting melons, tomatoes, and cucumbers. They sent money to me in Abu Ghraeb. This was for seven years and thirteen days. I was released October 22, 2002.

There were twenty-two Yezidi political prisoners in Abu Ghraeb from 1996 to 2002 under Saddam Hussein.   After the United States came to Iraq in 2003, they put a lot of my friends in prison.   In 2005 we built a mud house in Hrecko, Sunoni, Shingal.

When Paul Bremmer was serving in Iraq as the United States commander, he instructed the Iraq government to give lump sum payments to a list of Saddam's former political prisoners who had worked with America.   Over a three year period, in 2007, 2008, and 2012, I was paid approximately $90,000 to $100,000 dollars. Using this money, in 2010, I built our house in Hrecko. I finished it in 2013. Our house was destroyed by explosives by Daesh on or about September 22, 2014, because I had been a political prisoner.

Abbas Haji Hafko built his own house, worth a value of approximately $130,000 dollars. It was also destroyed with explosives. We were considered to be a threat, because many of Saddam Hussein's people are now with Daesh.

I feel my life is in danger now even though we are in a camp in Kurdistan. All Yezidis' lives are in danger. I just want a safe country to live in so I do not have to worry about Daesh.

Because no one in Hassan's immediate family was kidnapped and raped by Daesh, his family does not qualify for any asylum programs for Ezidis. UNHCR rejected his family's request for resettlement in Canada. Ten family members live in their small caravan in an IDP camp near Zakho.

His son, Falah Hassan, a police officer, took his own life with his gun in February 2017. Falah left behind a stunned and grieving family and his pregnant wife and infant daughter whom he had named Damoa which means "tears". They are trapped with no possibility to return to Shingal and no hope of getting asylum in a safe country.

Roboski Saved Yezidis with Help of PKK

On September 3, 2014, I drove to Roboski (Turkish name: Ortasu), a poor mountain village in Turkey on the border of Iraq where I have many friends. My first visit to Roboski was in 2012, when I met Ferhat Encu. He became the spokesman for the Roboski family survivors of the infamous Roboski massacre on Dec. 28, 2011. His seventeen-year-old brother was killed in it. The US flew the drone then passed the location to Turkey which flew two F-16s and killed thirty-four innocent men and boys carrying petrol on their mules over the mountain ridge from Kurdistan, Iraq to Turkey. The government called it an operational mistake, but never apologized.

In 2012, I went to pay my respects, because I thought that at least one American should show up and say, "I'm sorry for what my country did." I returned many times to investigate and report on the Roboski massacre.

At the Roboski School, on September 3, 2014, I found 350 weary Yezidis taking shelter from the sun in three long tents. They had been fleeing for one month and had just arrived from walking over the mountain. In spite of many children, everyone was quiet and lackluster with vacant stares. They were exhausted physically and emotionally and were at the mercy of strangers.

Twenty-four-year-old Sheikh Alyas, an environmental safety specialist, used to work for the US Army as a interpreter. His family of fourteen people had stuffed themselves into their Opel car and driven seven hours from Zorava, Shingal, to Syria then Zakho, Iraq, where they abandoned their car. After sleeping in a school in Zakho for ten days, they paid a pickup truck driver $100 dollars for the 40-minute drive into the mountain north of Zakho.

A uniformed PKK guerilla guided them on foot to a temporary camp in the mountain where they slept two nights. The PKK provided them with blankets and water and refused money. From there they walked nine hours over the mountain to Roboski school in a mountain village in Turkey.

A friend informed Alyas by phone that Daesh had burned his family's house. The idea of ever returning home was finished.

The first thing every Yezidi family told me was, "If it were not for the PKK (Kurdistan Workers' Party) helping us all along the way, from Shingal to here, there would not be one Yezidi left alive today." This was the same litany I heard repeated in every refugee camp in southeast Turkey. In those first weeks, the Yezidis would have kissed the ground the PKK walked on.

For five hours people told me their stories of running for their lives like I was a UN representative. They expected me to send help. They expected me to *do something*. I did not want this responsibility, but neither could I look away. I had an awful pit in my gut.

I published my first of many stories about the Yezidi genocide. In the three years that followed, there was never a day that was not a struggle filled with crises; never a day I was not tired and discouraged and wanted to quit. It was the desperate pleas and gratitude from the Yezidis that kept me going. We grieved together and held each other up.

I found Ferhat Encu (who is *not* in the PKK) distributing food from the back of a pickup truck in the school parking lot. Inside, Lezgin Encu was dispensing medicine to sick children. There was no presence of UNHCR (United Nations High Commission on Refugees), Europe, or the International Red Cross. The Turkish government never spent one dollar to support the Kurdish-run camps in southeast Turkey.

Every Kurd in southeast Turkey filled his car with rugs, blankets, pillows, clothes, shoes, medicine, and food and showed up at the refugee centers. They did not wait to be asked. They did not need to be organized by the government or a charity. They just knew what they had to do. In the 1990s, Turkey destroyed 3,000 Kurdish villages in southeast Turkey, displacing more than one million people. Kurds knew all about genocide and running. That is why Kurdish hospitality is like none other in the world. It is a moral imperative. When people are running for their lives, you have to help.

Every family in Roboski, Turkey, owns at least two or three horses. These horses are traditionally used for their border trading which Turkey calls smuggling. All Roboski families sacrificed by diverting the use of their horses from trading to meet the refugees each morning at the unguarded border on the mountain ridge above their village. The weak and elderly were transported by horse or car or tractor to the Roboski school. It began with a trickle of twenty people and grew to as many as 4,000 people in one day.

The small village of Roboski, with only 1200 people, welcomed, sheltered, and fed 20,000 Yezidi refugees in three weeks. Nearby villages of Gulyazi, Yemishli, and others sheltered another 4,000 people. Hikmet "Reber" Alma led the aid effort in Gulyazi. Each day they coordinated with town managers throughout southeast Turkey to send buses to pick up the Yezidis. In this way, Yezidis were dispersed to Cizre, Sirnak, Siirt, Batman, Bismil, Marden, and Diyarbakir.

On September 4, 2014, Turkish soldiers dismantled the tents in preparation to open Roboski school. The last group of 1500 Yezidis crossed over on September 7 and were bussed directly to Sirnak. The Turkish soldiers began bombarding the mountain border, effectively stopping Yezidis from entering Turkey.

About 4,500 Yezidis who had crossed into Turkey and were picked up by Turkish jandarme (soldiers) were sent to the Turkish-run Midyat refugee camp.

In 2015, Ferhat Encu was elected from Sirnak district to the Turkish parliament. In 2016, the Turkish parliament removed diplomatic immunity from parliament members. It then arrested twelve Kurdish parliament members, including Ferhat Encu, with the typical charge of associating with a terrorist organization. In 2017, the four-year prison sentence against Encu was upheld. Ferhat Encu, who organized the humanitarian rescue of 20,000 Yezidis from Shingal, is a great humanitarian who sacrificed his own freedom to save both Kurds and Yezidis from genocide. Encu was released in 2019 after serving two-and-a-half years for standing up for truth and justice.

Traumatized Yezidis in Turkey Recount Atrocities

I will cast terror into the hearts of those who disbelieve. Therefore strike off their heads and strike off every fingertip of them. Quran verse 8:12

In September 2014, I visited all the Kurdish-run Yezidi refugee camps in southeast Turkey: Roboski school, Hilal school, Sirnak, Siirt, Batman, nine Batman villages, Bismil, Mardin, and Diyarbakir. Yezidis gathered around me, six deep, waiting to tell me their story. Some were holding the ID cards of their dead loved ones. They had a great need to tell the world.

I spent days listening and looking at the photos of dead bodies of their loved ones. In every camp there was an interpreter who had once risked his life working for the US Army when it was in Iraq from 2003 to 2011.

Ido Mato was my interpreter in Hilal. Ido's family got away from Daesh, but his neighbors, three women and one man, were captured. In 2015, Ido smuggled into Bulgaria where he was held, beaten, and starved by Bulgarian police for three weeks before being released. He made it to Germany where he received asylum with the help of a human rights attorney. The judge wanted to return him to Bulgaria under the Dublin Accords, but a high court ruled that immigrants could not be returned to Bulgaria due to inhumane treatment. Because of this ruling, Bulgaria was off the hook for resettling immigrants.

Naam's thirteen-year-old son, Adnan, was killed August 3 in the street by Daesh when they opened fire into a crowd with automatic rifles. Adnan's friend ran to Naam's house and told her Adnan was dead. The family of ten fled within minutes without being able to retrieve Adnan's body.

Alyas Darwesh was a shepherd. Daesh kidnapped him and his son when they were guarding their sheep. Daesh cut off the son's finger. The son escaped to Zakho. Daesh used Alyas' phone to call his father, Darwesh, and demand money. Darwesh had no money to pay a ransom. He does not know if his son is dead or alive.

Haji Khuder's thirty-seven-year-old son, Saado, worked in the Iraq government in Shingal. When a group of government workers was on their way home from work, Daesh stopped them. They identified the Muslims in the group and told them to go home. Then they shot dead the remaining twenty-two Yezidi government workers. A friend brought Saado's body to his father's house. He left a wife and two small children.

The family of Ghanow Hussein Ghanow and his wife Shamah Salih Amar owned a chicken production business in Sunoni. They valued the modern equipment, building, and 8,000 chickens at $45,000. Her two sons risked their lives to return from the mountain on August 5 and 7 to feed the chickens. On August 7, they were captured by Daesh, but managed to escape when a plane flew overhead scaring off their captor. After they fled, their Arab neighbors joined with Daesh and took over their chicken operation.

The family fled with only the clothes on their back, leaving behind their business and house worth $40,000. They sold their car worth $8000 dollars for only $1100. Their son in Germany had sent them $20,000 toward a new house they were building. They left the cash behind in a wooden box. Another son was in Peshmerga, so with his Peshmerga unit they returned twice in an attempt to retrieve the $20,000, but they were attacked by Daesh. The mother told her son, "We love you more than we love the money. Do not try again."

Daesh attacked the village of Duguri, with a population of 4,000, on the north side of the mountain. Many of the Duguri residents fled to the mountain or direct to Syria. Saido Ali Hamad owned a butcher shop for twelve years. He speaks six languages. Saido was not in Duguri on August 3, but his wife and relatives fled on foot toward Syria leaving behind their two sons who were sick and could not walk. They were Sassem, age three, and Qassim, age four. Saido's grown cousin stayed with them. Daesh killed the two little boys. The cousin is missing.

For two days, Ismail Alo Silo was my interpreter in Batman as I listened to dozens of atrocities. When I wanted to finish at 11 PM, emotionally exhausted, Ismail turned to me and said, "You haven't listened to my story. May I tell you?" Of course, I said, and turned back from my car. Twenty people sat quietly in a circle under the stars in the parking lot.

Ismail Alo Silo was born and lived in Qine Mehrkan before moving to Tal Qassab in 1975. He and his brother's families were among six families of about 200 people escaping to the mountain from Tal Qassab (population 30,000). They stopped to rest by Qine Mehrkan, the village where Ismail was born, in the shadow of Shingal Mountain. They did not stay when they heard that Daesh was coming. In Qine Mehrkan Daesh killed eighty men and two babies including nineteen of Ismail's uncles and cousins. They kidnapped thirty-one women and thirty-six children.

The families of Ismail and his brother reached the mountain where there is a Yezidi shrine called "Amadeen". It was later exploded by Daesh. On the third day, in fear that the place was not safe and after losing all those uncles and cousins, the two families left. Their mother was ill and could not walk and they could not carry her, so Ismail's grown son, Sami, and his older brother, Faisal, stayed behind with her and five other old men and women. When Faisal and Sami went to get water from a well 500 meters from the shrine, Daesh shot at them.

When Ismail's family was leaving, Daesh shot at them, but they escaped. Ismail recalls "the moment I was crying because of the little quantity of water we had, and my brother's wife was encouraging me. I thought we all will die. We had only a half-liter of water left for fifteen persons. After I called my brother and told him that we will die, he brought four-and-a-half liters of water and stayed with us until we got to a safe place. The next day my son Sami joined us because he saw Daesh nearby and had to leave my mother."

The brother returned to their mother and stayed forty-five days on the mountain. In 2017, Ismail remained an IDP in Kurdistan. Ismail is the head of a family of ten people, including his ill ninety-year-old mother who made it to safety.

This was the selflessness with which Yezidi interpreters helped me, in spite of their own suffering. In February 2017, Daesh released a propaganda video showing two of Ismail's cousins who had been kidnapped and sent to Daesh military training. They were used as suicide bombers. Rest the souls of Amjad and Asad Elias Ma'ajo from Tal Qassab. Their father, Elias Ma'ajo, was killed with five other sons on August 3, 2014.

Beheading of the men was an effective technique used by Daesh to terrorize the entire Yezidi population. It worked. They ran.

Twenty-eight-year-old Ferman Khalaf was a Yezidi Iraqi border policeman from Khanasor. Nearly two months before Daesh took control of Mosul, on April 17, 2014, they attacked thirty-seven Iraqi border police near Tal Afar. Thirteen were killed, eight escaped, and sixteen were injured. He received five bullets. They ran into a building and collapsed in death. Ferman and two others survived. He had a bullet wound so big near his heart that he put his hand inside the hole to stop the bleeding.

The room was dark when Daesh entered. They shot the police to be sure they were all dead. Ferman received three more shots. The man next to him was still alive. He stood up and surrendered to Daesh. Daesh made a video with him before killing him. In spite of eight bullet wounds and the pain from his big toe being shot off, in spite of the terror of listening in the dark, Ferman pretended to be dead next to his companions' bodies while Daesh slowly beheaded the survivor who surrendered. It took ten minutes.

Namir Yusef Osman was trapped with his two sons and eight daughters on Shingal Mountain with no food or water. On the third day, his eldest son, Saeed Namir, age twenty-three, volunteered to return to their village of Gohbal to get food. He was captured at the foot of the mountain. Yusef watched helplessly as three men with long swords killed his son by chopping him across the back of his neck.

Passing the phones around is part of the common experience of telling one's terrible story. Everyone has photos.

One man in his thirties received a gruesome photo sent from his uncle's phone. The message said, "This is what will happen to you if you don't leave." The young man passed me his phone to show me the photo. His uncle's body was covered in blood. The decapitated head sat two feet away, tipped over on one ear, facing the camera. There was blood everywhere and ragged, raw flesh on the torso and head.

The next photo was of a stripped woman lying dead on her back. Both of her breasts had been sliced open to the ribs from top to bottom. I did not see a pool of blood under her. I bowed my head and hoped they killed her with a bullet first to stop her heart from pumping. "Where did you get this photo?" I asked the man. "I took it myself," he said. I pinched my lips and silently handed the phone back.

Another man passed me his phone with a photo of three bodies in the street burned to a black crisp.

There were photos of dead children who died on Shingal Mountain from dehydration. Their bodies were left behind. Over 300 children died on the mountain, as well as many elderly and disabled.

There was the photo of the little boy with his pants pulled down to his ankles, hanging over the side of a building with a rope around his broken neck. And another one of a mother and her small daughter, both hanging over the side of a cliff. There were photos of bulldozers shoveling up piles of bodies on the street.

There was the photo of a naked Yezidi woman being held horizontal by two men. One of them was pulling her head back by her long blond hair. They had sliced her aorta. A second cut was vertical down her chest, opening up her throat. They were draining her blood into a surgical steel pan. I heard that the Yezidi prisoners were being forced to give their blood to use for the injured Daesh terrorists.

The worst photo was of three tiny, naked babies laid out side by side for the photo. They had been sliced open between their legs. This is the photo I can never forget. This is why I know Daesh are not just ordinary terrorists. They are criminal psychopaths.

If one wanted to document the Daesh atrocities, all one would have to do would be to collect all the photos stored on Yezidis' memory cards. Even if they lose their phones, they can never burn the images out of their memory. There were 360,000 displaced Yezidis. They all have a tale of terror. These stories are typical.

When trauma happens, tears are delayed by shock and the survival instinct to escape. Trauma is masked with dry eyes, a flat voice, a stone face, a vacant stare, a rocking motion, a trembling hand. Every Yezidi was terrorized and traumatized. They had no opportunity to wail at a graveside and express the full breadth and depth of their grief.

Sare's daughter Bassima, son Barzan, and husband Khalil were captured by Daesh terrorists in front of her eyes. The rest of the family ran for their lives. They were from Duguri.

I put down my notebook and hugged Sare. With my hug, her face of stone contorted into sobs, and she collapsed in a dead faint. Sare's mother took one look at her daughter and fainted, too. Over the weeks and months, I came to learn that fainting and hysteria attacks are daily phenomenon with the Yezidi survivors.

There was daily group weeping and wailing for an estimated 6,000 Yezidi woman and children being held captive by Daesh and sold in slave markets. The worst stories of the kidnapped women and children were yet to be heard. Every family had its list of missing.

Twenty-year-old Adiba Qassim made a list of twenty-eight of her female relatives. They thought they would be safe if they remained behind in Khanasor. Daesh kidnapped them and took them to the village of Qaser Al Mehrab. Adiba pointed out four cousins in a Daesh propaganda video in which 200 men in rows were being forced to convert to Islam.

Diler Havend Khalaf, twenty-two, was in medical school when 100 people from his village of Tal Qassab Kevan were captured, twenty-seven of whom were his relatives. His cousin was sold into sexual slavery in Raqqa. His sister, Viyan, and her two toddlers from Kocho were being held in Tal Afar. She had managed to make one secret phone call. Her husband, Basman, was missing, probably killed by Daesh.

One girl who had been captured by Daesh managed to make a secret phone call to her father and report that she had been raped for eighteen continuous hours. She promised to kill herself when she got the chance. They did not hear from her again. Word of suicides by the kidnapped girls began leaking out.

Daesh's plan was to exterminate the Yezidis off the face of the earth.

Ido Mato spoke for everyone, "We will go anywhere. Just don't send us back to Iraq. We can never return. We cannot live among Muslim Arabs who killed us and drove us out. Shingal is surrounded on all sides by Arabs. We are terrified. We want to go to Europe."

But the Kurds had other plans for the Yezidis.

Adiba's List of Kidnapped from Khanasor

"I used to have a nice life until Daesh attacked us in Shingal," explained twenty-year-old Adiba Khudaida Qassim. "Now our life is finished," added her younger brother, Maher.

I met Adiba in September 2014, when she was living with thirty-two of her relatives in the Yezidi refugee camp in Sirnak, Turkey, with 1400 other Yezidis. She preferred not to talk about the traumatic end of her life in Shingal. The atrocities were too unspeakable for words. What she wanted most was for me to know who she was when her life was in full bloom. She did not want me to see only the image of her with unwashed hair, wearing donated clothing, living and sleeping with her family in two rooms in a former Army barracks. She wanted me to know there was more substance to her than that. She eagerly practiced speaking English and French with me.

Adiba showed me pretty photos of herself standing on Shingal Mountain on a beautiful spring day and another one picnicking with relatives. In another photo she shows me a woman laden with elaborate gold necklaces, belts, and bracelets. She is literally wearing her family jewels.

In Shingal, because people do not trust the banks who had previously stolen their money, most people keep their life savings in the form of gold jewelry. This explains why the Yezidis who fled the Daesh attack with the clothes on their backs were destitute. They left their gold behind in their houses which Daesh gangs looted and burned. They hardly had time to put their shoes on and run.

If one studied Adiba's FaceBook page, one could follow her life as it descended from joy to sorrow to death and atrocities worse than Dante's hell. Like any young person, Adiba posted links to her favorite singers, actresses, and movies. She watched Lion King 2 and Arab Idol. Her profile photo was of an innocent young woman wearing a flowing red dress, walking through a lush green meadow with the wind in her hair and a butterfly at her side. It was a self-image of beauty, nature, and freedom. She could be your own daughter.

Adiba is a product of the Yezidi religion which promotes a philosophy of love and harmony with all people and nature. She had posted a photo of two little children walking arm-in-arm on a beach. Another photo was of heart-shaped cookies with pink sprinkles on top. All that optimism and cheerfulness was before Daesh attacked.

After Daesh attacked Mosul, Adiba's mood turned somber. She often posted "I am sad" on her FaceBook page. She changed her profile photo from a little girl dressed in a gauzy white dress playing the violin to a little girl with tears streaming down her cheeks. After she reached Sirnak, her FaceBook banner photo showed the backs of six little boys lying face-down in odd positions on a rocky, dusty mountain. There was no explanation that they died from dehydration on Shingal Mountain along with hundreds of others.

Adiba showed me on her phone a photo of twenty relatives posing on the flat plain beneath Shingal Mountain, dressed in their finest clothes. Three late model cars are parked behind them. There are red circles drawn around seven heads. I asked why.

Daesh is all she said and crossed her wrists with clenched fists.

Her family heard that Daesh was advancing, so on August 3, at 11 AM, her family left home and climbed Shingal Mountain before Daesh arrived in their city of Khanasor. Sixty-three people who stayed behind were captured, taken to Tal Afar, and forced to convert to Islam.

Adiba showed me the Daesh propaganda video on her phone of Yezidi men converting to Islam. There are thirty rows of men standing, praising Allah, then kneeling down. She paused the frame to show me her four cousins in the second and third rows: Hussein Rashow Saedow, and his brothers Hassan, Nasser, and Rayed. Also, taken were their father, Rashow Saedow Ali; sister, Fayza Rasho Saedow; Hassan's wife, Gulan, and their five children, Falah, Salah, Kefah, Sabah, and Evline; and Nassar's son and his son's wife and their two sons, Nuri and Nawzad and also two daughters.

In those first few weeks, Adiba's family received word from the men forced to convert to Islam that Daesh was still killing more Yezidis, even though they had converted.

Then Adiba showed the video of her hometown Khanasor before the Daesh attack. It was once a clean, beautiful city with a wide main street. Her family's two-story house had a circular marble staircase and brass railing.

Farhan Mahlo, who had been interpreting for us, asked to see the video. His face flushed and tears rolled down his cheek. Adiba snatched the phone from him before he could finish. Every Yezidi can look stone-faced at the most horrible photos of brutal murders, but the sight of their once normal life breaks them into utter despair. Strolling down the sidewalk in the city they loved, their homes, their schools, their friends, BBQs on Shingal Mountain, dancing at wedding parties . . . all, all is gone forever. They mourn the loss of their life.

Twenty-eight of Adiba's female relatives from Khanasor were kidnapped. Along with others, they had fled to Shingal Mountain. When they tried to come off the mountain and walk fifty kilometers to Syria, Daesh captured them and took them to Tal Afar. The captured females made calls to their families until their last communication on August 15.

Adiba carefully wrote down the list of twenty-eight names and ages in my notebook. The women must be rescued. This remained everyone's top priority. Yezidis who were crowded in the room to listen to the list of twenty-eight missing females, then passed their phones to me to share their photos.

Passing phones is a ritual at the end of telling their stories. Every Yezidi has photos of the genocide on his or her phone. When I asked if we should prevent the children from seeing the photos, the parents just shrugged and replied, "They saw everything in real life. Even the little ones know what happened."

I curled my lips inward over my teeth and silently passed the phones back. No words were adequate. One can only react with a bowed head as one is forced to confront mankind's capacity for evil. I put the back of my hand over my mouth in an instinctual gesture of horror and killed the moan in my throat so it came out as a stifled whimper.

No person should ever have to look at photos like these, because once viewed, one can never scrub the images from one's head. They are photos of the most unspeakable atrocities . . . babies beheaded and others sliced open between their legs, eyes gouged out, breasts cut off, piles of bodies being bull-dozed off the road, baskets of heads, headless men hung by their legs from telephone poles, long rows of people lying down being shot in the back of their head by a line of executioners, pickup trucks piled with bloodied bodies, a little boy with his pants pulled down hanged by the neck over the side of a building.

Once you know, you can never un-know. Acts of genocide stay with you for a lifetime, making you stare into vacant space when people are speaking to you and toss and turn at 3 AM until dawn arrives and exhaustion overcomes you. Even sleep is disturbed with dreams of being pursued and running away, but there is no escape from the memories. One may curl up fetal style day and night, but never be rested. Restlessness becomes a permanent condition. One may never again feel at home in this world. One might hope for amnesia, but forgetting is not an option as long as Yezidis remain missing. One cannot easily move on with the act of living.

In 2016, Adiba borrowed $18,000 to smuggle her younger brother, sister, and parents to Germany. She was the last to leave Sirnak refugee camp in December 2016, when Turkish military attacked the Kurds and destroyed 75% of Sirnak. Adiba returned to Duhok, Iraq, to work as an interpreter.

Beytussebap Was Our Shingal

In November 2014, I suggested to my interpreter, Farhan Mahlo, that he bring his wife along to visit Beytussebap (pronounced Beytushebap), but he was vehement in his refusal. "I will never take my wife to meet a Kurdish woman. I hate all Kurds. I do not trust them."

"You are wrong, It is the PKK and the Kurds who have saved you. They feed you. They give you clothes and shelter from their own pockets without one dollar of government help. If it weren't for the Kurds, you would be dead," I lectured him.

We took a three-hour bus ride from Sirnak on winding roads into the mountains of Beytussebap. I pointed out the flocks of sheep on the mountain meadows in the early morning light. "I miss my sheep," was all Farhan said with a forlorn longing.

Autumn had turned the leaves golden yellow. The bus turned off the main road and snaked its way upward along a rushing river. We were eye level with the clouds. Farhan had motion sickness all the way from Sirnak which turned into painful dry heaves by the time we arrived. The Kurdish DBP political party in Sirnak had arranged for their leader in Beytussebap, Hazim Cin, to meet us. Our bus driver delivered us to his house. Farhan translated while curled up under a blanket, his head near the warmth of the coal-burning stove.

After an extravagant lunch in our honor, Hazim and his mother helped me complete the list of thirty-five villages and farms that were evacuated and burned in Beytussebap by the Turkish government in the early 1990s. Only the town of Beytussebap itself was spared destruction. The villages are no longer on any map. They will never be listed in a Turkish text book. The government destroyed 3,000 Kurdish villages in the 1990s.

1. Basaka 1	13. Güzhışk	25. Kahniya Beşker
2. Basaka 2	14. Gühüsok	26. Kanireş
3. Beri Kişli 1	15. Hacelya 1	27. Kendala
4. Beri Kişli 2	16. Hacelya 2	28. Mehre
5. Derasutlhe	17. Hale	29. Merkıtke
6. Dule	18. Hanik	30. Pertavin
7. Evrak	19. Hındirunis	31. Pirdoda
8. Ferasin	20. Hırabé Mergi	32. Tanga Hana
9. Gırgav	21. Hoze	33. Zerbel
10. Gouik	22. Isirwan	34. Xelka
11. Gova Mala Haci	23. Kaçit 1	35. Zorava
12. Gozney	24. Kaçit 2	

In these staggering mountains, sunset comes by 4 PM and the deep canyons fall into blue shadow. Abdul arrived to pick us up. We drove carefully up the steep, rutted road toward Meydan. A truck had slipped sideways on the muddy road leaving barely enough room for us to pass. I sucked in my breath and squeezed my eyes shut as we crept past the truck with not a foot of extra road between us and the gorge.

"The government refuses to give us a paved road to our village," Abdul explained.

Abdul's family was gathered at the door to greet me with bear hugs like a favorite aunt. His wife gave me the new baby to inspect. His older brother, Yakup Aslan, and their mother walked through the ankle-deep mud from Yakup's house to meet with me. Abdul had seven children under the age of fifteen.

I introduced Farhan and explained he was Yezidi and his family was living in Sirnak refugee camp in one small room. They asked Farhan about the attack on Shingal Mountain. No Yezidis had come to their remote mountain village, so they were eager to hear what happened.

I was working in Duhok when Daesh attacked Shingal on August 3, 2014, at 2 AM. People woke up in the morning to discover the Peshmerga, who were supposed to be defending us, had left during the night. My parents, my brother, wife and kids fled in the car to Shingal Mountain where they left the car then walked three hours up on the mountain. They had no food or water, so the next day my father went in search of food in an abandoned village. He was driving his car toward a village when he saw Daesh gangs on the road ahead of him, so he drove his car into a ditch and slumped over the steering wheel pretending he was dying in a car accident.

So Daesh did not touch him. After they left, he returned to the mountain without food. The next day he went again and succeeded at buying food in a shop and returning to the mountain. I was in touch with them by phone and had their coordinates. So I downloaded a map of Shingal Mountain from Google Earth and drove to the Syrian border, then drove to the base of Shingal Mountain. This was before the mountain was completely surrounded by Daesh forces; before everyone was trapped on the mountain.

I climbed up and found them. We slept one night, then I brought them to my uncle's home on the mountain. He has a garden with grapes and figs. At 3 AM, we walked off the mountain in the dark. I carried my six-month-old baby on my shoulders and held the hand of my two-year-old boy. We walked from 3 AM to 3 PM in 44C heat to the Syrian border. My shoulders were burning with pain. It was during that walk that I resolved to keep going until we reached Europe. I told my father, 'Muslims will never stop killing Yezidis. We cannot live in the Middle

East. I am taking my family to Europe. I hope you will come with me, but I am going, with you or without you.'

At the border, the PKK put us in a car and sent us to Zakho. From there we walked up the mountain and slept three nights in a PKK camp. They gave everyone food and water and blankets. But we had only two blankets for six of us, because there were 3,500 Yezidis waiting to cross into Turkey.

During the night the PKK guided us to the mountain border and we walked into Turkey where we were met by people from Roboski. They put the people who couldn't walk in cars and on mules. We walked nine hours to the school. After one night, buses took us to Sirnak. Now six of us live in one little room. We all made it. We are safe, thanks to the PKK. If it wasn't for the PKK, we'd all be dead.

We left behind everything: four houses, one car, one pickup truck, 112 sheep, and two kilos of gold. That is about $76,000 dollars. Now I cannot afford a pack of cigarettes. They gave me a pair of used shoes, but they leak. I am ashamed to ask for another pair. Who will help us? I don't know.

My uncle's house was near the mountain in Judela. It was worth $30,000 dollars. Daesh blew it up. Now my uncle is in a camp in Duhok. Their tent was flooded last week.

I don't care about anything but my computer. It had all my photos on it. . . .all my memories of my life. Photos of my childhood. Photos of my mother holding me, of my wedding day. Photos of my house, my city Tal Ezeer, my school mates growing up, high school graduation. Photos of when I worked as an interpreter for the US Army during the war. Photos of when I was given awards for my performance. . . when my first son was born. I have lost all my memories. That is the worst. I have nothing now. How can I ever start over when I do not have a lire in my pocket? I was always strong for my wife. Now, what can I do?

Abdul's wife shifted the baby on her lap and reached over to squeeze Farhan's hand. "You have your children. We will be your family, too, here in Turkey." At this gesture, Farhan wiped a tear from his eye. It is the kindness of strangers that always disarms us.

Yakup and Abdul's mother poured tea for everyone while Abdul's daughter set out plates of sliced apples for dessert.

I turned to Yakup, "I have waited one year to hear your story, Yakup, about what happened here twenty years ago. Finally, I have Farhan here to translate. Will you tell us?"

"We used to live in Ferashin, up in the highlands with our sheep," he began. "Oh, Ferashin is like paradise. In the spring the river is full from melting snow. The wild flowers are a yellow carpet. In June everything is green and the grass is high. You must come back to visit next summer and stay in our tent. All the

houses have been destroyed. Now we open our tents up there to live in the summer with our sheep, but back then, when I was a young man, our village was there.

"We were one of the last villages in Beytussebap that the soldiers destroyed. It was September 1995."

Farhan was translating. He reacted to Yakup's story with an "Oh" and another "Oh" and another. Each sentence wounded him. Yakup's voice trailed off. Everyone was silent. Yakup's mother picked up the story. I prodded Farhan to translate. His eyes were glistening.

"They bombed around the edge of Ferashin for ten days with Cobra helicopters. Also, the helicopters were used to deliver four or five thousand soldiers. They were bombing near our sheep and killing some. Each day they would come to us after bombing and pressure the men to join the Village Guard to fight the PKK, but the men refused, so the next day they would bomb again. They told us we were protecting the PKK, so they had to destroy our village. They promised to build us new houses if we would join the Village Guard. They tried every kind of threat and promise, but no one would join the Village Guard.

"Finally, after ten days of bombing, the Turkish soldiers came to us with their guns and ordered us to leave. They threatened to burn us alive inside our houses if we did not leave. They forced us out of our houses with only the clothes on our backs.

"The soldiers beat and kicked the men down. It was terrible. They stomped on top of their bodies until the men were nearly dead and could not move. They accused them of being PKK, but this was not true. We were all shepherds. Ferashin had only 1,000 people with over 100,000 sheep and cows. Our family had 500 sheep. We had a good life in Ferashin.

"They burned all the houses with everything we owned. "They stole our animals and said it was because the sheep belonged to the PKK, but this was a lie. The sheep belonged to civilians. All our wealth was in our animals and our land. How could we start over without them?

"We left without even carrying any food with us. The United Nations had made two tent cities that the soldiers ran. One was named Kanimasi. It was five kilometers from our village and had 200 or 300 tents. It was created in 1992. Every year in the early 1990s, Turkey was destroying the villages in Beytussebap and sending the people to these tent camps. Ferashin was last. All 300 families from Ferashin walked to Kanimasi.

"The soldiers gave us two pieces of bread and two kilos of sugar per family. They enforced a food embargo on Kurds from here all the way north to Erzurum and Kars. We were allowed barely enough food each month not starve to death, but not enough to give to the PKK. They warned us not to let the PKK enter the camp.

"Eventually the families moved away to Sirnak, Mersin, Adana, Van, Entebbe, and Hakkari. We stayed four months in a tent then moved to Mersin. We worked for Turks and were poor. About 4,000 people moved to Iraq where the UNHCR made Makhmour refugee camp. Our tribe is called Gewdan Ashiret. It has 40,000 people; about half still live in Turkey. My grandfather was named Zoradesht. He was famous.

"Only fifteen families joined the Village Guard and moved into the town of Beytussebap which had not been bombed. The soldiers promised to build them new houses, but broke their promise. After five or ten years, they finally built this village, Meydan, and gave a house to each Village Guard family."

Yakup picked up the story from his mother.

"We got tired of working for Turks in Mersin. In 2004, Prime Minister Erdogan said we could return to our villages. What villages? They were destroyed, but we missed Ferashin, so in 2008, we returned. We came back to our memories. My brother, Abdul, bought this house from a Village Guard. The Village Guard moved away because people do not like them. They are not safe here anymore.

"Now Kurds are very strong. We do not want Village Guards living among us. Maybe there are a few left here. Maybe some people work secretively for the government and don't wear a uniform. We have to be careful. If it was not for the Village Guard system, the conflict between Turkey and the Kurds would not have lasted more than five years. The PKK would have finished this problem.

"I bought some land and built my house near Abdul's house. We are poor here, but it is our home, our culture, our land. We will never give it up. We can speak our own language here. What can Turkey do to us now? They already destroyed everything we had. We have nothing to fear, because we have nothing more to lose. Only last year they stopped shooting at us from that military outlook up on the mountain."

Now Yakup was telling his story for Farhan. I was forgotten. We all had damp eyes. Yakup's mother looked at Farhan, and gently explained, *"You see, Farhan, Beytussebap was our Shingal. We understand very well what happened to you. That is why we Kurds have to save Yezidis even if we have nothing ourselves."*

Abdul's wife disappeared into her bedroom and returned with a beautiful, green velvet dress for cold winter days and a big bulky pullover sweater to match. "This is for your wife," she said. He refused, but she insisted with a lie, "I don't wear it anymore."

"I will bring my wife to visit you," he replied and gave her a hug.

In 2015, Farhan's family, along with his parents, reached Germany and received asylum. Amy Beam was banned from returning to Turkey after visiting Beytussebap and has not been able to visit the family since then. She was falsely accused of overstaying her residence permit even though she had six weeks remaining on it. Secretly, she was told it was because of her Kurdish politics. In 2019, Turkey's highest court ruled the entry ban was illegal.

First Warning Signs: Yezidis Must Return to Shingal

I visited twelve Kurdish-run Yezidi refugee camps in southeast Turkey in September 2014 and met with every camp manager. Each manager had recently been released from prison as a political prisoner. Prime Minister Erdogan, in an effort to bolster votes for his AK party in the forthcoming elections, released over one hundred Kurdish prisoners from May through July 2014. The camp managers had served between two and ten years in prison. Some were journalists and human rights activists, others PKK militia. All had been accused of being terrorists.

Straight away they joined the Kurdish BDP party. These were the Kurds saving the Yezidis in Turkey. The Yezidis were grateful, but a disturbing pattern quickly emerged. Every camp manager insisted on these conditions:

- The Yezidis would wait in camp until Shingal was safe to return.

- No Yezidis would go to Europe.

- Yezidis were referred to as "our Kurdish brothers," never as Yezidis.

It was clear the Kurdish camp managers were following a directive from higher up, either from the Kurdish BDP party or the PKK leadership in the Qandil Mountains in Iraq on the border with Turkey. I knew then that there was a plan. A terrible foreboding hit me as I realized the Kurds, whom I so loved and defended, were planning to use the Yezidi refugees as pawns to gain the disputed territory of Shingal for their own in Kurdistan. They were going to call the Yezidis "Kurds" and justify annexing Shingal on the basis that it was "Kurdish land." This aspect of genocide in which the Yezidi ethnicity was denied is referred to as *Kurdification*.

To ensure that Yezidis stay put until they could be returned to Shingal, the camps were isolated far from cities with poor transportation and communication. When Kurdish camp managers both in Turkey and Kurdistan, Iraq, were asked for permission to erect cell phone towers, their identical answers were, "Now is not a good time. Maybe later."

As for the Turkish government, Ankara refused to spend one dollar on the Yezidi refugees in the Kurdish-run camps. Turkey wanted to defeat this Kurdish initiative, like every other Kurdish self-help effort in the country. Except for a half-dozen medical charities, Turkey refused visas to more than 100 foreign humanitarian organizations. It levied heavy duties from $7000 to $10,000 dollars on container trucks coming with aid from Europe.

In each town and city the mayors are elected, but a governor is appointed from Ankara. In theory, the mayors run their city, but in actuality they lack control over their budgets. The governors control the budgets and approve program requests.

The governors of Sirnak, Batman, Diyarbakir, and Mardin provinces refused to give authority or funding to the Kurdish-run municipalities who managed the camps with Kurdish volunteers. If Ankara could not take control of the camps and replace Kurdish municipality guards with Turkish soldiers to run them, then they would not support them financially.

All the expenses of providing for the Yezidi refugees were borne by the local municipalities (Belediyesis) and donations. Every Kurdish family and business gave and gave and gave. Ankara's sole donation was a pitiful 100 tents, 500 blankets, and 500 toys to Fidanlik Park camp twenty kilometers south of Diyarbakir.

In spite of being cared for by the Kurds, by November 2014, the Yezidis' deep loyalty to their Kurdish saviors began to erode, because the camp managers continued to insist they were Kurds and they would return to Shingal. These policies worried the refugees and festered like a sore. Inside the camps, Yezidis elected their own leaders and discontinued meetings with the camp managers.

The Turkish government built a camp to house 15,000 Yezidis in Nusaybin on the border with Syria. They enticed Yezidis with the promise of schools, a UNHCR office, and monthly allowances for buying their own food inside the camp store. Only 1500 Yezidis moved to Nusaybin. Another 3,000 were being housed in tents in Midyat camp, also funded by Ankara and guarded by Turkish soldiers. The majority of Yezidis continued to place their bets with the Kurds.

Under Turkey's 2013 Law on Foreigners and International Protection, a person fleeing a dangerous condition coming from a non-European country is considered a "conditional refugee". This describes the Yezidis from Iraq. Turkey is required to give them "temporary protection". When the dangerous condition which forced them to flee ceases to exist, they must return home. Turkey's law denies residency or citizenship to conditional refugees. So Yezidis had to either return to Iraq or go to a third country. It was pointless for them to get comfortable and start new lives in Turkey.

Under the international law of "non-refoulement" refugees could not be forced back to Iraq to live in a dangerous situation where their own government could not guarantee them protection. Insisting that the traumatized Yezidis return to Shingal was like expecting Jews after the World War II Holocaust to return to Auschwitz, the site of mass extermination in gas chambers. It was impossible to fathom.

The responsibility for resettlement is vested with the United Nations High Commission on Refugees (UNHCR). With few exceptions, the UNHCR did not resettle any Yezidis. They, too, took a "wait and see" position. Yezidis would return to Shingal when it was safe.

In reality, the UNHCR, with one office in Ankara, Turkey, was overwhelmed with over one million refugees in Turkey, mostly from Syria. They simply could not manage the crisis. Those Yezidis who registered with UNHCR were given interview dates as far as 12 years in the future. According to UNHCR statistics, the average number of years that refugees live in a camp is 17.

As for Yezidis in the camps in Kurdistan, they were considered internally displaced persons (IDPs), not refugees. By international agreement, they, therefore, did not qualify for UNHCR resettlement as refugees.

On November 20, 2014, the European Parliament convened a special session to discuss the situation of the Yezidis. The EU passed a resolution that included the "*establishment of an international fund to be set up in order for the Yezidis to return to their lands and for the infrastructure to be restored.*" The EU also resolved that "*an autonomous Yezidi region be established in order for a just and lasting political solution to be secured in the Kurdistan region.*" No mention was made about what countries would provide this rebuilding fund nor who would provide protection for an autonomous Yezidi region. No motion to grant asylum was considered.

For three-and-a-half years, the need to defeat Daesh divided everyone and destroyed trust, but there was one uniting belief that all political parties, governments, militaries, and militia forces agreed upon:

Yezidis have to return to Shingal when it is safe.

On March 23, 2015, Yezidis in all the refugee camps in Turkey and Iraq, as well as the capitols of Europe demonstrated for asylum in Europe and international protection in Shingal. In Zakho, Iraq, and Nusaybin, Turkey, demonstrators were attacked by Asayish security police, beaten, bloodied, and arrested. One Yezidi whose cousin was arrested from Jam Mishko camp near Zakho described the attack. "The Asayish arrested about fifty persons and held them for 24 hours using all types of torture, hitting them on their feet, cheeks, back, and hands by pipe sticks and hand grips."

The Yezidis' request to go to Europe was to be silenced and ignored. They gave up hope that the UNHCR would resettle them and turned to smuggling themselves to Europe.

Sworn political enemies were in agreement that Yezidis are Kurds and they have to return. This included the Kurdistan Regional Government, Baghdad, Turkey, the United States, political parties such as PYD, PDK, PUK, and militias such as PKK, YPG, YPJ, YBS, PMU, Peshmerga, the Iraqi Army, the European Union, and coalition forces fighting Daesh. Each group was vying for control of Shingal. This competition intensified over the next three years, growing into a proxy war between western powers and Russia and Iran. The Yezidis were the sacrificial pawns.

I met in June 2015 with Gharib Hassou, the representative to Kurdistan of the PYD political Kurdish party from Syria. I went to relay the desires of the Yezidi refugees in Turkey. Gharib spent ninety minutes insisting that Yezidis are Kurds, and YPG were going to save them and return them to Shingal. He could not be budged in his thinking. I warned him that this position would alienate Yezidis from Kurds.

Mr. Hassou explained, "If Yezidis go to Europe, it will be a second genocide against them. They will lose their land, their culture, their music, their friends, their religion, and their community. The Yezidi culture will cease to exist. We are fighting for their land and for their future existence as a people. What are we sacrificing our lives for if they all want to go to Europe? We want them to return and be part of Kurdistan."

Even the Yezidi Diaspora living in Russia, Georgia, Armenia, Europe, Canada, and America agreed the Yezidis had to return. They were the children of Yezidis who had fled in the 1980s and 1990s after previous genocides against their parents and grandparents. Most of them had never lived in Iraq, but they had a yearning to have a symbolic homeland. They were part of the small minority of Yezidis who identified themselves as Kurdish. Some of these self-proclaimed Yezidi Kurdish leaders actively lobbied foreign governments to deny asylum to Yezidis.

When asked if they wanted to go live in Shingal, their answer was, "Oh, no, I live in Los Angeles" . . . or London or Hannover or Tbilisi. They wanted the *refugees* to return, but *not themselves*. They were already citizens of another country.

The Yezidi political, religious, and military leaders, also, agreed that Yezidis had to return to Shingal. The only people who did *not* agree were the displaced and traumatized Yezidis living in tents and caravans. Yezidi refugees began grumbling amongst themselves that they had no leaders who spoke for them.

In 2016, Yezidi religious leaders, including Tahsin Bag, Prince of Yezidis, and his son, Hazim Tahsin, member of the Yezidi Spiritual Council, met in Germany to establish the amount of gold that would be required for the mandatory dowry in Europe. No mention was made of raising money to free over 3400 Yezidi woman and children in the hands of Daesh. Qassim Shesho publicly denounced Hazim Tahsin for never spending 10,000 dinar (less than $10 USD) to help a single Yezidi woman who had escaped from Daesh.

The Yezidi military leaders, Peshmerga Commander Qassim Shesho and his nephew Haider Shesho, commander of the independent Yezidi militia, both have German citizenship. Years before, they fled from persecution with their families to Germany. Qassim Shesho had been a political prisoner under the Saddam regime. Yet, Qassim Shesho, with his own family living safely in Germany, stated his position that it should be illegal for Yezidis to leave Iraq. When I challenged him, he grudgingly admitted that the survivors who had been raped should be allowed to leave.

The Yezidi refugees in Iraq and Turkey continued in their insistence that they were going to Europe.

Vian Dakhil, the Yezidi MP who was revered for having first alerted the world to the genocide, lost her base of support when she continuously stated Yezidis are Kurds and should be part of Kurdistan. Yezidis accused her of selling out to President Barzani's PDK political party in Kurdistan. By 2016, Yezidis were publicly attacking Dakhil and stating she was free to speak for herself, and choose to be Kurdish, but she did not represent the voice of Yezidis.

A small group of Yezidis went to Iran in January 2017 to solicit military support. In an effort to head off a Yezidi alliance with Iran, Baba Sheikh, the religious leader of Yezidis, made this televised statement: "I made a promise to Mr. President [Barzani] and I will not break my promise. We are Kurdish. Our language is Kurdish and maybe some people from Baghdad and Shingal went to Iran. Nobody is talking for Yezidis, but me. I am talking in the name of Yezidis and myself."

So despised was Barzani by Yezidis that demonstrations were held in Berlin, Germany, and Greece in 2017, attacking him and Baba Sheikh. Some Yezidis disparagingly referred to Baba Sheikh in private as "Baba Shit".

The Yezidis pondered their dilemma as to how to respect and preserve their religion while simultaneously wresting political control from a religious family clan that derived its authority based on the outdated concepts of lineage and monarchy. Many IDPs felt these leaders did not represent their demands or ethnic identity. How could Yezidis build their own democratic country based on a religious dictatorship? Non-religious political parties began to form in tents and living rooms from Shingal to Germany.

The debate as to whether Yezidis are Kurds caused a bitter divide between Kurds and Yezidis. Had Kurds acknowledged that Yezidis are a distinct ethno-religious group, they might have continued to enjoy the support of the Yezidis. Yezidis might have trusted to return to Shingal and become part of Kurdistan, but by insisting that Yezidis are Kurds, and silencing them in camps, the opposite result was achieved. Yezidis lost trust in Kurds and demanded their own independent territory so as to protect their identity. As the tide turned against Yezidi leaders, Baba Sheikh did an about-face. In July 2017 he declared an autonomous country of Ezidkhan. His appointment of a Prime Minister passed with little notice.

While waiting for Daesh to be defeated and Shingal to be safe for return, an estimated 40,000 Yezidis smuggled themselves to Europe before the borders were closed. By 2016, the cost for smuggling illegally averaged $12,000. By 2017, it was virtually impossible to smuggle oneself to Europe. European countries refused visas to virtually all Iraqi IDPs.

Smuggling was replaced with bribes for visas. The average bribery price for a Schengen visa to visit a European country was $12,000 USD. The moment they arrived in Germany, they requested asylum, then applied for their family in Iraq to join them. By the end of 2017, Germany announced it would stop its program for family reunification. Those who succeeded in getting asylum in Germany remained separated from their families stuck in tents in Iraq.

Why Yezidis Plead for Asylum and Refuse to Return to Shingal

The Kurdish policy position that Yezidis would return to Shingal "when it is safe" grew stronger. I gathered a group of refugees in Turkish camps to list their reasons in October 2014. To the last Yezidi, each emphatically stated *I will never return to Shingal.*

By 2018, these reasons remained unchanged and strengthened with nearly four years of supporting evidence. While Yezidis from the Diaspora and others who had lost many or all family members fought valiantly to reclaim and return to Shingal, those IDPs living in tents and caravans for a fourth winter, grew more despondent and continued to plead for asylum in other countries.

One father summarized the sentiment of everyone, "If I have to choose between saving Shingal or raising my two boys in a safe country, I will choose my children. I will take them anywhere in the world to grow up in a safe country, even as far as Australia."

1. Yezidis Are a Different Ethno-religious Group

Although Yezidis speak Kurdish and share cultural similarities with Kurds, Yezidis insist they are a different ethnic and religious group from Arab Muslims, Kurdish Muslims and Christians. They have one god. They believe in peace and brotherhood, but, like Jews, they do not marry outside of their religion. Daesh accused them of being "infidels" or "kuffirs". Shingal is surrounded on all sides by Arab Muslims and Turkmen. Yezidis were targeted by Arabs for extermination because of their religion. Kurds insisted they were Kurds, another aspect of genocide.

2. A History of Yezidi Genocide

There have been at least 73 previous massacres committed against Yezidis in the last 1400 years since Muhammad founded Islam. The Yezidi community suffered one of the worst attacks in 2007 when 312 people were killed, more than 600 were wounded, and 1000 families left homeless when four trucks loaded with explosives destroyed two Yezidi towns. Yezidis do not believe the history of massacres will change, and thus, they can never again feel safe living in Shingal or anywhere in the Middle East.

3. Kurdish Peshmerga Abandoned Yezidis

The Iraqi army was not allowed in the Shingal region prior to the August 2014 attack. The PDK Peshmerga defense force fled in the early morning hours of August 3, 2014, even before the civilians, thus leaving Yezidis exposed to the attack by Daesh. Yezidis swear they can never again trust Kurdish Peshmerga forces.

4. Arabs and Kurds Betrayed Their Yezidi Neighbors

Yezidis were betrayed by the Arab Muslims in Iraq, especially from neighboring Arab villages in Shingal, because many Arabs joined Daesh and many others assisted Daesh attack Shingal in August 2014. When the Daesh gangs were attacking the villages in Shingal, some Yezidis took refuge in the homes of their Arabic or Kurdish friends and neighbors. While some did protect their Yezidi neighbors, other Arabs and Kurds turned the Yezidis over to Daesh. In Shingal, some of the guides who led Daesh to the Yezidis who then killed them were Muslims from Shingal from Kechala, Sarhokia, Jankulia, Khatonia, Kutowea, and other tribes.

5. Terror and Atrocities Used as a Strategy of War

Daesh's strategy was to create a state of terror through savage, unprovoked, and unexpected attacks including beheadings, physical attacks, firing machine guns into people gathered in the streets, and mass executions by bullets to the back of the head while Yezidi victims kneeled or lay on their stomachs awaiting their death.   Men in Siba Sheikh Khudir village were beheaded and hanged from their legs on electricity poles. There were reports of Yezidis buried alive. Allegedly, 40,000 Daesh fighters and their families escaped capture and were living freely in Kurdistan in 2017.   Without international protection and prosecution of the guilty, Yezidis cannot live safely anywhere in Iraq, including Shingal and Kurdistan.

6. Yezidis Forced to Convert to Islam or Die

All captured Yezidis were forced to convert to Islam. Males who refused were killed. Women and girls were sexually enslaved. Very young children were sold to adoptive Arab parents. Boys were sent to training camps to become Daesh terrorists. Daesh ideology comes directly from verses in the Quran calling for all Muslims to engage in jihad against all non-Muslims until Islam is the only religion in the world. The population of non-Muslims in Iraq is less than 1%. Yezidis do not feel they can ever live safely surrounded by Muslims.

7. Yezidis Raped and Sold into Slavery

Approximately 5,270 Yezidi women and children were abducted in 2014. Females were sexually enslaved. At the end of 2017, more than 2,000 women and children were still missing. Slavery and rape of non-Muslims captured during jihad against non-Muslims are part of radical Islamic ideology condoned by verses from the Quran. The Iraqi constitution is based on Shariah law, derived from the Quran and Hadith teachings. This makes all non-Muslims second-class citizens without protection of their civil and human rights.

8. Houses, Businesses, Cars, and Money Looted

Daesh and other Arabs and Kurds looted all the Yezidi homes of all valuables, appliances, wiring, lighting and plumbing fixtures, and burned or exploded hundreds of houses. Yezidis left everything behind. They have no houses, jobs, cars, businesses, neighbors, money, gold, computers, possessions, schools, or hospitals. The infrastructure is destroyed. The area is unsafe with live explosive devices. The refugees are without hope for their religion, ethnic customs, and community continuing in Shingal. The older the person is, the less likely he or she is to wish to leave Iraq, yet there is nothing to return to in Shingal and no money with which to return and rebuild. They face living in camps until they die. Many IDPs, including teenagers, say they are waiting and wishing for death.

9. Safety in Shingal Is a Moot Issue

Many well-meaning supporters of Yezidis, including Yezidis living in Europe, Kurdish political parties, foreign governments, and military forces express the position that the Yezidis should return to Shingal "when it is safe". The question of safety is now a moot issue to Yezidis. The Yezidis left behind dead family members and fled in terror. They have been betrayed by their government and their Arab and Kurdish Muslim neighbors. Their trust has been destroyed and can never be restored. They can never feel secure and live without fear in Shingal. They can never live in psychological peace.

In summary, Yezidis need a choice between asylum or return to Shingal with international protection, compensation, massive rebuilding funds, prosecution of the guilty, and self-administration. By 2018, none of these options had been offered by the international community.

First Responders Were Once Refugees

There have been 73 recorded genocides against Yezidis in the last hundred years. The attack of August 3, 2014, in Shingal was number 74. The Yezidis say theirs is the oldest ethno-religious group in the Middle East. There were once twenty-three million Yezidis in Mesopotamia (now Iraq). Now that number has dwindled to half-a million, with less than half-a-million more displaced in the Diaspora.

The first Islamic State was declared by Muhammad in the year 622. The teachings of Muhammad are the foundation of Islam and are codified in verses in the Quran. Since that time, Islam spread from Asia to North Africa and eastern Europe. The entire Middle East was converted. It once had been predominately populated with Jews, Christians, Assyrians, Armenians, Greeks, and Yezidis.

The first Islamic State began to convert or kill non-Muslims in 622. They had three choices: convert to Islam, pay an extra tax called "jizya," or be killed. Many, including the Kurds, converted to Islam to save their lives. The Yezidis did not have the option of paying an extra tax. They could only run, convert, or face the sword. This Islamization explains how the Yezidi population dwindled to under a million and how the Kurds became Muslim. Those who did not convert remained Yezidis. Daesh used these identical tactics against Christians and Yezidis in 2014.

Genocides against non-Muslims continue to this day, which is why Yezidis say they can never be safe living in a Muslim country, especially one whose constitution enshrines Shariah law. The population of Yezidis in southeastern Turkey was around 80,000 until the 1970s. The estimated population of Yezidis in Turkey before Daesh attacked Shingal was 350.

If the reader is not convinced about the religious motivation for the Yezidi genocide, he or she need only do some reading about the beginnings of Islam and the Christian Crusades. The 1400-year decimation of the non-Muslim population under Islam is a religious war that has no end in sight.

Refugees who grew up in Germany were in their thirties when Daesh attacked Shingal in 2014. Hundreds of Yezidi-Germans moved into action within the first few days. They knew what was needed without having to be told, because they had once been refugees.

Some collected aid to take to the displaced Yezidis in Iraq and Turkey. Others mounted political action campaigns. Some returned to Shingal to take up arms against Daesh. Every Yezidi in Europe and North America shifted into emergency mode to save their people.

In the 1980s and 1990s, Turkey destroyed the Kurdish and Yezidi villages and cities in eastern Turkey. The Yezidi refugees fled to Europe or Iraq. There is not a single Yezidi resident in most of the former Yezidi villages in Turkey today.

After the attack, Batman local government, under the direction of Fikret Taskin, BDP party member, refurbished 94 houses in nine Batman villages in the country-side thirty kilometers from Batman city. They housed 500 Yezidi refugees. In the early 1990s these former Yezidi villages were forcibly evacuated by the Turkish government. They had been empty for over twenty years.

In each deserted Batman village there was one family living to oversee the empty houses. These village managers contacted the current house owners, mostly living in Europe, for permission to use their houses rent-free for the Yezidi refugees. In exchange, Kurdish volunteers repaired the electricity, installed new windows, and painted the houses inside and outside entirely with donations.

Ali Sedo Rasho, a well-known Yezidi historian, took asylum in Germany in 2009 when Iraq became unsafe for him because of his writing. In Bielefeld, Germany, Ali immediately began organizing activists and speaking to elected officials to urge them to help save the Yezidis. Ali's daughter's family and his brother's family of three generations fled from Shingal to Batman in 2014. They were among those housed in the Yezidi villages that had been abandoned under the Turkish genocide in the 1980s. When Ali applied for a visa to go to help his daughter and blind grandchild, Turkey denied his visa.

Ali Sedo's own home in Shingal, worth $100,000, was exploded by Daesh in September 2014.

Haider Shesho left his family in Germany and went directly to Shingal where he organized an independent militia of 3,000 Yezidis. After Kurdistan jailed him for nine days, demonstrations in his support erupted all over Kurdistan and Europe forcing KRG to release him. He remained the commander of his growing militia, but was careful to say he was Kurdish. He wore both the Yezidi flag and Kurdish flag on his uniform.

Qassim Shesho, Haider's uncle, also left his family in Germany. Years before they had fled from Saddam Hussein. Qassim Shesho became the KRG Peshmerga commander in Shingal with 8,000 Yezidi volunteers who signed up after the attack. He grew up on Shingal Mountain above Sherfadin shrine, which he made his headquarters. Qassim wore no insignia of any sort on his uniform. When asked why he wore no flags or insignia on his uniform, Commander Qassim answered, "I have never worn a flag for any country, and I never will."

Shereen Alkalo was twenty when terrorists kidnapped and executed twenty-three innocent Yezidis in front of her home in 2007 in Mosul, Iraq. It was a convincing threat against her family. Her family escaped with an hour's notice to Shekhan city near Mosul. They lost their house and went overnight from rich to poor. Shereen, a young mother living in Germany, immediately began writing witness' stories when Daesh attacked in 2014.

Turkey denied visas to over 100 foreign NGOs who wanted to help the refugees. Only about a half-dozen NGOs, such as Doctors Without Borders, were granted visas. Hefty taxes of $7000 to $10,000 were assessed for container trucks coming from Europe with donations. Turkey effectively blocked the trucks loaded with donations from reaching the Yezidis in refugee camps by applying duties that individual humanitarians could not afford to pay.

The Mennonites' container truck of aid from Pennsylvania, US, was trapped for forty days between the border of Turkey and Iraq. It could neither go forward nor backward. The cost of the truck was $1000 per day.

Mejdin Kurt was nine when his family was forced to flee from Turkey in 1989. He and his wife, also a refugee, collected fifty tons of clothing and money to pay for transportation. When their first container truck arrived in Turkey in October 2014, the government wanted to asses a duty of $7500. Mejdin called me in Sirnak for help and after four days and many meetings, we got the duty waived and they distributed the aid in Sirnak refugee camp.

Mejdin is but one of hundreds of displaced Yezidis in Europe who were first responders to those Yezidis attacked in Shingal. This is Mejdin's story about when he was a refugee. Every Yezidi in the Diaspora can tell a similar story.

Mejdin Kurt (born in 1979)

I am from Dênwan (Turkish: Çörekliköyü), a small village near Midyat, which belongs to Mardin in the southeast of Turkey (northern Kurdistan). I lived there as a young child with parents and seven brothers and sisters. We did mixed farming. In this area we did not have any infrastructure or industry. We lived apart from the rest of the world. Most of us had no formal education.

For us it was normal to be oppressed by the Turkish soldiers or a policeman or by Muslims. I will never forget the oppression of the Muslims. Some Muslim friends of my father used to always say, "You are good men, but unfortunately you are not Muslim!" Or they would not buy from the Yezidis in the marketplace. If they did, they would cheat us by paying a cheaper price. Take it or leave it.

In our village there lived only Yezidis, but we had many Christian villages and some Muslim villages surrounding us. We had good relationships with the Christians, but not always with the Muslims. Between 1985 and 1988, a lot of our villagers moved from Dênwan to Europe for a better life. Most of them came to Germany, because some of our villagers knew that Germany would host guest workers in the 1960s and 1970s.

We children worked very hard. We also took care of the villagers' animals, because there were no more young people remaining in Dênwan. All of them had moved. That was the reason why my dad said that I had to go to our uncle in Germany. My dad never wanted to leave his homeland. He did not choose to leave.

In 1989, we sold some of our goats and sheep to raise money to smuggle to Germany. My dad sent just me, my eleven-year-old brother, and my thirteen-year-old sister. I was only nine. We had never left our village before. It was hard for him to send his children away, but he did it out of love to give us a future.

My dad took us to Istanbul where we waited two weeks in a hotel until finding someone to help us. At long last, we found someone, and my father paid a lot of money to him. Then we took a flight from Istanbul to the Czech Republic. In the Czech Republic we waited another two weeks for a smuggler to help us get to Germany.

The first attempt failed. When the smuggler brought us to a river to cross, there were a lot of security guards that night. After this, the smuggler disappeared, and we spent a few more days in the hotel. Suddenly a good friend of our uncle fetched us from there and brought us to our uncle in Upper Palatinate, Germany. The friend of our uncle was from the Green Party. At that time, the Green Party helped the refugees a lot.

Seven months later there was an attack on our village. The Muslims or soldiers killed two men and injured one woman. One of them was my father's uncle. Their bodies were riddled with twenty bullets. My father barely escaped the bullets. After this tragic incident, everybody left the village in the direction of Europe. The village and most Yezidi villages in southeast Turkey remain empty to this day. My parents came with my siblings to Germany and we were reunited.

Now we live far away from our homeland, and we all are missing it. All of the older generation miss their homeland and have psychosomatic illnesses. The family members usually live far apart and we cannot act out our traditional customs. We miss our culture, not just our homeland.

The younger Yezidi generations have been assimilated in Germany. We have an enormous number of academies. But we have one big problem that disturbs everyone's thoughts: *How can we protect the future of Yezidis and our culture?*

Twenty-five years after Mejdin smuggled to Germany, the Yezidis were still smuggling to Europe for safety from Islamic extremists and still longing for their homeland.

Tambours, Jihad and the Spread of Islam
Barakat Ali Khalaf, September 2, 2016

The *Encyclopaedia of Islam* states that the *"spread of Islam by arms is a religious duty upon Muslims in general ... Jihad must continue to be done until the whole world is under the rule of Islam ... Islam must completely be made over before the doctrine of jihad [warfare to spread Islam] can be eliminated."*

I am Barakat Ali Khalaf. I have been playing the tambour since I was eleven. It is a holy stringed, wooden instrument similar to a lute, with a gourd-shaped body. Now I have memorized 250 historical songs which preserve the history of genocides against Yezidis.

In the days after Daesh went on their killing rampage through the villages and city of Shingal on August 3, 2014, they returned and stole everything from our houses. Photos showed up on the internet of stolen refrigerators, stoves, washing machines, TVs, and furniture being sold by Arabs in big open air market places. They even ripped out kitchen and bathroom sinks. Nothing remained in any house except broken glass and scattered pieces of torn clothing. They burned and exploded many of our houses.

When I returned to see the damage to my home after Khanasor was freed from Daesh, I found all three of my tambours smashed. Instead of stealing the tambours, Daesh left the pieces in every house as a symbol to insult our religion. I brought the necks for memories, nothing more.

But if we want to be sorry about something, there are a lot more important things than this, such as what happened to our girls and our women and children, innocent people like old people. Daesh killed people and cut their heads off and committed many crimes against Yezidi people.

They broke everything, because they wanted to wipe out our culture. They wanted to break everything, not just our tambour, but what it represents to us. Daesh knew from the Arabs around our area that the tambour is holy as a religious instrument in our culture. We kiss it before we play a song. For many years our fathers and grandfathers were saying the tambour is a holy instrument in our culture. If you are not serious and talented enough on it, then you are not allowed to play it.

Many genocides happened to us in the past. We knew they were repeating. Those people who were attacking us tried to break everything we have. They burned our books, so that is why we depend on keeping the songs in our mind. They can destroy my tambours, but they cannot destroy my memory. Someone gave me a new tambour, and now I am singing again. I wrote a new song in memory of the 74th genocide entitled, "Dedication for the Kidnapped."

These historical songs are mostly about genocide. Those songs that are not about genocide are about love, but those love stories are giving you a history lesson of when Yezidis were in Turkey and had to run away. A majority of Yezidis in Kurdistan, Iraq, originally came from Turkey.

The Kurdish people originally followed the Yezidi religion, not Islam. Yezidi people were attacked by the Ottoman army who tried to steal their land and force them to convert to Islam, but they refused like we are refusing right now. I remember my father telling me about these stories and teaching me our history when I was a boy. He said there used to be 366 Yezidi villages around Siirt in southeast Turkey. Yezidis were forced to run from Turkey to northern Iraq.

When the Ottoman soldiers attacked the local population, they gave them two choices. Either you are going to be Muslim or you are going to be killed. Since they did not want to be killed, children and old people who were unable to run had to convert. So that is how the Yezidis became Muslim Kurds. The Kurds *used* to be Yezidis.

The able-bodied Yezidis like us and our fathers ran. They survived in the mountains. We Yezidis have always been Yezidis and will always remain Yezidis. We never converted to any other religion. We do not read the Quran like Kurds. We are peaceful people who believe in God, so we don't want to convert to any other religion. We still live near mountains to be prepared for the next genocide.

After the Republic of Turkey was created in 1923, Turkey continued the practice to force Yezidis to convert to Islam. Turkey changed the names of Yezidi villages to Turkish names, destroyed Yezidi temples, and defaced Yezidi graves. Muslims refuse to trade with Yezidis or eat food prepared by Yezidis. They call it haram. To this day, right here in Duhok, Muslims will not eat food prepared by Yezidis, so we cannot get any jobs in restaurants. The restaurants will not buy fish from a Yezidi fisherman, so they have to sell their fish for half-price to a middle-man. It is considered *haram* (not allowed) to eat eggs from a chicken owned by a Yezidi.

In the 1980s Yezidi villages in Turkey were attacked and Yezidis had to run for their lives once again. Many went to Germany. By 2014 the Yezidi population of Turkey was only 350 people. When Daesh attacked in 2014, we had to run again from Shingal back to Kurdistan. My family stopped in Duhok, but twenty-five thousand Yezidis kept going. They walked over the mountains from Iraq to southeast Turkey.

Shingal was not originally the homeland for Yezidis. When they came from what is now Turkey to escape the Ottomans, they settled in towns like Bashiqa and Shekhan near Lalish, the site of our holy shrines. I, myself, am originally from Khattari which is in the Kurdistan region, nearby Mosul. As the Yezidis kept being attacked over the decades, they ran to Shingal Mountain. If you go to see our old villages from a few decades ago they are just ruins. Most of them were at the foot of the mountain or actually on the mountain.

After Saddam Hussein controlled Iraq, he pushed our villages off the mountain to five or ten kilometers back onto the flat Nineveh plain, farther from safety. Yezidis have always been near mountains to run to safety. We have been running for centuries. There is no safe haven for us in the Middle East. We love all people, so we do not understand why no country protects us.

I have read that seven hundred years ago our population used to be 63 million, and now we are under one million. If we do not get protection, then we cannot go back to Shingal. If we leave Iraq, we are worried that we will disappear from this earth.

Commander Qassim Derbo Shoots Daesh Oil Trucks

A Peshmerga officer, who asked to remain anonymous, told me that when Daesh had control of the city of Sinjar, the Peshmerga were shooting at the oil trucks from their position on Shingal Mountain overlooking Highway 47. Daesh trucks used this highway to drive between Mosul, the Daesh capital of their so-called Islamic caliphate in Iraq, and Raqqa, their capital in Syria, a distance of 370 kilometers (230 miles).

An American military team showed up on Shingal Mountain to train the Peshmerga. They ordered the Peshmerga commander to stop shooting the oil trucks. "If you shoot one more truck we will shoot you," they threatened. "But don't take my word for it, go ask Qassim Derbo directly."

After visiting with Hassan Derbo and getting the story about the Doshka memorial on Shingal Mountain, I drove into Sinjar city and was ceremoniously ushered into see Hassan's brother, Commander Qassim Derbo. Qassim Derbo was officially in command of all 8000 Peshmerga in Shingal. His role seemed to be managerial as he worked in the large building headquarters for Peshmerga training and administration, complete with security guards at the iron gate and even inside his inner office.

Do not confuse Qassim Derbo with Qassim Shesho whose headquarters is next to Sherfadeen shrine near Sunoni. Commander Qassim Shesho was in the field commanding Peshmerga on the front lines.

Qassim Derbo greeted me like every other government director and commander in Kurdistan and Shingal. He sincerely thanked me for coming half-way around the world to help them defeat Daesh. His photographer took a photo of us drinking tea together.

"I've come to ask only one question. Is it true that the Americans ordered you to stop shooting Daesh's oil trucks transporting oil from Mosul to Raqqa?" I asked.

Qassim Derbo explained that the Americans accused him of shooting at civilian vehicles that were not carrying oil.

"I knew what I was doing. I knew every truck or tanker I shot at was carrying oil. Daesh had many ways to disguise what they were carrying. Often they transported the oil stored in other containers besides barrels or oil tankers."

"Highway 47 runs from Mosul in the east through Tal Afar, Sinjar, then to Raqqa, Syria, in the west. At the west end of the mountain, it is called Shilo Road. Between August 3, 2014, and November 12, 2015, when Sinjar was liberated, this road was heavily trafficked with cars and every kind of truck. More than 1000 vehicles passed every day from morning until night. This road was Daesh's route for oil and supplies."

"We could not stop all the oil trucks, because we did not have enough ammunition, but we hit one or two per day. We had two Doshka cannons. The Doshka 24 has a firing range of ten kilometers The Doshka 12 has a range of three to five kilometers. Our position was only three to six kilometers from the road. On December 20, 2014, we seized a Doshka 12 from Daesh. We seized another Doshka 12 after we liberated Sinjar on November 13, 2015. That brought our total to four Doshkas."

"The American team came to train our Peshmerga soldiers. They taught us how to call in coordinates for coalition air strikes. The Americans flew a small drone one-foot in diameter. We have several people who coordinate strikes with the coalition forces. We called in coordinates of Daesh locations on a daily basis to the coalition. Occasionally, they would strike one of the locations."

It was no secret that from Kobane in Rojava, Syria, to Shingal, coalition airstrikes were bombing holes in the desert sand for the benefit of journalists. This fake "targeting" was common knowledge among the entire population that caused a furious disappointment with the Americans in whom Iraqis placed so much hope. Qassim Derbo tried to stop the Daesh oil trucks with his four Doshkas and volunteer soldiers.

In a single hour the road from Mosul to Raqqa could have been closed by coalition airstrikes. It is nothing short of mind-boggling that this route was allowed to remain open for fifteen months for Daesh to transport oil, food, supplies, arms, terrorists, and abducted Yezidi girls and children between the Daesh capitals of Mosul and Raqqa.

In October 2015, Financial Times reported that only 196 of 10,600 air strikes by US-led coalition forces were conducted against oil infrastructure since August 2014 and that Daesh earned $1.5 million dollars per day in oil sales. The world price of oil fell from $100 to $35 per barrel before climbing back to $50. Daesh was trucking crude oil to Syria and selling it for $25 to $35 per barrel.

Yezidi Peshmerga and YPG and YBS militias in Shingal said that for two years they had been like actors in a Hollywood movie, just waiting for the Americans to decide when to finish the war and finally divide up the country. The analogy to being in a movie, waiting for the ending, was a common refrain.

Everyone I interviewed from all sectors agreed that Iraq was a failed state and had not functioned as one country for several years. When I asked my pilot friend in the Iraqi Air Force when the division of the country into Shia, Sunni, and Kurd would finally be officially recognized, he answered, "When the Americans decide." By late summer 2016, he said all air force missions and targets were being directed by the Americans.

One might think the story of Yezidi Commander Qassim Derbo being ordered not to shoot the oil trucks is just a footnote to history. In reality, this is the smoking gun.

Where should I begin to tell this tragedy?   When Caesar crossed the Rubicon? Let us begin when the gasoline automobile was invented in the 1890s. King Leopold II of Belgium claimed the Belgian Congo to steal rubber for the production of automobile tires.   Leopold brutalized, enslaved, and killed ten million Africans between 1885 and 1908 in the collection of rubber.

The automobile became a beast that is devouring the world with oil wars one hundred years later. The United States invaded Iraq in 2003 on the now-famous lie of finding weapons of mass destruction. The real goal was to claim the oil in Iraq, mostly in Kurdistan.   Because America ended the despotic rule of Saddam Hussein in 2003, the Kurds gave loyalty to America, but a dozen years later many felt betrayed.

One day in 2016, a senior government bureaucrat who had been imprisoned and tortured as a young man by Saddam Hussein gave me a history lesson, jotting notes on a napkin. In 1986 an American team came to them with their plan for the future of the Middle East.   Syria would be destroyed. Iraq would be partitioned into three countries including one for Kurdistan. Turkey's strength would be knocked down. Here we were, thirty years later. The plan took longer than anticipated, but it was coming to its conclusion.

On September 15, 2006, while the US was occupying Iraq, US Secretary of State Condoleezza Rice presented a map to a meeting in NATO's Military College in Rome, Italy. She called it the map of the New Middle East. This map was prepared by Lieutenant-Colonel Ralph Peters, a retired colonel of the US National War Academy. It was published in the Armed Forces Journal in June 2006.

It showed Iraq partitioned into three countries: Kurdistan for the Kurds, then one for the Sunnis and one for the Shias. Most of the oil is in the disputed territories of Kirkuk and Shingal and in Kurdistan, the semi-autonomous state in northern Iraq where Kurds live. The Kurds are loyal to America. If Kurdistan could become an independent country, it would be easy to control and export the oil.

The Kurdistan of this New Middle East map included western Iran and eastern Turkey where at least half of Turkey's twenty million Kurds live. Turkey raised a fire storm over this. There would be no Kurdistan for Kurds in Turkey! The map vanished for a decade, but reappeared in mass media one week after Daesh took control of Mosul, June 10, 2014.

From 2003 until 2011, the United States occupied Iraq. In December 2011, the American forces left Iraq without having partitioned Iraq into three countries. Some Yezidis claim Shingal was the stumbling block.

In 2013, the KRG economy was booming in anticipation of oil revenues. Hi-rise condos selling for one million dollars dotted the Erbil skyline. In January

2014, Baghdad cut the central budget allocation of 17% of oil revenues to KRG by 50%. By March 2014, Baghdad stopped sending money to KRG.

In May 2014, KRG completed building two oil pipe lines running directly from Kirkuk and Baiji, Iraq, to Ceyhan, Turkey, and began delivering oil. Baghdad called it smuggling because KRG was not sharing oil revenues with the central government. Baghdad threatened to sue anyone who bought oil directly from the KRG.

When a tanker filled with oil sailed from Ceyhan, Turkey, to Galveston, Texas, Baghdad filed a court case in the United States. The tanker returned to Europe and sold the oil to Israel. After all those years of war, the United States was still not getting oil from Kurdistan, at least not directly. In May 2014, media reports announced it would not be long before Kurdistan would begin to sell its oil.

On June 9, 2014, Daesh took control of Mosul, then swept west through central Iraq, Shingal, and all the way to Raqqa, Syria, to declare its Islamic caliphate. Right after Daesh controlled Mosul, Peshmerga took control of Kirkuk, and Kurdistan began selling its oil. Within three months, Iraq was unofficially partitioned into three sections among Kurds, Sunni, and Shia. Shingal, homeland of the Yezidis, remained a disputed territory although Peshmerga was controlling and claiming it for Kurdistan.

Shingal was a geographic inconvenience, located on the direct oil tanker truck route between Mosul and Raqqa. Yezidis had to go. Both oil-rich KRG and western countries who coveted its oil and minerals sacrificed Shingal by allowing Sunni Muslim extremists and psychopaths to commit genocide against the Yezidis.

Turkey was accused of supporting Daesh. The American journalist, Serena Shim, reported in 2014 that Turkish Daesh terrorists were smuggling themselves into Syria by hiding inside World Food Organization trucks. Shortly after, she died in a suspicious car accident.

On October 18, 2015, Jacki Sutton, acting Iraq director for the Institute for War and Peace Reporting (IWPR) in Erbil, died in a suspicious "suicide" in the Istanbul airport. Officials claimed she hanged herself with her shoelaces from the hook on the back of the door on a toilet stall because she was upset about missing her connecting flight to Erbil. The day before she had just secured a million dollars in funding to train Iraqis to use social media to counter violent extremism.

The Kurdistan economy that was booming in 2013 was bankrupt in 2014 because of the inability for Erbil and Baghdad to resolve their dispute about oil revenue sharing. KRG sank into debt. By June 2014 the KRG could not pay salaries to government civil servants nor to the Peshmerga soldiers fighting Daesh. The United States sent financial support to Baghdad to fight Daesh, but not one dollar found its way to KRG to pay Peshmerga salaries.

A remarkable thing happened in Kurdistan which demonstrated the resilience and solidarity of Kurds. The entire government sector showed up for work five hours per day without salaries for the next two years. Every three months, they got paid for one month, or approximately $300 US dollars, barely enough to buy food. There were no exceptions, from bureaucrats to teachers to surgeons in the government hospital. Many Peshmerga volunteered six to twelve months without a salary. To earn money, they would take two weeks off to drive a taxi, then return to the front line.

The KRG continued to sell its oil in Turkey via its pipeline while Baghdad continued to freeze KRG's budget. By January 2016, KRG could no longer sustain itself economically while supporting more than one million Syrian refugees and internally displaced Iraqis. Teachers went on strike to demand their salaries. Malcontent and hopelessness set in.

In January 2016, KRG did an about-face and signed an agreement with Baghdad to give Baghdad all its oil in exchange for Baghdad paying all the withheld money owed to KRG. The year passed without implementing the agreement. The stalemate continued.

At the same time that the United States was sending aid to support the Kurdish YPG who were fighting Daesh in Syria, Turkey was flying missions into Syria killing the YPG. Yet the United States supported Turkey in its war against Kurds in southeast Turkey, where up to one million Kurds were displaced when their cities were destroyed by their own government.

Masoud Barzani, the Kurdish president of Kurdistan, offered no objection to Turkey's war on Kurds in Turkey, even when Turkish war planes crossed the border into Iraq and killed PKK militants in Qandil Mountains. The KRG wanted to maintain good relations with Ankara government at any cost, because Turkey was buying KRG's oil. KRG needed the oil revenue for salaries. Secret reports claimed Masoud Barzani was siphoning off oil proceeds for himself.

The KRG also wanted the YPG and PKK to leave Shingal, but they refused. President Barzani ordered the Peshmerga to force the YPG and PKK out of Shingal, but the Yezidi Peshmerga commanders refused to use force to remove them. It was, after all, the YPG and PKK who had saved the Yezidis after Daesh attacked them. When pressure did not work, beginning in 2016, the KRG blocked vehicles from taking food and medicine to Shingal with the strategy to starve them off the mountain.

Foreign fighters who had joined YPG to fight Daesh were imprisoned in Kurdistan, if caught. Their home countries also charged them with joining a terrorist organization when they returned home. The United States removed its open tourist visa policy for citizens of any country if their passport showed a visa entry stamp to Iraq. The US State Department warned US citizens not to travel to Iraq, even though Kurdistan was safer than Kansas.

The US placed Iraq on its list of sanctioned countries meaning it enforced an economic blockade against Iraq. Western Union made it virtually impossible to send money to anyone in Iraq with the excuse that the money might be funding terrorism, rather than helping its victims. The displaced Yezidis wondered why volunteers were not coming to help them recover from their suffering.

In 2015, Turkey criticized Russia for bombing the Daesh trucks, oil tankers and depots in Syria. One week after Turkey shot down a Russian fighter plane, Russia accused Erdogan and his family of involvement in the oil smuggling.

Russia criticized the US for not stopping the oil trucks. The United States government rejected the premise that the Turkish government was in league with Daesh to smuggle oil. In order to support those accusations, on December 2, 2015, the Russian Defense Ministry released satellite images proving that Daesh trucks were moving oil from Iraq, to Syria, and then to Turkey.

The US was under pressure of public opinion to match Russia's efforts to stop the terrorists' oil smuggling. On November 16, 2015, US warplanes destroyed 116 Daesh oil trucks in Syria. Forty-five minutes prior, leaflets were dropped advising drivers to get out of their trucks and run away.

It had taken the US an astonishing 15 months to decide that in order to cripple Daesh it had to strike the oil trucks. In the following two weeks, Russia and the US vaporized a combined 1,300 Daesh oil transport vehicles. By this time, Daesh had become the richest terrorist organization in the world, financed by illegal oil sales to Syria and Turkey where the oil then changed hands and was sold on the world market. At the same time that the United States and Russia were both fighting Daesh, Russia was supporting the presidency of Assad in Syria while the US and Turkey were trying to overthrow him.

Powertrans is an oil company. In 2011, Turkey granted it the exclusive right to import and export oil to and from Turkey. President Erdogan's son-in-law, Berat Albayrak, was appointed the Minister of Energy in Turkey in November 2015. In November 2016, Wikileaks released hacked email exchanges from 2012 through 2015 between Albayrak and Powertrans. Emails strongly indicate that Albayrak controlled the Powertrans oil company. The argument that Turkey supported Daesh grew stronger.

On November 12, 2015, Peshmerga retook Shingal in one day. They were prepared to go further south, but were ordered by the US to remain in their positions and actually retreat from their position on Highway 47 near the Syrian border. Daesh continued to use their position in Shingal to run as many as 500 trucks a day, full of oil, from Kirkuk to Turkey, where it was sold at a discount. The US would never grant Peshmerga's daily requests to bomb them.

In April 2016 on a talk show, US President Donald Trump stated, "We have got to get the oil, because that's their (Daesh's) source of wealth." On the NBC TV Today show (4/28/16), Trump said, "Now, they (Daesh) have fortified oil reserves and they've prepared. And we'll still take the oil, and we should be taking the oil and we're not."

By the end of 2016, multi-national oil companies in KRG were laying off employees and walking away from their investments in Kurdistan. Cartoonists and pundits were describing the Middle East as one giant clusterfuck.

In 2017, US President Donald Trump sent his Secretary of Defense, General James Mattis, to Iraq to assure Iraq that Americans are "not in Iraq to seize" oil. Gordon Duff, senior editor at *Veterans Today*, told Press TV that in the course of one year after the 2003 invasion of Iraq, the US "stole 40 percent of Iraq's oil that was sent out through the Kirkuk pipeline to the Mediterranean port, south of Ceyhan, Turkey. It was loaded on ocean-going tankers owned by, well oddly enough, mostly ExxonMobil corporation." The former ExxonMobil CEO, Rex Tillerson, was serving as President Trump's Secretary of State in 2017.

Duff explained, "Those tankers would be loaded, supertankers one after another, with Iraqi oil that was never paid for and then again you have the issue of ISIS (Daesh) and their 12,000 trucks that the US never saw." The stolen oil is also being sold at a "highly discounted price" to ExxonMobile, "and that would be Rex Tillerson." Duff noted that General Mattis, himself, "knows all about this."

On March 13, 2018, President Trump fired Tillerson without warning. Tillerson had met the week before with Turkey's President Erdogan for six hours.

For three years while the war against Daesh was being waged, KRG revealed it was exporting 150,000 barrels per day to Ceyhan, Turkey. In October 2017, Baghdad used military force against Peshmerga to take control of Kirkuk away from Kurdistan. Crude oil prices jumped immediately from $45 a barrel to $65.

According to a PUK Peshmerga Colonel, Baghdad checked the meters on the pipeline and discovered that KRG had been piping 450,000 barrels per day to Turkey for three years, not the 150,000 it publicized. Even at a discounted price of $40 per barrel, that equals $12 million US dollars per day unaccounted for.

There are two ways oil was leaving Iraq: north from Kirkuk to Ceyhan, Turkey, by pipeline controlled by KRG or west by Daesh oil trucks from Shingal to Syria and then to Turkey. Whoever could control the Shia Crescent from Iran to Shingal to Syria could build pipelines to the Mediterranean.

Iran, which is a Shia government like Iraq, sent both oil and arms to support Syria's Shia government. In logic that was sinister in its beauty, Iran was accused of supporting the Sunni-inspired Daesh in Iraq. With Daesh in Iraq, this gave Iran the justification to invade Iraq to defeat Daesh. Iran armed Yezidi militias to retake Shingal in 2017 along with Iranian-backed Shia Hashd al-Sha'abi militias from Baghdad and Iran.

With the war in Syria dragging on, the plan for exporting oil west to a Mediterranean port was revised. In December 2017, Iran and Iraq signed an agreement for Iraq to export its crude oil *east* through the Iranian territory – a scheme that would remove Baghdad's reliance on the KRG to export its oil through a pipeline to Turkey.

The reason no US military officials ever visited the front lines in Shingal was because they knew that Kurdistan's Peshmerga forces were never going to be allowed to go forward and would, under their agreement with Baghdad, be pushed back by the Hashd al-Sha'abi to the 2003 borders. This is exactly what happened in October 2017 after the Kurdistan referendum for independence.

For two years I maintained to my Yezidi friends that the genocide against them had been because of oil, not religion. But after listening to hundreds of Yezidi witness testimonies, it is clear that the Yezidi genocide occurred, also, as ethnic cleansing by fundamentalist Sunni Arab foot soldiers who swallowed the brainwashing of performing jihad against non-Muslims. Daesh, using extremist Islamic ideology to recruit, incite hatred, and justify rape and murder, was intent on destroying the Yezidi culture and religion.

Religious fanaticism was exploited to partition Iraq in order to deliver the oil to world markets. In the deal, the Yezidis were sacrificed.

Daesh Tunnel Discovered in Sinjar

Mirza Bakir Pisso's testimony as recounted by Amy Beam, May 18, 2016

The battle to retake Sinjar city from Daesh was on November 12, 2015. There was a fierce fire fight in the devastated historic old town on the north side where the road from the mountain enters the city. Daesh was shooting from inside a pink, two story house on one corner. PKK and YPG were shooting from behind sandbags and steel barrels diagonally across the intersection, a mere thirty meters away. Sinjar was declared liberated on November 13 by Peshmerga.

Mirza Bakir Pisso moved back to Sinjar with his wife and three youngest children a few months later. "We thank all the people in Kurdistan who helped us for two years, but now we want to come back to our house." His older children remained in their tent in Shariya camp. Mirza was among the first fifty families who decided the danger of living in Sinjar was worth the risk to get out of their tent. They had lost so much already, returning was an act of sheer defiance.

Moving back required total independence living off the grid with a generator, heating and cooking oil, and hauling water in large jugs. The blue sky was hidden by dark smoke, like a foggy day. Black soot covered everything. Instead of growing wheat, the fields surrounding Sinjar were being burned off for a second year to explode live bullets and IEDs.

Walking down the deserted street, overgrown with weeds, Mirza explained, "Ali Khuder al-Tayif, a Sunni Arab from the Meteoti tribe, moved to Sinjar in 2007. He was my neighbor. He lived on the next road. Asayish captured him many times, and then they released him, stating they did not have enough evidence to hold him. Then he became an Emir in Daesh."

So when David Shumock, a volunteer with the small Peshmerga special forces unit just a few kilometers to the southwest of the city, stated they were trapped on August 3 between Daesh to the north and Daesh's Toyota pickup trucks advancing from Baaj to the south, here was some proof of that. Daesh was already living inside of Sinjar waiting for the attack.

Ali Khuder al-Tayif and other Sinjar residents raised their black flags even before their partners in crime arrived from the south that morning. By 9:30 AM on August 3, 2014, Daesh controlled all of Sinjar. Most residents escaped on foot and by car, but Daesh captured at least 1,000 Yezidis and corralled them into a new government building used to issue national identity cards (jensias).

Mirza explained, "My father, Bakir Pisso, and my wife's father, Shamo Kolas Mirza (born 1941), escaped that morning from Gir Zerik and made it to our house in Sinjar. When I decided to escape with my wife and children, Shamo and Bakir, decided to take their chances and remain in our house. They hoped Daesh might not hurt the old men. Both of them were captured and later transferred to Tal Afar."

"From Tal Afar, Shamo escaped west on foot, but was recaptured when nearly at the mountain. Daesh threw his body on the ground, drove over him, breaking his arms and legs, then shot him afterwards. They tossed his dead body into the room in Tal Afar where the other Yezidi men were being held prisoners. 'This is what will happen to anyone else who tries to escape,' they warned."

The Emir established his headquarters in the houses of Mirza's uncles and sister right down the road from his own house. Houses in the entire city were connected with shared walls. Mirza and his kids walked me through the houses, quite literally. Holes had been broken through the concrete walls so one could stoop through the holes and walk through four houses without ever having to go outside and risk being seen by overhead drones. "These other holes were for air conditioning units," Mirza explained.

The interior concrete walls were covered in Arabic writing made with black markers. On one wall was a schedule with the exact times of day for praying to Allah. On many walls was written "Allah is great. There is no god but Allah. Muhammad is the profit of Allah."

Prayers specifically for Daesh fighters to recite were written on pieces of paper carefully glued onto cardboard that lay scattered on the floor along with books with Islamic prayers.

Like graffiti, Daesh names were scrawled everywhere from floor to ceiling in that primeval need to record one's existence for history: I was here. Abu Bakir, Abu Saif al-Ansari, Abu Abdullah al-Ansari, Raid al-Ansari, Abu Ayisha. They were dated May 17, 2015. six months before Sinjar was cleared of Daesh forces. I took photos of the self-incriminating evidence.

"This is the room where the Emir slept and sometimes fought," Mirza showed me. The walls were stacked high with sandbags to stop bullets. "He slept here on the floor surrounded by sandbags."

The next room was the Daesh courtroom identified by an Arabic label at the door. "Here is where they hung the Daesh flag." One could see the clean rectangle on the wall where the flag had been nailed. "The judge stood over in that corner when people were brought before him. He had a microphone to address all the people under his control."

We ducked through the hole in the wall to the next room. It was labeled "Daesh police headquarters". Next to it was a room with diesel stains where they had cleaned their weapons.

The next room was used for storage and the kitchen. The last room was piled with dirt. Mirza explained, "This is where they put the dirt from the tunnel they dug so it would not be seen from the street."

Mirza took me on a flashlight tour of the sixty-meter tunnel under the houses. It was more than a meter wide and two meters high. He explained, "Daesh forced Yezidi prisoners to dig the tunnel. I knew two of them, just boys.

After the tunnel was dug, Daesh killed them so they could not give evidence against them."

The tunnel went in two directions. To the left were mats and blankets. To the right was the main tunnel where Daesh hid themselves. An electrical wire was strung along it for lights. There was a hole overhead, so in an emergency the Emir could jump straight down.

"We are under my sister's house now," Mirza said. "This is as far as we go. The tunnel may be wired with explosives."

We climbed out of the tunnel and walked through his family's houses until emerging out of the hole in the wall into a field of rubble. Mirza explained, "This house belonged to my cousin Haji. Daesh destroyed his house, so he went to the States."

Mirza pointed to a building across the field. "In this building behind us, they were making IED explosives. When Peshmerga came inside the city, we came with them inside the house. There were many documents I gathered and gave to Commander Qassim Shesho. He visited this house and thanked me. Some groups from the US, France, and Peshmerga checked everywhere for explosives. It is safe now."

Mirza pointed, "There was another tunnel under that building, but it collapsed when the American Coalition bombed it. Behind us is my uncle's house. He, his wife and son are under Daesh control in Raqqa. Most of my family is missing. Daesh killed my seventeen-year-old son, Mazin (born 1997), along with sixty other Yezidis fleeing Gir Zerik on August 3. They fought until their ammunition was finished."

"We need help from countries like America."

The Anfal Campaign - 1988 Kurdish Genocide

After I was banned from Turkey by the Sirnak Foreign Police for my writing in support of Kurds, I moved to Kurdistan, northern Iraq. The police there were a complete opposite to police in Turkey because they are Kurdish. In Turkey, the police are Turkish and are assigned for five years to work as rookies in eastern Turkey before working anywhere else. Teachers must serve two years. In eastern Turkey, one always had the sense of living in an occupied country. The police were not your friends. Arriving in Kurdistan in June 2015 was like breathing the fresh air of freedom after the oppression of Turkey. Everyone everywhere thanked me for coming to help, even the police.

The immigration police major in Erbil who gave me my residence permit asked me one question. He said, "Are Yezidis Kurds? I only have the TV and newspapers to read, and I do not know if it is true."

"Yezidis say they are not Kurds," I replied. He thanked me for coming to Kurdistan, gave me his name, and told me to call if I needed help.

I settled into a motel apartment in Duhok. One night as I came downstairs to the lobby at 11 PM to ask when the internet would be working again, two plain clothes detectives were speaking to the receptionist. They were showing a document to him with my name on it.

"She's right here," Maher said, pointing to me. "Amy, they are Asayish. They want to ask you some questions."

Asayish are the special investigative police in Kurdistan, akin to the FBI in America. The mere word "Asayish" makes people pinch their sphincter.

I walked behind the reception counter and stood next to Maher who translated for us. "Tell them I have some questions of my own before I answer them."

Maher was visibly shaken, "But Amy, you *have* to answer their questions. They are the Asayish. Do you know who the Asayish are?"

Yes, I knew. In December 2014, they were accused of bloodying up and jailing some Yezidis in a Zakho IDP camp because they were carrying signs and demonstrating in support of the PKK who had saved the Yezidis when they were trapped on Shingal Mountain.

"Just translate," I told Maher. "Did you come here to arrest me?"

"No," one answered.

"Good. Do you think I have committed a crime?"

"No," again.

"Why do you want to talk to me?"

"Madam, we saw your name on the hotel list. You are an American. It is our job to know what you are doing here. We just want to know what's your job? Who pays you? It will only take five minutes."

"No one pays me. I will not talk to you unless you promise to sit down and listen for one hour. I do not have a job description. I cannot explain in five minutes."

Maher whined, "Please, Amy. They are the Asayish. Just answer their question."

"Just translate, Maher," I ordered.

It is their job to know what my job is. After some drama in which I lost patience and stood up, yelling and shaking my finger at them, they understood I was a self-supporting, independent volunteer.

"I came here to help those poor women who have been kidnapped and raped by Daesh. It is one year since the attack. Are you telling me that you *still don't know* there was a genocide against the Yezidis? Shame on you for thinking I have to be paid to come and help young girls who were raped."

I sprinkled "genocide," "rape," and "Kocho" generously throughout my tirade. They knew enough English to get my message. They apologized and begged me to sit down.

"You are very interested in writing about Yezidis. Why don't you write about what happened to the Kurds?" they asked.

I surprised them by asking the first one, "Did you lose any family members under Saddam?"

Between 1986 and 1989, Saddam Hussein's military conducted the Anfal campaign which was a massacre against the Kurds. Estimates of deaths vary between 50,000 and 182,000. In one day, they dropped gas bombs on the town of Halabja, killing 5,000 Kurds. In March and April 1991, the Kurds rose up against the tyranny of Saddam's Sunni Ba'ath party. They stormed the prison in Sulaymaniyah where Kurdish and Shia political prisoners were held. The prison is preserved as a museum with wax figures shown being tortured. This period is called The Uprising.

Under Saddam's brutal military response to The Uprising, over one million Kurds fled to neighboring Iran and Turkey. There are no Kurds in Kurdistan whose family was not affected. The adults remember walking in cold driving rain and mud when they were small children. They returned one month later when the United States secured the borders of Kurdistan and made it a no-fly zone. That is why Kurds give their loyalty to America.

The Asayish answered my question, "Yes, I lost my two brothers."

I asked the other man. He answered, "I lost my father and uncle."

"What village are you from?"

They described their village behind the mountain, still standing empty twenty-four years after The Uprising, because the IED bombs have not been removed.

"I am very sorry for your loss. If you take me there with a bomb removal expert, I promise you, I will write the story of what happened to your families."

They stayed three hours, until 2 AM, and we parted as friends with their promise to help me anytime I needed anything, including driving me anywhere.

If one plans to volunteer in Kurdistan, it behooves one to learn the Kurds' painful history of a hundred years of genocide. In every office, at ever security check point, I was regularly asked, "Do you know how many Kurds died in 1988?" When I knew, their attitude reversed itself and support was extended to me. I never failed to ask a Kurd about his own family history. Everyone in Kurdistan has suffered. Everyone has a big story. Many were tortured in prison. This is why I supported Kurds to have their own independent country of Kurdistan.

Volunteering in Kurdistan was a three-step process which never varied. First came the challenge. All sorts of prohibitions and procedures for obtaining permissions blocked most people. I refused to be deterred. After overcoming the challenge, I formed bonds of trust and friendship with dozens of Kurds who helped me in my work. The directors of the Iraqi ID and passport offices were invaluable in their help.

The third step was when people who were helping me contacted me asking for my help. Many bureaucrats implored me to help them leave Iraq. Disillusionment and hopelessness was gripping Kurdistan. The economy that was booming in 2013, was bankrupt in 2015. I advised everyone to stay and build Kurdistan.

One night a Kurdish police officer called me in a panic to meet that very hour. He had the opportunity to smuggle his family of four to Germany for $25,000. It was his entire life savings. The smuggler was employing high-pressure tactics on him. He had to decide by the next day or lose his chance. I convinced him to stay since he had a house, a car, and a job. "Kurdistan will not always be like this. The war will end. The economy will recover. The oil will flow. There will be opportunity. Don't run."

We talked about the importance of living in one's own culture. A year later, he was still at his job. Many people told me that my very presence in Kurdistan brought them hope, because it seemed like the world had abandoned them.

Yezidis Mass Exodus to Bulgaria Fails

In the first three months in the refugee camps in southeast Turkey, Yezidis were psychologically paralyzed, waiting and weeping. "When will someone tell us where we are going?" was a persistent refrain. From the very beginning, I could foresee their grim future. "Never," I told them. "No one is ever coming to your rescue. The sooner you understand that, the sooner you can make a plan."

They began to take the bus to Ankara and register as refugees with the UNHCR. By December 2014, the waiting list for an interview for resettlement with UNHCR was twelve years. The UNHCR was overwhelmed and could not meet the needs of nearly two million refugees in Turkey.

Kurdish camp managers continued to tell Yezidis they would return to Shingal when it was safe. This thought terrified Yezidis, so they stopped waiting for the UNHCR to resettle them. In October, a Yezidi representative met with "Hassan" at the Bulgarian consulate in Ankara. He told the officer their plan to charter buses and try to cross the Bulgarian border without documents. Hassan replied, "As you like. If you want to go, I cannot prevent you."

Hassan asked the Yezidi representative to please inform him when they planned to go to the border. Yezidis naively trusted him and gave the consulate advance notice. Hassan promised to call the border and ask for the Yezidis not to be treated badly and that violence not be used.

A group of Yezidis from Diyarbakir refugee camp also met with the Ankara-appointed Governor of Diyarbakir and shared their plan with him. The Governor gave them permission to leave Diyarbakir, but he assumed no responsibility for their safety or success at the border. He advised them to charter the buses from the bus garage and have them come to their camp. The Yezidis paid $2000 USD for each of three buses. Everyone in the camp of 4,500 Yezidis contributed.

On December 21, 2014, two hundred Yezidi refugees from Diyarbakir Fidanlik Park rode thirty hours to the Bulgarian border arriving before dark. Seventy of them were children. At the border all 200 Yezidis walked across the border without documents. Both Turkish and Bulgarian border police used violence to push them back into Turkey.

One woman stated that the Turkish police pointed his gun at her baby. She grabbed his weapon and said, "If you want to kill someone, kill me, but do not kill my children."

After police pushed and pulled them back into Turkey, they returned to their buses and were transported by Turkish security forces to Adana on the Syrian border where men were separated from their families. All were imprisoned. Each family was given a hefty fine before being returned to Diyarbakir Fidanlik camp.

Yezidis began to understand the seriousness of their predicament. Truly, no one was coming to their rescue. Europe did not want them. Turkey did not want them. No one cared that there had been a genocide. Yezidis were going to be forced back as pawns to annex Shingal to Kurdistan. There were no Yezidi refugees in Turkey willing to return to Iraq.

On March 23, 2015, Yezidis demonstrated for asylum and international protection in every refugee and IDP camp in Kurdistan and Turkey. They were joined by demonstrations in Russia, Germany, and Belgium. In Kurdistan, Iraq, demonstrators were dispersed by police using water cannon. One Yezidi whose cousin was arrested described an attack upon demonstrators from Chamishko camp in Zakho, Kurdistan:

"The Asayish (Kurdistan security forces) arrested about fifty persons of the demo and for 24 hours held them under torture, hitting them in their feet, cheek, back, and hands by pipe sticks and hand grips. They did not release the ones who were affected by hitting so that they can heal and no one will know what they did with them.   They arrested them because they were saying 'Hol hola Tawus Melak' and saying Apo in support of the PKK imprisoned leader. The ones saying Apo are still gone."

In spite of demonstrations, no countries responded to grant asylum to Yezidis.   Over 4,500 Yezidis in Diyarbakir camp prepared themselves for a second attempt to cross the Bulgarian border. They called it the Mass Exodus. Word spread secretly to the other camps until 20,000 Yezidis were committed to going to Bulgaria.

It was too big to remain secret.

A well-known Yezidi religious leader. also in the PDK party, met with ten Yezidi men in Nusaybin refugee camp.   According to reports from people in the meeting, he allegedly gave each one $100 dollars to call off the Mass Exodus. After he left, one of the Yezidi refugee leaders in the group took the money from everyone, tore it into small pieces and threw it into a trash can. None of them was going to join PDK and betray the Yezidis.

"We will cross into Bulgaria or die trying," said many Yezidis. "We will never go back to Iraq and live surrounded by monsters. We've had 74 massacres against us. We will not return to wait for number 75. We want to go to a safe country to raise our children."

Other Yezidis gave notice to the government that if Turkey tried to return them to Iraq, they would all join the PKK.   This was an interesting twist since it was the Kurdish PKK militants who most insisted they would go back to Shingal.

I met with Gharib Hassou, Rojava's PYD party representative in Kurdistan, to convey the Yezidi sentiments of refugees in Turkey, but he would not be swayed. The YPG and YPJ militias are the fighting forces of the PYD political party in Rojava.   They are closely aligned with the PKK from Turkey.   They were leading the fight against Daesh in Syria and Shingal.

Gharib explained, "If Yezidis go to Europe, it will be a second genocide against them.   They will lose their land, their culture, their music, their friends, their religion, and their community.   The Yezidi culture will cease to exist.   We are fighting for their land and for their future existence as a people.   What are we sacrificing our lives for if they all want to go to Europe?   We want them to return and be part of Kurdistan.   The Yezidis must return to their land and save their culture.   The world will not resettle 400,000 people."

The refugees were confused, frightened, and desperate.   All their own Yezidi leaders, who insisted they return, were former refugees, most of whom now had German citizenship.   Yezidis in the Diaspora did not want to live in Shingal themselves, yet their spokespersons insisted those who had been displaced had to return to the scene of the massacre.   Yezidis said their leaders had sold them out.

Many refugees asked me for my advice.   I counseled everyone not to go. They would not succeed and would lose their money.   They were hopeful, however, of entering Bulgaria or at least camping out between borders to gain international media attention.

On June 26, 2015, Yezidis from refugee camps in southeast Turkey began their Mass Exodus to the Bulgarian border.   They had arranged to charter buses for every camp, but Turkish authorities intervened along with the Kurdish camp managers.   From a planned 20,000 Yezidis who hoped to join the mass exodus, only 2,000 were allowed to leave their camps.

Refugees in Batman and Sirnak Kurdish-run camps, as well as Midyat and Nusaybin Turkish-AFAD camps, were prevented from leaving.   In Nusaybin and Midyat government camps, anyone who left prior to the day of the exodus was threatened they could not return.   In Midyat camp, security officers severely beat a man who had to be hospitalized.   Three women who wanted to join the exodus were also beaten.

Most set out from Diyarbakir camp.   In Diyarbakir camp, hired buses were stopped from arriving.   Fifteen hundred people began walking (a 24-hour trip by bus).   Three buses with sixty-five people per bus made it to the Bulgarian border, but Turkey refused to let the Yezidis exit the country.   They were sent back to the Istanbul central bus terminal.   Another twenty-eight buses were prevented from going further than the Istanbul central bus station.

In Istanbul, the Yezidi leaders met with the Governor of Istanbul and HDP Kurdish party representatives who said they would attempt to take the Yezidi request to President Erdogan.   However, while the refugees were waiting on the grass, Nusaybin camp managers worked into the night preparing tents for their return.   After waiting through the day, all of the refugees were sent back to Nusaybin camp, defeated and demoralized.   Leaders of the exodus attempt were prevented from entering the camp for several hours, but were eventually allowed in.

The refugees were assigned to clean tents and given new bedding and an electric space heater. Those Yezidis who held ID cards issued by Diyarbakir camp were returned the next day from Nusaybin camp to Diyarbakir camp. Diyarbakir camp population shrunk from 4,500 to 3,000 people. The Turkish government had succeeded in getting another 1,500 Yezidis out of the Kurdish-run camps and into the Turkish government-run camp.

The food situation in Diyarbakir camp continued to deteriorate as Yezidis subsisted on a diet of tomatoes, cucumbers, and bread. One six-month-old baby required emergency dialysis treatment for infected kidneys due to bad water and malnutrition. The hospital administrator in Diyarbakir denied medical services until the Kurdish medical doctors' association intervened to save the baby's life.

Yezidis were trapped in Turkey. "How can we leave?" they asked me.

"Study a map. You can go by land or by water. . . walk through the mountains or take a boat."

January 3, 2017, Diyarbakir administrator, appointed by Ankara after the Kurdish co-mayors were imprisoned on charges of associating with terrorists, closed Diyarbakir camp. Fifteen hundred Yezidis were forced out.

Basima Darweesh Khudher, Yezidi Woman Captured Twice

Thirty-four-year-old Basima Darweesh was captured by Daesh, along with her husband, in Sinjar city on August 3, 2014. She has not seen nor heard from her husband since then. She was transferred by Daesh to a village named Mafree in the district of Zumar. Zumar is between the disputed territory of Shingal and Kurdistan in the north of Iraq.

First she was held captive by Daesh, then she was imprisoned by Kurdistan government for more than three years. The Kurdistan government accused her of collaborating with Daesh which resulted in three Peshmerga being killed by Daesh when they entered a house in which she was held captive. The testimony of a secret eye witness exonerates Basima by stating that no Peshmerga were killed in this operation.

On October 26, 2014, Zerivani Peshmerga soldiers surrounded Mafree village which was under Daesh control. Zerivani Peshmerga headquarters is in Erbil under the command of General Najat.

During the operation to free Mafree, the last house from which gun fire was coming was in the center of the village. Peshmerga surrounded the house and threw a hand grenade into the room from where the shooting was coming. The grenade killed the last Daesh inside the house. After the shooting stopped, a woman's voice cried out "hawara" which means "help" or "save me" in the Yezidi language. It is not used by Kurds. So immediately, the Peshmerga knew it was a Yezidi woman.

Peshmerga told her to go to the roof of the building and remove her clothes. They then ordered her to come out. According to a secret eye witness, Basima Darweesh came out naked, trembling and crying. Her body had bruises on it indicating torture. She fell down on the ground.

According to the government version of the event, Basima was asked if the house was empty. She answered "yes." At least three different stories were spread of what happened next. One version states that when Peshmerga went near the house, Daesh shot from inside the house and killed three Peshmerga on the outside of the house. One of them was a three-star officer. Another version states the Peshmerga entered the house and were shot and killed inside by Daesh. Yet a third version states that three Peshmerga entered the house and were killed by an explosion.

An eye witness came forward to Jaber Ali Beg, a journalist he trusted, "to be comfortable with his soul." The eye witness statement says unequivocally that no Peshmerga were killed or injured in the operation in Mafree village. The witness says that prior to arriving in Mafree, three Peshmerga had been killed and some injured in a different location. These deaths were unrelated to the operation in Mafree which captured Basima without any Peshmerga casualties.

The eye witness states that when Basima came out of the house, the Peshmerga commander yelled insults at her about her honor and was insulting the Yezidi religion. An Arab man, who was part of the Peshmerga operation because he was familiar with the village, covered Basima's naked body. Basima was then put in a car and held there, with her hands tied to the car, for 24 hours.

Then she was transferred to Duhok with four other Yezidi women. In Duhok, the four others were released. Basima was held for seven days and interrogated by a man who called himself Shirvan. During this time she stated she was hanged under a staircase by rope tied around her wrists. Basima stated she was hit and blindfolded when she signed some papers. She could hear Shirvan's voice along with others. Allegedly the papers she signed, written in Kurdish (which Basima cannot read or write) is her confession to collaborating with Daesh.

Basima was then transferred to the prison for women and children in Erbil, capital city of Kurdistan, where she gave birth to her baby girl on March 16, 2015. She had been pregnant with her new husband when they were both captured by Daesh, August 3, 2014.

In May 2015, Basima was transferred to the Directorate of Anti-Terrorism prison which is housed in the Asayish (security police) headquarters in Erbil. Her roommate in prison was the twenty-four-year-old wife of a high-ranking Daesh leader who had been killed in Syria.

Basima's sister was told that if their brother would come to the prison, Basima could be released to him. In June 2016, Basima's brother, Jassim, went to Erbil and met with prison director General Rostum, director of the Directorate of Anti-Terrorism. General Rostum told Jassim that Basima could be released to him if he would bring a letter from the Yezidi Spiritual Council. The letter was to confirm that Basima is Yezidi and guarantee that she would be welcomed back into the Yezidi religion and community after she was forced to convert to Islam.

The Yezidi religious leaders in Lalish center did not provide this letter to Basima's brother. Their position was that for over one year it was a well-known fact that the Yezidi religious leader, Baba Sheikh, had made a pronouncement that all kidnapped Yezidi women and girls who escaped from Daesh captivity would be welcomed back as holy women by the Yezidi community even if they had been forced to convert to Islam or had been raped.

Jassim failed to get the requested letter. Basima's family appealed to me (Amy L Beam) for help, since my humanitarian work for two years focused on assisting the kidnapped Yezidi survivors get their Iraqi IDs and passports. In July 2016, I requested and received the desired letter from Hazim Tahsin, chairman of the Yezidi Spiritual Council.

The way I got the letter was to corner Hazim on a Saturday morning when he arrived for a meeting at Lalish. When I revealed who I was, his face was astonished. "Oh, you're the one who posted that interview with Qassim Shesho last week!"

"Yes," I confessed. Qassim Shesho, in Kurdish, stated that Hazim Tahsin has not spent 10,000 dinar (about $9) on any Yezidi women survivors.

"You have no idea how much trouble that interview has caused me," Hazim said.

"Oh, I imagine it did," I quipped. I promised to give Hazim a chance to rebut the accusation. Hazim gave me the requested letter to guarantee Basima's safety.

I delivered this letter to the prison in Erbil on July 31, 2016.

I went in good faith to meet with General Rostum, Director of the Anti-Terrorism prison, to make a plan for Basima's release and security. At the gate to the prison in Erbil, Asayish guards refused to allow me to see General Rostum or any assistant. They were furious at Basima's nephew for having brought me to the prison gate, which theoretically is a secret location. So I sent the letter from the religious leader, Hazim Tahsin, inside to the director.

Both I and Basima's nephew were ordered to leave and never return. However, the Asayish kept my passport which I retrieved the next day with the help of the US Consulate. I was threatened that I would be charged with interfering with State security and put in prison if I got a lawyer for Basima or ever mentioned her name again.

The Asayish told us there was no point for the family to bring Basima a lawyer because no lawyer would be allowed to meet with her. They stated she already had a "secret lawyer" that her family did not know about. This was the Kurdistan Regional Government, not Daesh, holding her in secret.

I took the story to Amnesty International, Human Rights Watch, The International Committee for the Red Cross, and the United Nations.

In June 2016, General Rostum had told Basima and her brother and sister that Basima had been investigated and found innocent after one-and-a-half years in prison and no charges would be brought against her. He stated they were holding her for her own security, because Yezidis might kill her if she were released. While the General was making plans with Basima's brother for her release if he brought the letter from the Yezidi Spiritual Council, the prosecutor in Duhok court was telling an entirely opposite version of the story to his law students as late as September 2016.

Khairi Khider, a prosecutor in Duhok who calls himself Kurdish Yezidi, stated with self-assurance that he is the chief investigator in Basima's case and she was guilty of collaborating with Daesh and causing the death of three Peshmerga. He said she would never get out of prison.

Amnesty International published Basima's story and called upon KRG President Masoud Barzani to either bring formal charges against Basima or immediately release her. Basima immediately went before a judge. She was told again that she was innocent, no charges would be placed against her, and she was being held for her own security. She was then physically coerced to sign papers written in Kurdish which she cannot read. She was transferred back to the prison for women and children.

Basima was assigned a lawyer by the court in August 2016. That lawyer told her that her spoken statement of innocence did not agree with the papers, written in Kurdish, which she had signed. An independent lawyer brought by the family and Amnesty International was prevented from meeting with Basima.

Human rights organizations called for Basima and her child to be immediately released since no charges had been brought against her. After a court hearing and appeal, no charges were placed against Basima. She and her child were released from Erbil prison in mid-2017 and disappeared. Even her lawyer did not know where she was. She was secretly transferred to a house in Sulaymaniyah, Kurdistan, where she lived under constant surveillance for another seven months. When she overheard people talking about killing her, she escaped to Turkey where she remained in hiding with her daughter.

Basima Darweesh Khudir had been imprisoned in Kurdistan for three-and-a-half years without being charged. Basima immediately contacted Amy Beam for help in May 2018. She registered with the UNHCR in Turkey for resettlement, but the UNHCR office in Turkey was closed in September 2018.

When she was traveling to Ankara for an interview with the French consulate, Turkish police detained her overnight. As Turkey became more oppressive toward refugees, the government made it illegal to travel with permission outside of the area where they were living. After one year of effort, France turned down her request for asylum. She remained in hiding reduced to searching for food from garbage bins and back doors of restaurants.

Nayef Jaso, Kocho Manager, Describes August 15, 2014, Daesh Executions
Nayef Jaso Qassim, October 26, 2015

The flat plains of Nineveh, where Yezidis live, is the bread basket of Iraq. In the center is Shingal Mountain, surrounded on all sides by 100 kilometers of wide open, rich agricultural land and many small villages. Sinjar is the Arabic name and Shingal is the Kurdish name. There are no trees for shade. The only canopy is the expansive blue sky. We grow the barley and wheat for flour for the entire country of Iraq. We are mostly farmers and shepherds with large herds of sheep. Some men take jobs in the cities of Duhok and Erbil.

August in Iraq is the dry season. The wheat and barley crops have been harvested and trucked to Erbil silos. Temperatures soar to a stifling 45C. The green grasses die and turn brown. The ground hardens and cracks from drought. A grayish-brown fog of dust hangs in the atmosphere like a heavy blanket, lowering visibility and causing people chronic breathing problems.

I am the manager of Kocho village. My name is Nayef Jaso Qassim. I was born in 1958, one year after Kocho was founded by my father, the leader of the al-Mandkany clan. People tell me I look younger, but after what I have seen in my lifetime, I feel as old as the desecrated earth of Shingal itself.

I have witnessed the most treacherous betrayal that I could not have imagined was possible. Even though the Yezidis have recorded 73 genocidal attacks upon our people, the 74th was unlike all others. It destroyed the lives and properties of over 400,000 Yezidis. It destroyed our ancestral homeland. Shingal is finished.

Four of my sons were killed. I lost seventy-one relatives in Kocho, all sharing my family name of Qassim. They are either dead or missing. Twelve of them had married into our family. Only two of the kidnapped women on my list have escaped. One is the wife of my dead son.

Now my mission is to tell the world the truth about the attacks on Shingal in August 2014. I defy any individual or government or Daesh terrorist to silence me, because truth is on my side. I will never stop telling what happened. Only God himself can silence me.

Yezidis share many customs with the Kurds and the Arabs, including managing our villages under the tribal or clan system. We do not elect mayors. The leader or manager of the village is a senior man from the clan. As the town manager, I am given great respect by the town's people who are all my cousins to one degree or another.

I make decisions that affect the well-being of the entire town of 1,735 people. Being manager carries great responsibility to protect and provide for my people. A leader must also take counsel from his advisors. So I am often in council meetings with the eldest men in Kocho, the fathers of each family. On important matters I must consult with the town's people to reach consensus and have their support. We have a big hall for these gatherings.

On July 28, 2014, my wife and I flew to Istanbul. My elder brother, Ahmed Jaso Qassim, who is actually the head of our al-Mandkany clan which includes Kocho and four other villages, returned on July 27 from his work in Duhok to manage Kocho in my absence. His first wife and their house is also in Kocho.

We Yezidis have our own festivals, separate in custom and dates from the Kurds and Arabs around us. One of our annual events is the Chilla Eid feast after forty days of religious fasting by our spiritual leader, Baba Sheikh. It is celebrated during the hottest days of summer after the crop is harvested. On August 2, one day before the Islamic State terrorists attacked Shingal, my brother Ahmed Jaso hosted a luncheon at his house for fifty guests. It included twenty-two Arab neighbors of whom fifteen were managers of the surrounding Arab villages and one Kurdish village. Ahmed sacrificed sheep for this special occasion. There was every kind of special food prepared.

Women and children were not present at this special luncheon. All the village managers were friends and equals. This was a luncheon for Ahmed's associates and neighbors to share in the Yezidis' harvest. It was like The Last Supper, but instead of there being only one Judas who betrayed Jesus, thirteen out of the fifteen Arab village managers betrayed my brother and the entire al-Mandkany clan less than fifteen hours after smiling in his face, dining at his table, and eating his sacrificial sheep.

These are the clan leaders of neighboring Arab villages who had lunch with my brother Ahmed Jaso August 2, 2014:

1. Nofel	8. Muhammed Radife
2. Khalef	9. Muhammed Imad
3. Jarallah	10. Mallik Al Nuri
4. Abdullmajud	11. Muhammed Abaz
5. Khaton	12. Zed
6. Khalal	13. Farhan Jarallah
7. Tarik	14. Jasim

Not only were my brother, Ahmed, and I friends with the managers of the surrounding Arab villages, but our wives and children also were friends. We danced at each other's weddings and visited in one another's homes. Our children played together. We grew up together. We did business together. I regularly traveled together to Baghdad and Mosul with the Arab village managers for meetings with the government.

Our fathers' friendship goes back to 1948. The Yezidis used to live with Arabs in Kinissee which is only eight kilometers to the east of Kocho on Baiji Road. There were never any problems between the Yezidis and Arabs in Kinissee. In 1956, Yezidis built Kocho and they all moved out of Kinissee. Kocho is surrounded by 13 Arab villages and one Kurdish village. Since 1957, when Kocho was founded, our fathers, and then we, have been friends with our Arab neighbors with not one problem between us. Our problems started only when Daesh came. We call the Islamic State "Daesh".

When Shingal was attacked on August 3, 2014, my wife and I took the next plane from Istanbul back to Erbil. While we were flying home, some people from Kocho tried to get away in their cars. Daesh captured them and massacred a total of 150 people in three different locations. The others turned back.

I wanted to drive immediately from the airport to Kocho, but my brother, Ahmed Jaso, told me on the phone to stay in Duhok. It was already too late to return. Peshmerga had left Kocho and it was now surrounded by Daesh. Daesh was everywhere in control of Shingal cities and villages. Over fifty thousand Yezidis were trapped on Shingal Mountain without enough water or food.

The road from Sunoni, on the north of the mountain, across the flat open plain to Kurdistan, was jammed with cars and trucks packed with families fleeing to safety. The Peshmerga pickup trucks were leading, with Yezidis following close behind. Four-wheel trucks were passing on the side of the road over the hard ground, over-taking the slow traffic and turning the two-lane country road into a four-lane one-way road. It would be impossible to drive against the flow of traffic that inched northward at only a few kilometers per hour. Every civilian had to pass through several PDK checkpoints before entering the safety of Kurdistan which has protected borders in northern Iraq.

So I stayed here in Duhok, Kurdistan, from where I was in constant telephone contact with my brother, Ahmed Jaso, trapped in Kocho.

We did not know Abu Hamza, the Daesh leader who came to meet with Ahmed Jaso on August 5, but he came with my Arab friend Khalef Al Ayad and one other man. Khalef Al Ayad is the manager of Pisqi Jemali village which is three kilometers east of Kocho. Abu Hamza is from Khaider city, south of Mosul. They drank tea together in the meeting hall next to Ahmed's house.

Abu Hamza demanded we convert to Islam and gave us three days to decide. We tried to get outside help to rescue the village. We called the Arab managers who had been Ahmed's luncheon guests on August 2, and asked them to help us by going to talk to the Daesh leader in Mosul. I do not know the name of this bigger Daesh leader, but his wife's father is named Salam Mala Allo.

The Arab managers from our neighboring villages, whom we asked for help, talked to the brother of the Daesh leader in Mosul. They promised to do something to help us, but no help arrived. We remained besieged.

On August 8, Abu Hamza returned pretending to help us. Ahmed Jaso and the men of Kocho listened to what Abu Hamza had to say. The meeting hall was full. Hamza told us we did not have to convert to Islam after all. He told us to go about our normal lives, but we did not believe him. We knew they were Daesh.

For twelve days my brother and I and all the people of Kocho were desperately phoning people everywhere in Iraq and in the world asking to be rescued. My friends who were interpreters with the US Army took our message to Congress and the government in Washington, D.C. and to Europe. We called members of the E.U. parliament. Yezidis living in Europe went to the European Court in Brussels and pleaded for help for Yezidis, especially to rescue Kocho. We contacted every embassy. There were even demonstrations in Brussels in front of the European Court and in Hannover, Germany.

We called government leaders and military commanders in Kurdistan and Iraq and begged to be rescued, but the Iraqi government gave us no response and did not care. We were racing for time. We never rested.

So I sent my message to the Shia Grand Ayatollah Sayyid Ali al-Sistani, the most respected religious leader in Iraq. Only a few days earlier, on August 1, six grand ayatollahs had publicly announced their support to Ayatollah Sistani because Sistani was calling for a democratic Iraq in which each person could vote. Sistani called for Prime Minister Nouri al-Maliki to step down or be voted out of office.

Sistani sent my message to Prime Minister Maliki: "Kocho needs to be rescued."

The next day the Secretary to the Ministry of Iraq, close to Maliki, called me from his phone, 07802200011, and asked me if I was Nayef Jaso, the manager of Kocho.

I said, "Yes." We talked.

After our talk, the Secretary of the Ministry of Iraq signed an order to rescue Kocho. This order was sent to the operations control room for the Iraqi Army in Baghdad. This happened sometime between August 8 and 12. My sources told me that Americans were in the control room along with Iraqis.

I will never trust Americans again.

I had connections within the PDK political party. I sent them the same message, "Kocho needs to be rescued." I gave them a plan. They said they would send it to the military operations room in Erbil, capital of Kurdistan. There were Kurds, Arabs, and Americans in that control room. I did not see the Americans in the operations room in Erbil with my own eyes, because I was in Duhok, but my intermediary swears that American military personnel were there.

I asked for 14 planes to include ten helicopters, two Apache attack helicopters, and two military fighter jets such as F-16s. The helicopters were to be used to evacuate the people of Kocho to Shingal Mountain. The Apaches and the F-16s were to protect the helicopters during their operation. I said, "I have 200 Yezidi men of my own forces on the ground in Kocho. They will protect the helicopters when they land."

We got no sure reply to our request to be rescued.

On August 12, I called my brother Ahmed in Kocho and told him, "It's a plan. I do not know what will happen in the future, but I am sure it is a plan. Take whatever steps you can to save yourselves. No one is coming to your rescue."

On August 13, Daesh returned and brought some rice and food to the village. They also brought more guards to surround the village night and day. Only 3% were foreign. Only 7% were from other areas of Iraq. Ninety percent came from the Arab villages in Shingal. They were our neighbors.

The operations room said to my intermediary contact that they were watching Kocho intensively. They promised if more than two cars go to Kocho, they would bomb the cars.

I told my brother on the phone, "On August 15, Daesh will give you their decision. Either you can change your religion or they will kill everyone or you can escape to the mountain." Daesh did not say this, but I understood.

On August 14, Ahmed hosted a luncheon meeting with five of the 15 Arab managers from surrounding villages in an effort to avert an attack. They were Nofel, Khaton, Tarik, Jarella, and Farhan Jarella. These were the same friends who had come for lunch on August 2. Abu Hamza attended, too.

On August 15, at 9 AM many cars entered Kocho from three available directions. Cars came from Tal Afar to the north, heading south on Baiji Road. Others came from Baiji southeast of Kocho, heading north. Others came from Baaj, southwest of Kocho. They had loudspeakers on their cars and announced they would take everyone to the mountain. It was very hot that morning, so they brought ice and distributed it. They told everyone to bring their gold and cars and report to the school which is on the northeast corner of Kocho.

From 9 AM planes were flying overhead. The operations room in Baghdad watched and did nothing even though there were lines of cars and pickups surrounding and entering into Kocho.

They took the women and children to the second floor of the school. The world knows by now that they were all kidnapped and the women and girls were beaten, raped, and used as sex slaves. Some of them have escaped, but nearly 3,000 Yezidis are still being held captive.

Daesh kept the men and adolescent boys on the ground floor of the school. They checked the hair under the arms of some of the boys to determine age. Young boys went with their mothers.

Abu Hamza asked Ahmed one last time, "Do you want to change your religion?" My brother told everyone, "You are free to choose."

No one agreed to change religion except for one family that was not from Kocho. They were allowed to leave. Daesh said to the others, "We know you are not going to convert to Islam."

Until they collected the mobile phones, I was always in touch with my son, Mufit Nayef Jaso, who was only twenty. He was the last one to have his phone taken, because he was hiding it in his pocket with a wire in his ear. He was in constant communication with me. He was giving me the details of what was going on in the school. How they separated the men from the women and children. How they collected everyone's gold and cash and took their ID cards (hawea).

When they started taking the men out of the school and driving them away, my son told me they were shooting everyone. I told my son, "They will kill you." Then they took his phone.

I was in Duhok meeting with a man named Khairi Hamoka. He was sitting right next to me. He was talking on the phone to the operations room in Erbil. As my son told me what was happening, I was telling Khairi, and Khairi was telling the operations room. They knew everything that was happening in real time. The operations room said they were watching from the drones overhead which were controlled from Baghdad.

Khairi relayed the question from the operations room to me, "What will Daesh do?"

I answered, "They will kill everyone." I told them, "Bomb everyone, the women, the children, the men."

The man from the operations room asked, "You gave us orders to bomb and kill everyone in Kocho? What is your relationship to them?"

I said, "They are my family, my children, my relatives. I will write a report and put my fingerprints on it that I gave the orders to bomb."

The operations room said, "Human rights will not allow us to do that."

So they watched and never did anything to stop the executions that went on for an hour from 11AM until about noon. Two planes flew overhead watching until late afternoon. [Another witness swears it was unmanned drones, not planes, flying overhead.] Inside my head, I was screaming for help. I felt helpless. No! No! No! Please stop them! Please bomb them! Where was God?

When they took my son's phone, I called my Arab friend who lives in Pisqi Junoovi, two kilometers from Kocho. I told him to go see and listen for sounds of shooting. My friend called me back and began to cry on the phone and said, "Yes, you are right. They are killing them. I see one person running away. He is coming toward Pisqi Junoovi."

I asked my friend to care for him. When he arrived, my friend called me again and let me speak with him. He was Alias Salih Qassim, the father of Basman who is missing and presumed dead. Alias was shot in the knee. Alias told me they were shooting everyone. I told him to take care and promised we will try to get you and take you to the mountain.

This information was passed immediately by Khairi Hamoka to the operations room in Erbil.

Daesh took the men in their own cars and pickup trucks parked at the school to four locations at the edges of Kocho. The first location was to the water storage pool on the side of the perimeter dirt road at the edge of southeast Kocho. The first group of men and boys was shot in the back of the head at the edge of the pool. This is the group Alias was in. He ran directly east to escape.

The second group was in the same location, but Daesh made them get into the empty pool where they were executed.

The third and fourth groups were executed about 300 meters away from the first group on the southeast corner of Kocho, next to the perimeter dirt road where it turns to the west and wraps around the village.

The fifth group they took to a farm one kilometer north of Kocho. [According to a survivor, this was actually the fourth group to leave the school, but it may have taken longer to get there or shoot them because Daesh made a video first.] They put about fifty men into the empty pool and shot them. Three men escaped with multiple bullet wounds.

The sixth group was executed on the southwest corner of Kocho.

During the executions, the men in the cars saw others who were dead or being shot and they jumped from the cars and the back of the pickup trucks in an attempt to escape. On the northwest perimeter of the town, twelve men got shot and killed while running away.

Later, Daesh brought other kidnapped Yezidis to live in Kocho. They are witnesses to the locations of the four execution sites and the twelve bodies of men who jumped from the trucks.

Kocho had a population of 453 males aged 15 years and older. Of these, 19 men and teenagers escaped the execution lines with bullet wounds. These men have identified 84 people who were killed next to them. There are another 350 men who are considered missing because no witness has identified them as killed. This includes my brother, Ahmed Jaso Qassim, leader of our clan. No one has heard from any of these 350 men since the attack of August 15, 2014. We will not have closure until we can enter Kocho, uncover the mass graves, and perform DNA testing.

Four months after the attack, in December 2014, I visited the US Embassy in Baghdad. It's a town, not a building. It is rumored they have 5,000 American soldiers there. We argued for two hours. I made him listen. The US government cannot claim that it does not know what happened in Kocho.

I am sure if I live long enough, I will see the videos, taken from the planes, of the men and boys being executed in Kocho. There is no difference between the US military command and Daesh. Daesh represents Sunni Arabs.   America, Turkey, Qatar, Saudi Arabia, Kuwait, and the United Arab Emirates will not kill Daesh. We do not want to return to Shingal if Sunni Arabs are there. If we do not have weapons, our children will fight with pens.

No one has seen me shed a tear, because my life's mission now is to tell the world the truth about Kocho. The US Embassy offered me a visa, but I turned it down. I will stay right here in Iraq.

After nearly five years of pressure by Nayef Jaso and Nobel Peace Laureate, Nadia Murad Bassee, on March 15, 2019, a ceremony was held in Kocho with the United Nations Investigative Team for Accountability of Daesh crimes (UNITAD) to begin exhuming the mass graves. Twelve sites were opened in March. Remains were sent to Baghdad for analysis and DNA testing. Survivors continued to wait for news about their missing family members. By mid-2019, 3000 Ezidis remained listed as "missing".

Approximately 100 mass grave sites were identified throughout Shingal with evidence and exposed bones being destroyed by rains, floods, animals, and huge fires intentionally set to destroy thousands of acres of farmers' wheat and barley crops. One eyewitness stated Peshmerga forces had previously removed many bodies and took them to Halabja, Kurdistan, site of Saddam Hussein's chemical attack that killed 5,000 Kurds on March 16, 1988.

Abu Hamza al-Khatouni, the Daesh leader, was reported to have died in Duhok in early 2019.

Boy Soldier Who Escaped Daesh
Name withheld

I reported to Kocho School with my family at noon on August 15, 2014. They collected the men in the hall near the principal's office. I stayed with my father. I was fourteen, born December 24, 1999. They took my father away from me and took him to the car. I struggled to go with him, but they stopped me twice, and sent me upstairs with my mother and little brothers.

After they had driven all the men away, they took all the women and children to Solagh Institute at 4 PM. At midnight they came and separated the older children from their mothers. Some mothers tried to hide their children. They filled two buses with girls and two buses with boys who were seven and older. Before the buses moved, they took each boy outside of the bus and checked him and asked his age. They removed the older boys. We were about forty boys from age seven to fifteen. They took us to a big two-story house in Tal Afar.

We saw other children in the windows of the school near to our house. They had been there since August 3rd. We joined them and stayed in that school forty days, then they took us to our mothers in a different school, and I was reunited with my mother. Then they transferred all of us to Qaser Al Mehrab which was two or three kilometers from an airport in Tal Afar. We lived there three or four weeks.

Then they transferred three full buses of children and women without their husbands to Raqqa, Syria. They put us in a big house where we stayed for twelve days. There were already about twenty Yezidi women and children there. The single women aged seventeen to nineteen pretended to be married by holding a small child and telling Daesh it was theirs. There were not many girls. They were all younger than eight or nine.

We were about 200 people guarded by three or four men. There was not enough space for us in this house. The boys, ages fourteen and fifteen, could not sleep with our mothers. We slept on the stairs. Some Daesh asked us why they brought us because we were big.

The Daesh leader, called the emir, came every two or three days and took two or three single girls. The girls cried and resisted, but Daesh dragged them into the car. They took the girls to Syria to sell. In the last two days in Qaser Al Mehrab, they took all the women including my mother. For the second time I was separated from her.

The next day, they took me and a group of boys ages ten to sixteen to Mahad Farook Al Shari Lie Ashbal (Legal Institute of Farouk for Cubs) in Seluk, Raqqa, Syria. We were nearly thirty boys. There were also about forty children of

Muslim parents there and five teachers. It was the beginning of November. We were waiting for new text books to arrive.

We stayed in Seluk fifteen days, and then they took us to Tal Abeya on the border of Turkey and Syria. We lived one month in Tal Abeya Institute which was actually a hospital. We heard lectures from three books: the Quran, Faka, and Akido.

We had to memorize verses from the Quran. They would always show us a verse in the Quran to prove the religious basis for how we had to behave. It is really true that they taught us that we would get 72 virgins in heaven when we die. From the Faka book we learned about religious study and practices such as how to wash ourselves before prayers. From the Akido book we studied about Daesh, kuffirs (non-Muslims), and the goals of Daesh. The goal is to build an Islamic caliphate and kill all non-Muslims.

We were forty Yezidis who had been captured. More than half the students were Daesh children. When I was in Kocho, before the attack on Shingal, I heard on the news that Daesh fighters were from eighty countries. I did not believe it, but now I do.

When I was in Syria, I saw whole families who moved from other countries to join Daesh and send their kids to Islamic jihad schools. They came from Egypt, Tunisia, Morocco, Uzbekistan, Iraq, Syria, Saudi Arabia, Qatar, Caucuses, China, Kazakistan, Turkey, Somalia, Sudan, India, Germany, and the Netherlands. I even saw British and black Americans who joined Daesh.

All of the Daesh leaders came from Saudi Arabia, but they did not bring their families.

From Tal Abeya we moved to Isa, Syria, near Kobane where we stayed one month. We had daily lectures there, just like in Tal Abeya. From Isa we moved back to Seluk. That is where Daesh made their propaganda video at the Farouk Institute for Cubs in Seluk in February 2015. They wanted to show that we had converted to Islam and were prepared to fight for Daesh and they wanted to recruit more people from other countries. I had been held in captivity six months by the time they made the video.

Not all of us were Yezidi captives. Some of us were really Muslim children, but by now Daesh treated everyone like a Muslim. I knew I was Yezidi, not Muslim, but I had to act like a Muslim so I would be safe. This included praying five times a day. I began to wonder why Yezidis do not pray like Muslims.

For the propaganda video we dressed in clean uniforms of a tan and khaki camouflage pattern. The long-sleeve shirts came to our knees like dresses. Underneath we wore pants that ended above our ankles. We all wore a black headband with Arabic writing on it in white letters reading, "There is no God but Allah." We stood at attention in about six lines of eleven boys. After we did some calisthenics, they brought a microphone to some of us who volunteered to speak to the camera and to recite from the Quran.

I was deciding what to do. Some little boys were eager to speak and show how they memorized verses from the Quran. In my heart I knew it would be a shame to speak in support of Daesh and Islam, but in my head I thought I should speak in front of the camera so that someone would know where I was. I stepped forward and talked enthusiastically into the microphone.

Our classes at the Farouk Institute were divided by skills. We had three rooms in a village near Seluk named Judada. We got certificates. The smartest students were moved back to Seluk city center. I was one of the top ten students. In Seluk, every month they took us near the PKK. PKK snipers shot at us but we did not get shot. I saw a YPJ girl through the binoculars.

Once a month in Seluk, they would take us out for a chicken barbeque and we would practice shooting Kalashnikov guns.   They took all five Yezidis to Seluk city center. We were the top five students.

We stayed one month in Seluk and had more lectures. PKK Kurdish militia were near to us. When PKK was near, our leaders went to fight and we were transferred to Seluk to protect it. By that time, I felt PKK was the enemy. I made friends with the Muslim boys and did everything I was supposed to do so I would not get in trouble. We never got any news, so we did not know that PKK had rescued the Yezidis when Daesh attacked Shingal. I did not learn this about PKK until I escaped, and my family told me.

PKK was controlling part of Tal Abeya, so we moved to Raqqa. In Raqqa, our first two weeks we lived on the ground floor and continued our studies until Ramadan Islamic fasting ended.   After Ramadan ended, thirty of us moved to weapons training camp. They chose the oldest boys who were mostly from Syria. Ten more Yezidis joined us. Now we were fifteen Yezidis and fifteen Muslims, although they treated us like we were all Muslims.

There were three training camps. Camp #1 was for beginners. It was near Firat River and the ancient ruins of Kala Jobba castle near Tabbaqa. We were in the mountain and took our training hidden under the trees. We slept in green tents. We dug tunnels and caves underground.

When the planes flew overhead, we stayed in the caves or tents. There were always drones flying overhead. We could hear the planes bombing near us. Day by day our numbers increased from thirty to 109 boys. We were then transferred to camp #3 on the Firat River. We ran past camp #2 which was only for Daesh leaders.

We were all from Syria except for two from Qatar, one from Iraq and fifteen Yezidis also from Iraq. We were training to kill everyone who was not Muslim. They gave us a weapon and told us it was to be with us at all times like a third hand, even in the toilet or kitchen. It was an old weapon that was no good. It was forbidden for us to have a knife or a pistol. According to Islam, we were taught that Muslims are forbidden to hold any iron in one's hand to show to another.

All of us wanted to go fight, but our leaders said no. We had to take more training. Every three weeks, we could have leave to go home and visit our families for two or three days. Of course, we Yezidis did not leave camp, because we had been taken from our families. The other Muslim boys would go home for a visit. Many did not return, because Daesh would not take us to the battle front. Our numbers shrank from 109 to 60.

One night they transferred us by bus to camp #4 between Halab and Taboq and Kalep Dipsey Farage camp. We stayed there one month until we escaped. They gave us all our freedom. If we had money we could buy a phone. They gave us just a little money for a candy or coke. They promised we would graduate in one month and be Daesh fighters.

When we were in camp #3, we washed in the river. In camp #4 we had to boil our water to wash ourselves and our clothes. If we had any problem in camp or lied and said we are sick and cannot train, they took away our water for one week.

I had to follow any order my leader gave me. Every night two people took guard duty. We had a schedule for who was on duty. For two days they took our weapons at night and put them in the warehouse. They told us if we needed them, go to the warehouse.

One night some cars came. They were shooting, and we thought they were al-Nursra. I was sleeping in my tent. They ordered us to get our weapons and go to the cars. Someone said to crawl to avoid bullets. I got my weapon from the warehouse, but it would not shoot, so our leader said run to our camp car. We had one car and sixty people. We ran to the camp car. Then the shooting stopped and the "enemy" left.

Then our leader held a meeting with us. Our leaders had taken the pins out of our guns. It was not really al-Nursra shooting at us. It was Daesh, and they were testing us. Our leaders insulted us and said none of us had acted right. We should have said "Allahu Akbar" and shown group spirit to fight. He said we were a bad group because we were afraid.

I found out where my mother and little brothers were being held by Daesh, so I went to visit them for one week. She wanted to give me her phone, but I refused it because I wanted her to escape before me. Later, when my friend went to visit his mother who lived near my mother, I told him to bring my mother's phone. So I had a phone and it was allowed by Daesh because they treated us the same as the Muslim boys in training with us.

My friend decided to visit his mother, and I went with him. They drove us near a place and dropped us off. We had lied. My friend's mother had escaped three months earlier. We were far from the mountain.

We went to an Arab neighbor family. My friend explained he had come to visit his mother, but she was gone. They knew she was Yezidi. We asked if we could rest three days with them before returning to camp. We prayed with the family as if we were real Muslims. On the third day, we escaped.

Using the phone my mother had given me before she escaped with my brothers, I called my friend who was in Kurdistan. He arranged for a smuggler. Two men came in a taxi while we stood in the road. They asked our names and we told them. We asked by name if our friends had sent him and he said yes. So we went with the driver who hid us, then took us on bad secondary roads to Qamishlo in northern Syria. He took us to the PKK who were expecting us, so they did not shoot. The driver was paid $20,000 dollars for helping us to escape.

From Qamishlo my friend met me and drove us to the Asayish (security police) in Sunoni, Shingal. We gave our report and slept there one night. In the morning I went to the IDP camp near Zakho, Kurdistan. My relatives took me to Duhok where we stayed a few days with Amy Beam. She and Jiyan Havind took me to get my Iraqi IDs and passport so I could join my mother and two younger brothers who were already in Germany on the program for women and children survivors who had been traumatized by Daesh. They left for Germany one week before I escaped.

I was sixteen when I escaped. I left behind thirteen other Yezidi boys in Daesh military training. My father, four older brothers, four uncles, an aunt, and eight cousins are still missing. Now that I am free, I heard that people warn others who befriend me not to trust me. They say I might have been brainwashed, and I might stab them in their sleep. Amy defends me. After all I suffered and all the pain I carry, this really hurts me. I am not a Daesh terrorist. I am a Yezidi survivor.

Teenage Yezidi Boy Escapes from Daesh Training

Ayad Khalaf Hussein, June 26, 2016

My name is Ayad Khalaf Hussein. I was 13 when Daesh attacked my village of Kocho (Shingal, Iraq) on August 15, 2014. We knew that Daesh was in Kocho and driving through our village from August 3, 2014, when Daesh attacked the rest of Shingal. They had Kocho surrounded. On August 15, at noon we were at home about to eat lunch. We were told by our neighbors that everyone in Kocho had to gather at the Kocho school. We did not take anything with us, except two bottles of water, some bread, and our two phones, money, gold and IDs. We were seven people.

We drove to the school in our new two-door pickup. My father put the car keys in his pocket. The school is a green and white two-story building. My older brother, Zadan, and my father were held on the ground floor with the men. I was sent with my mother, two sisters, and younger brother to the second floor with classrooms.

We were not searched at the door when we entered, but once inside the school, Daesh searched the men on the ground floor and took their gold, money, and phone. I had forgotten my phone at home. My brother, Zadan, and my father gave up their phones. Daesh said, "We have a device to see all the electronic items on you." They threatened that If they discovered anything on us, they would not let us go to Shingal mountain.

They told the women to go to the second floor with classrooms. My family was in a classroom with no chairs, so we sat on the floor. We were about thirty women and children. We were in fear, wondering what would happen next.

There were more than ten boys on the ground floor. Daesh told them they were too young to stay with the men. They sent them to the second floor. When those boys came upstairs, they told us that Daesh gave the men the choice to convert to Islam, but they all refused.

There were two women watching from the upstairs balcony. They told us they were taking the men outside. I was not able to see when they were taking the men out. I did not hear any sounds other than the cars driving away. At that time, I did not know what they did to the men.

After about one hour, when all the men were gone, Daesh moved everyone from upstairs to the ground floor. While we were on the ground floor, a couple of young boys about age fourteen came running back to the school. Daesh had told them they were too young, and so they returned to the school.

The boys told us that they heard some bullets being fired and saw dirt flying. I thought everyone was killed. We started a great wailing and crying. We were very loud in the school. There were about six guards with guns in the school.

One of them fired his gun into the air and told us to be quiet. So everyone fell silent. We were scared.

After about four hours in the school, they took us in our own vehicles to Solagh Institute, about one hour away. Inside Solagh Institute, I, along with all the other children, were separated from our mothers. The last thing my mother said to me was, "Take care of yourself. Be careful."

It was dark and I was sleeping when Daesh picked me up and carried me by force to two big buses. They put me in one. There were fifty or sixty boys, all from Kocho, from ages seven to fourteen in the buses. They drove us to Tal Afar city where we arrived at midnight.

In Tal Afar they put us in a school next to a silo. I stayed with the boys from Kocho on the third floor. There were many women there from different Yezidi villages. I recognized some from Tal Qassab which is close to Kocho. For breakfast they fed us bread and cheese. The other meal was soup and rice.

Sometimes Daesh would come in cars. They would put the women in a room for Daesh to see them. They would move among them and choose the most beautiful ones, then take them away in their cars. The women were always crying. We boys were crying, too.

Abu Muhammed, a Daesh man from Tal Afar, would beat the boys, but I stayed hidden most of the time, so he did not beat me.

During our time there, Daesh taught us about the Quran and how to pray. We had no news from the outside. I did not know what had happened to my mother. I could see and hear drones were always flying overhead.

After thirteen days, Daesh returned all of the Kocho boys to our mothers in Tal Afar school. I was reunited with my mother, Wadha Khalaf Kalo, and seven-year-old brother, Yamin, who had stayed with my mother, but my two older, teenage sisters were gone.

After one day, we were taken to Qassel Kayo village in the province of Tal Afar. I then stayed with my mother and brother for the next six months. We stayed three months in Qassel Kayo. There were fifty people from Kocho village living in one house. You can read my mother's story to know about this period. So I will not repeat it, because her story is the same as my story, except how I was trained in Islam when we were held in one room for three months.

From Qassel Kayo we were taken to a Daesh military medical care center called Al-Tubia-Al-Askaria. It held many pharmaceutical supplies. We were the only people held prisoners in a room in the basement. There were three adults and four children held in that room. It was 3 meters by 2 meters. It did not have a toilet or water. For the toilet we used a can the size of one used for baby formula. We had light one hour per day. There were no windows, not even in the steel door. We had three blankets for seven people.

There were four to six rooms in the passageway outside our room, but we were the only people living there. Some rooms had medical supplies in them. Daesh would let me and my younger brother out of our room to wash and go to prayers five times per day. I stole an empty plastic water bottle and would fill it with water and sneak it to the others in my room. They gave us only bread to eat once a day. We were all so weak, we could only lie there. We thought we would die in that room. Sometimes they would give us half of a potato or one egg.

My mother did not wash for three months. Maybe twice a week the guard would let her out of the room so she could walk in the hallway. There was a toilet in the hallway. One time she fainted and they took her upstairs to breathe fresh air at a window for a few seconds.

After the two other mothers and their two children were removed, there was only my mother and my brother and me left in the room. We begged the guard for more food, so he let us go to the kitchen where we escaped. On the street we stopped an Arab taxi driver. He demanded money and gold from us, but when we said we had nothing, he drove us immediately to a Daesh headquarters where we were beaten for an hour, then returned to the same prison room.

A few days later, around February 2015, we were sold to a Daesh man from Holland. He called himself Abu Omar. We had already been held captive by Daesh for six months: three months in Tal Afar, Iraq, and three months in our basement prison room in Raqqa, Syria.

Abu Omar took us to his house. His real name is Nuradeen. He had moved with his wife and three children from Holland to Raqqa, Syria, where he joined Daesh. His wife is named Mariam. She was pregnant. Their children are Omar (boy, 8 yrs.), Hafsa (girl, 5 yrs.), and Safia (girl, 3 yrs.).

My mother and I talked about escaping, but I told her that I would stay until I could find my two sisters and get them free. I was willing to sacrifice my freedom for them.

Abu Omar bought my mother to be a servant, cooking, cleaning, and washing and ironing clothes; but he had other plans for me to be trained as a Muslim and a Daesh fighter. Immediately, he took me to a Daesh training center and left me there for two months. I was thirteen. That was the last time I saw my mother and little brother until I escaped six months later.

While I was in Daesh training, my mother and brother escaped. My two sisters escaped two weeks later. The reason my mother did not wait for me to return from training was because Abu Omar was threatening to also send my younger brother, who was seven years old, to Daesh training. My mother felt she had to get him out of there as fast as possible.

At the training base in Syria, we lived by a strict schedule, always praying five times per day. We woke up around 4 AM to pray. This was followed by physical exercise and sports. After that, we had a lesson in the Quran and other religious books. Then we had breakfast.

After breakfast, we had two more lessons; one in the Quran and the other was math and biology. We also studied Arabic reading and writing. I studied hard, because Daesh promised that the best students would be allowed to walk freely outside in the park. I was one of the top ten students. Our teacher was Abu Khalid, from Egypt. He was about thirty. He had brought his whole family with him from Egypt. At night he would go home to his family.

They also gave us lessons in military training like handling a Kalashnikov and marching drills. Our "guns" were fake. They were made of solid wood. We wore Daesh uniforms with the pant legs about six inches above our ankles.

Daesh made a propaganda video of boys being trained by Daesh. Four of my cousins from Kocho were in that video, but it was made at a different training camp. At my training camp, I was the only Yezidi boy. The other boys knew I was Yezidi, but said it was good that I became Muslim. I became friends with the Muslim boys, not causing any trouble. I behaved like I was Muslim, doing everything I was supposed to do, just like them, but inside I knew I was Yezidi. I always knew I was a prisoner.

I was allowed to go out walking in Raqqa, alone, but I think I was being watched. At that time I was young and did not think of escaping, because I had no idea of how I could escape. I was alone in a big city.

Raqqa is a very nice city, but we only had electricity for one hour per day. Daesh made it illegal for anyone to watch TV. If they saw a satellite dish on anyone's house they would destroy it and give a $500 dollar fine. The food was very bad, unlike food in Iraq.

After two months of Daesh training, Abu Omar, the Daesh man from Holland, came and got me and took me home to his wife, Mariam, but by then my mother had escaped with my little brother. I stayed with Abu Omar's family for another two months, until Mariam was about to deliver her baby. Then Abu Omar returned me to the Daesh training base. Daesh had moved it to a different location in Raqqa, but it was the same teachers and training procedures. The oldest boys were no more than fifteen years old.

One time we shot real Kalashnikovs at small stones as a target. I was allowed to shoot only two bullets because ammunition was limited. I missed the target. They taught us how to take apart the Kalashnikovs and clean them.

They taught us that Yezidis are "kuffir" (infidels), but I never believed them. I wondered to myself how they could accuse Yezidis, who were innocent like myself, of being kuffir.

When I was at this second Daesh training location, a number of times people came and said they had seen me before. They showed me a photo that looked like me, but it was a photo of my cousin who was a prisoner in Aleppo. One day, a

Daesh man from Saudi Arabia bought me. He was called Abu Osama. His real name is Khalil. He had long black hair and a big beard. He took me to a Daesh headquarters.

I lived with Abu Osama for five months. He was one of about ten religious teachers living together with us. One was Kurdish and the others were Arabs. They told me, "Why don't Yezidis worship God, like us, praying every day? Yezidis have abandoned their religious obligations."

I began to wonder myself, "Why don't Yezidis pray like Muslims?" but I never stopped knowing or feeling that I am Yezidi. Abu Osama went all around Raqqa giving lectures in mosques about Islam. He always kept me at his side. He was kind to me. He gave me money and even bought me a phone.

When he bought me the phone, the men I was living with all agreed on a plan. The Kurdish man told me to use the phone to call my family and find a smuggler to come and get me. They pressured me to do this, but their secret plan was actually to catch the smuggler, which they did. I was told he was later released for a ransom. (This interviewer was told differently, that two smugglers who came on two different operations to rescue him were captured and killed.)

In order to get a phone signal and internet signal, I had to walk to an internet cafe. I was allowed to call my family. I told them that I wanted to stay with Daesh and that they should return to Raqqa (controlled by Daesh) to be with me. I could not say the real truth, because the Kurdish Daesh was sitting next to me in the internet cafe, listening.

One time, when the Kurdish man had to go fight with Daesh, I was able to go alone to the internet cafe. I remembered the phone number of a cousin. I immediately dialed it and when my cousin answered, I told him I wanted to escape. He gave me the name and phone number of a smuggler. I called this smuggler who then gave me the phone number of another man. I called that number and we made a plan for when and where to meet in Raqqa. We met and he took me to a house.

(The details of how the escape occurred cannot be revealed, because it would endanger lives and hinder future escapes.)

The cost of buying my freedom was $20,000 US dollars. I returned to Qadia camp, Kurdistan, Iraq, on June 6, 2016. My mother and one of my sisters flew back from Germany to meet me. They are in a program sponsored by Badden-Wurttenburg, Germany, for therapy for Yezidi survivors who escaped from Daesh.

Dr. Amy Beam and Jiyan Havind (AAJ organization) spent three weeks taking me to many offices in Duhok to make my report to the police, to get my official letters stating that I was a prisoner with Daesh, to get a court document giving me permission to leave Iraq to join my mother in Germany, and to get my birth certificate, Iraqi ID, citizenship card, and passport so I can travel.

I was a prisoner with Daesh for 22 months. During that time I learned to speak English from a Daesh man from the U.K. I also met Daesh fighters from Syria, Tunisia, Germany, France, Egypt, Saudi Arabia, Iraq, and other places.

My father and eldest brother are missing since the attack on Kocho. I would like to know what happened to them. I would like to join my mother, two sisters, and younger brother who escaped before I did and are now living in Germany. They are all I have left in this world.

In December 2016, Ayad joined his mother and siblings in Germany.

Mother and Children Imprisoned in Basement in Syria

Wadha Khalaf Kalo (born 1971), June 22, 2016

I am from Kocho and was taken prisoner there when Daesh attacked Shingal. My husband is missing along with all the men of Kocho, most of whom were shot and killed. I spent nine months with Daesh; three months in Iraq and six months in Syria.

After we were attacked August 15, 2014, by Daesh in Kocho all the women and children were separated from the men and our teenage sons. From Kocho school we were transferred to Badoosh prison in Mosul.

Daesh did not force me to marry one of them. I wore a big baggy sweater that made me look fat and a scarf on my head wrapped like an Arabian grandmother wears a scarf. I have a bad knee, so I limped and said I am an old grandmother, even though I was only 41, so they did not take me.

From Badoosh prison, I was taken to Qassel Kayo village in the state of Tal Afar. My sons Ayad and Yamin were with me. There were fifty people from Kocho village living in one house. Fahima Murad Mulham, my husband's cousin, was with us. We were free to walk in the village, but there were Daesh security guards around the perimeter of the village. We had to dress in all black and also cover our faces. We saw ten to sixty armed guards in any one day.

After we were there for two weeks, nearly ten cars full of Daesh arrived and took all of us from the house to the Qassel Kayo school. Daesh searched the whole house, so no one could hide. We knew that Daesh was coming ahead of time, because the children were going every day to the Daesh school and coming home with news. Previously, Daesh had taken everyone's phone, but one phone was hidden. We all used it. So we wrapped the phone and the charger in a bag and buried in it the ground behind the house.

There were nearly 500 women and children held in the school. When we were in the school, Daesh took between twenty and thirty girls they liked and they never returned with them. Sometimes Daesh took women who were married with children. They took them and raped them. If the woman was not a virgin, then they would believe her that she had children and return her to the school. Also, some single girls were returned to the school. We were about 300 children and 200 girls and women.

I stayed in the school for four hours. For the first three or four hours Daesh was with us and taking the girls and women they liked. After four hours, I was still in the school with my two sons. Daesh had not taken me. Then Daesh said to those of us remaining that we should return to the house we were living in.

Daesh took all the women and children to the school five times and repeated this procedure. There were about 300 women like me living in Qassel Kayo whom Daesh did not touch. The fifth time Daesh took me and my two sons, Ayad and Yamin, to Raqqa, Syria.

In those three months in Qassel Kayo we cooked our own food that Daesh brought us. We had only rice, bread, and tea to eat. Each month each person got one potato or only half a potato and one egg. We were so weak. We were starving and always crying.

I thought Daesh would kill me and everyone in Qassel Kayo. I had very bad psychological problems, so Daesh took me to a doctor. I told him "*You* are my psychological problem." We begged Daesh for food and kept asking, "Where is my man from Kocho?" They said they did not know. We were living in a house that had belonged to a Shia Arab, so we used their clothes and soap. We had a good shower in the house.

All the Daesh in Qassel Kayo who guarded us were from Iraq. Some were Arabs from Shingal. I did not know any of them, but some of my relatives from Kocho village recognized some of them. The Daesh living in Qassel Kayo laughed at us.

Daesh took my son Ayad from me and took him to Syria. I was crying and said, "I must be with my son."

They left behind just some old women in Qassel Kayo. In Qassel Kayo, Daesh told us if we don't pray, they will kill us, but I never prayed. We said, "Kills us."

Daesh took me to Raqqa, Syria, on November 11, 2014, with my youngest son, Yamin. We were in four buses. There were seventy people in each bus, so we were about 280 people. We spent nine hours on the way. We went through Hasaka Island in Dicle River.   In Raqqa they took us to a farm. We spent ten days there with nearly 1,000 kidnapped Yezidis. It was so bad. We did not have food. It was cold and we did not have clothes to change or stay warm. We tore blankets to wrap the babies in.

After ten days, Daesh took us to a 12-story prison. They put seven of us in a room in the basement. We were three women and four children. For three months we did not see the light or take a shower. Ayad and Yamin were with me. Our room was three by two meters. It had no toilet or running water. We used a small can used for baby formula as a toilet. Each day we got one meal of bread. They did not give us water. We lived in one room without anything. We had only three blankets. I continued to have psychological problems.

My son, Ayad, was forced to learn to pray like a Muslim with Daesh guards. He stole an empty water bottle. When he would go to wash himself before prayers, he had a towel around his neck. He would secretly fill the bottle with water and bring it to us.

I was so sick that one day a Daesh guard took me out of my room and took me upstairs to breathe air from the window, then he returned me to the room.

We had one electric wire in the room. Daesh told us it was hooked to a car battery. We charged a small light with it. When the light died, Ayad knocked on the door to tell the guard. The guard would say they had no charge. We had light only one hour per day.

One day a Yezidi woman named Hunaf Abdullah Sala from Tal Banat visited us. (Hunaf got free from Daesh before me.) She was also kidnapped, but forcibly married to a Daesh man. She was working as a servant. She gave us soap and dates to eat. We asked her about her situation and what was happening on the outside. She told us that Daesh would keep all the old women like us, so we all began to cry. Daesh saw we were crying and told us not to cry. He said, "Muslims are good, you have dates to eat."

Hunaf spent half-an-hour with us. Her news was so bad. She told us that the kidnapped women were forced to marry Daesh. We felt so bad and were crying.

Baran and her seven-year-old daughter, Suzanne, shared my cell. Baran's grown daughter, Eva, and her baby were also with us. Later, after two months in this prison, Daesh took Baran and Suzanne. Twenty days later, Daesh took Eva and her baby. The next day I wanted to escape. It was a Friday. On Fridays, all the Daesh went to Friday prayers. They forgot to lock my door which was solid metal. We could not see out.

After Daesh took Baran and her daughter, Daesh did not always lock our door. One day we opened the door and said we were so hungry. We asked if he could bring us food. The young Daesh man let us go to the kitchen. Ayad knew where the kitchen was because he got out of the room at prayer time. When we got to the kitchen, we ran away.

The taxi driver knew we were Yezidis. He said he would keep us, but he wanted us to give him money and gold. I did not have any money or gold, so the driver took us to another Daesh center in Raqqa. The Daesh manager beat us and sent us back to prison.

The next day one Daesh man from Holland bought us. He went by the name of Abu Omar. His real name is Nuradeen. His wife was Maria (her real name). His wife was pregnant. She was also from Holland. I was used as his servant. We stayed three months in this house.

They had three children, aged 7 (boy), 5(girl), and 3 (girl). When we were in this house, we were always so hungry. Every day the planes bombed near to our house. Our windows were broken. Daesh took my son, Ayad, from me in April 2015. I was afraid they would also take my youngest son, Yamin, aged 9.

Nuradeen's wife gave me black clothes to wear, because they wanted me to do the shopping. They let me go with Yamin, alone, to do the shopping. I asked the wife to give me a phone to call my family. She gave me a phone with Nuradeen's knowledge. I called Ayad's cousin, Nassir, in Duhok. Nassir gave me

Abu Shujja's phone number. Abu Shujja is famous for getting the kidnapped women and children free.

I told Nuradeen that I want to see my family with Daesh in Tal Afar. I wanted to visit them. Nuradeen said it is okay. So I called Abu Shujja. He arranged for a man to come in his car to get me in the bazaar on Tal Abiyat Street. I told Nuradeen that if I ran away I was going to my family in Tal Afar. Nuradeen said it was okay because my family is with Daesh.

The driver took us from Raqqa to Tal Abiyat, Syria. We stayed only a few minutes in Tal Abiyat, then transferred to another car with the same driver. We spent two days in a house in Tal Abiyat. Sheep were living in this house. After two days we went by car to the Turkish border. The border was closed, so we could not drive into Turkey. The driver left us there and returned to Syria. His two sons walked with us all night into Turkey. We had no shoes because our feet were swollen, so we left our shoes behind. We crossed a small stream and walked through hills. When we saw the sunrise, we crossed the border.

My niece, Jiyan, and nephew, Muhammed, met us in Jezeera Botan, near the Zakho-Silopi border. They took us by a small bus to Sirnak camp to see my sister and her family who were refugees in that camp. We showered and stayed three hours. Then we went to Zakho, Iraq, and went to Qadia camp. We stayed in Qadia camp one week, then my two daughters, Ahfra and Dallal, escaped from Syria. After living in Qadia camp five months, I went to Germany with Yamin, Ahfra, and Dallal under the Badden-Wurttenburg program for traumatized Yezidis who had been kidnapped by Daesh.

On June 6, 2016, my son, Ayad, escaped from Raqqa. I returned to Iraq for a month to get him. He was so happy to see me, he could not stop hugging me, but we could not get his visa. I had to return to Germany without him. He joined me a year later and is doing well in school.

How Kidnapped Yezidi Women and Children Were Rescued

In the first few months after Shingal was attacked, a few women and girls escaped from Daesh without outside help. They climbed out of an unlocked upstairs window when their captors were sleeping or at work or off fighting. Their captors often drugged the girls with pills. Some girls put these sedatives in their captor's food.

Once outside on the street, the Yezidis flagged down a taxi or took refuge in a neighbor's house, taking a risk to find a sympathetic Arab. Some were captured again, returned and beaten. Some succeeded. Those Yezidis who were left behind in the same house were often accused of being part of the plan and were beaten. The fear of causing harm to others left behind was a deterrent to escaping. That method of daring, independent escape quickly ended.

There were many women and girls who tried repeatedly to escape and suffered many beatings before succeeding. One girl told of being taken into a Daesh court for repeated escape attempts. The Shariah judge said if she tried to escape again, he would have her foot cut off. Eventually, she made it to freedom.

On November 3, 2014, the Kurdistan government said that it had purchased the freedom of 234 Yezidi captives from Daesh in return for $1.5 million paid to intermediaries. This was the first large group of Yezidis rescued. A government representative stated, "We are not paying any money to Daesh. We pay the people who are helping us and it doesn't matter to us whether they buy them from the Daesh. What matters is rescuing the person."

Hadla Ahmad Jaso, one of the abducted adult daughters of Ahmad Jaso, al-Mandkany clan leader presumably killed in Kocho, explained failed negotiations between Daesh and Baghdad. In December 2014, Daesh transferred her along with 5,000 other captive Yezidi men, women, and children to Galaxy Wedding Hall and nearby areas in Mosul. They told everyone to wash up and gave the mothers diapers and toys for their small children. There was far too much food brought to the hall. A Yezidi man from Hardan asked Daesh why there was so much food and what they planned on doing with everyone. Daesh told him they were gathering 8,000 Yezidis to sell them to the Iraqi government for $8 million US dollars.

Negotiations failed after twenty-one days. According to Daesh, Baghdad offered $6.5 million US dollars which Daesh refused. The man from Hardan mysteriously disappeared from their midst, but not before sharing the plan. On the 22nd day, in early January 2015, families were sent back to Tal Afar, single girls and young married women were sent to Raqqa, Syria. Everyone was dispersed again.

The plan for a mass exchange was corroborated by a Yezidi woman who was captured with a large group on Mount Shingal on August 3, 2014. Their Daesh captor said, "We are going to sell all the Yezidis back to the government."

Seventy-seven-year-old Preskee Ismail Atto from Gohbal, corroborated without prompting that Yezidis were moved from Qaser Al Mehrab village to Galaxy Wedding Hall in Mosul in December 2014, and then returned after twenty-two days to Tal Afar and put in Shia houses.

After the failed negotiations, on January 18, 2015, Daesh released a group of approximately 200 elderly, ill, or disabled Yezidis. After the first release, the city of Tal Afar, under control of Daesh, received uninterrupted electricity while the rest of Iraq endured power outages at least three times per day for hours. Preskee Ismail Atto explained that they had electricity in the kitchen for baking bread twenty-four hours per day after the first group was released. She was released in the second group of 217 elderly, handicapped, and ill on April 4, 2015.

As for the young and healthy Yezidis, they had to plan their own escape. A phone was essential for getting free. When the Yezidis were captured, some hid their phone or SIM card in their clothing. One phone would be shared among all the women and girls. Their captors stripped the Yezidis in search of their phone or SIM card. So they would wrap it in plastic and bury it in the yard or hide it in their baby's diaper or behind the refrigerator. Mosul residents, after their liberation in 2017, said anyone caught with a phone would automatically be charged with conspiring with the Iraqi government and face execution.

Viyan Havind convinced her captor in Tal Afar to take her for a visit to her home in Kocho so she could retrieve her wedding album. She hoped to secretly get a SIM card, but her captor never took his eyes off of her. She failed to get a SIM card, but she got her four-inch-thick wedding album and her husband's soccer trophy, both of which she carried with her when she escaped on foot to Kurdistan.

When Daesh learned that women were still making secret phone calls, they cut the electricity so that the women could not charge their phones. One girl described how her brother explained to her over the phone how to cut an outside electrical wire coming to the house and join wires together with the phone charger to get electricity for a phone call.

Captives would steal SIM cards and phones. Family members who were free, had to remain in Kurdistan, rather than go to Turkey, so that they could keep their phone number operational in hope of receiving a phone call. They also had to top up credit on the secret phone being held by the captive Yezidi. Some family members waited months and even years for that crucial phone call from their captured family member. When the captive Yezidi could place a call to a friend or family member, she or he was given the name of someone to call to plan the escape. This was a middle-man with contacts within Daesh territory.

For most Yezidis who returned to freedom, their escape was planned by their own family. Often the YPG in Syria was involved in sending the smuggler. The person on the outside would hire a driver or guide who was living in Daesh territory. This driver or guide was typically an Arab friend from before Daesh declared its caliphate. A meeting place was determined.

When the captive had the opportunity to get away, she would call the driver to come for her. She would have to risk walking outside dressed all in black with her eyes covered, without being accompanied by a man, and hope she could make it to the meeting point and the waiting car. The most dangerous part of the escape was leaving the house and walking a few blocks without being caught. In Daesh territory, a woman was not allowed to go anywhere without a man.

Two young women were captured walking alone to the waiting get-away car a few blocks away. Their driver was captured and killed. The women were returned and beaten.

Once safely inside of a car, the Yezidis would be driven to a safe house or another waiting car. In order to get out of Daesh territory, they were driven on indirect routes over dirt track roads or guided on foot on trails to the front line with Peshmerga forces. The final walk to safety might take six to nine hours. Methods of delivering Yezidis from Daesh territory to the Peshmerga front line and freedom were varied and creative. The escape distances were not far, between twenty and 100 kilometers, but driving time might take hours or even a few days to avoid being stopped at a security check point. Yezidis, once free, cannot publicly tell the details of how they escaped for fear of endangering lives of those who helped or those who remained behind.

The YPG militia forces in Syria were often involved in planning and implementing the rescue. The captive might be passed from one guide to the next before reaching freedom. Every helper along the way required payment, although YPG and PKK say they did not accept payments for themselves. Because the smugglers were risking their lives, the payments were high. A one-hour taxi ride might cost hundreds or thousands of dollars instead of a normal twenty dollars.

Walking was dangerous because it was dark and land mines were strewn everywhere. A secret special forces Peshmerga team, with Coalition support, had been sent to Hawija, controlled by Daesh, to extract Katherine who was Nadia Murad's cousin. The plan went awry when the girls did not run in the expected direction. Lamiya Aji Bashar, was only meters from freedom when her companion, Katherine, age twenty, stepped on a land mine. Katherine and eight-year-old Almas died. Lamiya was blinded in one eye and deeply scarred by shrapnel. She underwent surgery in Germany.

Lamiya became a spokeswoman for Yezidis, along with Nadia Murad, for which they shared the European Parliament Sakharov Prize for Freedom of Thought in 2016. Nadia Murad became a United Nations Peace Ambassador.

Other unpublicized extractions of Yezidi captives succeeded in secret   and dangerous Peshmerga operations at no cost to the families.

A handful of middle-men or brokers established networks for moving the Yezidis from Daesh territory to freedom in Kurdistan. The cost in 2015 averaged $3000 dollars per person. By 2016 this cost had doubled. Like with any commodity, the more times she was resold, the higher her ransom price became. In extremely difficult cases, families paid $20,000 for one person as in the case of a child whose first two smugglers were captured and killed. Any smuggler who was caught was executed by Daesh. Most were publicly beheaded as a deterrent to others. At least three smugglers of survivors who told their stories in this book were captured by Daesh, sentenced by a Shariah court, and executed.

One woman and her three children were held in Raqqa by the Daesh man who forcibly married her and made her convert to Islam. One day he took his suicide vest and went on a mission. Days later she got his suicide note delivered to her with $500 and a message to raise her kids as Muslims.

The Daesh court awarded her a small monthly stipend as the widow of a Daesh fighter. She was allowed to live alone with her children. When she contacted her Yezidi husband in Iraq and planned an escape, her smuggler was captured. The court ordered execution for him and prison for her. He was beheaded in front of her. She was warned the same would happen to her if she tried to escape again. Her prison sentence was commuted and she remained in Raqqa under Daesh control.

Because the Yezidis were uncooperative rape victims, their owners tired of them and sold them. It is not so easy to keep a prisoner in one's own home for an extended period. The entire family would have to remember to call one another by their fake names, but many Yezidis found their captor's IDs and discovered their real names and nationalities in hopes of placing criminal charges against them. Eventually, most Yezidis were offered for sale.

According to an Associated Press (AP) story, Yezidi girls were being offered for sale on the internet using an encrypted app called Telegram. One ad offered a Yezidi "Virgin. Beautiful. 12 years old.... Her price has reached $12,500 and she will be sold soon."

The middle-men, referred to as smugglers or brokers, got involved in the business of returning Yezidis to freedom by buying them from their Daesh owner. Contracts of sale were registered with the Daesh courts. Yezidis were considered slaves who could be legally bought and sold under Shariah law. Arab or Kurdish brokers might keep Yezidis in their safe house for days or weeks until negotiating payment from their family. The family was threatened that if they did not come up with the money, the Yezidi woman or girl might be sold into Syria where she would be even more brutally sexually used and abused.

Some brokers or wholesalers photographed and gave them numbers to advertise them to potential buyers. Osman Hassan Ali, a Yezidi businessman who successfully smuggled out numerous Yezidi women, said he posed as a buyer in order to be sent the photographs. He shared a dozen images, each one showing a Yezidi woman sitting in a bare room on a couch, facing the camera with a blank, unsmiling expression. On the edge of the photograph is written in Arabic, "Sabaya No. 1," "Sabaya No. 2," and so on.

The middle-man who bought Yezidis would make the phone call or let her call her family, then negotiate payment. He would help in the planning to transfer her to safety. Commonly, the person holding the payment was in a different location. Payment would be made once a phone call was made saying the captive was free. So Yezidi captives "returned" in a cooperative plan rather than "escaped" to freedom.

As soon as a Yezidi would return from captivity, dozens of other families would come to question her in search of their own missing loved ones. The rescued person would tell the names and locations of those left behind. Making lists and sharing information was a constant activity within the refugee and IDP camps.

Brokers were both loved and vilified by Yezidis. The middle-man and drivers in Daesh territory risked their life if caught. A handful of Yezidi smugglers became famous for rescuing several hundred women and children. They were also accused of profiting on this dangerous enterprise. One girl who was held prisoner was allowed by her Australian captor to keep her gold jewelry. When she got to the Peshmerga front line and safety, the Yezidi smuggler stole it from her.

Some Yezidi captives regularly called their families who were free in Kurdistan and talked with the permission of their captors, but the family had no money to pay for their release and the captive had no opportunity to secretly escape. The risk of capture was a severe beating, being sold to Raqqa as a sex slave, or even death.

One sixteen-year-old girl being held prisoner in Mosul called her twelve-year-old brother every week for months and talked for an hour at a time. She said she could not reveal her address, because Daesh said they had software on the phone that was recording the phone conversation. Her family made no plan for her return, because they did not know how. Even for those captive families who lived free inside of Daesh territory, escaping was dangerous because the towns were surrounded by Daesh observation points and there were security check points on all the roads.

Kocho teenager, Ardawan Nasser Qassim Elias, was held prisoner for seven months. He volunteered to work on the poultry farm for Daesh since his family were poultry farmers. Ardawan and the other laborers simply walked away one night to freedom when their Daesh guards were off fighting.

Some brokers bought many Yezidis, then photographed each one and sent their photos to Yezidis who were free in hopes of locating the families. In the summer of 2016, photos of fifty small children were widely circulated by phone and internet in search of their parents. They were all for sale. Most of those children were bought by their family and returned to safety.

The Yezidi Affairs Office was established in Duhok by Kurdistan Prime Minister Nechervan Barzani. It was funded by the Kurdistan government and run by Khairi Bozani. Family members reported their kidnapped loved ones to this office or to the Genocide Office, who took official police reports of the missing persons. In the early months of paying for the return of kidnapped Yezidis, the government paid money in advance. The price averaged $3000 US dollars per person.

After a few months, advance payment was discontinued. Because anti-terrorism laws in most countries prohibit paying ransom, even to intermediaries, the financing to buy back captives was slow and secret. Families had to raise the money themselves. Some private donors and also organizations, including one in Germany and two from Israel, gave bridge loans. The family had to pay the money in advance. Some families bought back as many as forty abducted family members, one by one.

The brokers or smugglers, also, often offered to loan the money with the agreement that it would be paid back when the family got reimbursed from the government. The government reimbursement amount rose from $3000 to $5000. Families waited three to six months to be paid.

By November 2015, reimbursements to families were discontinued. Either the Kurdistan government could no longer afford it, or it succumbed to international pressure under anti-terrorism laws. In June 2016, KRG again began quietly reimbursing families at a price of $4500 to $6500 per person.

In July 2016, Peshmerga Commander Qassim Shesho told me, "With regard to my own way of rescuing Yezidis, I called the honorable Sidat, the brother of the honorable President Barzani. He himself asked the president and sent $300,000 dollars that we used to rescue sixty of our girls and women, each one for $5000. We do have a way through a friend to coordinate with Daesh, so we can buy another 500. If our party or a charity organization or Americans or Europeans give us support, we have found a way, through friends, to buy about 400 or 500 girls and children and women from them."

But no countries offered financial help.

Money was not paid for everyone who escaped Daesh, especially with PKK help. It must be mentioned that the PKK claimed that it had rescued the same sixty persons claimed by Peshmerga Commander Shesho. Tensions between

Peshmerga forces and militia forces, especially the PKK, remained high. The PKK, YPG/YPJ, and HBS militias, made of Yezidis and Kurds who were living on Shingal Mountain, sent secret teams into Daesh territory to scout for homes where Yezidis were being held captive. In March 2016, one HBS Yezidi soldier said, "We go in to the house with guns blazing. Someone dies. We have rescued twenty-three Yezidis like this."

Many Yezidi families lost communication with their loved one, such as seventeen-year-old Sameh Pissee Murad from Kocho who could not raise $25,000 for his mother and brother before they disappeared in Syria for another year. The excruciating emotional pain of losing contact with one's mother or wife or daughter left the Yezidis psychologically dysfunctional and depressed.

When Mosul, then Tal Afar, Hawija, and Raqqa in Syria were liberated, Iraqi military or Peshmerga or YPG militias rescued many captive Yezidis during the battles and Coalition airstrikes. Many Yezidis, such as Haifa Barakat Mahmud, walked out the door to freedom after their captors were killed in battle. Sixteen-year-old Amina, orphaned by Daesh, was burned over eighty percent of her body by a Coalition airstrike that killed her captor. Iraqi police rescued her. Unfortunately, the civilian death toll in Mosul was estimated to be as high as 40,000 from the liberation.

On December 9, 2017, Iraqi Prime Minister Haider al-Abadi announced that Daesh was totally defeated in Iraq. The next day, the United States congratulated Iraq on defeating Daesh. But where had Daesh fighters disappeared to? Some were allowed escape routes out of Iraq. Others shaved their beards and returned home, many to Shingal and Kurdistan. A PUK Peshmerga colonel said they had a list of 40,000 names of Daesh men living freely in the Duhok province. The journalists and governments stopped using the label of "Daesh," but the ideology of Daesh remained. On December 13, 2017, a group of Arabs, possibly Daesh fighters, killed a young shepherd named Watban in Shingal.

Between 2,000 and 3,000 Yezidi women and children were still in captivity. For Yezidis, the genocide was not over. The number one priority of every Yezidi was a plea to the world to find and rescue their missing loved ones.

The Price of a Yezidi Bride

Daesh rapists were not the only ones selling Yezidi girls.

I met with Hazim Tahsin, a member of the Yezidi Spiritual Council, one week after many prominent Yezidis had met in Germany in July 2016. I asked Hazim what the subject of their meeting had been, assuming they would be developing a political platform for the future of Shingal or strategy for returning the captive women. To my gob-smacked amazement, Hazim told me they had spent the week setting the dowry price in gold for marriage in Europe. Since so many Yezidis had fled to Germany, it was necessary to set an official dowry price. In 2017, it was 75 grams of gold which equaled $3000 dollars for 24 karat.

My Yezidi friend and interpreter had smuggled with his bride to Germany by way of a rubber dinghy to Greece. He insisted he could not marry his fiancée until he paid her father the Iraqi dowry price of $2400 US dollars. I argued vehemently that paying a dowry was no different than Daesh selling a woman as a sex slave. But he would not be swayed. He said it would be a shame not to pay her father.

He paid his future father-in-law the dowry price of $2400 dollars. Yezidis share this same dowry tradition with Kurds and Arabs. Many support it, including the women. The logic is that the father will use it to pay for the wedding of his son. Weddings are the financial responsibility of the groom's family.

In Russia, Georgia, and Armenia, where many Yezidis live, the dowry practice is implemented differently. Fathers of both the man and the woman to be wed give something to the young couple to help them get their start in married life. The gold given by the man's father is called *qalen*. The gold given by the bride's father is called *jayhess*. A rich father might give an apartment or furnishings or car.

The Kurdish dowry practice in Iran differs in amount and purpose. In Iran the dowry is paid directly to the woman before marriage. It can typically be $100,000 dollars. This money belongs to the bride to be her support in case her husband ever abandons or divorces her. It is akin to paying alimony *before* the wedding.

After the genocide, most Yezidis were bankrupt, making it impossible for young people to get married if a dowry had to be paid. If the Yezidi religious leaders pressured fathers to require a dowry, this could force young Yezidi men to marry non-Yezidi women, thus further contributing to the demise of Yezidis. More modern-thinking fathers defied the religious edict and stated publicly that they would refuse to accept dowries for their daughters. They would not stand in the way of young people in love from getting married.

In cases where the father insists on a dowry, many Yezidi couples get around the dowry by running off and eloping without their parents' consent. The man is said to "kidnap" his bride from her father's house. In reality, they make a secret plan to elope. After secretly running away and spending three days at a friend's home, they each inform their family of what they have done. The parents have no choice but to accept that the deed is done. The bride is no longer a virgin, so it is impossible to force her to return home. This Yezidi and Muslim cultural practice of a man "kidnapping" his bride is far different than Daesh kidnapping Yezidi girls for sex slaves. Yezidi "kidnapping" actually is a form of marriage based upon true love of two young people determined to be together.

Nadia Murad Basee and the West's Refusal To Pay Ransom

The knowledge that on a daily basis over 3,000 Yezidis were being raped and tortured seared the soul of every Yezidi. Yezidi activists beseeched every western government for funds to help them free the kidnapped women, girls and children. Western governments were united in their refusal to pay ransom to free the Yezidis.

In March 2016, I was part of a delegation that met in London with UK parliament members. I took Salwa Khalaf Rasho, an eighteen-year-old Yezidi girl who had been held captive for eight months, to testify. Haider Shesho, Yezidi commander of 3,000 independent militia fighters, also testified. We asked for aid to fight Daesh and funds to return the kidnapped Yezidis. With a $15 million dollar fund, 2000 Yezidis could be freed very quickly. No military action would be required.

Our recommendations were presented to the UK House of Commons for consideration. Rt. Hon Dominic Grieve QC MP, on the UK's Intelligence Committee, stated the "United Kingdom policy is not to pay ransoms to kidnappers either directly or indirectly."

On May 11, 2016, UK MP Tobias Ellwood, Parliamentary Undersecretary of State, responded in writing:

Ransom payments to terrorists are illegal under both UK and International law because it amounts to financing terrorism. This includes any payment where there is reasonable cause to suspect that the money, or other property, may be used for the purposes of terrorism. In terrorist kidnap cases, payment of a ransom to an intermediary could well result in at least some of the funds being used for the purposes of terrorism. As such, it would be inconsistent with our policy to support people smuggling in any context, even in this tragic case.

Nadia Murad Bassee Taha is a Yezidi woman from Kocho who was kidnapped and sexually abused at age 19. After Nadia escaped, she courageously pleaded to the UN Security Council on Dec. 16, 2015, to rescue 3,700 Yezidi women and children. Here is part of her testimony:

Prior to 3 August 2014, I was living with my family, my brothers and sisters in the pretty, quiet village of Kocho. But then the Islamic State attacked our region, and we found ourselves facing a true genocide. A large number of those forces of evil had come from different States with weapons, equipment and uniforms. Their aim was to eliminate all Yezidi existence under the pretext that — according to them — we were infidels.

The Islamic State did not just come to kill us, women and girls, but to take us as war booty and merchandise to be sold in markets for a bit of money, or even for free. Those crimes were not committed without design; they were part of a premeditated policy. The Islamic State came with the sole aim of destroying the Yezidi identity through force, rape, recruitment of children and destruction of all of our temples, which they took control of. All of this can be interpreted only as an act of genocide against our identity, in particular against Yezidi women. Rape was used to destroy women and girls and to ensure that they could never again lead a normal life.

On 15 August, elements from the Islamic State summoned us to the village school. They separated the men from the women and children. I saw them from the second floor of the school as they took away the men and killed them. Six of my brothers were killed, while three survived the mass killing. We, the women and children, were taken by bus from the school to another area. They humiliated us along the way and touched us in a shameful way.

They took me to Mosul with more than 150 other Yezidi families. There were thousands of families in a building there, including children who were given away as gifts. One of the men came up to me. He wanted to take me. I looked down at the floor. I was absolutely terrified. When I looked up, I saw a huge man. He was like a monster. I cried out that I was too young and he was huge. He kicked and beat me.

A few minutes later, another man came up to me. I was still looking at the floor. I saw that he was a little smaller. I begged for him to take me. I was terribly afraid of the first man. The man who took me asked me to change my religion. I refused. One day, he came and asked me for my hand in what they called "marriage". I said that I was ill; most women were menstruating because they were so scared. A few days later, this man forced me to get dressed and put on my makeup. Then, on that terrible night, he did it.

He forced me to serve in his military company. He humiliated me daily. He forced me to wear clothes that barely covered my body. I was not able to take any more rape and torture. I decided to flee, but one of the guards stopped me. That night he beat me. He asked me to take my clothes off. He put me in a room with guards, who proceeded to commit their crime until I fainted.

I was finally able to escape three weeks after my abduction. I currently live in Germany. Thankfully, Germany provided me with the necessary medical attention, for which I thank that country.

But this is not just about my suffering; it is about collective suffering. Daesh gave us two options: become a Muslim or die. And even men who agreed to become Muslims out of fear for their lives were killed, their women enslaved and their children recruited. Sixteen mass graves have been discovered so far. One of them contains the remains of eighty women — including my mother — whom they did not desire and so decided to kill. More than 400,000 people have been displaced, and over 40 per cent of our land is still under the control of Daesh.

Our liberated areas are uninhabitable because of the devastation, and Yezidis have no confidence that they will ever live on their land again. Just last week, more than seventy Yezidis drowned during their perilous journey to Europe. Thousands are looking for a way out, and a great many see migration as their only option. The Islamic State has made Yezidi women fodder for human trafficking. To the Security Council today, I lay out our demands, and I very much hope that humanity has not yet come to an end.

First, we demand the liberation of the more than 3,400 women and children still suffering and living under the mercy of the merciless.

Secondly, we demand that the incidents that took place, including the murders, collective slavery and human trafficking, be defined as genocide. I am asking the Council today to find solutions to the issue of genocide before the International Criminal Court.

Thirdly, demand the liberation of all of our areas, including my own village of Kocho, so that we can bury our dead. We demand the establishment of international protection for the Yezidi areas and for the minorities under threat so that, one day, we can return to our regions and live in peace. I also request the allocation of an international budget, under international supervision, to compensate the victims and rebuild the region.

Fourthly, we ask that members open up their countries to my community. We are victims and we have the right to seek a safe country that safeguards our dignity. Every day, hundreds of people risk their lives. We entreat you today to consider the resettlement option for the Yezidis and the other minorities under threat, especially the victims of human trafficking, as Germany has done.

Fifthly, and finally, we ask the Council, please, to put an end to Daesh once and for all. I suffered the pain they inflicted on me. I saw their evil. All those who commit the crimes of human trafficking and genocide must be brought to justice so that women and children can live in peace — in Iraq, Syria, Nigeria, Somalia and everywhere else in the world. These crimes against women and their freedom must be brought to an end today.

Nadia's press coverage gained momentum. She went on a grueling world-wide tour pleading for help from heads of state and parliaments. Time magazine named Nadia one of the most influential people in the world in 2014. She was awarded the Václav Havel Human Rights Prize in 2016 and was also named a U.N. Goodwill Ambassador for the Dignity of Survivors of Human Trafficking.

After more than three years, Nadia was still pleading through her tears. Why wouldn't her tears stop? Her appeals were met with respectful sympathy and photo opportunities, but not one nation helped to free the kidnapped women and children.

U.N. Secretary General Ban Ki-Moon honored Nadia in a special ceremony as he, too, hugged her and smiled for his photo while she literally cried. Nadia, herself, repeatedly said she did not care about all the honors bestowed upon her. Her singular, unrelenting, urgent desire was to rescue the women, girls, and children.

Ban Ki-Moon's position on Nadia's request was an unspeakable shame, defiantly supported by all the leaders of the world's democracies. Nadia enlisted the help of human rights lawyer, Amal Clooney, who also addressed the U.N. and stated she was ashamed of their failure to help the Yezidis.

On June 2, 2016, Ban Ki-Moon addressed the UN Security Council on sexual violence in conflict. He threw flames on the fire by deceitfully stating, "It is estimated that the Yezidi community gave the Islamic State up to $45 million in ransom payments in 2014 alone."

Yezidis began accusing the KRG of misappropriating "the missing $45 million dollars," when, in fact, there was no evidence of there ever being a fund of $45 million. It was irresponsible for the UN Secretary General to make such an unsubstantiated claim. The definition of "up to" a certain amount means anything that does not exceed that amount. Is $1 million dollars considered "up to" $45 million? Was this wording intentionally selected so as to deny the claim of $45 million dollars when challenged?

By the end of 2014, no more than 400 Yezidis had been freed or escaped from Daesh without a ransom. Even at a price tag of $5000 per person, that would equal only two million dollars. This deceit by the U.N. Secretary General was a clear threat to any government or organization that if they attempted to pay ransoms to free the Yezidi captives, they would face sanctions or prosecution under anti-terrorism laws.

Khairi Bozani, Director of the Yezidis Affairs Office in the Kurdistan Regional Government, sent an open letter to Ban Ki-Moon challenging his statement as "too vague and uncertain." He also stated that Yezidi officials and community members have called on Ban Ki-Moon repeatedly, pleading with him to save them from Daesh shootings, beheadings, and kidnappings.

"After all these crimes were committed against Yezidis and their calls for help [remained unanswered], we would like to ask you, have you done anything for them other than expressing your concern about the fate of the minority?" Bozani questioned.

Daesh oil sales into Turkey in 2014 and 2015 averaged $35 million dollars per month. This accounted for half of all income for Daesh. The amount of ransom money paid by families to free 2000 Yezidis could not have exceeded $10 million dollars in two years and was probably half that amount. Yet, the western countries remained adamant that they would not pay ransom to free the Yezidis because that would be funding terrorism.

In November 2015, the Yezidi Affairs Office stopped officially paying families when their family members returned from Daesh. In June 2016, one week after Ban Ki-Moon addressed the UN Security Council suggesting Yezidis had paid $45 million dollars in ransom to terrorists, the Yezidi Affairs Office quietly paid $4000 each to some survivors who had returned from Daesh the previous year.

In September 2016, the US Congress approved 1.15 billion dollars in sales of tanks and heavy arms to Saudi Arabia. In January 2017, the U.K. approved 100 million pounds (130 million dollars) in sales of heavy arms to Turkey after its 2015-2016 armed campaign against its Kurds displaced estimates of one million people. Both of these countries are majority Sunni Islamic and have been widely accused of supporting Daesh terrorists.

By 2018, an estimated 3,000 Yezidis were still in the hands of Daesh. Some remained in regular phone contact with family members who were unable to raise the money to pay for their return. The Yezidi communities were bankrupt and could not find $5 to top up their phone, let alone $5,000 for ransom for a girl who was being raped for more than two years.

Nadia Murad was awarded the 2018 Nobel Peace Prize. In her acceptance speech she stated, "The international community should provide international protection under United Nations supervision. Without this international protection, there is no guarantee that we will not be subjected to other genocides from other terrorist groups. The international community must be committed to providing asylum and immigration opportunities to those who have become victims of this genocide."

Rape Survivors Suffer Family Separation in Germany

In 2015-2016, the state of Baden-Wurttemburg, Germany, accepted 1,100 vulnerable Yezidi women and girls from Iraq who were kidnapped and sexually abused and tortured by Daesh.   Participants also included a dozen teenage boys who had escaped mass executions or military jihadist training. The budget was $95 million dollars for a two-year program.

Baden-Wurttemberg's intent was to provide a model therapy program that other jurisdictions could replicate. Regardless of this program's controversial policies, Germany deserves praise for being the only jurisdiction in the world that offered a program for traumatized Yezidi women, girls, and children. Something *was* better than nothing.

In Germany, they were assigned to live in group houses or apartment complexes turned into refugee centers. There were 24-hour security guards. At 10 PM doors were locked. This was similar to all the refugee centers throughout Germany, but there were some special differences for the Yezidi women and children.

In 2016, I spent five weeks visiting women and girls in this program to see how they were doing. I had met them in Iraq when I got their passports for them and went to follow-up their progress. Based on conversations and observations, there were signs of psychological healing including improved grooming, smiling and laughing, replacing their black clothes and head scarves with European clothing, removal of head scarves, improved self-confidence, independence and ability to handle money, taking public transportation without a male relative, and learning the German language. The women, however, identified several problems with the program.

They bitterly resented being separated from the adult male members of their family who were not permitted to accompany them to Germany. This included women's husbands. Psychologist Dr. Jan Ilhan Kizelhan, a Yezidi himself, stated that in setting the criteria, they made a decision not to accept men because of the stigma of loss of honor for raped women.   The small number of 1100 made it impossible to accept everyone who was traumatized.

Jaed Murad Khero, a boy whose father, cousin, and uncles were massacred on their family farm, survived with a few teenage male cousins who were locked in their kitchen. Jaed watched through the window to see his father and uncles shot in the head. Twenty-eight female family members and relatives were abducted by Daesh.

Jaed stated, "I asked for help from a lot of organizations and even from Mirza Dinnayi who made the selections for Germany, but no one helped me. My future was Mirza's to decide, but he destroyed me." Female survivors in Jaed's extended family went to Germany, but Jaed was left behind in his tent in Iraq along with 200,000 other Yezidis who had not been abducted and raped. They were deeply traumatized, but there were no asylum programs for them.

Many of the women and girls who went to Germany in the B-W program saved their monthly government stipends of 320 euro per person and sent money home to their husbands and fathers in Iraq so they could smuggle themselves to Germany to join their family. When male family members smuggled themselves illegally to Germany and were processed as refugees in different cities and states, they were prohibited from joining their families. The traumatized women were not re-united with their fathers, husbands, and sons even when all of them were spread across Germany. By 2017, it was virtually impossible to smuggle into Germany.

This problem remained at a severe level, trapping women in a chronic condition of severe psychological suffering and preventing healing. With bitterness, women said, "First Daesh took us away from our men, and now Germany is doing the same thing." The women who were interviewed stated it was more important to be re-united with their families than to be housed with other Yezidi survivors.

Some women ran away from the program. Others got lawyers to leave the German therapy program and apply for asylum in Germany. One woman traveled from Stuttgart to Hannover where she married her boyfriend from Shingal and moved into his apartment. When she was five months' pregnant, German police returned her against her will to Stuttgart.

The same policy applied to parents of young Yezidi men and married couples who had smuggled to Germany in advance of their parents. If their parents got fingerprinted in a different state or city, they could not be relocated to join their children. Yezidi families remained separated throughout Germany.

Germany was overwhelmed with 1.1 million immigrant arrivals in 2015 and was unable to respond to personal family requests for reunification. Yezidis' psychological suffering continued in Germany, in spite of their deep gratitude to the German people for helping them when other countries refused them.

When Yezidi survivor Nadia Murad addressed the United Nations Security Council, Dec. 15, 2015, it gave courage to the other Yezidi girls who had escaped sexual enslavement. They contacted me and invited me to come with a camera so that they, too, could tell their stories of Daesh captivity to the world. They no longer wanted to hide behind a scarf.

When I arrived in Freiburg, Germany, Viyan's kids, now age two and four, leaped into my arms. All the girls in the house came to hug me. Each was eager to tell her story. On the third day of my visit, Viyan's social worker and psychologist showed up to meet me. I was glad to meet them and discuss Viyan's progress, until I discovered they were there to kick me out. Neither of them, in fact, knew anything about Viyan's personal story of eleven months in captivity with Daesh. They had never had one counseling session with her. They were only there to tell me the rules that visitors could not stay overnight.

They threatened Viyan and the other girls and women with having their monthly German government stipends withdrawn if they allowed me to publish their stories on the internet or interview them with a video camera without hiding their faces behind a scarf.   If the girls did give me an interview, they were ordered to make me pay them money for the interview. These were women I had been helping for nearly a year.

I was so distressed at this treatment that I immediately phoned Dr. Jan Ilhan Kizelhan, the psychologist who helped design this program. He explained he was not involved with the German government policies of house guests and interviews.   This was standard German policy for refugee centers. Kizelhan advised me to call Mirza Dunnayi, the program director who had interviewed and selected the girls in Kurdistan. I thought surely Mirza, a Yezidi himself, would defend the girls' right to tell their stories to the public.

Mirza defended the policy of silencing the girls. He explained that they should not tell anyone they were Yezidi because of the stigma associated with being kidnapped and raped. They must keep their story, their Yezidi identity, and their address a secret, thus further contributing to their victimization as if they had done something wrong.

In a heated phone conversation, Mirza said to me, "Are you going to be responsible when Daesh comes and harms Viyan's kids?"

I protested the policy of instilling fear into their heads in the safety of Germany.   The denial of their Yezidi identity further perpetuated the genocide against Yezidis.

Viyan is an articulate, strong, and courageous woman. She called a local Yezidi activist and we went to a nearby house where she recorded her video testimony.   When I returned to Viyan's group home, the other girls and women had changed their minds about telling me their stories, after having been threatened by the social worker and psychologist. I was treated as the enemy by the staff for wanting to give the Yezidi survivors a voice. The policy was to silence them.

I had come to visit Viyan after promising her for five months that I would drive her to visit her uncle and his family in another German city. Viyan was told she could not go with me.   We went anyway for a great family reunion for one week.

Salwa Khalaf Rasho was another courageous Yezidi survivor of kidnapping and rape. I accompanied her by plane from Cologne, Germany, to London where she appealed for help to members of the U.K. parliament.   We flew back to Germany, and I drove her home to a city in Stuttgart. We arrived at midnight after public transportation was closed.

It was a dilemma for Salwa to give me her address so I could deliver her to her doorstep.   Any Yezidi who revealed her address was under threat of being expelled from her building.   Many girls had heard of this happening to one Yezidi woman.   Salwa finally agreed to let me drive her home if I promised not to park in front of her building.   She had a key to sneak in the side door undetected.

The policy of concealing their identity and address effectively prevented the Yezidi survivors from making any normal friendships in the town where they were living.   It also kept human rights activists, humanitarian groups, and journalists away.   The survivors were isolated and had virtually no visitors. Going to Germany was like having to give up one's whole life and enter a witness protection program under a false identity.   Who were they if they could not be themselves?   How could they invent a new past?   How could they make a new friend?   How could they pretend the genocide had never happened?

The justification for concealing their address, at least, had some merit.   The wave of immigrants from 2014 to 2016 grew to two million in Germany.   The majority of these immigrants were Muslims fleeing war in Syria, Afghanistan and northern Africa.   Islamization crept into Germany.   A small group acted out their discrimination against non-Muslims and gave rise to a growing backlash in Germany against immigrants.

Isolated attacks upon Yezidis occurred.   Yezidi men who were housed in apartment buildings and large sports halls with predominately Muslim immigrants were particularly vulnerable.   Whether to speak up about the genocide or to conceal one's Yezidi identity or at least one's address was a real dilemma for the Yezidi women and girls.

The survivors in the Baden-Wurttemburg program as well as all those in refugee centers were not permitted to have overnight visitors, including their own husband, family, or friends.   So if their family members could not afford a hotel room, then they could not afford to visit them from elsewhere in Germany.   There are security guards in each house or building who check who comes and goes and deny permission for outsiders to enter the building unless they have a friend living there.   All visitors must leave by 10 PM when doors are locked.

The house managers' behavior toward visitors differed from one location to another.   In Ulm, the manager was extremely open and welcoming to my overnight visit with my Yezidi friends whom I had helped in Iraq from the time they escaped from Daesh.   The social worker and psychologist explained that the training they had received when the program was initiated was that they should not ask the Yezidi survivors to tell their stories.   They should focus on providing a sense of security and integration into the German culture.

The therapy program in Germany hired Kurdish-speaking interpreters and therapists who were Muslim.   After having suffered a genocide at the hands of

Muslims, the Yezidi women absolutely refused to trust non-Yezidi interpreters or to confide in Muslim therapists.

There is a lot that has been written about the lack of psychological help for the escaped Yezidi women who have been traumatized by war and rape. Their husbands were killed. Their children were stolen. Their homeland was destroyed. Their lives were shattered. Weekly chat in a therapist's office could never ever fix this.

There was some justification in the policy of not having counseling sessions with the survivors. The very act of recalling the savage treatment received at the hands of their Daesh captors was enough to trigger an attack of hysteria. Forgetting their deep trauma was the best therapy. Only time could ease their suffering.

The escaped women gathered in each other's rooms while their two-year-olds played. They shared their experiences of captivity and escape and formed their own support groups. These women were not broken. To the contrary, their hearts were on fire with rage. They wanted Daesh to be *destroyed*, not *contained*. The genocide forced Yezidis to begin to break free from orthodox ideas of shame. Where previously, a woman who was raped would have been shunned, after this genocide, hundreds of Yezidi men offered to marry any Yezidi woman who would want to marry. Couples who had been in love before the woman was kidnapped, reunited and held public weddings as a symbol of defiance against Daesh.

In February 2016, admission to the Baden-Wurttemburg program for survivors was closed, leaving more than 1800 survivors trapped in Kurdistan without help. Even when additional family members escaped from Daesh, very few were able to join their sisters and mothers in Germany.

In 2017, the United Nations High Commission on Refugees held interviews in Duhok, Kurdistan, to refer families for resettlement to Canada, Australia, and the US. Canada took 1200 survivors and family members. Males were included. The United States accepted ten families as a trial program. Australia accepted some who had private sponsorship.

Most of the survivors remained trapped inside of Iraq as IDPs. 196,000 Yezidis were living in tents and a few in caravans (trailers). No countries in the world opened their doors to displaced Yezidis as a class of people who had suffered a genocide. In 2016, Florida Representative Alcee Hastings introduced H.R. 379 Justice for Yezidis Act to the US Congress to create a special class of religious minorities in Iraq who could apply for humanitarian asylum in the US. It languished in committee as Yezidis languished in tents. One young man told me, "I know that we will die in these camps before we go the USA. We are suffering from psychological and physical problems."

Yezidis Flee from Turkey's War on Kurds

My friend Farhan Mahlo, who had interpreted for me in Beytussebap in 2014, made it to Germany with his family and parents in November 2015.

When the Turkish government opened a government-supported refugee camp for Yezidis in Nusaybin, in November 2014, Farhan and his family, along with 600 people from Sirnak camp, moved to Nusaybin camp on the promise of better food, a school and a UNHCR office in the camp. By then, the waiting period for a UNHCR appointment to apply for asylum in a third country was seven years. I cautioned him against going to Nusaybin.

When he arrived, I asked him about his situation. There was no UNHCR office as promised. "How is the school?" I queried. "And the teachers?"

"They took our computers, but they will return mine in two weeks, because I will be one of the teachers. I have to download the Turkish school curriculum and teach it." A conundrum. . .Turkey's school is taught in the Turkish language. Yezidis speak Arabic and Kurdish. Turkey outlaws public education in Kurdish.

Their first winter passed in Nusaybin camp. Another winter was approaching. Turkey broke the two-year peace with the Kurdish Workers' Party (PKK) and mounted an unrelenting attack against Kurdish cities and villages, bombing, burning, and shooting live bullets into peaceful demonstrations. The civilian death toll mounted weekly while Turkey blocked over 100 news websites and imprisoned journalists so the outside world could not witness its genocide against the Kurds.

In July 2015, when the Yezidis attempted a mass exodus with buses to the Bulgarian border, Farhan's family joined in. When they were sent back from Istanbul by Turkish authorities, Nusaybin camp refused at first to let his family return, accusing him of being one of the leaders of the failed exodus.

In October 2015, a section right next to the Yezidi tents in Nusaybin camp was turned into a military camp to house tanks and soldiers. Farhan feared open war would break out soon between the Turkish government and the Kurds. With tanks parked next to their tents, they knew they had to flee once again. His fears came true.

By mid-November 2015, Nusaybin was under curfew for two weeks. Seven civilians were shot dead in the street in one week. Food was not entering the city. No one could leave their house, not even to retrieve their dead or wounded family members lying in the streets. The co-mayor of Nusaybin cried out on social media for international help to stop Turkey's renewed siege. On December 6, a police tank was blown up killing six police officers. On December 7, another two teenage boys and an elderly woman were killed, allegedly by security forces.

Nikki, a single working mom in Canada, had contacted me earlier in the year and asked how she could volunteer from home. I suggested she become friends and a lifeline for a Yezidi family. I put her in touch with Farhan and their friendship developed. One year later, Farhan appealed to her for help to go to Germany. With some trepidation, Nikki asked me if I thought Farhan was trustworthy. I vouched for him, and she did something she had never dared before in her life. She sent a whopping $2000 US dollars to Farhan.

With this and money he had earned teaching, Farhan and his family left their few possessions behind and took a twenty-hour bus ride to Izmir on the west coast of Turkey. He, his wife, two sons, a sister, brother, and nephew crossed in a rubber boat to the island of Samos, Greece, on November 9, only days before Nusaybin turned into an open war zone. They sailed from Kosadesi, Turkey, at 11 pm and arrived four hours later to Samos Island. It was an easy crossing. They paid $3000 for seven people.

They were met by Doctors Without Borders and other volunteers, taken to the police station to be processed and fingerprinted, then taken to a camp. They stayed more than one week, waiting for their travel documents. In the end, they left without the documents. Without documents from Greece, they were stopped and questioned hard for two hours at the Macedonia border, but were finally allowed to enter.

After entering Macedonia, they traveled without immigration checks by bus to Macedonia, Serbia, Croatia, Slovenia, Austria, then Germany. It took them 16 days from when they left Turkey by rubber boat with only the clothes on their backs and life vests.

When they arrived, Farhan bought a German SIM card but quickly finished the credit on internet messages. They found a refugee camp in Stuttgart with free WiFi.

That is when Farhan contacted me for help. He was out of phone credit and out of money. They still had 370 kilometers to go to reach his brother in Cologne, northwest Germany. Weekday train fare could be over 100 euro per person. There were five adults and two children. I went into action contacting friends I knew in Germany.

Another Yezidi, whose parents were killed in Kocho, offered to buy a weekend pass for 60 Euros. It would be good for up to five people on Saturday and Sunday. Children traveled free. He would pay for the ticket at the Hannover station and send a PIN code to Farhan who would pick up the ticket in the Stuttgart train station. Before, he could buy the ticket, a sympathetic German in the train station bought the ticket for Farhan's entire family! Such was the kindness of Germans in 2015 to the refugees fleeing genocide.

On November 29, 2015, Farhan sent me a photo of the family in his brother's room in Cologne. Their journey to a safe country had taken, not only 16 days, but 16 months from when Daesh attacked Shingal, August 3, 2014. The family received asylum in October 2016. They were now eligible to work in Germany.

In December 2016, German social services approved their move into a house near his parents who had taken the dangerous trip across the waters to Greece shortly after he had. They were learning German. Because they acted fast, they were resettled and starting their new life two-and-a-half years after the attack on Shingal.

In 2017, they received three-year temporary German passports which allowed them to travel. They are the fortunate few who escaped before the borders closed. They are grateful to those who helped them on their long journey and to the generous German government and people for a chance to start a new life.

Others were not so lucky.

In late 2016, the Turkish government arrested and imprisoned nearly every democratically elected Kurdish mayor in southeast and eastern Turkey, including Diyarbakir, on charges of supporting a terrorist organization. In the mentality of the ruling Turks, every Kurd was a terrorist. Governors appointed from Ankara central government took over control of the Kurdish towns and cities which were occupied by Turkish military.

On January 3, 2017, the last Kurdish-run refugee camp in Turkey, south of Diyarbakir, was forcibly closed by the Turkish government, and 1500 Yezidis were again displaced. Those who had money to smuggle themselves went to Europe, risking death along the way. Those who were too poor, too old or disabled returned to Iraq.

Smuggling through Bulgaria and the Dublin Accords

After one year in refugee camps, it began to dawn on Yezidis that no one was coming to their rescue, including the UNHCR. The Yezidis' attempt at mass exodus to Bulgaria on June 25, 2015, and again on December 21, 2015, had ended bitterly. In its annual report for 2015, Amnesty International found that "NGOs reported that people in search of international protection who were trying to enter Bulgaria through checkpoints were rejected." As a consequence, Yezidis began smuggling to Bulgaria on foot through the forests and mountains north of Istanbul, Turkey, referred to as the green border.

Western media stirred up an irrational fear and backlash against immigrants, saying that Daesh jihadists are escaping to Europe and beyond, sneaking in with all the refugees fleeing Daesh. Their "proof" was that many of the media photos showed mostly young men with no women and children. However, this is because the young, single men were sent by their families to be the first ones to get to Germany, get a room, and apply for asylum. A child under age 18, could apply for their parents and siblings to join them. Alternatively, their families might enter the E.U. illegally when they knew they would have a secure destination at which to arrive.

After having faced the kidnapping and rapes of Yezidi women in Shingal by Daesh, no Yezidi woman would dare to travel alone on the dangerous smuggling routes. First, the young unmarried brothers smuggled themselves to Germany and rented rooms. Then their married siblings and parents followed behind.

According to the Dublin Accords, a fleeing immigrant must be registered and fingerprinted in the first country in the European Union in which he or she enters. The only E.U. country which shares a border with Turkey is Bulgaria. All the immigrants were intent on getting to Germany which in 2014 and 2015 had an open door policy under Prime Minister Angela Merkel for people fleeing war. Germany was becoming the new homeland for Yezidis.

Immigrants did everything to avoid being caught and fingerprinted by police in Bulgaria. If they were fingerprinted in Bulgaria, and then made it to Germany, the German government would be required, under the Dublin Accords, to return them to Bulgaria.

Bulgaria is a beautiful but poor country. It was not equipped to handle the influx of illegal immigrants, nor did it have a program to resettle them. Whether it was intentional or not, Bulgarian authorities beat, starved, and temporarily imprisoned the refugees, ensuring that no one would want to stay in Bulgaria. Bulgaria also avoided fingerprinting them.

As early as 2014, administrative courts in Germany in one asylum appeal case after another ruled against returning refugees to Bulgaria because of inhumane conditions, brutal treatment, and inability to provide minimum standards of safety. Bulgaria's tactics were working. Word spread quickly that smuggling through Bulgaria was dangerous. It became a way-station to Germany.

In 2015, one million asylum seekers entered Europe. According to statistics from the Immigration Office on Migration (IOM), 27% were under the age of 18. Of those children, 6% were from Iraq. One-quarter of the child refugees applied for asylum in Germany. More than half of all refugees arriving in the E.U. were fleeing war from Syria, Afghanistan and Kosovo. The Yezidi refugees, continued to be a minority among the Muslim immigrants. Estimates are that 35,000 Yezidis arrived in Germany by 2017.

Khalef Kassim

Khalef Kassim (not his real name) was one such case. He was the only single young male in his family, so he was the one who took the risk to smuggle to Germany. Yezidi families referred to this risk as "sacrificing" their son. Once one family member could get asylum in Germany, then he could apply for asylum for his family to join him under Germany's family reunification program. If the refugee was under age 18, he could apply for asylum for his parents.

Khalef paid $11,500 US dollars to his guide to smuggle him into Bulgaria illegally. In a group of 25 Kurds from Syria and Yezidis from Iraq, they walked through the trees until they were twenty kilometers inside the border of Bulgaria. It was cold and raining. The police caught them that night at 4 AM when they built a fire to warm up.

Police took them to Elhovo camp where they were locked up for twenty days. Within the first 38 hours they were fingerprinted. There was no shower, not enough food, and no drinking water except from the faucet in the toilet room. Khalef had to buy his own food so he would not starve. There were twenty people per small room, so Khalef slept outside on the ground in the cold. He did not wash his body for his entire stay. When he asked for anything, like to charge his phone, security police hit him. He suffered repeated beatings and inhumane treatment.

After twenty days, two police transferred him and others to another camp. When they arrived, they took them into a building to apply for asylum. A government worker asked them in Kurdish, "Who wants to stay in the country and who wants to leave?" For those people who wanted to leave Bulgaria, the translator told the guard at the door to open the door and let them leave.

After the inhuman treatment suffered in Bulgaria, Khalef did not waste time saying goodbye to Bulgaria. It took him six weeks to get to Germany, mostly by walking. He traveled through Serbia, Croatia, Slovenia, and Austria to arrive in Stuttgart, Germany, where he applied for asylum. He was provided a shared room in a house, 329 euro per month, and an ID good for three months while he waited for his asylum interview. He went daily to German language class.

After three months, he was informed he had to return to Bulgaria because he had been fingerprinted there. They gave him a date to be ready to leave. Khalef promised to kill himself if he had to go back to Bulgaria, Turkey, or Iraq. At night he awoke from nightmares of being beaten by police. He was depressed and cried often from fear of being returned. Finally, in a deteriorating psychological state, he called his German teacher for help.

She took him to a hospital where he was admitted for observation and stayed two months. When he returned to his room which he shared with three Yezidis in a house of 25 men, he discovered that two Muslim immigrants in the house had broken into their room, smashed the mirror, broken into the cupboards, and stole their few possessions. Khalef was surrounded everywhere by Arabs and did not feel safe, even in Germany, because it was Arabs who had killed and kidnapped Yezidis. He remained deeply traumatized.

The court denied his asylum, stating he had to be returned to Bulgaria. He maintained that he would kill himself if sent back to Bulgaria. With the help of a lawyer, his asylum was finally granted on appeal. After two years, he remained alone and unable to bring his parents and little siblings to Germany.

Bassam Martin Sadoo

My family of five was trapped on Shingal Mountain for eight days with no food and water until the PKK opened a corridor to Syria. They took us by car to Syria and then we went to Zakho. There were no tents or organization, so after two months, we paid a smuggler $200 per person to cross into Turkey.

We stayed in Sirnak refugee camp in an old Army barracks for one year. I saw nothing was changing in the camp or in Iraq. I was only seventeen, but I felt my future was lost. For a long time the Turkish government and Kurds were fighting each other. The Turks were gassing, shooting, and bombing the PKK Kurdish militants and, also, the innocent Kurdish civilians. We Yezidis were trapped in the middle. Kurdish volunteers were running our camp and providing us with food. If Turkey killed the Kurds, we did not know what would happen to us. That is why so many Yezidis were leaving each day.

By the end of 2015, Sirnak camp was abandoned because of the Turkish attacks. My family, whom I left behind when I smuggled to Germany, had to flee back to the danger of Iraq. Finally, in 2016, the Turkish military and police bombed and destroyed 75% of Sirnak city and displaced 100,000 Kurds. If we say something to support Kurdish people, the Turkish government will come and arrest us. Even in Kurdistan (Iraq), who says anything will get arrested.

That is why I left in September 2015. Turkey was not safe, and I did not see a future. I did not register with the UNHCR because the waiting period for an interview was eight years, and then still there was no guarantee we would get out of Turkey.

I called a smuggler in Istanbul. He agreed to take me and my friend to Germany for 8,000 euro each. We took a bus to Istanbul, and he met us at the bus station. We only had 500 euro between us. He agreed that we would pay him the money when we arrived in Sophia, Bulgaria. We had a plan to run away, because we had no money and neither did our families. We lost everything in Shingal.

We took a small bus which dropped us near to the border of Bulgaria. There a group of five smugglers from Afghanistan led us to Bulgaria. Our group had 15 passengers. There were many other groups, too. Our guides said, "You guys have to follow us. Don't get lost."

We walked one hour through the forest in the mountains to get to the border of Bulgaria. There was no road. We walked at night and slept under the trees in the day. We had some bread, cake, and candies we had brought with us. After we crossed the border, cars came and took us to Sophia. Getting to Sophia from Istanbul took two-and-a-half days.

In Sophia, they locked us in a house. That explains why there were five smugglers guiding us. They had to prevent us from running away without paying our money. That was when my problems began with the smuggler. Each passenger had to pay the smuggler in Sophia or contact his family and tell them to pay the smuggler in Istanbul.

The smuggler in Istanbul was running the operation. He had communication with smugglers in every country. He conducted all of his work on the phone.

In Sophia each passenger in our group paid his money, then left. Only my friend and I remained locked in a room. We had a problem with our money. The price from Istanbul to Sophia, Bulgaria, was 2,000 euro per person. But we did not pay any money in the hand in Istanbul. We had promised to pay in Sophia. The truth was, we did not have any money to pay the 8,000 euro per person to get to Germany.

We told the smuggler our money was not ready yet. He said, "You are lying to us." I told him that we know we made a mistake. The person in Istanbul told the smugglers in Sophia to take us and lock us in another place. It was the worst place I ever saw in my life. They did not give us any food. When we asked to go outside to the toilet at night, we managed to escape.

In the city center of Sophia, the police picked us up at 4 AM. They knew we were refugees. They hit us and told us they would take our fingerprints and return us to Turkey.

I said, "Okay, I want to return." That was hard, but we had lost our opportunity. Then the police said, "Give me $500 dollars, and I will let you go."

So I gave him 500 euro, and they dropped us in another location. Now we had no money. We went to the taxi driver in Sophia center. The same place where the police picked us up. We called someone to come and pick us up.

The smuggler in Istanbul already knew we were missing. He had called both of our families saying, "We are looking for your son. If we catch him, we will kill him."

The smuggler in Istanbul has communications with all the smugglers in Sophia. If they double-cross him, they will be in trouble. So we got caught again. They locked us up while my family collected 2,000 euro to save my life. After my family paid the money, I was set free.

I made a big mistake. Each Yezidi wants to go out from hell, but the road to freedom is so dangerous.

I knew a smuggler in Sophia, so I called him and told him what happened to me. He said he would help me. He sent me to the Serbian border where there were organizations helping the refugees for free. They sent us by bus and train to Croatia, Slovenia, Austria, then Germany. The Yezidis did not know organizations were working at the borders, so Yezidis were paying thousands of euro unnecessarily to smugglers to get to Germany.

The organizations took us to Munich, and then to a refugee camp in Trier. The refugees were being dispersed all over Germany. Germany did not care where you might have a friend or family. They said I have to register in Trier, but I did not want to, so I just left. I took a train to Hanover where I have a friend who took me to a refugee center where I registered.

I stayed there eighteen days before I had my first interview. We did not speak each other's language, but luckily we could have the interview in English which I know. They gave me a card to get money.

I told them I am Yezidi. I got a court date in three days for my interview for asylum. At the court interview the man asked me if I had seen massacres. I told him yes. I had seen massacres between Khanasor and Sunoni in Shingal.

They asked more questions, and then they took my fingerprints. After that, they gave me a green card. That means I did an interview in court and I had to wait for asylum.

In one month I was transferred from the temporary camp to Wolffenbuttel main camp where I live now. There are not too many people here. Each person gets a room. I have a roommate. After fifteen days, I got a post. Someone knocked on my door. When I opened the post, it was asylum. I was so relieved!

It took three months. After that, I went to another place to get a date to get fingerprinted for my passport. I got my temporary German passport and ID eighteen days after that. So, it was easy. The reason I got my asylum and passport in only six months is because not very many refugees come to this small town. I did not have to wait long for my appointments like other refugees in the big cities.

I had to register in school to learn German. When I learn to speak German, I can either get a job or go to school. Now I can stay in Germany and travel anywhere in Europe, so I took a train and visited Paris. It is so great to be free and safe, but I am all alone. There are not many Yezidis living in Wolffenbuttel, so I miss my culture and my language. I am so thankful to Germany for giving me a new start on life, but I miss my family so much and hope they can join me.

By the end of 2015, the organizations stopped receiving refugees from Serbia, because Bulgaria put up fences at the border with Turkey. There are no more smugglers on the Bulgarian route. The only choice left is to go by sea from Turkey to Greece, and that is even more dangerous than Bulgaria was for me.

In February 2016, Turkey stopped giving visas to people in Iraq, so they are trapped in Iraq and cannot get to Turkey unless they pay a smuggler the same way we did in September 2014. It is one big circle, like a game. My family is back to square one in the same place we were when we ran from Shingal. They are living in a tent in Kurdistan, Iraq. If I want to see them, I will have to fly back for a visit.

Smuggling through Greece to Germany

I first met Nayf in September 2014, when he called me with a desperate plea to come to Diyarbakir refugee camp in Turkey and alert the United Nations to their dire food shortage. They had recently arrived from Roboski, Turkey, after the PKK had guided them to the mountain pass from Iraq.

Six months later, Nayf left Diyarbakir camp to live in a camp in Iraq and look for work. In February, 2015, he helped me distribute $2999 US dollars to 35 kidnapped women, and some orphaned girls, who had escaped Daesh captivity and rape. That is the maximum limit that Western Union would send to Iraq in one transaction. It took two weeks of appealing to supervisors to waive Western Union's policy that they would not transfer money to Iraq if the donor does not know the recipient face-to-face. Western Union's policy is that unless the person is known to the donor, it must be a scam.

The private donation came from an elderly man nicknamed "Easy" in Prescott, Arizona. He explained the people of Prescott had been deeply moved when they learned about Kayla Mueller, a young American woman from Prescott who had been captured and raped for months by the Daesh supreme leader, Abu Bakr Al-Baghdadi, before being killed. "Easy" wanted to help the kidnapped Yezidi women. (Easy went on to anonymously contribute thousands of dollars over the next three years to Yezidis.)

Nayf carefully compiled a list of thirty-five women and girls who had escaped from Daesh, and we distributed $85 dollars to each of them.

In the summer of 2015, Nayf took a dangerous job working on cell phone towers within 500 meters of Daesh in Shingal. He earned a meager $600 dollars per month. One day when talking on Skype, he told me he was depressed and feeling suicidal. He explained his girlfriend was going with her family in the Yezidis' attempt at a mass exodus to Bulgaria.

I sent him loads of information and advice about the Bulgarian border and urged him to persuade her family not to go, because they would waste money and be sent back. "Do you love her?" I asked, to which he answered, "Yes."

"Does she love you?"

"Yes, she does," he replied.

"Are you sure?"

"Oh, yes, I am very sure she loves me," he replied.

"Then ask her to return to Iraq and marry you," I advised.

Nayf rejected this, explaining how in their culture they had to wait and he would have to work several years, save money, then the mothers both had to agree, and then there was the matter of paying the mandatory $2400 dollar dowry to her father.

"That was before the genocide. Since then the rules have changed. If she goes to Bulgaria without you, and you are not married to her, you may never see her again. If she gets asylum, she will not be allowed to request her boyfriend join her. She can only bring her husband. Marry her now. You lost everything in your life. Don't lose the only thing you have left: the woman you love."

After two weeks of nightly counseling and prodding on Skype calls, Nayf announced that both his mother and hers had agreed over the phone to their engagement. Her family would not try to escape to Bulgaria. His university-educated girlfriend returned to Iraq and found a job as a nurse in one of the Yezidi camps. They began planning their escape to Europe.

In November 2015, they quit their jobs, and registered their marriage before leaving Kurdistan so that they would not be separated when they arrived in Europe. They headed to Izmir, Turkey, with her family for the illegal boat crossing to a Greek island.

A court in Germany had ruled that asylum-seekers who first entered the E.U. in Greece could not be returned to Greece due to Greece's inhumane treatment of refugees. After so much negative publicity about refugees drowning, Greece changed its policy to register the refugees and send them on their way to the Macedonia border, assured that they would not be returned because of the court ruling. Greece was off the hook.

On December 5, Nayf sent me a message, "Half-way to Kos Island, the boat turned back due to high waves in the black of night. My wife cried all the way. We will not try again. I am afraid she will be traumatized for life if she has to do this again. What will we do? We quit our jobs. We can't go back."

Even though he was on dry land, this university-educated electrical engineer was drowning in desperation. I was his only lifeline.

I studied the map of the Greek islands and understood immediately that they had chosen an island near Bodrum, Turkey, that was too far south, exposed to big waves from the Mediterranean. Using FaceBook messenger, I sent him a map and explanation. "Go further north where the islands are protected. You will find flat water. Your smuggler friend gave you bad advice. Get your money back."

The next day he arranged to go in a wooden boat out of Cesme, near Izmir. That day he flew from Izmir to Istanbul where his friend refunded his $4000 dollars. He turned right around to the airport, flew back to Izmir, arriving at 9:15 PM, where he dashed to the harbor. The boat was scheduled to leave at 10 PM. Alas, when they saw the boat, it was old and looked unsafe, so they rejected it. He still had the money in his pocket. He continued to search for another boat until finding one going the next night.

At 3:50 AM, December 8, 2015, Nayf landed safely in the Greek Island of Chios in a rubber boat with his new wife and her family of six. When they landed, there were already fifty refugees sitting on the shore. There were no volunteers to meet them. He sent me another FaceBook message with a GPS map showing his location, "Please try to give me the organization position or send someone to help us if you can."

They had landed at Paralia Agias Fotinis on Chios Island. I searched Twitter for the latest news on Chios and sent him this:

> *Today, December 7th, 500 toasted cheese sandwiches and 600 eggs with bread were shared at Tabakika registration area, DIPETHE registration area and at the port. Right now, 60 kilos of lentils (almost 600 portions) are being cooked and they will be distributed tomorrow. - From the social kitchen*

I translated some phrases into Greek, sent them to him, and told him to knock on a door before the other fifty people: *Please may we have bread and water? We are Yezidis from Iraq. Where is the new refugee center? Can you help us get there?*

Three hours later came his message, "We are registering now."

Their documents were checked. They were finger-printed, photographed, and registered, and then given a piece of paper as documentation. By the next night they were on the New Star Ferries ship to Athens, a three-hour cruise. In his pocket Nayf had the bus tickets to Macedonia on Greece's northern border.

After hundreds of refugees drowned in the Aegean Sea, in November 2015, the Greek government opened refugee centers called "hot spots" on six islands to handle the daily wave of asylum seekers arriving by small boats. The refugees were documented and registered before being allowed to continue their journey or turned back to their country of origin. Those eligible to receive international protection because they were fleeing war could stay. Those who were economic refugees were sent back.

That week Macedonia closed its borders which resulted in demonstrations and a new spontaneous refugee camp. It built razor fences at the Greek border to stop the immigrants. Only immigrants eligible for international protection were allowed to enter. A dangerous precedent was being established: borders within the E.U. If all the member countries of the European Union were to build fences at their borders and install border crossing security checks, then the concept of a united European Union with open borders would be finished.

Nayf and his wife traveled to a rural town in northern Germany before registering for asylum. They were immediately assigned a free apartment since they were a married couple. Ten months later their baby girl was born a German citizen. All medical services had been free. They were both learning German. Easy, the donor from Arizona, sent $2,000 to help them get a start in their new life.

Twenty-seven months after the attack on Shingal and one year after entering Germany they received asylum and work permits. After they save some money, they are planning to bring Nayf's parents to Germany under Germany's family reunification program. They are a success story of Germany's model fast track for immigrants becoming productive citizens.

Others were not as fortunate.

The root of the problem is not the generous German people still apologizing for their grandparents' sins, nor the immigrants. The problem is the other countries of the world that turned a blind eye not only to the suffering of the refugees, but also to that of the German people. Of all countries in the world, Germany stands far above others in taking in immigrants fleeing war.

Rather than come to the aid of Germany, the member states of the European Union signed a draconian agreement with Turkey to send $2.1 billion euro to Turkey in exchange for stopping all refugees from leaving Turkey for Europe. In the first week Turkey arrested 1300 people trying to leave Turkey on rubber dinghies headed to Greece. Turkey virtually stopped the boats from leaving its shores to get to Greece.

In the cruelest strategy for self-preservation, the E.U. further rewarded Turkey's campaign of terror against its own Kurdish citizens by promising to waive visa requirements to Europe for Turkish citizens and to renew suspended talks for Turkey to enter the European Union.

In February 2016, Turkey effectively closed its border with Iraq by requiring visa applications in Erbil for the next year. Ninety-nine percent were denied. The Yezidi IDPs were trapped in Kurdistan. By 2017, many European countries had internal border checks on trains and buses, making it hard for asylum-seekers to move between countries and make their way north. Some even erected fences.

United States politicians dithered about whether to allow asylum-seekers from Iraq to enter the US, disregarding the death and destruction the U.S. had caused in Iraq based on the 2003 lie that Iraq had "weapons of mass destruction".

In January 2017, both Canada and the US each succumbed to political pressure and announced token programs to take refugees and displaced persons from Iraq. Canada took 1200 Yezidis and Syrian Kurds. The US took ten families of Yezidi survivors in February 2017. Meanwhile 200,000 Yezidis continued living in IDP camps in Kurdistan as the war against Daesh dragged on.

On December 9, 2017, Iraq declared that Daesh had been defeated in Iraq. Germany suspended its family reunification program, began denying asylum for Ezidis in Germany, and ordering many to be sent back to Iraq saying it was now "safe to return." The future was not looking good for Yezidis.

Drowning at Sea: A Greek Tragedy
Qawal Hassan Khuder, July 14, 2016

I am Qawal Hassan Khuder, age forty-six, from Sunoni, Shingal. When Shingal was attacked by Daesh on August 3, 2014, my family fled and went to a refugee camp in Turkey. When Turkey became unsafe in December 2015, we had to flee again, because the government was attacking the Kurds with tear gas, live ammunition, and bombardments. We were depending on the Kurds to protect us and feed us, but the government was attacking them in all the towns in southeast Turkey.

We knew how dangerous it was to attempt to get to Germany by crossing the water to Greece, but we were desperate.

On December 8, 2015, we attempted to cross illegally by boat from Bodrum, Turkey, to Greece with my family of seven and my brother's family of six. We were wearing orange life vests. I paid $200 dollars for my own family's vests. I paid the smuggler $2500 per person for my family. The little children went for two for the price of one. I paid a total of $13,500 dollars from my own savings for seven people.

We left between 10 and 11 PM and traveled approximately nine kilometers Over twenty passengers were wearing life vests. The boat was an old, unseaworthy, wooden boat with two decks. After one hour, two-meter waves pounded our boat and broke it into pieces. It happened very fast. One minute we were on the boat, then next thing we were in the water with pieces of the boat pushing us under. It was a black night and I could not see my family.

I was in the water for two-and-a-half hours, so I know the life vests I bought were not fake like what caused other people to drown, but I could not find my family. Although it was early December, the water was not cold enough to cause hyperthermia, but the waves were high and crashing on us.

I and my daughter were fished out of the water and taken with twenty-one to twenty-three survivors to Fairmakosi, Greece, a military base. The boat captain was taken into custody. I and others identified him to the police. I do not know what happened to him.

The police or an NGO volunteer took a swab from my cheek and my daughter Sahar's cheek for DNA testing.

Then an NGO (I think American) took me and my twelve-year-old daughter, Sahar Qawal Hassan, to Marilyn Hotel on Leros Island and paid for our hotel and gave us food. One hour after arriving at the hotel, police found the bodies of three members of my and my brother's families.

Out of thirteen people in our families, only my daughter and I survived. Three bodies were recovered. Eight people are missing even though we were all wearing life vests. The youngest ones were only one and two years old. They drowned from the waves that pounded them and pushed them under.

The Iraqi consulate in Greece gave me a one-way visa to fly back to Iraq with the bodies of my son Mushtaq (age 16), my brother Haji Hassan Khuder (age 40), and Haji's baby son, Aham (age 1). We left for Iraq on Dec. 22, 2015. I buried the three in Sunoni, Shingal. My twelve-year-old daughter Sahar, who survived, went directly from Greece to Germany and applied for asylum.

I lost my wife, Tufaha Mirza Khalaf (age 48), and four children named Mushtaq (16), Mashaar (14), Malik (9), and Mithaq (4). I also lost my brother, Haji Hassan Khuder (39), his wife, Hadia Hussein Faris (35), and their four children named Amanda (8), Rahaf (5), Aham (3), and Anmar (1).

I later heard that some people who were in the water in the Aegean Sea were taken to Greece and Turkey and over 1,000 are locked up in Adana and Izmir prison. Amy Beam went with me to Erbil on August 4, 2016, to visit the Turkish consulate. I requested that Turkey search for my missing family members in Adana or Izmir prisons. Several months later, the consulate told me they found no information about their whereabouts, dead or alive.

After visiting the Turkish consulate, we went to the German consulate in Erbil. Dr. Beam asked them on my behalf for a visa to join my daughter in Germany. They were firm and said absolutely no visas for family reunification are being issued. Don't bother to apply. "It's a sad case," they agreed, "but we get 2,000 requests a week for visas for family reunifications. They are *all* special cases. Ask us in five years," was their reply.

An hour later, en route home from Erbil to Duhok, our taxi driver was speeding over 140 km/hour. Amy yelled at the driver to slow down or he would kill us. Five minutes later we had a terrible car accident. Amy was sitting in the front passenger's seat. Her vertebrae was crushed, and she could not walk for six weeks.

I felt so bad, because I insisted she sit in the front seat for her comfort even though I am very tall and was cramped in the back seat. I wished I had been in the front seat, not Amy. I asked God why he did not let me die. Amy came to Iraq just to help people she doesn't know, and then that accident happened to her, just as if she had been on the battlefield. The woman in the other car died in the Duhok Emergency Hospital in the bed next to Amy.

My sister and her husband were also injured in the car accident. Her husband was an interpreter for the US Army in Iraq, so they just immigrated to the United States. I am completely alone and without hope living in the camp.

While Amy was recovering for the next two months, unable to walk, sometimes I visited her and just sat next to her in her room for hours even though we cannot talk to each other because of the language barrier. Like me, she had no family to sit with her. I did not know where else to go, what else to do with myself, but just sit silently, staring at the wall without moving an inch for hours. Time moves so slowly. I listened to each second tick on the clock. I turned to stone. My life is lost. I don't know how to see my daughter again, and she is all I have to live for. The world has lost its humanity.

In 2015, 3,692 migrants drowned trying to smuggle to Greece. At least 821,000 refugees and economic migrants reached Greece's eastern islands. Nearly all continued north, hoping for a better life in European countries. Greece closed its borders along with Bulgaria. Turkish and Greek coast guard ships patrolled the Aegean waters to prevent the boats from making it to Greece. The European Union reached an agreement with Turkey in March 2016 to stop the immigrants. Turkey stopped giving visas to Iraqis. So Qawal was trapped in Iraq.

In January 2017, Qawal finally got a three-week business visa to Germany and was reunited with his only surviving daughter, Sahar, fourteen months after their family was lost in the Aegean Sea. In 2020, Qawal discovered that the bodies of his eight missing family members had been recovered the same night that the boat went down. They were buried on a Greek island in three different U.N. grave sites with numbered markers. No one had informed him.

Kidnapped Yezidi Boys Forced by Daesh To Be Suicide Bombers

In February 2017, Daesh released a propaganda video with the intent to inflict maximum pain to Yezidis. In the video are two Yezidi boys who were allegedly used as suicide bombers.

The boys denounced their parents and Yezidis as infidels. They stated they would explode themselves among the infidels. We then see an aerial view from a drone of two separate suicide truck bombs exploding. There is no way to verify if the boys were the ones actually in the suicide trucks allegedly in Mosul.

The boys are Amjad and Asad Elias Ma'ajo both born in 2002. They lived in Tal Qassab on the south side of Shingal Mountain. On August 3, 2014, everyone from Tal Qassab fled to the mountain. On the mountain, near Qine, more than 35 people from these boys' family were killed or kidnapped at 10 AM. According to Ismail Ali Silo, a cousin, the boys' father and five brothers were killed. The others were kidnapped, including Amjad and Asad Elias Ma'ajo.

Daesh followed a very systematic method of separating and categorizing the Yezidis. Men 16 and older were killed. Boys between six and fifteen were sent to jihadi school to study the Quran and extremist Islamic ideology. After months of Islamic indoctrination, they were transferred to Daesh military training camps in Syria to be brain washed and trained as boy soldiers. In reality, they did a lot of calisthenics, were given fake wooden guns for practice, and were closely guarded.

Girls and single women between ages nine and thirty-nine were sold into sex slavery. Married women were forcibly "married" to one Daesh man (sometimes more than one). They could keep their children under age 3 if they cooperated with their captor. In Daesh lingo, "married" means "raped." Children between three and eight were sold to childless Arab couples. Six-year-old Ayman Amin is a boy who was sold for $500 dollars when he was four. Ayman was rescued from his "adoptive" Arab parents in January 2017, when the Iraqi Army recaptured northeastern Mosul. Older women and handicapped were used for slave labor.

I interviewed two Yezidi boys who escaped Daesh military training after two years. One boy had been featured in an early Daesh video of military training of boys. He spoke enthusiastically for the camera. When he spent several days with me immediately after being released, he explained that he used the opportunity to speak on the propaganda video in the hope that his mother would see it and know he was alive.

The other boy told me that the top ten students in his training class in Raqqa would get the special privilege to walk around in Raqqa accompanied by a Daesh trainer. He got to go to the internet point and call his mother. On the first opportunity when his Daesh companion was called to fight, this young boy called home and made a plan for his escape. He immediately was directed to a safe house and escaped to Kurdistan after two weeks.

Both of these young men were delightful to be with. Both explained that they pretended to convert to Islam and be like the other true Muslim boys in order to survive. They never gave up the hope of escape and reunification with their families.

It is my belief that Amjad and Asad Elias Ma'ajo, the two Yezidi boys in the Daesh suicide video, never stopped loving or missing their families and never stopped knowing they were Yezidis. Because their father and five brothers had already been killed and most of the women and children kidnapped from their family, this was their escape from Daesh.

They were parroting words that were fed to them, because their speeches were standard Daesh propaganda lines used repeatedly. It is possible that this was the trade-off they faced in exchange for making a final video for their mother.

The link to the Daesh propaganda video is
https://www.facebook.com/AmyLBeam/videos/10211347125051289/

The Stolen Children Were Rescued Last

The last Yezidis to be rescued from Daesh captivity were the young children. Since many had no memory of their previous life or parents, they could not participate in their own rescue. Several hundred children between the ages of infancy and eight years old were taken from their mothers and housed in Tal Afar school until sold to adoptive parents, some of whom were unable to conceive children. Yezidi mothers were often permitted to keep their babies and toddlers to care for them and nurse them. Amina recalls being driven away with other women in buses to Raqqa and last seeing her two small boys in the Tal Afar school yard with the other children.

These stolen children were raised as Muslims. They had their names changed to Arabic names. They came back speaking either Arabic or Turkish. A few returned speaking English, learned from their foreign Daesh "adoptive" parents. Their mother language of Kurdish was forgotten.

The rescued pre-teen girls hid their faces behind black scarves. The rescue of the children was more daring and dangerous. It came at the end of three years as Daesh was defeated in Iraq. Many of the rescued children were orphans. According to the Directorate of Yezidi affairs in Duhok, Kurdistan, in 2016 there were 2745 orphaned Yezidi children who had lost one or both of their parents. When orphans returned from Daesh, some neighbor would take them into their own family. The idea of adoption outside of the Yezidi community was out of the question.

Seven-year-old Ayham Azad Alias from Tal Banat returned speaking excellent English from an American woman whom he lived with in Syria, along with her Daesh husband whom he called Abu Yousif. He had been featured in a Daesh propaganda video talking about kuffirs (non-believers) and loading bullets into a gun. When Abu Yousif was killed by an airstrike, his American wife arranged to return Ayham to the safety of Kurdistan. Ayham's younger brother, Anis, was born in Sinjar Hospital on August 3, 2014, the day Daesh attacked. He was identified by an unusual birthmark on his face. He returned from Tal Afar at age three speaking Turkish. Neither of them spoke Kurdish to communicate with their father, sister, or grandmother.

The father borrowed $25,000 from Yezidis to pay for their return. Khairi Bozani in the Yezidi Affairs Office said the government had no money to help with the rescue or to reimburse him. Their mother, Wazeera Ahmed Yousif from Tal Qassab, has not been heard from since 2014 when Daesh took her sons from her in Tal Afar. Although these boys were held separately, when it came time to sell them to their father, Daesh was able to locate each one. They returned together with the help of YPG forces in Syria.

When Mosul was liberated in a fierce, deadly, and prolonged battle in January 2017, a local Arab family told Iraqi army forces about a Yezidi boy living with Sunni Arab parents. He was quickly found by the Iraqi Army. The Arabs admitted buying him for $500 and raising him as their Muslim son for eighteen months. It was the wife's idea to adopt a child. The couple had no children, and she heard that Daesh was selling orphans in the town of Tal Afar, forty kilometers (twenty-five miles) to the west. She went alone and paid for him out of her earnings as a teacher.

Ayman Ameen Barakat had been captured at age four and spoke only Arabic when rescued and reunited with his grandmother, Basma. Basma was also abducted by Daesh, but was released with a group of elderly. Eleven relatives, including Ayman's real parents and brother, all from the Yezidi village of Hardan, are still missing.

The local Rudaw TV news channel portrayed the Arab couple as loving parents who had rescued Ayman and cared for him during the war to defeat the scourge of Daesh. The adoptive Arab mother bragged, "He was really smart. I taught him to pray and perform ablutions. Do you know how much of the Quran he memorized?"

They cried along with Ayman when he was separated from them. The Arab couple begged for visitation privileges or at least the chance to talk to him on the phone. The Yezidi family denied their request.

Should I feel sorry for that "nice Arab couple"? Far from being treated like they had rescued a child, the Arab couple should face criminal punishment for knowingly buying a stolen child and making no effort to return him to his birth parents for two years. The adoptive mother was even aware of the location of Ayman's teenage sister who had also been taken prisoner.

Little Lazim was only three when he was captured in Kocho, August 15, 2014, along with the females in his family. Lazim's grandmother, Hanifa Halo Alo, was killed the next day at Solagh Institute with eighty older women. His father, Qassim Avdo Ali, age forty-four, is one of the nineteen men who survived the mass executions in Kocho. Qassim lives in a camp near Zakho, Kurdistan. He rarely speaks. His wife, Ghalia Saado, was returned from Daesh captivity in April 2015. Lazim has three missing older brothers, Hazim, Bassem, and Salam. His aunt Alia Saado is also missing.

In June 2017, Lazim's family raised $8000 dollars to pay for Lazim's return from Tal Afar. At this time, the liberation of Tal Afar was about to begin. Daesh members were shaving their beards and looking for ways of escape with their own families. Lazim was taken from Tal Afar to Syria by the wife of a Daesh terrorist. In a daring rescue, Lazim was snatched from her in Syria and transported to Turkey. From Turkey, his handler took him to the border of Iraq on June 18, 2017.

When Lazim saw his father, he did not recognize him, nor could the two communicate. The father speaks Arabic and Kurdish, but Lazim was speaking Turkish which he learned in Tal Afar from the Sunni Turkmen who had him. An argument ensued at the border. The Turkish security smacked the father and he fell down. Lazim was yanked back to the Turkish side. The handler refused to pay a $300 dollar bribe to the Turkish border police officer and Customs officer.

Lazim's father, Qassim Avdo, was ordered to go to Sirnak Court in Turkey to get custody of his son. I got Qassim's Iraqi passport in one day. On June 19, he went to the Turkish consulate in Erbil who denied his visa to enter Turkey. Instead, the Turkish border police escorted him to the Sirnak court which ordered a DNA test to prove he was Lazim's father. He visited his son, gave a hair strand and a blood sample, then returned to Kurdistan, Iraq. He waited three months for the DNA results from Istanbul. Lazim waited in a state-operated orphanage. He must surely have felt he had been kidnapped.

In September, Lazim was reunited with his parents and older brother Bassam. He must learn to speak Kurdish. The family was approved by the UNHCR for resettlement in Australia. They continue to search for information about Lazim's missing brothers and aunt.

Nadia was only seven days old when her village of Siba Sheikh Khudir was attacked on August 3, 2014. Her father and grandmother were killed. She was taken along with her mother, Sabri Nafkhosh Ali Harba, and sisters to Mosul.

When Tal Afar was liberated from Daesh in July 2017, one family identified a Muslim widow who had children thought to be Yezidis. An older sister went with the Iraqi intelligence police to the home. Nadia was positively identified by her sister from her peculiar, dark birth mark. The widow insisted the children were her own, but when pressured, she admitted she had bought Nadia in the street for $10. The other children were also identified as Yezidi. In Islam it is permitted to buy children to raise them as servants and later use them for sex.

Three-year-old Nadia returned with a long, sad face to relatives whom she did not know. She speaks only Turkish, learned from the Turkmen people living in Tal Afar. For Nadia, it must feel like she has been kidnapped. In fact, Nadia has a long Yezidi genealogy going back six generations. Her full name is Nadia Dakhil Ramo Khudaida Bakir Hussein Kairani. Her mother is still missing.

I met eleven-year-old Layla (not her real name) three days after her rescue from Mosul. She returned speaking only Arabic. She was well-groomed and had little gold earrings dangling from her ears. The Daesh father of the Muslim family with whom she had lived for three years had been killed in an airstrike. She was rescued by the Iraqi Army. Layla was from Kocho. Her elderly grandmother had been released by Daesh on April 4, 2015, with other elderly, ill, and handicapped prisoners. Layla's little brother and sister had been rescued before Layla. They were living with the family of a very distant relative in a small concrete block room he had built. He was the only man, surrounded by one old woman and little girls.

We took Layla to my apartment, then shopping for clothes. While driving to Duhok, she chattered all the way. A survivor who has been sexually abused has an identifiable look about her. Her face is wooden. Her eyes stare. She is stone silent. Not a facial muscle moves. I knew immediately that Layla had not been abused. I asked her if she had ever visited Duhok before. With an air of superiority, she compared it to Mosul, "I prefer living in Mosul. It's bigger and better than Duhok."

In my apartment, she spilled a drink and jumped up to wipe it up. I commented to her, "I suppose you are used to being the one to do all the cleaning when you lived in Mosul."

Her answer revealed the awful truth. "Oh, I never did the cleaning. Someone else did that for us."

I understood, Layla had been illegally adopted and treated well as one of the children in the Arab family who bought her. Her transition back to her grandmother in dire conditions of poverty was going to be hard.

Nearly 3000 women and children remained missing in 2017. The children who have no memory of who they were before they were captured by Daesh, may never return. They are being raised as Muslims. Mohammed founded the religion of Islam 1400 years ago, with the stated objective to convert the world to Islam. Now, the non-Muslim population in Iraq is one percent.

How Yezidi Voices Were Silenced

There was a policy to silence the Yezidis from telling their stories about the genocide. The policy of the Kurdish camp managers in both Turkey and Iraq was to contain them in camps until "it was safe to return to Shingal." This policy was dictated at high levels, then enforced by camp security guards. Journalists were not welcomed.

My first experience was when I was called on my phone by several Yezidis I had met in Roboski school who urgently requested me to come to their camp in Fidanlik Park, south of Diyarbakir. Some people had not eaten in three days. Since they had no idea where they had been transported by bus, they told me they were in Diyarbakir. I drove to Diyarbakir and went to the Belediyesis (city hall) which is surrounded by a large park area. Most workers had gone home but I found a woman on the way out the door. I asked, "Where is the camp for the Yezidis?"

She said, "Oh, yes, they are here." She took me outside and pointed out a Muslim family having a picnic under the trees. This was so obviously a lie, I pressed her. She finally admitted about 4,000 Yezidis were in a camp south of the city. When I drove there the next morning, the security guards at the front gate would not let me get out of my car. They ordered me to leave, but I refused. "Not until I see the camp manager."

They called him, but he refused to come to meet me. I refused to get out of my car or leave. I watched a half-dozen cars, including TV stations, pull into the gate and be ordered to leave. No visitors! I called my Yezidi "inmates" on the phone and told them I was sitting in my car. Soon, about 300 Yezidis came to watch me sitting in my car. Then they all began shouting and demanding I be allowed to talk to them. All of them blocked traffic on the four-lane highway between Diyarbakir and Mardin.

The camp manager finally showed up and invited me to get out of my car. "See what you have caused," he pointed to the traffic backing up for miles.

"I did not cause that. You caused it," I countered.

"Just please get them to come out of the road so the traffic can move. You have my permission to walk through the camp and talk to whomever you want and take your photos."

Two buses had been blocked on the highway and the demonstrators told Yezidis in the buses what was happening. Within ten minutes, every Yezidi camp in southeast Turkey knew I was in the camp and began calling me.

After thirty minutes of walking through the camp, with dozens of people following behind me, I looked up to see I was surrounded by five armed soldiers. Number one and number two commanders both spoke English.

Number two growled roughly at me and said I did not have permission to be there. He ordered me to leave. I turned to the general with the stars on his shoulder and said, "I most certainly was given permission to be in this camp. Please instruct your officer to show some respect to me."

The general did exactly that, then most politely asked me if I would accompany him to the front of the camp where we could sit and talk. We were followed by about a thousand observers. When we got to the entrance, I was dumbfounded to see that about seventy-five armed soldiers were lined up shoulder to shoulder with their guns pointed directly at the Yezidis who lined up opposite them in a face-off. There were two military tanks with gun turrets and a police car. The driveway was lined with thirty cars. Apparently, every Kurdish party member had driven to the camp to see what the fuss was all about.

I turned to the commander and said, "Are you crazy! Order your men to lower their guns. These people are traumatized. They have been attacked by Daesh who murdered their family members. What in the world are you doing pointing guns at them!"

He ordered them at ease. We sat at a folding table for more than an hour while the commander called high and low all over Turkey to check out my story of who I was. When his last call was returned, he said to me, "Well, apparently you are who you say you are. You are a retired American woman who runs a tourism business in Mount Ararat. You have a Turkish residence permit and you live in Sirnak."

"Madam," he explained, "the camp manager called me and asked me to remove you from this camp. I am the commander of the Çınar jandarme post. We do not have any control over this camp, but we cannot leave until you leave. Would you mind very much leaving so my men can go home?"

It was by now dark and mosquitoes were biting. I asked for permission to speak to my Yezidi interpreters who had called me to come to the camp. Permission was denied by the Kurdish camp manager, and I left peacefully. The next day I published my story, *Yezidis Beg for United Nations Help in Diyarbakir.*

I went to the administrator for Sirnak city hall and told him there was a problem in Diyarbakir camp. I knew very well that all the camps were run and guarded by Kurds from the BDP Kurdish party. No Turkish police or jandarme were allowed inside. The Sirnak administrator was sure I was wrong about the jandarme. He could hardly believe his eyes when he saw the photo of 75 armed soldiers pointing guns at refugees. From this first experience, I understood that the Kurds did not want any publicity about the Yezidis whom they were keeping virtual prisoners in Diyarbakir until they could send them back to Shingal to claim their territory for Kurdistan.

The policy of silencing the Yezidis grew more aggressive as time passed. The first time I entered Qadia camp near Zakho, Kurdistan, Iraq, in 2015, I was directed to the manager's office. His assistant made me stand at attention like an errant school girl and read aloud the camp rules which were numbered. I had to initial each rule after reading it. To his surprise, after I finished, I told him, "These are excellent rules. I hope you enforce them properly."

The rules, in fact, stated that before any journalist could have an interview or take photographs, he had to get informed consent from the persons being interviewed, photographed, or videoed.   This is standard procedures in journalism.

The camp managers throughout Kurdistan, however, *mis*interpreted this to mean "no journalists allowed," "no cameras allowed." By 2017, the restrictions got even more onerous. I had to get a letter from the director of Bureau of Relief and Humanitarian Administration (B.R.H.A.) to enter any camp. He gave me the letter which stated I could enter the camp but could not interview survivors of Daesh captivity. Getting passports for survivors and interviewing them was my work! The B.R.H.A. director told me I had to get a letter from the court giving me permission to interview survivors.

Off I went to Judge Mustafa Mukhtar who helped all the Yezidi women in the court and asked for a letter. He said, "I will give you a letter as a favor, but why is B.R.H.A. sending you to the court for permission to interview survivors? We have no control over the camps. This letter is meaningless."

I am sure I was the only one that the Kurdistan government ordered to get a letter signed and stamped by the court in order to speak to survivors. It was just another ploy to stop my interviews and silence their voices. I carried it around with me.

In 2017, when I went to Shariya camp and met the manager, we had a nice hour-long introductory meeting. He asked me to publish his own story which I did. Hekar Tanahi had been born under a tree while planes were bombing his Kurdish village. He had lived in refugee camps in Turkey and Iran until he was twelve. His father was killed by Saddam Hussein forces when he was thirteen. He genuinely cared about the IDPs in his camp. On the day I went to interview one survivor, a security guard came to the tent to order me to stop the videoing and interviewing. I ordered him out of the tent. He returned and said I needed to have permission from the court. I asked him who said I had to leave the camp, and he said "B.R.H.A."

"Well, how in the world would the director of B.R.H.A. in Duhok know I am visiting in this tent?" He was mute. Every camp has spies in it loyal to the PDK political party. Behind the camp manager's back, the security guards make it their job to make sure no journalists get inside the camp.

To his surprise, I pulled out my court permission. He went off to show it to his superior. When he returned, he said the court permission "was not in the right format." I shouted him out of the tent. I am pretty sure the whole camp heard the incident.

"Let me explain something to you. Listen very carefully. I do *not* need an NGO, even though I have my registration. I do *not* need B.R.H.A.'s permission, even though I have their letter to enter the camp. I do *not* need the court's permission, even though I have that. And I most certainly do *not* need your permission to interview this woman. *You* cannot give permission for *her*. So unless you are running a prison camp here, the only person who can give me permission to interview her is *her*. Not even her mother or brother can give their permission. It is her story to tell if she wants to. And she does not need anyone's permission to talk to me or anyone else. *Now get out!*"

On his third visit to our tent, the guard ordered the interpreter to leave because it was his quitting time. My own interpreter had left on an emergency that morning and the camp manager had generously offered me the camp's interpreter. I told him if he would stay, I would pay him myself and pay for his taxi, but the guard threatened him with losing his job if he did not leave immediately. The interpreter hurried out taking with him the video interview on his phone camera.

I went to the security director, Haki, who knew me, and I raised hell. He told me to return the next day which I could not do. I had traveled from Erbil for this interview. I demanded that the security director call the interpreter and have him return to camp. After denying that he knew where his own employee lived, the security director miraculously figured out how to locate him. While we waited an hour for the interpreter to return from Duhok, the security director fed me dinner and we chatted. I finished the interview at 10 PM.

I told the interpreter to please ask the camp manager in the morning to go in person to apologize to the family of survivors whom I had interviewed so they would not be afraid and further traumatized. If not, my complaint would go to the Prime Minister's office. The manager, Hekar Tanahi, apologized profusely and promised they were free to talk to anyone they wanted to.

These scenes were replayed in all the camps I visited. In Berseve camp, I was requested by a sixteen-year-old orphan, Ahlam Albriea, to go visit her. She was in a tent with her aunt and uncle. Ahlam gave me a bear hug when I arrived and did not let go of my hand the whole time. She wanted to live with me. I had hardly arrived when the security guard came to her tent and ordered me to leave because it was his quitting time, around 6 PM. The family was intimidated. I drove my car down the deserted road and waited. They walked out of the camp and met me. I interviewed her in my car in the dark with the overhead car light.

Later I got her passport and referred her to the program for survivors in Germany. The next year I visited Ahlam in Germany.

In Qadia camp, the security guards routinely asked if I were a journalist. "No," was my answer. Then they asked if I had a camera. "No cameras allowed in the camp," he threatened. Most of my work with the survivors of rape was in Qadia camp. I had to interview them to collect all their names, birthdates, date of escape, and village so that I could get their passports and recommend them for UNHCR resettlement. The camp management was not the problem. It was the camp security guards at the entrance gate who blocked the journalists.

In Khanke camp I arrived on a Saturday. The camp manager was not at work on the weekend. The manager who said he was in charge was actually the manager of a little grocery store in the camp. He decided that no visitors were allowed on weekends, even though I was an invited guest of a family whose male family members had been massacred by Daesh. The teenager had begged me for months to visit him. I had to demand the grocery store manager call the camp manager at home. I spoke to him on the phone and he gave me permission to enter the camp. When we went to the tent, we were escorted by another person.

"Who are you?" I wanted to know.

"My job is to escort you to their tent."

When we got to the tent, he came in uninvited and sat cross-legged with me and the family. "What is your purpose here?" I wanted to know.

"My job is to make sure you do not use your camera or interview this family."

They spread out lunch and we ate. I asked about the *guard's* story. He was a Yezidi IDP living in the camp. He was one of four camp section guards. It was his job to know everyone's business. . . who comes and goes. For that he said he got paid $150 dollars per month. I gave him such a hard lecture about being a traitor to Yezidis who needed to tell their story to the world.

After lunch, I simply said, "Now it is time for you to go."

He left and I conducted my interview, but with only a hand-held phone camera. The family was too intimidated for me to put my big camera on a tripod in case the security guard came back. The family explained, "There are spies everywhere in the camp. We are not free to talk."

A Yezidi from Kabarto camp who worked in the office had overheard the Kurdish staff saying Daesh had not killed enough Yezidis. When the next war came, they would be sure to kill every last Yezidi. His co-workers complained to his supervisor that he should be fired because he could not be trusted.

When I visited survivors in Freiburg, Germany, I was kicked out of the house by the social worker who told me I was not allowed to interview Viyan whom I had helped back in Kurdistan when she escaped from Daesh. She had waited months for me to visit. Her kids flew into my arms when I arrived. I was the first visitor not only for her, but for the dozen other women in the house. The girls were threatened with losing their monthly stipend if they told their stories to me. Viyan and I had to go to a friend's house to video her story. When we returned, the other girls who had been eager to tell me their stories were afraid to speak to me.

In 2017, when I tried repeatedly to get permission to visit Shingal, my permission was denied by Kurdistan's Asayish (security police). I was secretly told it was because I was a "Yezidi nationalist." I was prevented from going to talk to the Yezidis living in tents on the mountain or those who had returned to their villages under Hashd al-Sha'abi control. I would not be allowed to be their mouthpiece even though my NGO was registered to do media work. Rudaw TV could go, but Amy Beam could not.

It was imperative that Yezidis be silenced prior to the Kurdistan referendum for independence. The fact that so many people told me their stories for this book is a measure of their courage.

This paternalistic attitude that Kurds took toward Yezidis was soon to backfire on them after the Kurdistan referendum for independence. The hostility of Yezidis for being exposed to the genocide in 2014 and then being silenced about it was an open secret.

When the Iraqi army pushed Peshmerga out of Kirkuk and Shingal, in October 2017, many Yezidis cheered silently. They were still living in IDP camps in Kurdistan. They were still reliant on the government for fuel, food, electricity, and water. Their silence continued as their anger and depression deepened.

In March 2018 on a visit to the State Department in Washington D.C., a producer from Voice of America (VOA) invited me to join a TV show to discuss religious freedom. He had two other guests: a Muslim working at American University in D.C. and a Chinese-Christian. He wanted me to discuss Yezidis and religion. After thirty minutes of chatting on the phone, the invitation was withdrawn. What I had to say about Daesh killing Yezidis because they are non-Muslim did not fit their agenda.

Humanitarians and the Starfish Parable

A man was walking down the beach one morning after a storm. Thousands of starfish were stranded on the sand. He came to a boy who picked one up and threw it back into the sea. The man asked the boy, "Why are you throwing starfish into the sea?" The boy answered, "If I don't throw them in the water, they'll die." The man said, "There are thousands of starfish on the beach. You can't possibly make a difference." The boy picked up another starfish. As he threw it back into the water, he said, "It made a difference for that one."

- adapted from The Star Thrower by Loren Eiseley

The distribution of 13 stove burners for mothers to warm their baby's milk left me trembling inside. I was swarmed by men and women in Sirnak refugee camp holding up their children, begging for a burner so they could cook. I learned then that distribution of aid is never fair, because there is never enough to serve everyone. Rather than feeling satisfied, I was shaken to my core. Barbara Shabo, from California, emailed me and asked if she could send me $100 to spend on the Yezidis. She had read my story about buying burners from my own pocket. Each cost $4.75.

Barbara and her husband, Alan, were children of Jewish Holocaust survivors from World War II. They felt a necessity to do something to help the Yezidis. I bought forty more burners for the camp.

Because of Barbara's initiative, I began accepting donations via PayPal, then getting the money to Iraq by debit card withdrawals. That was not easy, because the ATM bank machine in Duhok was removed. I had to take a three-hour taxi ride to Erbil to find an ATM machine. These were the challenges with which we worked to get donations to Iraq.

When twenty-six-year-old American Kayla Mueller was reported killed in Syria on February 6, 2015, it sent a shock-wave through her hometown of Prescott, Arizona. Kayla, a volunteer aid worker, was kidnapped in Syria by Islamic State gangs in 2012 and later held hostage by the self-proclaimed leader, Abu Bakir al-Baghdadi. Her death was verified when Daesh sent photos of her dead body to her parents.

In a visit home, Kayla had told the Prescott Kiwanis Club, "When Syrians hear I'm an American, they ask, 'Where is the world?' All I can do is cry with them, because I don't know." Her selfless humanitarian example and her death left those in Prescott deeply troubled and searching for ways to heal and help.

One retired man, who goes by the nickname of "Easy," was moved by Kayla's death. Easy had no family and was in declining health. His monthly income from a life of hard work and smart investing was more than he needed to live on. At 78, he was simplifying. There wasn't anything that Easy really needed, so he gave his money away each month. He helped immigrant families. He sent some kids to college. He gave away a commercial building to a charity that trains seeing eye dogs for the blind. Each month he mailed out checks based on reading the news.

When he read my stories published in KurdistanTribune.com about the plight of the Yezidis, he emailed me and said he wanted to donate $5000 to Yezidis who had been attacked by Daesh.

When I left Sirnak, Turkey, the camp manager's parting words were "We need your help to raise money to feed the 1500 people in this camp." This scared me. I was only one person.

I asked an accountant friend in Sirnak to ask the mayor for a bank account number for Easy to transfer the $5000 for food for the refugee camp. To my surprise, the mayor's answer came back "We don't want money from Amy. She might be a secret agent." An agent? For whom? I was flabbergasted.

The Sirnak Foreign Police did not want me living there. "No foreigners live here. Go live in Izmir or Istanbul," they had said. They wanted no foreign eyes to witness Turkey's assault on the Kurds. About four nights per week the police were forcing restaurants and shops to close early by tear-gassing the city center of Sirnak. I was tweeting the photos to the world from my balcony.

The day I returned from visiting my Kurdish friends in the mountain village of Beytussebap, the police entered into the immigration database that I had visited Beytussebap. They were following my every move. The police also entered a secret visa entry ban on me for overstaying my residence permit. This was a lie. I had six weeks remaining.

After being banned from Turkey for supporting Kurds, the Kurds in Sirnak betrayed me. It was a bitter disappointment to be blacklisted by Kurds running the refugee camp in Sirnak. It was a devious but brilliant tactic by the Turkish police to undermine my work there by planting a lie with the Kurdish camp managers and mayor's office suggesting I was a spy working against the Kurds. Or was it the news story that Turkey's M.I.T. secret police said I had met with people who may be associated with people who may be terrorists? Associating with a terrorist organization (PKK) is Turkey's boiler plate accusation for journalists and Kurds.

It was not until one year later that my accountant "friend" in Sirnak told me, "I am so sorry, Amy. We got some wrong information about you and believed it." By then both co-mayors had been removed from office and arrested by Ankara, and 75% of Sirnak, including my apartment building, was demolished by Turkish military bombardments in 2016.

In 2015, I moved to Duhok, Kurdistan, Iraq, where the Kurdish police welcomed me. Easy agreed to send his $5000 donation by Western Union to Duhok, Iraq. Western Union refused to send it from the U.S., stating their policy was not to send money to Iraq unless it was to a family member, because they risked sending money to terrorists.

It took Easy and me two weeks of elevating the problem to senior supervisors before Easy was allowed to send a maximum of $2999 dollars to Iraq. This Western Union policy never changed in the next four years. The US had a banking embargo on Iraq that prevented individuals from sending money to the refugees and IDPs. Even those who wanted to send cash to help IDPs could not. Western Union said they were protecting Americans from being scammed. The suffering Yezidis asked, "Where is humanity?"

We distributed Easy's $2999 dollars to thirty-four Yezidi women and girls who had recently returned from Daesh captivity. Nadia Murad, who later received the Nobel Peace Prize in 2018, was number three on the list. We sent photos to Easy of each girl or woman signing a receipt for the cash. Easy continued to donate $20,000 over the next three years. A handful of others donated, also, between $1000 and $3000 at a time. Most donated $50. A core group of 200 people continued to send repeat donations. I thought of them as my finance team.

Each person had his or her own motivation. Most of them were Jewish or evangelical Christians. For myself, I was not defending a religion. I was defending people who had been victimized and needed help. It was one year before I asked a Yezidi friend to explain his religion.

I asked two close, wealthy friends for donations. One was a wealthy philanthropist who donated to women's health issues. To my shock, they both declined to help with even $100. Their reason was that the problem of displaced persons, Yezidis in particular, was so big that no amount of money would make a difference for the future of the Middle East. They wanted their money to save the world. Maybe they wanted a plaque with their name on it.

The people who did donate or volunteer believed in the starfish philosophy. They were not hoping to save the world nor change the course of events in the Middle East. They were interested in helping individuals, one by one. This is what distinguished those volunteers who stopped their lives to help Yezidis. They believed helping one person did constitute making a difference.

Volunteers contacted me and asked how they could help. "Tell me what to do," they wrote. Very few volunteers stayed the course. I am not sure what they expected to do, but something filled with adrenalin. Most of the work is tedious and requires persistence.

There is a profile of the volunteer activists. Many were retired women, like myself, or disabled American vets who had fought in Iraq and loved Iraqi people. Most of us had a meager source of income, like my social security, or a vet's disability check. We were able to devote ourselves to the cause of saving the

Yezidis, because we could pay our bills to sustain ourselves. We were not many, maybe fewer than 100 non-Yezidi volunteer activists.

Among these activists, many sacrificed their own families when spouse or grown children demanded they choose between them or their work for Yezidis. Family members were shocked when activists chose their commitment to saving Yezidis. I know of marriages that broke up and children who disowned their parents.

Beverly Hinch Luttrell helped dozens of interpreters who had risked their lives on the front lines for Americans in Iraq between 2003 and 2011. They were promised citizenship in the US. She helped with their IOM applications when the US failed to keep its promise. She gave them hope over the phone when they despaired. They called her Mom.

Beverly explained, "My family had an intervention meeting with me, telling me I either had to choose them or the Yezidis, as I was spending too much time on the computer and ignoring them. I refused to choose, because my Iraqi friends needed help, whereas all my children were parents themselves and did not require my attention. They accused me of helping people I did not even know. To my dismay, that is the reaction I got from almost any American I told about the Yezidis."

Beverly chose to continue her volunteer work. Such was the passion with which activists fought to save Yezidis in crisis.

I, too, gave up most of my friends. August 3, 2014, was a demarcation line in my life: my life before and my life after Daesh attacked Shingal. When talking with friends from "before," they shut me down with "Amy, we don't want to hear about Iraq." For me, I lived and breathed it. I could talk of nothing else. It devoured me. I became more of a loner at my computer. My only friends were Yezidis in their tents who could understand me. It was as if the genocide had happened to me, too. Old friends urged me to leave Iraq, take a vacation, and stop thinking about the crisis. They meant well, but I loved my work in Iraq.

An amazing thing happened. Social media on the internet empowered Yezidis and activists worldwide. Through FaceBook, a network of tens of thousands grew, formed bonds and helped each other to help Yezidis. One by one, activists made the pilgrimage to Iraq, without sponsorship, or to the parliaments and congresses of the world to lobby for help.

I wake up to messages of love and gratitude every day. When Yezidis learned that I have no family, except one niece, they were absolutely stricken. The idea of being alone in this world without family is inconceivable to them. More than gold or possessions, family is the most valuable thing in life for Yezidis, and that is why they continued to be devastated by family separation. Yezidi families took me into their own families in Iraq, Germany, and America.

This love from people whose lives were destroyed was the wind beneath my wings to keep me going.

There was never one single day in three years that I did not swear to quit out of frustration, failure, weariness, and poverty. But every day someone would beg me for help, or I would have a small success with one individual or family. I did not choose this path. It chose me, and I could not look away from the suffering, not since the day Sara fainted in my arms. Her husband and two children were taken by Daesh. "What should I do?" she asked me, before fainting. I did not have an answer. "I'm sorry," sounded so inadequate.

I began to tell survivors, "I am sorry for what happened to you and your family. I know nothing will fix it and you will never forget. What I can do is to help you along your path by getting you your passport. It won't cost you anything."

With donations we got IDs and passports for more than 700 Yezidi survivors and interpreters. Many were resettled in Germany. At least a dozen interpreters' families made it to Lincoln, Nebraska, USA. I helped to get Basima Darweesh out of prison. I registered AAJ charity in Kurdistan in 2016. We gave away refurbished computers, clothes, shoes, beds, pillows, blankets, eye glasses, bicycles, food and more food, heating fuel, cash, school supplies, pampers, walkers for handicapped, pots and dishes, computer video projectors to show movies, mobile phones, internet credit, and transportation expenses.

We referred hundreds of people to other resources including legal services. We made medical referrals for free doctors' visits, and got life-saving surgeries for a cancer patient, a kidney patient, and a baby who needed dialysis.

When we gave cash in the hand to a survivor, she would ask, "When do I have to tell you my story?" Other journalists were paying for stories.

"My dear," I would reply, "You do not ever have to tell me your story. This money is a gift because you need it. But if you think it will help you to tell me your story, I will listen." Yes, they wanted the world to know. I video-taped many stories of capture and captivity. I helped dozens of journalists and film-makers find survivors to interview. I visited and documented mass grave sites.

We helped with donations to family members getting back their loved ones from captivity and to others who went to Germany. Helping Yezidis will be my most important life work. I surrendered to it. I did not take salary from the donations. I lived off my social security and the help of many people, such as restaurants in Sirnak and Duhok who did not charge me for my meals.

I met with government employees and elected parliament members in six countries to lobby for asylum and in-country rebuilding funds. I did all these activities and travel without taking permission.

Most people believe that someone else is responding to a disaster, some government or big charity like the International Committee for the Red Cross

(ICRC) or the United Nations High Commission on Refugees (UNHCR) or the European Union. It is hard to fathom that change begins with one person, not an institution. There are not enough institutions in the world to address the needs of 58 million refugees and displaced persons worldwide. Helping must become a global ethic. Every individual must take action without waiting to be assigned a task and without financial incentive. The disaster of mass displacement and migration might not have reached your country yet, but it will be there soon. It is every human being's responsibility to respond. Building walls, blocking borders, and blinding oneself to suffering is not a solution.

My message to those who feel moved to do humanitarian aid work is that you do not need permission. You do not need to apply for a job, volunteer with an organization, or be granted permission from a government. Just buy your plane ticket and go to Iraq. Everyone needs everything, regardless of their religion or ethnicity.

Every government will act like you must get its permission. Whenever a government official or camp security guard demanded to see my government letter of permission or a work contract, I wagged my finger, said, "Shame on you for thinking I need a job, a badge, and a paycheck to help girls who have been raped." It always ended by getting their support and friendship.

You do not need to leave your house to volunteer, because most of the work is done at the computer and on the internet phone. Guidelines for being an activist:

- You do not need permission. . . .not from your family, not from a government, not from an employer. You do not need someone to select your application. You need the will to act.

- You do not need to know the end result to get started. Just take the first small step.

- Do not take "no" for an answer. "No" comes disguised in many forms such as sending you to someone else for another signature or application form. They never ever say "no".

- Do not give up. You will be frustrated with bureaucracy. You will lose often, but sometimes you will win.

- Call or leave messages every day. Busy people do not have time to read messages and return calls, so keep sending them daily. State your request for action in your message.

- Direct your requests to the person who has authority to grant them. Start at the top.

- Build a contact list. Always save names, email addresses, phone numbers, and a note.

- Do not be deterred by rules. Yezidi cases require extraordinary remedies and exceptions to the rules. Lobby the decision-makers to change the rules.

- Ask for help. I always begin by saying, "I need your help," especially when I want to have a rule waived and when I have no money to pay for a service.

- Before asking an official for help, ask about his own background and family and offer empathy. It is hard to find anyone in Iraq who has not been displaced or lost family.

- Become a friend and advocate to one Yezidi family. Listen to their story and suffering. Be a sympathetic ear and a shoulder to cry on. Guide them along their path to recovery.

- Use FaceBook to contact your first Yezidi friend and join Yezidi activist groups.

- Be gentle when someone contacts you. You do not know if they were captive with Daesh or have missing or murdered family members. Everyone lost their homes and livelihood.

- Use software to communicate. FaceBook, Skype, WhatsApp, and Viber are favorites.

- Use a translation program to overcome the language barrier. Use simple words. Write short sentences. Yezidis speak Arabic and Kurdish. They read and write only Arabic.

In 2018, there were 196,000 Yezidis facing their fourth winter in tents in camps in Iraq and approximately another 150,000 living outside of camps. Each family needs its own friend and advocate. They need food, research, information, referrals, applications, health care, transportation, communication, and, of course, a source of income. It is hard for them to research online using a phone in a tent. Do it for them. This help can be given online from the comfort of one's home. Reach out.

Bribery and Bureaucracy To Document Survivors

I began in June 2015 taking survivors and their families to get their Iraqi IDs and passports. The wait in Duhok for applying for a passport was six months which increased to one-and-a-half years in 2017 and three years by 2018. One in three people out of 5.2 million people living in Kurdistan was either internally displaced or a Syrian refugee. They all wanted out of Iraq.

The burden of sheltering, feeding, and documenting nearly two million people created a bureaucratic nightmare. Compound this with the fact that the Kurdistan government workers were getting paid only once every three months because Baghdad was withholding monthly payments to Kurdistan. Government offices were open from 9:30 AM until 2 PM.

Nawzad Majid Suleiman, Director of the Duhok passport office, was sympathetic to peoples' losses and suffering regardless of whether they were Sunni, Shia, Kurd, Yezidi, or Christian. He never asked about religion or ethnicity. He never talked politics. If there were a hundred other humanitarians like Nawzad managing the government offices, Iraq and Kurdistan governments might function efficiently without the corruption of bribes. Unfortunately, Baghdad government removed Nawzad from office, along with many other directors, as punishment for Kurds daring to hold the Kurdistan referendum for independence.

In three years, I and my AAJ staff got about 700 passports for Yezidi survivors who escaped captivity and their families, families with missing or murdered family members, and interpreters who worked for the US Army between 2003-2011. The waiting period was waived for these categories. In Sulaymaniyah, the passport office, run by assistant director Major Awder Aziz, put on three shifts of workers and issued 10,000 passports monthly.

The difficulty with getting a passport was in getting the Iraqi nationality card known as a jensia. The process of getting identity papers in Iraq is possibly the most complex and thorough in the world. Without a jensia, people from Shingal . . . that is, mostly Yezidis . . . could not get a passport, and were, therefore, trapped in Iraq as stateless persons.

The first time I took a survivor to the Shekhan jensia office in 2015, the officer refused to give her a jensia until her husband left his job and took a two-hour taxi ride from Erbil to show his face and be fingerprinted, even though she had a copy of his jensia. Without her husband's presence, she was not going to get her jensia ID. It cost him $100 in lost income and taxi fare. He earned $300 a month.

A survivor had to go to six offices at least two times. With no public bus service, transportation costs could be several hundred dollars. First she had to go to the Genocide office to file a police report and get a document proving she had returned from Daesh captivity. Then she had to go to court. Then she had to get a hawea with the presence of her husband, and then the jensia before applying for a passport. Before getting those, she had to have her father's green card which proved what province he was born in. If she did not have it, jensia staff told her to go to Baghdad . . . a financial impossibility, not to mention a danger. Suicide bombers are a regular occurrence.

Women have to "belong" to a male, primarily her father, and his name must be on her hawea and jensia IDs. Her husband's name must also be on her hawea. Her children will belong to her husband. She has no legal authority over them. Getting each document, including a passport, requires a male relative to show his identity and verify the female's relationship to him. He could be the husband, father, brother, uncle or grandfather.

Many women returned from Daesh with no living male relative. Her husband, father, and brothers had been killed by Daesh. When they literally ran from their houses on August 3, 2014, many people left their IDs behind. If the woman could not produce the jensia of her missing husband or father, she, herself, could not get her hawea or jensia. She had to go to court to get a document called a *haja al kaimoma* stating her husband or father was missing and making her the legal guardian of her own children. Judge Mustafa Mukhtar never turned away a Yezidi woman. Even with this court document, the jensia office often refused to issue her a jensia.

In Iraq, ID cards indicate one's religion, inherited at birth, and one's clan name. Iraqi law states one may not change one's religion from Muslim, but non-Muslims may convert to Islam. In 2017, a new plastic biometric ID card was introduced which replaced the hawea ID card and the national identity card called a jensia. This new ID card can be obtained in one day in Duhok. It eliminated religion on the card. This was a major breakthrough for Iraq to move away from religious sectarianism. However, Iraq's Personal Status Law, based on Shariah law, still made it illegal for a Muslim to marry a non-muslim.

The old IDs had to include the names of the father, mother, and a man's wife as well as the clan or tribe name such as Mandkany tribe. At marriage, a woman does not change her name. She keeps her father's name. All her children take their father's name. So if a person is named Thamir Khalaf Qassim Khudaida, that means his father was Khalaf Qassim Khudaida and his grandfather was Qassim Khudaida. Another way to say this is that Thamir is the son, Khalaf is his father, Qassim is his grandfather, and Khudaida is his great-grandfather. So paternal lineage can be easily traced for generations simply by reading a person's name. A child's relationship to his mother cannot be identified by her name because a child does not carry the mother's name.

The new biometric ID card eliminated the name of a man's wife on his ID. Displaced Shingal residents (i.e., Yezidis) were not eligible to get the new biometric cards. They had to go to a special jensia office for IDPs.

Many forms of bureaucracy were used to block Yezidis from leaving Iraq. Even Yezidi leaders lobbied foreign governments to refuse asylum and lied by saying all Yezidis want to return to Shingal. The Iraqi constitution guarantees one seat in parliament for every 100,000 people of each ethnic group. This would ensure three seats for Yezidis, although in 2018 Yezidis were awarded only two seats. Yezidis did not want to lose their seats in Baghdad's parliament due to migration.

On another visit to the jensia office, I took eleven young women and teenagers and two babies. The man checking files and doing fingerprinting kept them sitting against the wall on a dirty concrete floor for two hours in 45 C (113 F) heat while men pressed up to his table with their files. We were the only women brave enough to apply amidst a sea of pushing men with no crowd control or lines. I kept going to the director's office to complain. The director, General Hussein Muhammed, ordered his worker three times to process our applications. Finally, I erupted loud enough to jar the earth out of its orbit.

I elbowed my way to the front of the table and forcibly pushed the men back. "Stand back!" I ordered in English. "These women have escaped from Daesh. They are from Kocho. Their husbands and fathers were killed in Kocho! How dare you men let them sit on the floor! Shame on you," I yelled. To the worker, I demanded, "You WILL fingerprint these women from Kocho now!"

The men were so astonished by my volcanic outburst that the room fell silent. The men stood back against the wall. They may not have understood my ranting, but they did understand one word. I could hear them murmuring "Kocho," "Kocho". The Kocho women smiled and clapped for me. My yelling brought security officers racing into our room. The worker, I, and security officers marched into the director's office. He slammed and locked the door. In a head-to-head confrontation, the director stabbed his finger at his worker and ordered, "You WILL process the applications of the Yezidi women."

We filed back to the room. The women got in line while the men stood back. It took him thirty-five minutes to examine the files and fingerprint eleven women. When he finished, I asked to take a photo with him smiling and shaking hands with me. He refused, but I insisted. I posted our smiling photo online with a big thank you to the jensia office. After that day, the women and kids were allowed to come into an inner office for processing. A year later this worker apologized to me. "I was not feeling well and the other workers had not shown up to work. I was wrong. I am sorry." Such were the battles I never stopped fighting on behalf of the Yezidis to get their documents.

The difficulty to get jensias, especially for women and children, contributed to a system of bribery. The government fee for a jensia is $4 dollars. The bribery price to get a jensia was $200 dollars in 2017. As long as staff in the jensia office, working secretly with people in the IDP camps, could earn money illegally, they had no incentive to give out the jensia application forms for free as required by law. The staff willfully withheld the forms.

In 2015, the price was 50,000 dinar ($40 USD) for one form. I, myself, was told by a senior assistant to General Hussein Muhammed, in the Shekhan office in 2015, that he would give me for free all the jensia application forms I wanted, if I would get him and his family visas for Germany. Of course, I could not get him visas, even if I wanted to.

I sat inside the office and watched in Shekhan in 2015 as the major in charge of making the jensias took them out of his inside jacket pocket and handed stacks of them to different business men in suits who came into the office with briefcases, delivered files, then took the jensias and left in ten minutes. At the end of the work day, this manager would take a half dozen yellow files, roll them up and take them home.

In 2016, it became nearly impossible to get any jensias from Shekhan unless one paid a bribe, which we refused to do. Yezidis inside Qadia camp were asking $200 dollars per person and easily getting jensias from Shekhan. The applicants never left camp and were never fingerprinted.

After the liberation of Mosul from Daesh in January 2017, the jensia office was moved from Shekhan to a parking lot in Duhok. By August 2017, the price for the jensia application forms had fallen to 15,000 dinar or about $12 dollars. The form is supposed to be free. They were illegally sold by the men making files in the parking lot.

In Duhok in 2017, staff worked from inside several connected caravans with three small windows to serve people standing on the outside. Applicants pushed in a shoulder-to-shoulder mob to get up to a window. There were between 300 and 500 people per day. There were no security guards for crowd control, no lines, and no shade from the sun. This was an impossible situation for a woman and children, so mostly only men got their jensias without paying a bribe. Between 100 and 300 application forms were distributed on Sundays only, but many weeks there were no forms and many weeks the office was closed.

Many Yezidis went repeatedly to the Mosul satellite office in Duhok in 2017 and were told there were no forms. "Come back next week." One man had returned ten times to the Duhok parking lot office for one form for his wife, but was unable to get a form. Without her jensia, she could not get her passport. That man was eligible to immigrate to the US as a former interpreter, but was prevented because of this problem. Thousands of Yezidis were losing their future because of this.

After the Kurdistan referendum, September 25, 2017, the Mosul jensia satellite office in Duhok was moved to Mosul, making it virtually impossible to get a jensia without paying a bribe. Only drivers with red badges issued by Asayish police were allowed to pass the security checkpoint at Shekhan to go to Mosul. Therefore, the drivers were the persons taking bribes and working with the jensia staff in Mosul.

Numerous families, mostly women and children, in Qadia camp stated in 2017 that they paid approximately $200 dollars per jensia to Yezidis living inside the camp who came to their caravan. They were never fingerprinted. They never left their caravan. The jensias were delivered to them in one or two weeks.

This system thrived because many people were prevented at checkpoints from going in person to Mosul. I, myself, as the director of a humanitarian organization registered in KRG, tried unsuccessfully for six months to go to meet with the director of the Mosul jensia office. Even with signed and sealed permission from the Governor of Mosul to meet with the jensia director, the Kurdistan Asayish blocked me from leaving Kurdistan to enter Mosul.

It was dangerous and costly for Yezidis to go to Mosul. Drivers charged anywhere between $150 and $200 dollars for a one-hour trip. So most of the jensias were obtained illegally through payment of bribes without fingerprints and without seeing the applicants in person, contrary to legal requirements.

Many Yezidis were accepted to immigrate with UNHCR or IOM, but could not. This had an especially deleterious impact on survivors who were sexually abused by Daesh. Although the UNHCR policy stated that IDPs did not need passports to be resettled, the reality was that, after the Kurdistan referendum, Baghdad airport officials would not let anyone leave the country without a passport.

Baghdad closed both of Kurdistan's airports to international flights, forcing people to fly to Baghdad in order to leave Iraq. Baghdad did not recognize Kurdistan's residency permits. They fined everyone not working for a humanitarian charity $450 dollars for overstaying their 30-day Iraqi entry visa and stamped their passports so they were banned from returning to Iraq. The policy was intended to drive out all foreign friends of Kurdistan.

In 2017, I appealed for help to obtain jensias to Kurdistan Minister of Foreign Relations, Falah Mustafa, to a senior advisor to PM Nechirvan Barzani's office, to Mosul Governor Nofol and others. I also explained the problem to the US State Department in Washington, D.C. and to UNHCR.

By mid-2018, Baghdad greatly reduced the number of new, blank passports it was sending to the Duhok and Mosul passport offices. A regulation was implemented that provided for getting an expedited passport within 48 hours for the government fee of 250,000 dinar ($210 USD). This fee was intended for emergency cases. The normal fee was 25,000 dinar ($20 USD).

However, with Baghdad sending as few as 1,000 passports per week to each office, the only way to get a passport was to pay the extra fee. Upon Baghdad's orders, not only did everyone who wanted a passport have to pay the extra fee, but many waited one month to get it. Illegal bribery was replaced by bureaucratic corruption built into the system, ensuring that only those with money would get passports and be able to leave Iraq.

By 2018, Yezidis were trapped inside Iraq, unable to obtain their jensias or passports. Baghdad ordered the Sulaymaniyah passport office to stop issuing passports to Shingal IDPs.

The borders to Europe were closed to smugglers. There were no open asylum programs for Yezidis as a class of persecuted people. Only Australia agreed to take survivors and their families. By 2019, Australia had resettled 2700 Ezidis. France accepted 100 survivors. In 2018, all European countries began denying asylum and returning Yezidis to Kurdistan, Iraq.

There were no international protection or rebuilding funds for Yezidis to return to their homes in Shingal. No government officials from Kurdistan, Baghdad, or the United States visited Shingal to see the situation. Many Yezidi youth said they were only existing, waiting for their own death. After five winters, they had lost hope of any country, including their own, helping them get out of their tent, much less out of Iraq.

Monthly suicides increased.

How America Abandoned Its Iraqi Interpreters

In 2003, the United States invaded Iraq to topple the dictator, Saddam Hussein. They thought it would be a quick victory. In December 2011, the US finally left Iraq . . . in ruins and sectarian warfare. During those years of occupation, tens of thousands of Iraqi citizens risked their lives working as interpreters for the US military on the frontlines, and guiding American soldiers and commanders through Iraqi politics, tribal disputes and social customs. The US government never accounted for how many Iraqi interpreters were hired, killed, or injured in spite of being ordered by Congress to produce the numbers.

Many were Yezidis, a small non-Muslim people living mostly in Shingal, northern Iraq. Approximately 400 interpreters died in action in Iraq, and more than 1200 were wounded. After British forces pulled out of Basra, the southern Iraqi port city, interpreters were rounded up and slaughtered en masse. After the US left in 2011, many others were targeted and killed for working with the US. In 2007, the US Congress created the Special Immigrant Visa (SIV) program and the P2 program to allow interpreters from Iraq and Afghanistan whose lives were at risk to immigrate to the US with their families and become lawful permanent residents (LPRs) upon entry.

The SIV program was for interpreters and translators who had worked at least one year for the US Armed Forces between 2003-2011. Beginning in 2008, Congress expanded the SIV program to accept 25,000 interpreters and their families over five years. Yet for fiscal years 2008 through 2012, only 1,645 applicants and their dependents were resettled in the US. That amounted to just over 6% of the allocated number of 25,000. The process was so bureaucratic and difficult that it was virtually impossible for any interpreter to complete his documentation process with IOM without English-speaking legal assistance.

Applicant processing for the SIV program came nearly to a halt in 2010. In the next six years only 36 Iraqi interpreters were admitted to the US. The ratio of dependents to applicants was approximately one-to-one, meaning the interpreter brought his wife, but not other family members. Since Iraqi families are typically large, this meant painful family separation from their loved ones.

A State Department email leaked by Wikileaks advised that interpreters should not be brought to the US because there might not be enough remaining in Iraq and Afghanistan when the US decided to return.

U.S. State Department memos leaked by Wikileaks confirmed the delay in processing interpreters' applications. On July 12, 2011, Eric P. Schwartz, Assistant Secretary of State for the Bureau of Population, Refugees and Migration (BPR) sent an email to Secretary of State, Hillary Clinton, in which he stated:

The NY Times will publish a story tomorrow that describes delays in US refugee and SIV resettlement processing from inside Iraq, and correctly notes that individuals have thus been subjected to substantially increased risks of persecution as they've awaited USG (United States Government) permission to depart. . . . The delays are real, and result from new DHS security screening procedures that involve the intelligence communities. . . . the additional procedures have indeed slowed the process, causing delays of many months or longer. Second, the cases of a higher number of Iraqis are being put on 'hold' due to security information that raises questions about the applicant's suitability, and the intelligence community has not devoted the resources that would be necessary to quickly resolve, one way or the other, the status of these holds.

In spite of Eric Swartz's statement of delays of months and that not enough resources had been devoted to the security screening, the Department of Homeland Security indicated in response to a question following the October 2011 Senate Judiciary Committee hearing that it did not need additional resources to expedite SIV petition processing.

At a December 2012 House Homeland Security Committee hearing, DHS testified that it takes between three and ten days, on average, to process an Iraqi or Afghan SIV petition.

The statement of three to ten days to process an SIV application can only be viewed as a blatant distortion of the facts to Congressional inquiries. Many SIV applicants waited between one and eight years for IOM to process their applications before being scheduled for the Department of Homeland Security (DHS) interview.

Many others who completed their interview with DHS and completed their medical exams were never called to fly to the US before their medical certificates expired six months later.   When and if they were finally called, they had to repeat their medical exams.

Those who applied in Ankara, Turkey, in 2014 and 2015, then later returned back to Iraq when the refugee camps for Ezidis in Turkey were closed, had to return to Ankara to complete their interviews and medicals. However, in 2016, Turkey stopped issuing visas to Iraqi citizens.

The Turkish Consulate in Erbil made a special exception to issue visas to six Yezidi families to return to Ankara for their interviews and medicals. In addition to the requirement to return to Ankara from Iraq, when the families were finally told their visas were approved, they were required to send their passports to the US Embassy Ankara using the Turkish post office and, also, to receive them back by the Turkish post office.

Each passport holder had to appear in person at the post office in Turkey both to send his or her passport and to receive it back with the US visa stamp. This was an impossibility, because they could not obtain visas to Turkey.

It took the US Embassy in Ankara one year to transfer their cases to Baghdad for interviews. Traveling ten hours by car from Kurdistan to Baghdad for two interviews with IOM and DHS cost a family $500 US dollars for each trip, including driver, hotel, and food. Few families had this money, so many had to cancel their interviews.

If the interpreter asked for his interview to be transferred from Baghdad to Erbil, he was not told that it would never be scheduled. The Embassy could not transfer the DHS interview process to Erbil, Kurdistan (three hours from the IDP camps), because all Embassy staff are required to live and sleep inside the Embassy or Consulate compound. The US Consulate in Erbil did not have enough beds for the DHS staff, thus DHS interviews could not be conducted in Erbil.

The SIV program ended to new applicants September 30, 2014. The number of visas after that date was limited by Congress to 2,500 at a rate of only fifty interpreters per year. In 2015, only 190 interpreters and dependents from Iraq and Afghanistan were resettled in the US. By 2018, some applicants were still waiting to be processed.

The P2 program was also created by the US Congress in 2007. It has no expiration date. It applies to anyone who worked at least one day for the US government or a US company in Iraq between 2003-2013. Tens of thousands of applicants have been waiting years to be processed.

From FY2008 through FY2015, 37,777 Iraqi and Afghan nationals had been issued SIV (3,126) or P2 (34,651) visas to the United States. Principal applicants accounted for just under 15,000 of the total; the others were dependent spouses and children. This ratio indicates tremendous suffering caused by family separation. Many eligible family members have been waiting more than ten years in Iraq to join their immediate family members in the US. This means many parents in Iraq may never again see their sons, daughters, or grandchildren. In 2017, President Trump referred to the immigration policy which allows family reunification as "chain migration" and vowed to end it.

Priority is given to (1) medical emergencies, (2) persons with protection concerns, and (3) Yezidis. Priority is also given for (4) humanitarian exceptions for including ineligible family members who cannot be left behind, such as an elderly widowed mother-in-law or a young single woman over age eighteen.

A widow in Baghdad whose husband was killed in battle was waiting ten years to join her three sons who had worked as interpreters. All three received credible threats to their lives. Early in the SIV program, they were resettled in the US. In spite of the priority given to "humanitarian exceptions," their elderly mother could not join them and see her grandchildren. They are not safe to return to Iraq for a visit with their mother.

The International Office for Migration's (IOM) role is to collect the required documents and conduct the first interview with the family members. When their documents are all collected, the case is referred to the US Department of Homeland Security, Citizen Information Services (CIS). A team comes to Baghdad several times a year to interview applicants. Those who are approved are then handled by IOM again which provides air transportation to the US. IOM does not make selection decisions.

By 2016, interpreters could not get the required letters of employment verification from their US employer, Global Linguistics Systems (GLS). GLS had posted stories on the internet stating that the company had gone out of business after the US withdrawal from Iraq in 2011 and had shredded its employment files for interpreters. What nonsense to describe shredding paper files in the electronic age.

It took my lawyer friend 24 hours to track down the Vice President of Operations for GLS. It took the V.P. ten minutes to verify employment of one of my cases. The employment that GLS had on record was 18 months longer than the period for which the interpreter had been paid as a GLS employee. I understood immediately that GLS had overbilled the US government for the interpreters, probably to the tune of millions of dollars. Thus, the company owners wanted everyone to believe they had gone out of business.

I sent some emails out to some US embassies, consulates, and GLS threatening to report GLS for fraud if they did not immediately send the letters of employment verification to the interpreters who had been trying to get them for two years. GLS could risk sending the letters which documented overbilling or risk being reported to the Government Accounting Office and Congress for fraud.

Miraculously, within two weeks, the letters of employment verification began arriving by email to the interpreters who had waited up to two years for them. Five interpreters shared their letters with me in one week. All of their letters documented employment from six months to two years longer than they had actually been employed. For one year we were able to get these letters from a helpful GLS employee, until the GLS staff position was eliminated.

The IOM process was so back-logged that by the time IOM had collected all the interpreter's documents, the letter of employment verification was more than one year old. Because of IOM's inefficiency, the interpreter was penalized and was once again required to get a new letter. Most of the Army commanders and supervisors of the interpreters were retired or dead. For many interpreters their applications were not processed due to this problem.

When Donald Trump became US President in 2017, he immediately issued an executive order banning immigration from seven Muslim countries, including Iraq. Some interpreters' families had already been approved and issued visas to travel. They had sold all of their belongings and then were denied entry to the US. Others were already en route to the US and were flown back to Iraq. In response to an angry outcry, the Trump administration amended its visa ban to allow immigration by the families of Iraqi interpreters who had served the United States government. Yet, in reality, very few Iraqi interpreters were resettled in the US after the ban.

SIV and P2 immigration was suspended until September 30, 2017, as the ban worked its way to the US Supreme Court which overturned the bans based on unconstitutional discrimination. President Trump went back to the drawing board and issued even more onerous immigration bans. Although Iraq was removed from the list of banned countries, immigration remained halted. The US added an additional lengthy security check.

The week of the Supreme Court ruling, many interpreters received form letters stating their scheduled interviews were canceled due to "technical difficulties." Others received notice that their applications were denied because they were deemed to be "security risks." No evidence was provided. There was no appeal process.

One denial was for an interpreter nicknamed Matt. He was denied a visa despite submitting a dozen letters of recommendation from American officers. One letter said he had not only saved American soldiers from a burning Humvee, and treated the wounded, but that he had been abducted in 2007 by a local militia and interrogated about working for the Americans. He was denied a visa and never told why.

By late 2017, refugee resettlement from Iraq to the US had come to a virtual stand-still. During the four-month period from December 1, 2017, through March 31, 2018, only thirty Iraqi applicants and dependents were issued visas and resettled in the US under the P2 program and 206 under the SIV program. In spite of a backlog of tens of thousands of applications, when I got a tour in April 2018 of the center inside the Baghdad US Embassy where interviews were conducted, it was empty except for a mother with two children.

The Embassy was waiting for policy direction from Washington, but the slow-down was the handwriting on the wall. The Trump Administration was not interested in accepting immigrants. Those Iraqi interpreters who had risked their lives for Americans were abandoned, living in tents with no home to return to and no escape from Iraq. Daesh had exploded the houses of anyone who had worked for the US Army. The interpreters felt bitterly betrayed. Their lives will always be in danger living in Iraq.

Immigration arrival statistics are public information at:

https://fas.org/sgp/crs/homesec/R43725.pdf

http://www.wrapsnet.org/admissions-and-arrivals/

Shingal and the Kurdistan Referendum for Independence

For three years after Daesh attacked Shingal, the Peshmerga forces sat still in Shingal, defending its front line and waiting for approval to retake the Yezidi villages on the south side of Shingal Mountain. Peshmerga commanders, as well as Iraqi army officers and an Air Force pilot, stated they were waiting for the Americans to give them orders. 196,000 displaced Yezidis waited in their tents in Kurdistan IDP camps.

Qassim Shesho commanded fourteen Yezidi Peshmerga battalions in Shingal. On May 15, 2017, Nayef Jaso, for whom one of the battalions was named, and his son Talab Nayef Jaso, who commanded the battalion (which was stationed in the vicinity of the cement factory, several kilometers east of Sinjar city), left the Peshmerga with the men under their command and joined the Yezidi Hashd al-Sha'abi. Nayef was the mukhtar (mayor) of Kocho where the largest massacre had occurred. He had every right to lead the liberation of his own village. Kurdistan government banished Nayef along with all Yezidis who remained in Hashd al-Sha'abi.

These former Peshmerga participated alongside the Shia Hashd al-Sha'abi in retaking Yezidi villages. Other Yezidi Peshmerga also left their units and formed a second Yezidi Hashd al-Sha'abi unit. Allegedly, Yezidis received 1400 guns from Iran. The Iraqi government officially pronounced the Hashd al-Sha'abi to be part of the Iraqi army although it continued to function as separate units.

On May 21, 2017, Hashd al-Sha'abi liberated the Yezidi villages of Tal Banat and Tal Qassab. On May 25, Kocho was liberated. On May 28, Elias Tala, a Yezidi Peshmerga company commander, left the Peshmerga with his men and joined the Yezidi Hashd al-Sha'abi. By May 28, all the remaining Yezidi villages were freed from Daesh including Gir Zerik, Tal Ezeer, and Siba Sheikh Khudir which had been the first villages attacked.

Yezidis were elated and secretly supported the Hashd al-Sha'abi, in spite of their Iranian backing. Haider Shesho joined his 3,000 forces with Hashd al-Sha'abi. Only Qassim Shesho professed allegiance to PDK Peshmerga and Kurdistan.

Peshmerga forces had been ordered not to participate in the liberation. The Baghdad-backed Hashd al-Sha'abi, also referred to as the Popular Mobilization Units (PMU), controlled the south side of the mountain. The YPG from Syria controlled the west end on the border of Syria, and the Yezidi YBS controlled Khanasor and Sunoni on the north side of the mountain. Peshmerga forces withdrew to Sherfadeen, on the north side, under Qassim Shesho's command.

The Kurdistan Peshmerga forces had lost control of most of Shingal by June 2017. Tensions were mounting. The Kurdistan government made it increasingly difficult for any Yezidis to return to Shingal or for food or medicine to be delivered to those Yezidis living in tents on the mountain in extreme poverty and suffering.

Against this political stand-off between Erbil and Baghdad, Kurdistan held a referendum for independence, September 25, 2017. The referendum consisted of only one question: "Do you want the Kurdistan region and the Kurdistani areas outside the region's administration to become an independent state?"

KRG Minister of Foreign Relations, Falah Mustafa, stated that the day after the referendum passed, KRG officials would go immediately to Baghdad to begin peaceful negotiations for Kurdistan to separate from Iraq. It might take one or two years. The referendum was to measure the will of the people.

When I asked him, "What about the question for Yezidis to decide if they want Shingal to be part of Kurdistan?" he diplomatically told me, "Later there will be a 'secondary referendum' where they can decide to belong to Kurdistan or Baghdad." In other words, *first* Shingal would be annexed to Kurdistan. The Yezidi issue was shelved.

Many Yezidis disagreed with their religious and political leaders who supported the PDK party and annexation with Kurdistan. Yezidis were divided about whether to pledge allegiance to Kurdistan or to Baghdad. Most rejected both options and pushed for a self-governed Yezidi region with international protection. They privately explained that *Muslims are Muslims*. In other words, whether Kurdish or Arab, those Muslims who followed the Quran could not be trusted.

Yezidis have a saying, "If Muslims were gold, they would make a hole in your pocket." In one Yezidi household after another, in my presence they referred to the "shitty Muslims." No sooner would they lump them all together, then they would make exceptions and tell me how Arabs or Kurds had helped them when they fled. This scenario was repeated endlessly. Yezidis pray for all people of all religions, but their deep sense of betrayal by neighbors they had trusted caused them a sort of schizophrenic distress. Their religious training was to love all people, but they no longer knew how to do that. Their only solution was to no longer live among Muslims.

The borders of Kurdistan included the disputed territories of Kirkuk and Shingal. There was never an opportunity given to Yezidis and other residents of Shingal to decide whether they wanted to be part of Kurdistan. KRG persisted in referring to Shingal as Kurdish lands and Yezidis as Kurds, no longer calling them Yezidi Kurds. Although in 2016 the United Nations and the United States had declared that the Daesh attack upon the Yezidis had constituted genocide, the KRG never took any responsibility for the genocide nor offered an apology for the consequences of the Peshmerga retreat on August 3, 2014. Without an apology and compensation, Yezidis refused to be partners with Kurdistan.

Only Israel backed Kurdistan's referendum for independence. Every other western country warned Kurdistan to postpone it. The referendum passed by 92.7%. Kurds were jubilant. Baghdad, the US and European countries refused to recognize the result. The disputed territory of Shingal and Nineveh continued unresolved. The promise of Article 140 in the Iraqi constitution, which ordered a referendum for the disputed territories to decide their future, was not fulfilled.

The United States, in an unexpected and extraordinary act of betrayal to the loyal Kurds who had fought to defeat Daesh, withdrew its support for Kurdistan under the pretense of protecting "the integrity of Iraqi borders" and the "Iraqi identity" . . . both fantasies with no basis in reality. Peshmerga had lost over 2,000 men in the fight to defeat Daesh.

The US publicly acquiesced to Turkey's demand that it halt its military and financial aid to YPG in Syria. After the Kurds had led the fight against Daesh, reclaimed Kobane and Raqqa, Syria, and lost so many lives, this betrayal astounded and demoralized Kurds who had been so loyal to America for decades. Their love for America turned overnight to anger and profound disbelief by Kurds and their supporters worldwide. Two months later, in 2018, President Trump ordered a US-supported Kurdish defense force of 30,000 soldiers be trained to patrol the Syrian border with Turkey.

One week after the referendum, Baghdad ordered all international flights to be halted at the Erbil and Sulaymaniyah airports inside of Kurdistan. On October 16, the Iraqi army, using tanks supplied by the United States to fight Daesh, attacked Peshmerga, killing more than 200 of its own Iraqi citizens, and retook control of Kirkuk and its oil production. KRG lost the revenue from its 450,000 barrels of oil per day it had been selling.

Iraqi Hashd al-Sha'abi militia, backed by Iran, Baghdad, and the US, pushed on to take control of Shingal along the Syrian border to Turkey. The Yezidi Peshmerga forces retreated to Sherfadeen. Yezidis were loyal to Yezidis regardless of the uniform.

David Shumock, an American vet who was a commander in Peshmerga 2nd Division Special Forces Quick Reaction Forces Brigade stated, "When Yezidi Qassim Shesho abandoned the front in October 2017, when the Hashd came, I was stunned. Our entire right flank, from our base to near the Syrian border was unmanned. We stood side by side with his men every single time there was fighting from November 12, 2015, until then. So, for them to say we did not support them was a lie. I supplied them with medicines and treated his men when they were sick or wounded. The only ones to stand with us were Colonel Hisham Birifki and Major Sarbast Bozani."

The Baghdad parliament issued thirteen proclamations to penalize Kurdistan for holding its referendum and prosecute the leaders who planned it. By November, the Iraqi army, including its Hashd al-Sha'abi units, under Iranian command, had pushed the borders of Kurdistan back to the 2003 borders. Baghdad began replacing senior government managers within Kurdistan as punishment for holding the referendum. The Kurds' bid for independence had failed.

President Masoud Barzani saw the US willingness to allow Iran-backed Iraqi forces to attack the Kurds as an inexplicable surrender to Iranian influence and a betrayal to the Kurds.

"We regard ourselves as friends of the people of the United States, as friends of the government of the United States, but ... we have to revise our relationship with those who are responsible for this," Barzani said.

The Kurdistan flags in Shingal were replaced by Iraqi flags. The larger-than-life poster of Masoud Barzani was torn down at the Doshka memorial site on the mountain. The real Peshmerga truck with its mounted Doshka was removed and replaced with a cement replica bearing an Iraqi flag. The narrative was changed.

Yezidis in Shingal asked Iranian Hashd al-Sha'abi forces and PKK forces to leave Shingal. They agreed, but refused to name a deadline for withdrawal. Shingal remained a disputed area. Yezidis continued to lobby for international protection, self-administration under Iraq, rebuilding funds to return to Shingal, compensation, asylum, and trials for Daesh criminals. None of these demands was met with anything more than token gestures. Canada accepted 1200 Yezidi refugees. The US accepted ten families in February 2017 under the UNHCR resettlement program. Promised rebuilding funds were ear-marked for Mosul and Sunni Arabs, not Shingal.

The road from Zakho, Kurdistan to Shingal remained closed by the Iraqi army after the referendum, preventing Yezidis from returning to their villages. The hospitals in Sinjar and Sunoni had no doctors, medicine, nor ambulance. There was little or no water or electricity, no schools, no agriculture, no source of income, and no international protection to prevent another genocide. The houses were gutted or exploded.

All humanitarian organizations were ordered to leave Shingal. Yezidis remained trapped in tents in Kurdistan and on Shingal Mountain, reduced to cooking over wood fires and eating dried food.

On December 9, 2017, Iraqi Prime Minister Haider al-Abadi declared that "Our forces are in complete control of the Iraqi-Syrian border, and I therefore announce the end of the war against Daesh."

However, according to Iraqi government officials, 40,000 Daesh fighters and their families had fled to Duhok, Zakho, and Erbil, Kurdistan where they were living freely. The names and faces of many were known. On December 13, a group of Arabs, possibly Daesh, attacked two Yezidi shepherds in Shingal, killing one and injuring the other. The extremist Islamic ideology of Daesh had not been eradicated.

On December 19 and 20, 2017, demonstrations occurred in Sulaymaniyah and Ranya against KRG. People protested lack of salaries, electricity and water. Hundreds of live bullets were fired by PDK and PUK Peshmerga into the crowd resulting in the death of five civilians. Uniformed Iranian police were also present and shooting. Some said it was an Iranian plot. Kurdistan was erupting from pent up frustration over lost hope, a ruined economy, and anger at government corruption. Everyone's future looked bleak. The notion of one united Iraqi identity was exposed for the fiction it was.

Yezidis were left with a conundrum. Both Arabs and Kurds had betrayed their trust. Neither Baghdad nor Erbil moved to restore the infrastructure of Shingal. The only viable solution was for Yezidis to have their own self-governance which no government supported.

Early in 2018, Iraqi President Abadi announced that the IDP camps would be closed within months and the displaced persons would return to their villages. This sent a scare through the Yezidi camps. Shingal villages had thousands of unexploded IEDs (bombs). Five people died in Tal Banat when opening the doors to their houses.

The Iraqi parliament declared 85% of Shingal was destroyed. Yet, out of $75 million US dollars pledge to the UNDP to rebuild Iraq, only $3 million was earmarked for Rabia, Sunoni, and Sinjar. Rabia was well-known to be a Daesh stronghold when Shingal was attacked. Not one dollar was allocated for repairing or rebuilding houses or buildings in Shingal. Shingal was depopulated.

Yezidis could not leave Iraq because all asylum programs for Yezidis were finished and smuggling was stopped by closed borders. They could not return to their villages because Shengal was not safe. They remained trapped, depressed and chronically ill in their rotting, leaking tents.

Islamophobia, Cognitive Dissonance, and Secularism

Since the genocidal attack by Daesh upon Yezidis in August 2014, I asked every Yezidi whom I met what he or she thinks is the solution for their future in Shingal. Their demoralized answer was unanimous: "There is no future in Iraq for Yezidis." In February 2018, my FaceBook survey of IDPs showed 99% of Yezidis want to leave Iraq because they have no hope after nearly four years of living in tents.

After the Kurdistan referendum, September 25, 2017, the US supported Baghdad with a policy to maintain "territorial integrity." The American model of secularism has failed in Iraq. The western concept of secularism has not been able to work in tribal societies. Neither Sunni Arabs, Shia Arabs, Kurds, nor non-Muslims want to live together.

Cognitive dissonance occurs when a person is presented with hard factual evidence that is contrary to his or her belief system. When confronted with these facts, a person may respond with anger, denial, rejection of the facts, hostility, name calling, and a refusal to hear more. Cognitive dissonance leaves one feeling physically distressed because one's core values are challenged. Cognitive dissonance is a term to describe utter astonishment and disbelief.

Yezidis' core belief is to love all people. They pray for all other religions and even pray for the birds and the trees before praying for themselves last. They were genuinely friends with their Muslim neighbors and associates. When trusted Arab neighbors and friends attacked them, they experienced cognitive dissonance, that is to say, deep psychological distress. They had to face the truth: some of their Arab friends had betrayed them and could never be trusted again. For Yezidis, Daesh is equivalent to Islam because its extremist ideology is derived directly from the Quran and Hadith teachings. Daesh, themselves, stated this as one of their pillars of ideological belief.

The majority of Daesh were home-grown terrorists. They were the Arabs who lived in the house on the next street or one mile away in the Arab village. After their defeat, many of them shaved their beards, grew a mustache, and were living freely in Kurdistan or Mosul.

Because it is impossible to differentiate between the innocent Arabs and the Daesh collaborators, the only way that Yezidis say they can feel safe in Shingal is for *all* Arabs to be excluded. Excluding Arabs is not enough to ensure there will not be another genocide. Yezidis beg for international protection, but no country is willing to provide that.

For the first two years after the attack of Shingal, I defended Muslims with the argument that they represent one-third of the world population. Not all Muslims can be bad. I still believe this. Many of my associates, dearest friends, and even my business partner's family in Turkey are Muslim.   All of the government staff that help me in my work for Yezidis are Muslim.

After listening to hundreds of stories of Daesh crimes, I began to read the verses in the Quran upon which Daesh ideology is based.   The school of Islam known as Salafism believes in fundamentalist application of Quranic verses and Hadith teachings of the first three generations of prophets, beginning with Muhammad, the founder of Islam.   Since Muhammad is considered to be the messenger of Allah (God), his writings are considered, therefore, to be the word of Allah.   No one is allowed to question or debate the word of Allah because Allah could not possibly be wrong.

Followers must obediently accept the Islamic verses.   In modern lingo, we call this brain-washing.   Salafism is sponsored globally by Sunnis in Saudi Arabia.   This ideology has been used to justify the violent acts of jihadi Salafi groups that included Al-Qaeda, Daesh (ISIS), and Boko Haram.

If we remove the label of religion from Islam or at least from Daesh, we might more easily be able to expose the radical Islamic ideology which Daesh used to justify the Yezidi genocide.   What if the racist Ku Klux Klan or the Nazi party had been registered as a religion?   Would we have tolerated their ideology of racism and genocide?   When ideology that violates human rights hides behind religious freedom, then society must condemn it without fear of being accused of religious intolerance or racism.   One must be able to express both facts and opinions without fear of being called an Islamophobe or prosecuted for hate speech.   One must develop more tolerance for opinions and facts that challenge one's cherished values.

Daesh ideology is the embodiment of extremist Salafist Islamic teachings which require jihad against "kuffirs" (non-Muslims).   Even after the Daesh terrorist organization is defeated, its ideology will remain.   In order to defeat Daesh terrorism, one must defeat this extremist Salafi interpretation of Islam.

One Muslim said to me, "I resent Daesh because they hijacked my religion."

If Muslims wish to have their religion respected by non-Muslims, then they themselves must renounce this ideology enshrined in the Quran and preached by Salafist Muslims.   When the Pope called Islam a "religion of peace," a group of former Muslims who had converted to Catholicism challenged him on it.

I have spent my life fighting in America for equality for Afro-Americans and women.   I do not intend to throw away fifty years of struggle for women's rights in order to pander to demands of Muslims in America.   The hijab is a symbol of Islamic ideology that suppresses women, considers nine-year-old girls old enough for marriage, and allows a man to have four wives.

The Islamic explanation for a woman covering her hair is that if she shows her beauty, men might not be able to control their desires.   Frankly, if a man cannot keep his pants zipped up if he sees a woman's hair, *I do not want him in*

America. A survey of Muslims living in different European countries found that approximately 50% of Muslims prefer to live under Shariah law rather than be governed by the democracies of the countries which gave them asylum.

The people of a country have a right to defend and preserve their culture. America's culture is one of openness (even excessive permissiveness), freedom of expression, and equality. It permits sex before marriage, music, cursing, smoking, drinking, dancing, and skimpy dresses. The hijab symbolizes everything that is counter to American core values.

President Donald Trump declared immigration bans against all citizens from seven Muslim countries in 2017. This adversely affected the non-Muslim Yezidis trying to immigrate to the US. Trump faced an onslaught of criticism. The US Supreme Court struck down his blanket ban because it discriminated against a religion. He came back with a revised immigration plan which would end "chain migration". Chain migration is his new term for family reunification. This policy would be disastrous for Yezidis.

Both the Iraqi constitution (Article 2a) and the Kurdistan constitution (Article 6), make Shariah law the official law. The Kurdistan constitution states that it is not allowed to:

First: Enact a law inconsistent with the provisions of the fundamentals of Islam.

Second: Enact a law inconsistent with democracy principals.

Both constitutions, also, establish equality before the law without discrimination based on gender, race, ethnicity, origin, color, religion, creed, belief or opinion, or economic and social status. In spite of this constitutional declaration protecting equal rights, Shariah law is mutually exclusive with democratic principles of equal rights for women. One cannot have it both ways. Islam is not a religion of democracy or equality. It is an authoritarian ideology that suppresses women's rights and freedom of expression.

Iraq is not a secular country. Its official religion is Islam. Where does this leave minorities such as the non-Muslim Yezidis who must be governed by Shariah law? Extremely vulnerable. They want to migrate to non-Muslim countries, but so do persecuted Muslims.

Mass migration of persons fleeing war in Afghanistan, Pakistan, Syria, and Iraq surged to two million in 2015 through 2017. Most asylum seekers to Europe were Muslim. Europe underwent an Islamization process which triggered backlash. In the name of religious equality, European countries passed laws against so-called "hate speech" to silence dissent against this Islamization process.

As activists attempted to raise the alarm against Islam in Europe and North America, a new pejorative term was coined: *Islamophobia.* Rather than debate the facts, name-calling is a classic response of cognitive dissonance to silence the truth. Over the decades many disparaging terms have been used against human rights activists and others with opposing ideologies such as *nigger-lover, Jew-lover, commie, conspiracy theorist, tin foil hat wearer,* and now we have *Islamophobe.* No one dared express the opinion that Islam was the basis for Daesh atrocities against civilization. Political correctness suppressed free speech. Anyone who dared to speak out against the dangers of Islam was targeted.

Muslim asylum-seekers demanded special rights such as extra breaks at work so they could pray and a special prayer room. Many use it for an extra cigarette break or to check their FaceBook messages, rather than to pray. Mosques were built and allowed to blare out the call to prayer five times a day, disrupting people sleeping in the middle of the night. When Yezidis who got asylum in Germany, Canada, and the US attended English language classes, many other students were Muslim. They set their reminder for call to prayer on their phones. A dozen phones would sound at once with "Allahu Ahkbar," traumatizing the Yezidis. They were assigned scarf-wearing Muslims as counselors, teachers, and interpreters. Yezidi women, who had been sexually abused by Daesh in the name of Islam, refused to use Muslim women for psychological counseling.

In Minneapolis, Minnesota, US, Muslims demanded the city's public swimming pools designate days for women-only and men-only. Women police officers were allowed to wear the hijab scarf instead of the standard police hat.

When I opposed special exceptions for Muslim women in the U.S. military to wear hijabs instead of the standard military uniform required of all others, I was attacked as "a truly tragic epitome of a bigot and prejudiced person; an Islamophobe."

Yet in Iraq, occasionally when passing through checkpoints, the soldier would severely question my driver, "Why isn't she covering her hair?" There is no religious equality in Iraq. Non-Muslims are considered non-believers and suffer daily discrimination. Quranic verses regularly quoted on TV promise that they will suffer eternal hellfire when they die.

In the West's zeal to enforce equal rights for religions, an increasing number of *special* rights were granted to Muslims which undermined the culture of the non-Muslim countries. A distinction needs to be made that *equal rights* does not mean *special rights*. Equal rights means everyone gets the same treatment, not special treatment.

In 2016 the Iraqi parliament outlawed the importation and sale of alcoholic beverages which are banned by Shariah law. The Minister of Higher Education issued a dress code for university students corresponding to modest Islamic dress with a head scarf. No more blue jeans, especially not on co-eds. The Iranian suppression of human rights began creeping into Iraq.

Yezidis insist that Daesh is Islam. Daesh ideology is rooted in extremist fundamentalist Sunni Islamic teachings which condone marriage to girls, the subjugation of women, and stoning to death of women for sex outside of marriage (although stoning in Iraq is now rare).

In order to defeat Daesh terrorism, Yezidis argue that this extremist Islam ideology itself must be defeated. Human rights, religious freedom, and equality for all must be written into a secular constitution, but Iraq has Shariah law as the basis of its constitution. Shariah law cannot be reconciled with democratic principles of human rights, religious freedom, and equality for women.

A Yezidi elder with a long pointed white beard and red checkered turban asked me, "Please explain to me why the Americans are letting Muslims build mosques in America."

"I can explain," I proudly answered. "The very essence of what it means to be American is the cherished values of religious freedom and equal opportunity for all people regardless of race, sex, age, religion, or sexual orientation. I spent my whole life fighting for these rights. It is why so many people want to go live in America where every individual has the right to be who he or she chooses to be.

He shook his head in astonishment at my naiveté, and then proclaimed, *"That stuff about religious equality is the stupidest thing I ever heard. If you let Islam build mosques in America, your enemy will destroy you using your own laws. Then they will replace your democracy with Shariah laws. Stop Islam before it is too late."*

Making Lists of Survivors, Dead, and Missing

In three years, I filled dozens of notebooks with lists of names. Starting from September 3, 2014, when I visited Roboski School in the mountain village of Turkey, Yezidis encircled me to tell me the names of their missing family members. I sat cross-legged on the ground taking names. They waited their turn patiently. Always, an interpreter among them who had once risked his life fighting side-by-side with the US Army would sit at my side. They thought I was *somebody*. They thought I might be from the United Nations or a journalist.

I knew I was *nobody*. What I had once thought of as my hobby, listening to peoples' stories like an arm-chair sociologist, turned into a humanitarian duty. The burden weighed heavily upon me. I trembled inside. I was not big enough, not powerful enough for this responsibility. Camp after camp, the displaced and traumatized placed all their hope in me to tell their story to the world and bring help. It was hard to leave the camps after hours of writing down names, because the line of waiting people was unending. People would hear I was in the camp and come to find me.

Sarah gave me the names of her husband and two children taken at gunpoint, and then she fainted in my arms. Adiba gave me her hand-written list of 28 abducted female relatives from Khanasor. Diler gave me his list of 26 missing sister, cousins, aunts and uncles from Old Tal Qassab. A Yezidi man who joined Peshmerga gave me his list in Shingal of 74 missing family from Khanasor. In Batman, Turkey, a man gave me three lists of 98 abducted children under age 14, abducted females, and murdered men from Tal Banat. Two of the children were used two years later by Daesh as fourteen-year-old suicide bombers. My interpreter in Batman, after two days, said to me, "You haven't heard my story yet." He gave me a list of his nineteen missing family members.

Faisal Muhmoud Khero, in Germany, gave me his list of twelve murdered men and twenty-eight abducted women and a baby from his brother Barakat's family farm north of Tal Ezeer. Two years later when some of the girls were returned in exchange for money, I made the list of survivors and got their passports. I celebrated small victories each time someone on a missing persons list returned from captivity.

I collected hundreds, then more than a thousand names of dead and missing from every village in Shingal. Private citizens began making databases. The Yezidi historian, Ali Sado, who had previously taken asylum in Bielefeld, Germany, recorded over 3,000 names of dead and missing by November 2014. Within two weeks I was hit with the stark reality that each Yezidi would have to be helped one by one by one. It would take years. I understood clearly that some would escape to a safe country, but most would be trapped inside of Iraq with a grim future. Ali Sado had witnessed more genocides than I. His succinct conclusion was, "Many more Yezidis will die."   In September 2014, Daesh exploded his house and that of his brother in Shingal.

By June of 2015, Yezidi Judge Qassim Osman Rafu and his son, Aram, in Sulaymaniyah, Kurdistan, had a database of 5,000 names.   The Kurdistan government pressured the judge to share it.   He continued to update it for the government.

For the next three years I continued to make lists of names.   There was a list of the eighty-four men known to have been killed in execution lines in Kocho. They were identified by the nineteen men who survived their bullet wounds in the Kocho executions.   The other 350 men were referred to as missing, though no one ever heard from any of them again.   I had the list of fifty-two Arabs who participated in the Kocho massacre.   Next to most names is the neighboring Arab village where the Arab lived.   There is an X next to those who pulled the trigger. The two men who drove the excavators to bury the bodies are on that list.   The man who allegedly killed Ahmed Al Jaso, the al-Mandkany clan leader, is named.

Ahmed's brother, Nayef Jaso, Muhktar (mayor) of Kocho, gave me a list of sixteen muhktars of surrounding Arab villages who came to an annual luncheon at his brother's house in Kocho on August 2.   On August 3, thirteen of these trusted Arab friends joined with Daesh and attacked Shingal.   I had the list of thirteen Yezidi boys left behind in a Daesh training camp when one boy escaped.   I did not know what to do with all these hand-written lists with which I was entrusted.

I had lists of young women who committed suicide in Daesh captivity rather than to continue the torture of being raped.   I had lists of abducted Yezidis being held in Tal Afar and Raqqa who were in phone communication with their families.   Their families were raising money for their return.

The Kurdistan government established offices to manage the lists.   The Genocide Office in Duhok was staffed by nine police officers, a judge, and several social workers. They recorded the stories of each person who had escaped from Daesh or who had missing family members. Since these were official police reports, their lists were confidential. The Yezidis Affairs Office in Duhok did the same.   It also made partial reimbursements to families of survivors who had returned from Daesh captivity by paying money to a smuggler. I took some of my lists to them, to rescue those in captivity, to no avail.

The Board of Relief and Humanitarian Affairs (B.R.H.A.) was established in 2015 by the Duhok government next to the court house. It also maintained lists and statistics on refugees and IDPs. BRHA manages the processes of emergency intervention, relief support and humanitarian assistance provided to IDPs and refugees.   It provides for camp construction, management and coordination for refugees, mostly from Syria, and IDPs, mostly from Shingal and Mosul.

In 2015, I referred lists of about 300 survivors who went to Germany.   I began my program of getting Iraqi IDs and passports for families of survivors who had returned from Daesh captivity and those families with missing members. The waiting period to apply for a passport in Duhok grew to one-and-a-half years. There were one point seven million displaced persons living in Kurdistan, Iraq. One out of three people was displaced. Replacing people's identity cards became a bureaucratic nightmare. My organization, AAJ, was permitted to get passports for survivors and their families without appointments. The Duhok passport director, Nawzad Majid Suleyman, supported my efforts as one of the greatest humanitarians in Kurdistan. My requests to the passport office looked like this (each followed by a list of names):

Family from Kocho, captured 15.08.2014. Father is missing or dead. They finished their 3rd interview in Erbil with UNHCR for immigration to Canada.

██████ *was married and living in Tal Qassab. She was captured by Daesh on the road from Sinjar to Sunoni, Shingal, on August 3, 2014, 9AM. She returned from Daesh captivity on April 7, 2015.*

She and her family were captured by Daesh on August 15, 2014, in Kocho. She and her mother, ████████████, *returned to Kurdistan from Daesh on October 12, 2016. Her father and some siblings are missing with Daesh. She, her mother, two sisters, and a brother-in-law have completed their third interview in Erbil with UNHCR to go to Australia.*

We request approval for passport processing for 12 Yezidi survivors who recently returned from Daesh captivity, plus one husband of a survivor. They are all from Khanasor.

Three survivors from Kocho who escaped from Daesh captivity after two years (Nadia Murad's aunt and cousins.) One survivor who escaped execution line in Kocho with bullets and made it to safety, September 2014. He searched for his mother and brothers for two years. They returned in October 2016.

We request approval for passport processing for 10 Yezidis. They were captured by Daesh on August 15, 2014 in Kocho, Shingal. They escaped 19.11.2016, from Tal Afar.

██████ *is mother of Edo, she was captured in 03.08.2014; escaped 24.04.2015*

Faisal Mahmoud Khero called from Germany to ask for help to get passports for his sister and two of her children who returned from Daesh. Twelve men in his family were killed by Daesh 03.08.2014, and 28 women kidnapped at their farm at the junction of Tal Ezeer. Faisal is the only surviving adult male. The German government promised him asylum for his family members who survived.

████ is a 16-year-old boy from Kocho who was sent to Daesh military camp. He escaped from Raqqa after two years with Daesh. He needs his passport to join his mother and younger brother in Germany. They escaped before he did. Their father is missing, presumed executed in Kocho.

████ needs his passport to cross the border to Sirnak, Turkey, where his son, Lazim, is being held by Turkish authorities. Lazim was only three when he was kidnapped and held for three years in Tal Afar. His smuggler brought him from Tal Afar to Syria to Turkey. The Turkish Customs officer refused to let Lazim cross the border to Iraq because he did not recognize his father. Lazim came back speaking Turkish. The father must go to Turkey for DNA testing before the court will release his son to him.

During the recovery from a genocide, individual tragedies are reduced to lists and statistics. In the rush to document survivors, there is little time to listen to details of their captivity and abuse. Unlike the foreign journalists who searched out stories of women who had been sexually abused to sell their stories for $1000 or $5000 or more, I was too busy getting their documents to listen to every story.

In January 2017, the UNHCR in Duhok, Kurdistan secretly began to take lists of internally displaced persons (IDPs) for resettling 1200 people in Canada. . . .a drop in the bucket to garner votes. My referral lists of families became even more succinct:

Family of 5 Kocho survivors; all men in family missing, presumed executed.

Orphan girl, age 12, rescued in Mosul, mother killed with old women in Solagh Institute, father killed in Kocho, siblings missing.

Boy 16, escaped from Daesh military camp; mother previously escaped, father and siblings missing.

My sleep was tormented with dreams of making endless lists. After four years, the genocide, with all its human suffering, was reduced to a footnote in history:

In August 2014, the Islamic State, known as Daesh, attacked Shingal, homeland of the Yezidis, an ethno-religious people. Daesh abducted or killed 6417 Ezidis. By 2019, 3317 survivors, mostly women and children, had returned from captivity, while 3046 remained missing, many killed by Daesh. The Ezidi population in Iraq of at least 360,000 remained displaced with no available solutions for recovery.

Genocide Recognized

In 1944, Raphael Lemkin, a Polish scholar of international law who fled the German occupation of Poland in 1939, coined the word *genocide*. Combining Plato's use of the Greek word *genos* for a race or tribe, Lemkin added the Latin - *cide*, which means "killer" or "act of killing" in Latin, as in *homicide* or *suicide*. Thus was born *genocide*. The first prosecution for genocide occurred in the indictment of the Nazi war criminals in the 1945-46 Nuremburg Tribunal. They were indicted for "War Crimes" which included the "deliberate and systematic genocide; viz., the extermination of racial and national groups . . . particularly Jews, Poles, and Gypsies."

It was not until 2002 that The International Criminal Court (ICC) was created at The Hague, in the Netherlands, to prosecute crimes against humanity including genocide. Article 2 of the Convention on the Prevention and Punishment of the Crime of Genocide (CPPCG) defines genocide as "a crime with intent to destroy, in whole or in part, a national, ethnical, racial or religious group." If you don't have intent, you don't have genocide; like the distinction between manslaughter and first degree murder, but on a mind-boggling scale.

The defined groups are by intention explicitly targeted for destruction, and such destruction is not the unintended outcome of the intent to achieve some other goal, such as in defensive operations or attacks on military targets during a war. According to the legal definition, interpreting an event as genocide depends on intent.

Daesh itself stated publicly that its intent was to destroy the Yezidis.

After two years of relentless campaigning, spearheaded by Yezidi survivor, Nadia Murad Bissee, countries began to recognize the Daesh attack on Shingal as genocide against Yezidis. Nadia was a teenager when her village of Kocho was attacked. Her mother and six brothers were killed. She was abducted and sexually abused for three weeks [erroneous reports say three months] before escaping. Nadia, a girl who had never left her rural village, traveled the world meeting with political leaders and heads of state to plead for help for Yezidis. She published her story, *The Last Girl*, in 2017.

Out of continuing public shaming for their inaction, eventually, many countries and organizations passed resolutions recognizing the genocide. Unfortunately, beyond these words on paper, they did little else to provide asylum, rebuilding funds, military protection for Shingal, compensation, or prosecution of crimes against Yezidis.

The genocide against Yezidis and other religious minorities was unanimously recognized by these governments:

Nov 18, 2014	Iraqi Council of Ministers
Jan 27, 2016	Parliamentary Assembly of the Council of Europe
Feb 2, 2016	European Parliament
March 14, 2016	United States House of Representatives
April 20, 2016	United Kingdom
June 15, 2016	United Nations Human Rights Council
June 16, 2016	Canada
Dec 8, 2016	France
March 23, 2017	Scottish Parliament
Jan 16, 2018	Armenia
March 8, 2018	Australia

The European Parliament stated that those who intentionally commit atrocities for ethnic or religious reasons be brought to justice for violations against international law, crimes against humanity and genocide. The U.K. member of parliament, Fiona Bruce, said, "Recognition of genocide brings with it obligations on behalf of the international community to prevent, punish and protect people.

United Nations Human Rights Council, Findings on Yezidi Genocide, 15 June 2016
[http://www.ohchr.org/Documents/HRBodies/HRCouncil/CoISyria/A_HRC_32_CRP.2_en.pdf]

201. ISIS has committed, and continues to commit, the crime of genocide, as well as multiple crimes against humanity and war crimes, against the Yazidis.

202. The genocide committed against the Yazidis has not primarily been accomplished through killings, though mass killings of men and women have occurred. Rather ISIS seeks to destroy the Yazidis in multiple ways, as envisaged by the drafters of the 1948 Genocide Convention. ISIS has sought, and continues to seek, to destroy the Yazidis through killings; sexual slavery, enslavement, torture and inhuman and degrading treatment, and forcible transfer causing serious bodily and mental harm; the infliction of conditions of life that bring about a slow death; the imposition of measures to prevent Yezidi children from being born, including forced conversion of adults, the separation of Yezidi men and women, and mental trauma; and the transfer of Yezidi children from their own families and placing them with ISIS fighters, thereby cutting them off from beliefs and practices of their own religious community, and erasing their identity as Yazidis. The public statements and conduct of ISIS and its fighters clearly demonstrate that ISIS intended to destroy the Yazidis of Sinjar, in whole or in part.

203. Like all genocides, it is born of the warped thinking that the world, as the perpetrators understand it, would be better without a particular group of people in it and that by doing the work of destroying what they consider impure, the perpetrators are creating a more perfect society.

204. ISIS commits the crime of genocide against individual Yazidis, as an incremental step in their overall objective of destroying this religious community. This is the genocide accomplished through the destruction of a nine-year-old girl in a A/HRC/32/CRP.2 37 slave market, surrounded by men waving their bids; of a woman and children locked in a room, beaten and starved; of a little boy trained to kill his father. It is a genocide perpetrated by male fighters so ideologically enslaved that they believe that by committing some of the most horrific crimes imaginable, they are bettering the society in which they live.

205. Over 3,200 women and children are still held by ISIS. Most are held in Syria where Yezidi women and girls continue to be sexually enslaved and otherwise abused, and Yezidi boys, indoctrinated and trained. Thousands of Yezidi men and boys are missing. ISIS's trade in women and girls and its recruitment and use of boys have never ceased. The genocide of the Yazidis is on-going.

On March 9, 2017, Nadia Murad, a survivor who was awarded the Nobel Peace Prize in 2018, addressed the United Nations in New York:

"I am physically and emotionally exhausted.... I have put my personal life aside to seek justice, rather than focusing on my own healing. I wish I could say this was worth it. My words, tears and my testimony have not made you act. I wonder whether there is any point in continuing my campaign at all. I cannot understand what is taking so long. I cannot understand why you are letting ISIS get away with it. What more do you need to hear before you will act?"

Acknowledgments

It is impossible to name all the hundreds of people who have helped me in my research and activism which culminated with this book. Without the help of Yezidi interpreters, I could not have worked one day. From my very first hour visiting a refugee camp in Roboski School in Turkey, Yezidis who had once worked as interpreters with the US Army volunteered to interpret. Wherever I went, there they were, helping me to help their people.

Barakat Ali Hichani has been my interpreter, friend, and staff leader in our passport project in Duhok for two years. His family lives in an unfinished building awaiting to be called for their final interview to immigrate to the US. Baderkhan Ali Kasim has worked closely with me for three years. His family lives in a one-room block building he built, also awaiting approval to immigrate to the US. I also thank interpreter Farhan Mahlo whose family received asylum in Germany. Farhan interpreted and consulted with me on many issues as I wrote this book.

I also thank interpreters Ido Mato, Sheik Alyas, Naim Ali, Tahsin Hassan, Rakan Edo, Nayf Elias, Saad Bakir, Salam Bakir, Sardar Hassan Ali, Erivan Mahdi, Shaalan Aldoskys, Jiyan Havind, Diler Havind, Ahmed Alias, Amin Bali, Ismail Silo, Saado Ali, Qassim Khalaf, Gian Aldonani, and Muhammed Ibrahim. Garreb Khalaf Mandkany not only interpreted, but returned to Iraq from his home in New Zealand to help rescue and document over forty female relatives captured from Kocho. I apologize to any interpreters whose names I have not listed.

I thank Ahmed Helmi Darweesh for the final editing and typing of the Arabic translation. He did a superb job catching errors and formatting.

I thank all the Yezidis, especially the survivors of kidnapping and witnesses to massacres and battles, who shared their painful stories with me, at the expense of reliving their trauma, and allowed me to use their real names to document the genocide against the Yezidis. I hope their strength will encourage others to tell their stories of the Islamic State's crimes against humanity. I hope this will lead to prosecutions. I give special thanks to survivor Viyan Havind who spent days sharing her story and explaining the devastation of asylum policies which create family separation and prolong their suffering.

I have a special place in my heart for the teenage boys from Kocho who escaped Islamic State jihadi training camps and shared their stories with me. They are like sons to me.

I thank Judge Qasim Osman and his son Aram Qasim, in Sulaymaniyah, Kurdistan, Iraq, who first explained to me the difficulty for Yezidis to get their Iraqi IDs and passports in Duhok. This steered me to my main passport project. I found no greater humanitarian in Kurdistan than Nawzad Majid Suleyman,

Duhok Passport Director, who treated all persons with compassion and fairness regardless of age, religion, sex, or ethnicity. I thank Nawzad and the entire passport staff for issuing several thousand passports to Yezidi survivors without appointments. Many of them now live in Germany, Canada, Australia, and the United States.

I thank retired Duhok Judge Mustafa Mukhtar who gave court documents to hundreds of Yezidi women whose husbands were missing or killed so they could have legal custodianship of their children and leave Iraq for a safe country.

I thank camp manager Yahya Maroof of Rwanga (Qadia) camp for his support and caring for Yezidis.

I thank Director Rebar Abdulazeez and Deputy Director Nesreddin Suleyman of the Duhok Residency Office for granting me one-year residence permits for three years.

I thank Peshmerga commanders Hamad Ajaj, Naim Ali, and General Hakar and their soldiers who showed me the mass grave sites in Shingal.

The Iraqi people are so grateful to anyone who comes to help them recover from the destruction inflicted by the Islamic State. Many Iraqis offered me services and goods for free. This included housing, restaurants, taxi drivers, shops, the pharmacy, the Duhok Kurdistan emergency hospital and doctors (after my serious car accident in 2016), translators, and Iraqi Airways.

I also thank those who believed in me enough to donate financial assistance to my charity registered in Iraq, without benefit of a tax deduction. My greatest thanks goes to my patron saint, Stan Hobbs in Prescott, Arizona, who donated $20,000 over a three-year period to keep my work going for the survivors. Stan was humbled and inspired by 26-year-old Prescott resident and activist, Kayla Mueller, who was captured by Daesh in Syria and later killed in an air strike. He wanted to help the Yezidi girls and women who had returned from Daesh captivity. Stan explained, "My mortgage is paid off, and I don't need so much to live on." Every month Stan wrote checks to small hand-picked charities he trusted. Stan passed away in 2019 after donating all of his assets to charity. If only the world had more Stans!

Without the daily messages of love and support from thousands of Yezidis on social media, I would not have had the endurance to go on. They continue to be the wind beneath my wings. The friends who helped from Iraq and four continents would take pages to list. I thank all of you for your humanity. I hope my contribution of this book will encourage governments, charities, courts, and the private sector to help in the recovery of Yezidis and Shingal.

~ Amy L. Beam

APPENDIX - Who's Who in Iraqi Sectarianism

Religion:

Sherfadeen - Religion of Yezidis who claim it is the oldest religion on earth in the cradle of civilization.   Yezidis' homeland is Shingal, Nineveh province, Bashiqa, Shekhan, and Lalish (holy center) in Iraq. Shingal is disputed territory between Iraq central government and Kurdistan in northern Iraq.

Zoroastrian - The Islamic conquest of Persia (637–651) led to the decline of the Zoroastrian religion.   Before the Islamic conquest, the Persians had been mainly Zoroastrian, however, there were also large Christian and Jewish communities. Zoroastrians were converts to Islam.   Boiler-plate descriptions, repeated ad nauseum, say the Yezidi religion grew out of Zoroastrian, but Yezidi scholars say this is not true. Yezidis also were forced to convert to Islam.

Islam - founded in Mecca in 622 A.D. by Muhammad. Sunnis and Shias are the two largest sects. Political alignments and conflicts among the Arab countries are based on different interpretations of Islam by the Sunni and Shia sects.

Sunni Islam - 87-90% of the world's 1.6 billion Muslims (as of 2010)

Shia Islam - 13% to 20% of the world's muslim population. There are four Shia majority countries: Iran (93%), Iraq (67%), Bahrain (70%), Azerbaijan (70%), also there are large Shia populations in Yemen, Syria, and Turkey. Daesh accuses Shias of being "kuffirs," i.e., non-believers.

Christianity and other religious minorities - less than 3% of population in Iraq

Languages:

Farsi in Iran

Arabic in Iraq, Saudi Arabia, Qatar

Kurdish dialects in Kurdistan regions

    Sorani - Sulaymaniyah and official language in Kurdistan, Iraq
    Kurmanji also called Badini - Duhok, Kurdistan and eastern Turkey
    Ezidian or Shingally - Shingal, Iraq

Countries and Their Religions:

Iran -previously named Persia, became an Islamic republic after the Islamic Revolution of 1979, 95% Shia majority, 5% Sunni minority mostly Kurds, Shariah law

Saudi Arabia - Sunni majority, Shia minority; Shariah law

Qatar - mainly Sunnis; Shariah law

Turkey - 97% Islam, secular government turning toward Islamic control, mainly Sunni and Kurds (eastern Turkey)

Iraq - Shia in south, Baghdad; Sunni in middle; Kurds in north (Kurdistan), Shariah law

Syria - majority Sunni

Kurds - the largest ethnic group of people in the world without an independent country, divided between **Turkey** (20 million), **Iran** (3 million), **Iraq** (5 million), and **Syria** (1 million); now they are majority Sunni Muslim, used to be Yezidis until Ottoman Empire forced conversion to Islam.

KRG - Kurdistan Regional Government is Kurdistan in northern Iraq; autonomous with its own parliament, officially named Kurdistan since 1991 border was created by U.S.

KRI - Kurdistan Region of Iraq, used by those who do not recognize Kurdistan's autonomy

Shingal and Kirkuk- disputed territories in Iraq - every party fighting for these oil-rich territories; Shingal is homeland for Yezidis; Kirkuk used to be Kurdish

Political Parties and Defense Forces:

PDKI - Kurdish political party in Iran

PJAK - Kurdish militia from Iran

PDK or KDP- Kurdistan Democratic Party, majority political party of President Masoud Barzani in Kurdistan, Iraq; strongest in Duhok and Erbil

Peshmerga - Official military defense force for Kurdistan, Iraq, and Shingal disputed territory until driven out of Shingal in 2017

PUK, Goran, Change Party - minority political parties in Kurdistan, strongest in Sulaymaniyah

AKP - Turkish political party in power in Turkey opposes the Kurdish struggle, led by President Erdogan

HDP predominately Kurdish minority political party in Turkey; most leaders, MPs, mayors in prison since 2016 failed coup and immunity was removed from parliament members

PYD - Kurdish political party in Syria

YPG - Kurdish People's Protection Units, PYD male militia fighting ISIS

YPJ - PYD female militia fighting ISIS

PKK - Kurdistan Workers' Party, Kurdish armed resistance from Turkey, on terrorism list in Turkey and U.S., headquarters in Turkey/Qandil Mountains, Kurdistan; Ocalan leader in prison

YBS - Sinjar Resistance Units made up of Yezidis; formed after the PKK removed Islamic State from the Sinjar region 2014 and established a defensive force with the local Yezidi population. Trained by YPG and PKK. Attacked March 3, 2017 in Khanasor, Shingal by Kurds and Turks from "Rojava Peshmerga" to drive them out of Shingal.

HPE - Ezidkhan Protection Units

Rojava Peshmerga - Kurds, Turks, and Arabs in NE Syria supported by Turkey and KRG (Masoud Barzani)

PMU - Popular Mobilization Units or Popular Mobilization Forces (PMF), also referred to as **Hashd al-Sha'abi**. Created by Iran and supported by Iraq to fight Daesh in Iraq; mainly Iraqi Shia militias, with some Christian and Yezidi units, aligned with Baghdad, freed the Yezidi villages south of Sinjar, May 21-27, 2017

FSA - Free Syrian Army in Syria, fighting President Assad Bashur's government, initially backed by U.S., opposed by Russia

IS - Islamic State, also referred to as ISIS, ISIL, Daesh (in Iraq and Syria), ISHID (in Turkey); dedicated to jihad to convert the world to Islam, destroy non-Muslims and moderate Shia Muslims and replace them with an extremist Islamic caliphate; supported by Sunni Muslims with extremist interpretation of Islam

Shariah Law - law based on Quran used in constitutions of Iran, Iraq, Kurdistan, Qatar, Saudi Arabia

Wahabism and Salafism (Salafi jihadism) - fundamentalist Islamic ideology, opposes all non-Muslims, strongest in Saudi Arabia

Kuffir - "non-believer," or infidel, a derogatory term for non-Muslims, especially Yezidis, targeted for death by Islamic State; also spelled *kafir* or *kuffar*

Mukhtar - a person appointed by the government in neighborhoods to perform administrative tasks and provide information to the government on individuals such as verification of one's address; in villages it is usually the tribal leader

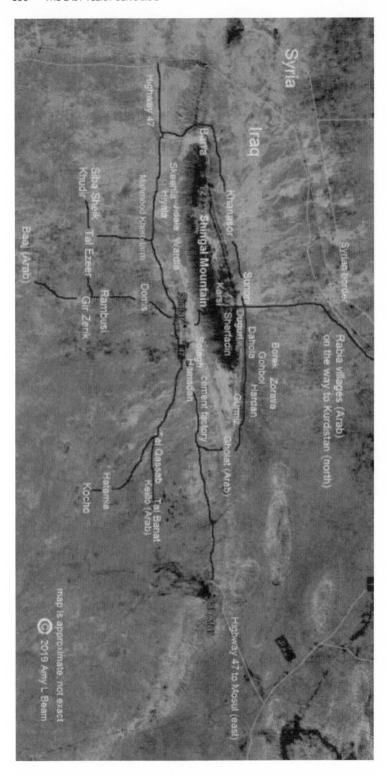

Made in the USA
Middletown, DE
10 March 2021

35041618R00215